Access® 2010

FOR

DUMMIES®

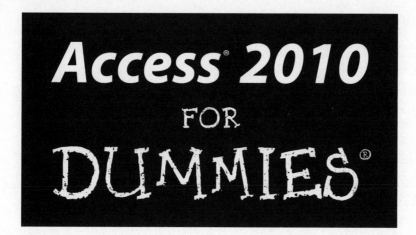

by Laurie Ulrich Fuller
and Ken Cook

Wiley Publishing, Inc.

Access® 2010 For Dummies®

Published by
Wiley Publishing, Inc.
111 River Street
Hoboken, NJ 07030-5774

www.wiley.com

Copyright © 2010 by Wiley Publishing, Inc., Indianapolis, Indiana

Published by Wiley Publishing, Inc., Indianapolis, Indiana

Published simultaneously in Canada

For general information on our other products and services, please contact our Customer Care Department within the U.S. at 877-762-2974, outside the U.S. at 317-572-3993, or fax 317-572-4002.

For technical support, please visit www.wiley.com/techsupport.

Wiley also publishes its books in a variety of electronic formats. Some content that appears in print may not be available in electronic books.

Library of Congress Control Number: 2010925160

ISBN: 978-0-470-49747-0

Manufactured in the United States of America

10 9 8 7 6 5 4 3 2 1

WILEY

About the Authors

Laurie Ulrich Fuller has been writing about and teaching people to use Microsoft Office for more than 20 years. She's been there through every new version of Access, as Office has evolved to meet the needs of users from all walks of life — from individuals to huge corporations, from growing businesses to non-profit organizations.

In the meantime, Laurie has personally trained more than 10,000 people to make better, more creative use of their computers, has written and co-written 30+ nationally-published books on computers and software — including several titles on Microsoft Office. In the last few years, she's also created several video training courses, teaching online students to use Microsoft Office and Adobe Photoshop.

Laurie's own firm, Limehat & Company, offers training and educational materials as well as graphic design, marketing, promotions, and Web-development services. She invites you to contact her with your Office-related questions at help@limehat.com, and to visit her Web site: www.limehat.com.

Ken Cook has built and managed a successful computer consulting business (now called Cook Software Solutions, LLC) since 1990. He began as a trainer — training numerous users (too many to count!) on a variety of software packages — specializing in Microsoft Office. Currently he "dabbles in training" (specializing in online synchronous training) but his main focus is creating expert Microsoft Office solutions and Microsoft Access database solutions for Fortune 500 and small business clients.

Ken is also a published author on Microsoft Excel, having contributed chapters on macros and VBA to *Special Edition: Using Excel 2000* and *Special Edition: Using Excel 2002* published by Que. Ken also contributed chapters on Microsoft Access to the book *How to Do Everything with Office XP* published by Osborne, and coauthored the previous version of this book; *Access 2007 For Dummies* published by Wiley.

Prior to his career in computers, Ken was a Product Manager for Prince Manufacturing, Inc. He is a graduate of Syracuse University with a bachelor's degree in Marketing. He can be contacted through his Web site (www.kcook pcbiz.com) or by e-mail (ken@kcookpcbiz.com).

Publisher's Acknowledgments

We're proud of this book; please send us your comments through our online registration form located at http://dummies.custhelp.com. For other comments, please contact our Customer Care Department within the U.S. at 877-762-2974, outside the U.S. at 317-572-3993, or fax 317-572-4002.

Some of the people who helped bring this book to market include the following:

Acquisitions, Editorial

Senior Project Editor: Paul Levesque

Senior Acquisitions Editor: Steven Hayes

Senior Copy Editor: Barry Childs-Helton

Technical Editor: Eric Legault

Editorial Manager: Leah Cameron

Media Development Assistant Producers: Angela Denny, Josh Frank, Shawn Patrick

Editorial Assistant: Amanda Foxworth

Sr. Editorial Assistant: Cherie Case

Cartoons: Rich Tennant (www.the5thwave.com)

Composition Services

Senior Project Coordinator: Kristie Rees

Layout and Graphics: Ashley Chamberlain, Samantha K. Cherolis, Ronald G. Terry, Christine Williams

Proofreaders: Susan Hobbs, Jessica Kramer

Indexer: Estalita Slivoskey

Publishing and Editorial for Technology Dummies

Richard Swadley, Vice President and Executive Group Publisher

Andy Cummings, Vice President and Publisher

Mary Bednarek, Executive Acquisitions Director

Mary C. Corder, Editorial Director

Publishing for Consumer Dummies

Diane Graves Steele, Vice President and Publisher

Composition Services

Debbie Stailey, Director of Composition Services

Contents at a Glance

Introduction *1*

Part I: Basic Training *9*
Chapter 1: Getting to Know Access 2010 11
Chapter 2: Finding Your Way Around Access 37
Chapter 3: Database Basics 59

Part II: Getting It All on the Table *79*
Chapter 4: Keys, Relationships, and Indexes 81
Chapter 5: Remodeling Your Data 99
Chapter 6: What's Happening Under the Table? 115

Part III: Data Mania and Management *139*
Chapter 7: Creating Data Forms 141
Chapter 8: Importing and Exporting Data 155
Chapter 9: Editing Data Automatically 169
Chapter 10: Gather Locally, Share Globally 181

Part IV: Ask Your Data, and Ye Shall
Receive Answers *201*
Chapter 11: Fast Finding, Filtering, and Sorting Data 203
Chapter 12: I Was Just Asking . . . for Answers 219
Chapter 13: I'll Take These AND Those OR Them 245
Chapter 14: Queries That Think Faster Than You 255
Chapter 15: Calculating with Your Data 267
Chapter 16: Flying into Action Queries 283

Part V: Plain and Fancy Reporting *295*
Chapter 17: Quick and Not-So-Dirty Automatic Reporting 297
Chapter 18: Dazzling Report Design 319
Chapter 19: Headers and Footers and Groups, Oh My! 345
Chapter 20: Magical Mass Mailings 367

Part VI: More Power to You 375

Chapter 21: Making It All Better with the Analyzer Tools 377
Chapter 22: Hello! Creating an Interface to Welcome Database Users 389

Part VII: The Part of Tens..................................... 399

Chapter 23: Ten Common Problems 401
Chapter 24: Ten Uncommon Tips 413

Index 421

Table of Contents

Introduction *1*

About This Book 1
Conventions Used in This Book...2
What You Don't Have to Read..2
Foolish Assumptions 3
How This Book Is Organized 3
   Part I: Basic Training 4
   Part II: Getting It All on the Table 4
   Part III: Data Mania and Management....................................4
   Part IV: Ask Your Data, and Ye Shall Receive Answers...............5
   Part V: Plain and Fancy Reporting...5
   Part VI: More Power to You 5
   Part VII: The Part of Tens...5
   Appendix: Getting Help 6
Icons Used in This Book 6
Where to Go from Here...7

Part 1: Basic Training *9*

Chapter 1: Getting to Know Access 2010 11

What Is Access Good For, Anyway? 12
   Building big databases 12
   Creating databases with multiple tables 13
   Databases with user forms 16
   Databases that require special reporting..............................18
What's New in Access 2010? 21
   New and improved features 21
   Reach out with SharePoint 24
How Access Works and How You Work with It 26
   Opening Access...26
   Selecting a starting point 28
   Now what?..34

Chapter 2: Finding Your Way Around Access **37**

Diving Right In 39

Working with On-Screen Tools in Access 42

    Clicking tabs 43

    Using buttons 44

    The File tab and Quick Access tools 46

    Accessing panes, panels, and context-sensitive tools 47

Customizing the Access Workspace 48

    Repositioning the Quick Access toolbar 48

    Adding buttons to the Quick Access toolbar 49

    Removing buttons from the Quick Access toolbar 51

    Minimizing the Ribbon 52

    Working with ScreenTips 54

Mousing Around 56

Navigating Access with the Alt Key 57

Chapter 3: Database Basics **59**

Database Lingo 59

    Data, no matter how you pronounce it 60

    Fields of dreams (or data) 60

    Records 61

    Tables 61

    The database 62

Field Types and Uses 62

Choosing Between Flat and Relational Databases 67

    Isolationist tables 68

    Tables that mix and mingle 68

Building a Database 69

Adding and Removing Tables 73

    One more, please 74

    Oops, I didn't mean to do that 76

Part II: Getting It All on the Table *79*

Chapter 4: Keys, Relationships, and Indexes **81**

The Primary Key to Success 81

    The lowdown on primary keys 82

    Creating a primary key 83

Making Tables Get Along 85

    Rules of relationships 85

    Relationship types 85

Building Table Relationships 87
    The Relationships window 88
    Table relationships 89
Indexing for Faster Queries 93
    Create your own index 94
    Adding and removing indexes....................................... 95

Chapter 5: Remodeling Your Data **99**
Opening a Table for Editing..100
Inserting Records and Fields 103
    Adding a record 103
    Inserting a field 105
    Deleting a field 108
Modifying Field Content..109
Name-Calling 110
    Renaming fields 110
    Renaming a table...112
Turn Uh-Oh! into Yee-Hah!..114

Chapter 6: What's Happening Under the Table?.................**115**
Access Table Settings 115
Field Data Formats..118
    Text and memo fields 118
    Number and currency fields..121
    Date/time fields 123
    Yes/No fields 125
Gaining Control of Data Entry 127
    You really need to put a mask on those fields 127
    To require or not to require..133
    Making your data toe the line with validation 134
Give your fingers a mini vacation by default 136

Part III: Data Mania and Management **139**

Chapter 7: Creating Data Forms **141**
Generating Forms 141
    Keeping it simple: AutoForm...143
    Granting most wishes: The Form Wizard 144
Customizing Form Parts 148
    Taking the Layout view 149
    The theme's the thing 150
    Managing form controls..150

Chapter 8: Importing and Exporting Data.......................**155**
  Retrieving Data from Other Sources 156
    Translating file formats 156
    Importing and linking 159
  Get This Data Out of Here.. 164
    Export formats 164
    Exporting table or query data 165

Chapter 9: Editing Data Automatically.........................**169**
  Please Read This First!... 169
  Creating Consistent Corrections 172
  Using Queries to Automate the Editing Process 174
    Looking for duplicate records 175
    Running the Find Duplicates Query Wizard 176

Chapter 10: Gather Locally, Share Globally.....................**181**
  Access and the Web 181
  Click! Using Hyperlinks in Your Access Database................. 182
    Adding a hyperlink field to your table 183
    Typing your hyperlinks.. 185
    Fine tuning your hyperlinks.. 186
    Testing links 187
  Embedding Web Content into Your Access Forms 187
    Adding hyperlinks to your form.. 188
  Publishing Your Data to the Web 194
    Publishing your Access tables 195

**Part IV: Ask Your Data, and Ye Shall
Receive Answers**... **201**

Chapter 11: Fast Finding, Filtering, and Sorting Data **203**
  Using the Find Command 204
    Finding anything fast 204
    Shifting Find into high gear... 206
  Sorting from A to Z or Z to A.. 208
    Sorting by a single field... 209
    Sorting on more than one field... 209
  Fast and Furious Filtering... 210
    Filtering by a field's content... 210
    Filter by selection 212
    Filter by Form 213
    Unfiltering in a form... 216
    Filter by excluding selection 217

Chapter 12: I Was Just Asking . . . for Answers 219

    Simple (Yet Potent) Filter and Sort Tools 220
        Filter things first..220
        Fact-finding with fun, fast filtering...222
        Here's the "advanced" part 224
    Select Queries 229
        Solid relationships are the key to getting it all
            (from your tables) 230
        Running the Query Wizard 231
    Getting Your Feet Wet with Ad Hoc Queries...236
        Adding the finishing touches...240
        Saving the query 242
        Running your query...242

Chapter 13: I'll Take These AND Those OR Them. 245

    Working with AND and/or OR..246
        Data from here to there..247
        Using multiple levels of AND 249
        Establishing criteria with OR...250
    Combining AND with OR and OR with AND 252

Chapter 14: Queries That Think Faster Than You 255

    Kissing That Calculator Goodbye via the Total Row 255
    Adding the Total Row to Your Queries..257
    Giving the Total Row a Workout...258
        Organizing things with Group By...258
        Performing sums 260
        Counting, the easy way 262
        Narrowing the results with Where 263
    Creating Your Own Top-Ten List...264
    Choosing the Right Field for the Summary Instruction 265

Chapter 15: Calculating with Your Data. 267

    A Simple Calculation 268
    Complex Calculations 270
        Calculate until you need calculate no more! 271
        Using one calculation in another 271
        Using parameter queries to ask for help 272
        Daisy-chaining your words with text formulas 275
    Expression Builder (Somewhat) to the Rescue 277

Chapter 16: Flying into Action Queries. 283

    Easy Update...284
    Add Records in a Flash 288
    Quick Cleanup...291

Part V: Plain and Fancy Reporting *295*

Chapter 17: Quick and Not-So-Dirty Automatic Reporting .... .297

Fast and Furious Automatic Reporting 298
    Creating a quick, one-table report 298
    Starting the Report Wizard 304
Previewing Your Report 309
    Zooming in and out and all around 311
    Pop goes the menu 313
Beauty Is Only Skin (Report) Deep 314
    The Print Options tab 314
    The Page tab 316
    The Columns tab 317

Chapter 18: Dazzling Report Design 319

Taking Your Report In for Service 319
Report Organization 321
    Structural devices 321
    Page breaks 324
Formatting This, That, and the Other 326
    Adding color 327
    Relocation, relocation, relocation 329
    One size does not fit all 331
    Spaced-out controls 332
    Borderline beauty 333
    Tweaking your text 337
Sneaking a Peek 338
Getting a Themes Makeover 339
Adding More Design Elements 341
    Drawing lines 341
    Pretty as a picture 342

Chapter 19: Headers and Footers and Groups, Oh My! 345

A Place for Everything and Everything in Its Place 346
    Layout basics 346
    Sections 348
    Grouping your records 350
    So you want more? 354
Customizing Properties 355
    Controlling report and page headings 356
    Adjusting individual sections 359
    Itemized adjustments 361

Chapter 20: Magical Mass Mailings. **367**
   Massive Mailings with the Label Wizard 367

Part VI: More Power to You 375

Chapter 21: Making It All Better with the Analyzer Tools **377**
   Convert Your Flat Files to Relational Tables with Analyzer 378
   Record Database Object Details with the Database Documenter 382
   Improve Database Performance without Steroids 385

**Chapter 22: Hello! Creating an Interface to Welcome
Database Users.** **389**
   The Comings and Goings of a Navigation Form 390
      Creating a Navigation form 390
   Am I in the Right Place? Testing Navigation Forms 393
   Maintaining the Navigation Form 394
      Edit a Navigation form item 394
      Delete a Navigation Form tab item 395
      Move a Navigation Form item 395
   Displaying the Navigation Form at Startup 396

Part VII: The Part of Tens 399

Chapter 23: Ten Common Problems **401**
   That's Just Not Normal 401
   You Type 73.725, but it Changes to 74 402
   The Words They Are A-Changing 403
   Was There and Now It's Gone 404
      Undo 404
      Search for the missing record 404
      Backup recovery 405
   You Run a Query, but the Results Aren't What You Expect 405
   The Validation That Never Was 407
   The Slowest Database in Town 407
   Your Database File Is as Big as a Whale 408
   You Get a Mess When Importing Your Spreadsheet 410
   We're Sorry; Your Database File Is Corrupt 410

Chapter 24: Ten Uncommon Tips **413**

Document Everything as Though You'll be Questioned by the FBI......414
Keep Your Fields as Small as Possible..415
Use Number Fields for Real Numbers...416
Validate Your Data 416
Use Understandable Names to Keep Things Simple.............................416
Delete with Great Caution 417
Back up, Back up, Back up 417
Think, Think, and Think Again...418
Get Organized and Stay Organized...418
There's No Shame in Asking for Help..419

Index *421*

Introduction

Y ou've picked up this book and are hoping it will teach you to use Microsoft Access 2010. Of course, as the authors, we believe this was a wise decision — or that (at the very least) it was some sort of divine intervention that led you to our pages. We're quite certain that this is The Book For You — but not just because we wrote it. Rather, we base this conviction on the fact that both of us have been teaching and using Access for a very long time, and we know how to share what we know with our students. That's right, you're now one of our students — at least that's how we feel about you as our reader. Now, we *could* be wrong here, but that happens so infrequently that we're hardly considering it. No, the reason you picked up this book is that you want to learn Access, and this is the best book to help you do just that. Really. No kidding.

Of course, being a normal human being, you probably have work to do, and whether or not we're right about this being The Book For You, you need Access. You need it to organize your data. You need it to store — accessibly, of course — all the information that's currently spilling out of notebooks, file drawers, your pockets, your glove compartment, everywhere. You need it so you can print out snappy-looking reports that make you look like the genius you are. You need it so you can create cool forms that will help your staff enter all the data you've got stacked on their desks — and in a way that lets you know the data was entered properly, so it's accurate and useful. You need Access so you can find little bits of data out of the huge pool of information you need to store. You just need it.

About This Book

With all the power that Access has (and that it therefore gives *you*), there comes a small price: complexity. Access isn't one of those applications you can just sit down and use, "right out of the box." It's not scarily difficult or anything, but there's a lot going on — and you need some guidance, some help, some direction, to really use it and make it sing and dance. And that's where this book — a "reference for the rest of us" — comes in.

So you've picked up this book. Hang on to it. Clutch it to your chest and run gleefully from the store. (Stop and pay for it first, please; we'd never want to encourage you to embark on a life of crime.) And then start reading — whether you begin with Chapter 1 or whether you dive in on your own and start with a particular feature or area of interest that's been giving you fits. Just read, and then go put Access through its paces.

Conventions Used in This Book

As you work with Access 2010, you're going to need to tell it to do things. You'll also find that at times, Access has questions for you, usually in response to your asking it to do something. This book will show you how to talk to Access, and how Access will talk to you. To show the difference between the two sides of that conversation, we format the commands as follows:

This is something you type into the computer.

```
This is how the computer responds to your command.
```

Because Access *is* a Windows program, you don't just type, type, type — you also mouse around quite a bit. Here are the mouse movements necessary to make Access (and any other Windows program) work:

- ✔ **Click:** Position the tip of the mouse pointer (the end of the arrow) on the menu item, button, check box, or whatever else you happen to be aiming at — and then quickly press and release the left mouse button.

- ✔ **Double-click:** Position the mouse pointer as though you're going to click, but fool it at the last minute by clicking twice in rapid succession.

- ✔ **Click and drag (highlight):** Put the tip of the mouse pointer at the place you want to start highlighting, and then press and hold the left mouse button. While holding down the mouse button, drag the pointer across whatever you want to highlight. When you reach the end of what you're highlighting, release the mouse button.

- ✔ **Right-click:** Right-clicking works just like clicking, except you're exercising the right instead of the left mouse button.

What You Don't Have to Read

Now that we've told you that you should read the book, we're telling you that you don't have to read *all* of it. Confused? Don't be. This section of the introduction exists to put your mind at ease, so you won't worry that you have to digest every syllable of this book in order to make sense of Access. And more than just being a required section of the introduction, the heading is true. You don't have to read the whole book.

You should read the chapters that pertain to things you don't know, but you can skip the stuff you do know or that you're fairly sure you don't need to know. If the situation changes and you eventually *do* need to know something, you can go back and read that part later.

If you only use Access at work, and you're using an Access database that some über-geek in your IT department created, chances are you can't tinker with it. Therefore, if you only need to know about using an existing Access database (or unless you have designs on that IT geek's job), you can skip the chapters on designing databases.

Of course, it might be nice to know what's happening "behind the scenes," but you don't have to read those chapters if you don't want to.

Foolish Assumptions

You need to know only a few things about your computer and Windows to get the most out of *Access 2010 For Dummies.* In the following pages, we presume that you . . .

✔ Know the basics of Windows — how to open programs, save your files, create folders, find your files once you've saved them, print, and do basic stuff like that.

✔ Have some goals that Access will help you reach. You either

   • want to build your own databases

     and/or

   • want to work with databases that other people have created.

✔ Want to use and create queries, reports, and an occasional form.

✔ Have either Windows Vista or Windows 7.

   If your computer uses Windows 98, 2000, or XP, you can't run Office 2010.

You don't *have* to know (or even care) about table design, field types, relational databases, or any of that other database stuff to make Access work for you. Everything you need to know is right here, just waiting for you to read it. Of course, you may *want* to know what's going on under the hood (so to speak). But if you do, you'll find that information in this book's pages.

How This Book Is Organized

Here's a breakdown of the parts in this book. Each part covers a general aspect of Access. The part's individual chapters dig into the details.

Part I: Basic Training

In this first part of the book, you'll find out what Access is, what it isn't, how it works, and how you open it up and start using it. You'll find out how to navigate and master the Access workspace — and people who've used previous versions of Access find out about all the new features and tools that are part of Access 2010.

Part I also takes you through the process of planning your database — deciding what to store, how to structure your database, and how to use some of Access 2010's very helpful tools for starting a database with templates and themes — cookie-cutters, to use a fun and accurate metaphor — for a variety of common database designs. Be prepared to pick up some helpful jargon, as you learn a bit about a few specialized terms that you really need to know.

Part II: Getting It All on the Table

Part II takes you a bit deeper, starting out with a chapter on setting up more than one table to store related data — and moving on with chapters on setting up relationships between those tables, customizing the way data is stored in your tables, and ways to control how data is entered into the tables in your database. You'll also find out about new tools that create new data in your tables — based on existing data — automatically.

Part III: Data Mania and Management

Here you find out all about *forms* — the customized interfaces you create to make it easier to enter, edit, and look at your database. You'll also discover cool ways to share your Access data with other programs and how to bring content from Word documents and Excel worksheets into Access to save time, reduce the likelihood of data-entry errors, and build consistency within all the work you do in Microsoft Office.

Speaking of saving time and building consistency, you'll also learn about the new Application Parts feature, through which you can recycle parts of your existing databases to build new ones. You'll also find out about using Access tables on the Web, and how to publish your database to the Internet. Look out, world!

Part IV: Ask Your Data, and Ye Shall Receive Answers

In Part IV, you get ready to ask questions such as, "How many customers do we have in Peoria?" and "How long has that guy in Accounting worked here?" Of course, you already know how to form and speak sentences that go up at the end (so people know you're asking a question), but when you ask a question in Access, the pitch of your voice rarely makes any difference. You'll need, therefore, to know how to sort, filter, and query your data to get at the information you're storing in your Access database. You'll also want to know more about Action Queries — and these, too, can be found in Part IV.

Part V: Plain and Fancy Reporting

Reports are compilations of data from one or more tables in your database. That statement might sound a bit scary, because "compilations" has four syllables and you might not be sure what a table is yet. Have no fear, however, because Access provides some cool automatic tools that let you pick and choose what you want in your report, and then it goes and makes the report *for you.* How neat is that?

Automatic reports weren't good enough for you, eh? If your job relies upon reports not only being informative but also attractive and attention-grabbing, Part V will be like opening a birthday present. Well, not really, but you'll find out about charts, printing labels, and putting everything from your logo to page numbers on your reports.

Part VI: More Power to You

Part VI gives more power in the form of the Access Analyzer, a tool that tunes up your database for better performance. It also gives you more power by showing you how to create a user interface that controls what people see, which tables they can edit, and how they work with your database overall.

Part VII: The Part of Tens

The format of these chapters is designed to give you a lot of information in a simple, digestible fashion so you can absorb it without realizing you're actually learning something. Sneaky, huh?

Appendix: Getting Help

This isn't really a whole part, but it's darn useful. Remember how your mom told you the only foolish question is the one you don't ask? In this appendix, accessible at www.dummies.com/go/access2010, you find out where to go to ask — namely, the online and built-in help resources that Access offers.

Note: We went to the trouble of typing up a ton of records in a few sample databases that are designed to show you the tricks of the Access trade. You can find all the samples at the aforementioned Web site, www.dummies.com/go/access2010.

Icons Used in This Book

When something in this book is particularly valuable, we go out of our way to make sure that it stands out. We use these cool icons to mark text that (for one reason or another) *really* needs your attention. Here's a quick preview of the ones waiting for you in this book and what they mean:

 Tips are incredibly helpful words of wisdom that promise to save you time, energy, and the embarrassment of being caught swearing out loud while you're alone. Whenever you see a tip, take a second to check it out.

 Some things are too important to forget, so the Remember icon points them out. These items are critical steps in a process — points that you don't want to miss.

 Sometimes we give in to the techno-geek lurking inside us and slip some technical babble into the book. The Technical Stuff icon protects you from obscure details by making them easy to avoid. On the other hand, you may find them interesting. (Your inner techno-geek will rejoice.)

 The Warning icon says it all: *Skipping this information may be hazardous to your data's health.* Pay attention to these icons and follow their instructions to keep your databases happy and intact.

Where to Go from Here

Now nothing's left to hold you back from the delights and amazing wonders of Access. Hold on tight to this copy of *Access 2010 For Dummies* and leap into Access.

- ✔ If you're brand-new to the program and don't know which way to turn, start with the general overview in Chapter 1.

- ✔ If you're about to design a database, we salute you — and recommend flipping through Chapter 4 for some helpful design and development tips.

- ✔ Looking for something specific? Try the Table of Contents or the Index.

Now, go ye forth and build a database!

Part I
Basic Training

In this part . . .

Don't worry, even though this part of the book is called "Basic Training", nobody's going to shout at you or make you do pushups. We promise. Instead, you'll find out what Access is, what it does, and how to get started using it.

The three chapters in this part of the book introduce you to what's new in Access 2010, help you get comfortable with the Access 2010 workspace, and show you how to start building your first database. You also find out about some essential terms and concepts that will help you figure out — and talk about — your database needs at work, with clients, or if you're trying to bore people to death at a party.

Ready? Then let's get started!

Chapter 1

Getting to Know Access 2010

In This Chapter

▶ Deciding when to use Access

▶ Discovering what's new in Access 2010

▶ Unlocking the basics of working with Access

▶ Figuring out how to get started

Access 2010, the most recent version of the Microsoft Office database application, is a very robust and powerful program. You probably already know that, and perhaps that power — or your perceptions of all that Access can do — is what made you reach for this book. We applaud your wise choice!

For all of its power, Access is also very — pardon the expression — *accessible*. It's pretty easy to use at the edges, where a new user will be; you don't have to venture all the way in to its core to get quite a lot out of the software. In fact, with just the basic functionality that you'll discover in this book, you'll be able to put Access through many of its most important paces, yet you'll be working with wizards and other on-screen tools that keep you at a comfortable arm's distance from the software's inner workings, the things that programmers and serious developers play with. Feel better now?

You don't have to use every feature and tool and push the edges of the Access envelope. In fact, you can use very little of everything Access has to offer and still have quite a significant solution to your needs for storing and accessing data — all because Access can really "do it all" — enabling you to set up a database quickly, build records into that database, and then use that data in several useful ways. Later on, who knows? You may become an Access guru.

In this chapter, you'll discover what Access does best (and when you might want to use another tool instead), and get a look at what's new and improved in Access 2010 (compared to Access 2007). You'll see how it does what it does, and hopefully you'll begin to understand and absorb some basic terminology. Now, don't panic — nobody's expecting you to memorize long lists of high-tech vocabulary or anything scary like that. The goal here (and in the next two chapters) with regard to terms is to introduce you to some basic words and concepts to help you make better use of Access in general — as well as better understand later chapters in this book, if you choose to follow us all the way to its stunning conclusion.

What Is Access Good For, Anyway?

What *is* Access good for? That's a good question. Well, the list of what you can do with it is a lot longer than the list of what you *can't* do with it — of course, only if you leave things like "paint your car" and "do the dishes" off the "can't do" list. When it comes to data organization, storage, and retrieval, Access is at the head of the class.

Building big databases

Okay, what do I mean by *big* database? Any database with a lot of records — and by *a lot,* I mean hundreds. At least. And certainly if you have *thousands* of records, you need a tool like Access to manage them. Although you can use Microsoft Excel to store lists of records, it limits how many you can store (no more than the number of rows in a single worksheet). In addition, you can't use Excel to set up anything beyond a simple list that can be sorted and filtered. So anything with a lot of records and complex data is best done in Access.

Some reasons why Access handles big databases well:

- ✔ Typically a big database has big data-entry needs. Access offers not only forms, but also features that can create a quick form through which someone can enter all those records. This can make data entry easier and faster, and can reduce the margin of error significantly. (Check out Chapter 7 for more about building forms.)

- ✔ When you have lots and lots of records, you also have lots of opportunities for errors to creep — duplicate records, records with misspellings, records with missing information — and that's just for openers. So you need an application such as Access to ferret out those errors and fix them. (Chapter 9 lays out how you can use Access to find and replace errors and search for duplicate entries.)

- ✔ Big databases mean big needs for accurate, insightful reporting. Access has powerful reporting tools you can use to create printed and on-screen reports — and those can include as few or as many pieces of your data as you need, drawn from more than one table if need be. You can tailor your reports to your audience, from what's shown on the reports pages to the colors and fonts used.

✔ Big databases are hard to wade through when you want to find some-thing. Access provides several tools for sorting, searching, and creating your own specialized tools (known as *queries*) for finding the elusive single record or group of records you need.

✔ Access saves time by giving you new uses for existing tools you may have used to import data from other sources — such as Excel work-sheets (if you started in Excel and maxed out its usefulness as a data-storage device) and Word tables. This saves you from re-entering all your data and allows you to keep multiple data sources consistent.

Creating databases with multiple tables

Whether your database holds 100 records or 1,000 records (or more), if you need to keep separate tables and relate them for maximum use of the infor-mation, you need a *relational* database — and that's Access. How do you know whether your data needs to be in separate tables? Think about your data — is it very compartmentalized? Does it go off on tangents? Consider the following example and apply the concepts to your data and see if you need multiple tables for your database.

The Big Organization database

A non-profit organization — one that rescues homeless pets — has a data-base of volunteers and contacts — past, present, and potential — and wants to keep track of a lot of information on them. For current and past volunteers, the people running the organization want to store information about the vol-unteering that was done, how much time they spent, what they did, and for whom. For potential volunteers, they want to keep track of when and how they've contacted them, whether with mailings and phone calls or at meet-ings. Imagine keeping all of that in a single table — with everything from the volunteer's name to what causes they support to where they live and how much time they can donate.

For a complex database like this one, you'd need multiple tables, as follows:

✔ One table would house the volunteer contact information — names, addresses, phone numbers, and e-mail addresses. It might make sense to add a Volunteer Number field, which would make each record unique, and it would be equally sensible to come up with a number format where one or more of the characters could be used to differentiate among different volunteer/contact types — past, current, or potential.

✔ A second table would contain the volunteer number again (as a way to link or connect the two tables) and also the volunteers' status informa-tion — how much time they have available to volunteer, when they're available, and which areas they can work in, geographically.

✔ A third table, again containing the volunteer number, would include the volunteer's preferences for activities — things they're good at, enjoy doing, and special skills or resources they can offer, such as training homeless dogs or providing space in a barn for rescued horses.

Because you don't have to fill in every field for each volunteer's record (in any table in the database) if you don't have a phone number or don't know how many hours someone can work, it's okay to leave those fields blank until you've obtained that information.

With these three tables in place, any type of volunteer or useful contact (past, current, or potential) can be entered into the database, and only the table(s) that apply to that person need be populated with data. When a potential volunteer becomes a current one, relevant data can be entered into the appropriate table(s). If a potential volunteer never becomes available to help out, you can delete that person's name when a prescribed length of time has elapsed — or perhaps you can set up a fourth table to hold archived volunteer records. The options are limited only by your needs and intended use of the data.

Failure to plan? Plan to fail

If you think carefully about your database, how you use your data, and what you need to know about your employees, customers, volunteers, donors, products, or projects — whatever you're storing information about — you can plan

✔ How many tables you'll need

✔ Which data will go into which table

✔ How you'll use the tables together to get the reports you need

Feel free to sketch your planned database on paper, drawing a kind of flow chart with boxes for each table and lists of fields that you'll have in each one. Draw arrows to show how they might be related — it's sort of like drawing a simple family tree — and you're well on your way to a well-planned, useful database.

Here's a handy procedure to follow if you're new to the process of planning a database:

1. **On paper or in a word processing document, whichever is more comfortable, type the following:**

   • A tentative name for your database

   • A list of the pieces of information you plan on getting from that database on a daily or regular basis

2. **Now, based on that information, create a new list of the actual details you could store:**

   List every piece of information you can possibly think of about your customers, products, ideas, cases, books, works of art, students — whatever your database pertains to. Don't be afraid to go overboard — you can always skip some of the items in the list if they don't turn out to be things you really need to know (or can possibly find out) about each item in your database.

3. **Take the list of *fields* — that's what all those pieces of information are — and start breaking them up into logical groups.**

   How? Think about the fields and how they work together:

   • If the database keeps track of a library of books, for example, perhaps the title, publication date, publisher, ISBN (*I*nternational *S*tandard *B*ook *N*umber, which is unique for each book), price, and page count can be stored in one group, and author information, reviews, and lists of other titles by the same author or books on the same topic can be stored in another group. These groups become individual tables, creating your relational database of books.

   • Figure out what's unique about each record. As stated in the previous point, you need a field that's unique for each record. Although Access can create this for you if no unique data exists for each record in your database, it's often best to have such a field already in place, or create it yourself. Customer numbers, student numbers, book ISBNs, catalog numbers, serial numbers — anything that won't be the same for any two records will do.

   With a big list of fields and some tentative groupings of those fields at the ready, and with an idea of which field is unique for each record, you can begin figuring out how to *use* the data.

4. **Make a list of ways you might use the data, including**

   • Reports you'd like to create, including a list of which fields should be included for each report.

   • Other ways you can use the data — labels for mailings, product labels, catalogue data, price lists, contact lists, and so on.

5. **List all the places your data currently resides — on slips of paper in your pocket, on cards in a box, in another program (such as Excel), or maybe through a company that sells data for marketing purposes.**

With this planning done, you're ready to start building your database. The particulars of that process come later in this chapter and in subsequent chapters, so don't jump in yet. Do pat yourself on the back, though, because if you read this procedure and applied even some of it to your potential database, you're way ahead of the game, and I'm confident you'll make good use of all that Access has to offer.

Databases with user forms

When you're planning your database, consider how the data will be entered:

- ✔ If you'll be doing the data entry yourself, perhaps you're comfortable working in a spreadsheet-like environment (known in Access as *Table view*), where the table is a big grid, you fill it in row by row, and each row is a record.

  Figure 1-1 shows a table in progress in Table view. You decide — is it easy to use, or can you picture yourself forgetting to move down a row and entering the wrong stuff in the wrong columns as you enter each record?

- ✔ You may want to use a *form* (shown in Figure 1-2) — a specialized interface for data entry, editing, and for viewing your database one record at a time — if

  - Someone else will be handling data entry.

  - Typing row after row of data into a big grid seems mind-numbing.

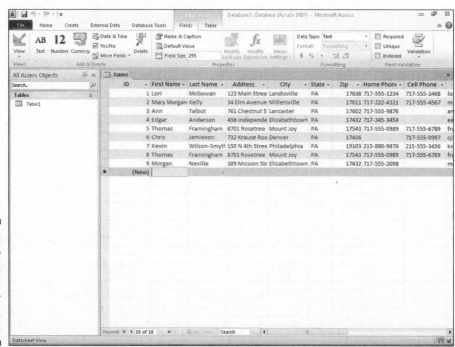

Figure 1-1:
Table view can be an easy environment for data entry. Or not.

The mind-numbing effect (and inherent increased margin for error) is especially likely when you have lots of fields in a database, and the user, if working in Table view, has to move horizontally through the fields. A form like the
one in Figure 1-2 puts the fields in a more digestible, vertical format, making
it easier to enter data into the fields and to see all the fields at once (or only
those you want data entered into). You can put those fields on the form in
the order that'll be easiest for the data-entry person — and that order would
not necessarily have to be the order they appear in the table.

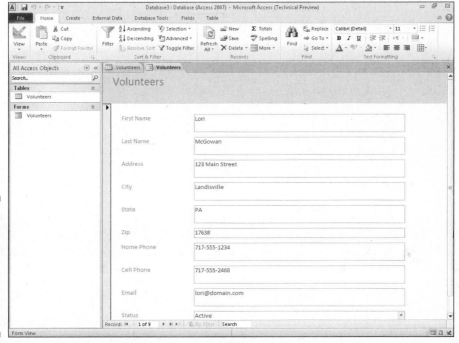

Figure 1-2:
Here's a
simple form
for entering
new records
or review-
ing existing
ones.

You can find out all about forms in Chapter 7. If your database is large
enough that you require help doing the data entry — or if it's going to
grow over time, making an ongoing data-entry process likely — Access is
the tool for you. The fact that it offers simple forms of data entry/editing
is reason enough to make it your database application of choice.

Databases that require special reporting

Yet another reason to use Access is its ability to create customized reports quickly and easily. Some database programs, especially those designed for single-table databases (known as *flat-file* databases), have some canned reports built in, and that's all you can do — just select a report from the list and run the same report that every other user of that software runs.

If you're an Excel user, your reporting capabilities are far from easy or simple, and they're not designed for use with large databases — they're meant for spreadsheets and small, one-table lists. Further, you have to dig much deeper into Excel's tools to get at these reports. Access, on the other hand, is a database application, so reporting is a major, up-front feature.

An example? In Excel, to get a report that groups your data by one or more of the fields in your list, you have to sort the database first, using the field(s) to sort the data, and then you can create what's known as a *subtotal report*. To create it, you use a dialog box that asks you about calculations you want to perform, where to place the results, and whether you're basing a sort and/ or a subtotal on more than one field. The resulting report is not designed for printing, and you have to tinker with your spreadsheet pagination (through a specialized view of the spreadsheet) to control how the report prints out.

In Access? Just fire up the Report Wizard, and you can sort your data, choose how to group it, decide which pieces of data to include in the report, and pick a visual layout and color scheme — all in one simple, stream-lined process. Without your doing anything, the report is ready for printing. Access is built for reporting — after all, it's a database application — and reports are one of the most (if not *the* most) important ways you'll use and share your data.

Because reports are such an important part of Access, you can not only create them with minimum fuss, but also customize them to create powerful documentation of your most important data:

- ✔ Build a quick, simple report that just spits out whatever's in your table in a tidy, easy-to-read format. (See Figure 1-3 for a sample.)
- ✔ Create a customized report that you design step-by-step with the help of the Report Wizard. (See Figure 1-4.) The report shown in the figure has the volunteers grouped by the State field (note DE comes before PA), and the records for each state are in ascending order by the City field. These options were easily put to work with just a few clicks.

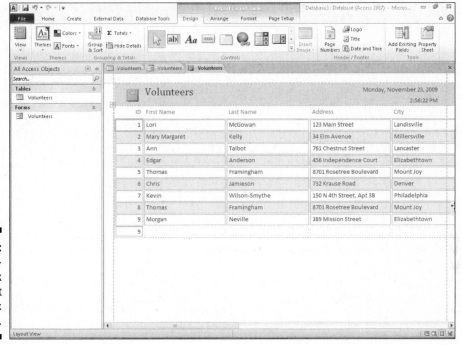

Figure 1-3:
Ah, simplicity. A quick report is just one click away.

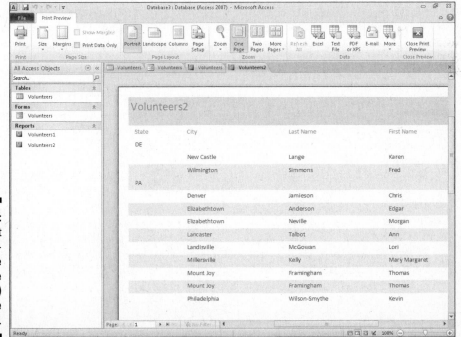

Figure 1-4:
The Report Wizard creates more elaborate (but simple) reports, like this one.

✔ You can really roll up your sleeves and design a new report — or play with an existing one, adding all sorts of bells and whistles. Figure 1-5 shows this happening in Design view — note that the report's title ("Volunteers Report") is selected: It has a box around it and tiny handles on the corners and sides of the box, which means you can reformat the title, change the font, size, or color of the text, or even edit the words themselves if a new title is needed.

So, you can create any kind of custom report in Access, using any or all of your database tables and any of the fields from those tables, and you can group fields and place them in any order you want:

✔ With the Report Wizard, you can choose from several preset layouts for your report, and it can all be customized row by row, column by column.

✔ Office Themes (see the Themes button on the Design tab back in Figure 1-5) apply preset designs that affect fonts, colors, and other graphical elements — automatically.

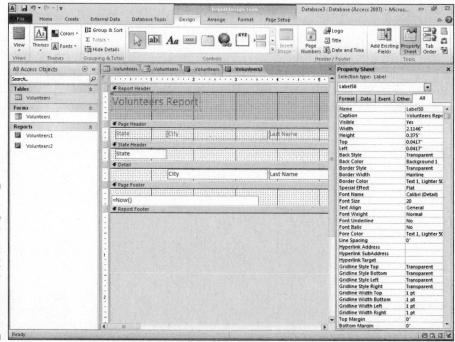

Figure 1-5:
You *can*
avoid
Design
view, but
to really
customize
things, you'll
need it.

✔ If you want to place your personal stamp on every aspect of your report, you can use Design view to

- Add titles, instructional or descriptive text boxes, and graphics.

- Set up customized headers and footers to include any information you want to appear on all the report's pages.

If all this sounds exciting, or at least interesting, then you're really on the right track with Access. The need to create custom reports is a major reason to use Access; you can find out about all these reporting options in Chapters 17 through 19. That's right: This chapter plus three more — that's four whole chapters — are devoted to reporting. It *must* be a big feature in Access!

What's New in Access 2010?

For users of Access 2007, the upgrade to 2010 won't seem like a big deal. Yes, there are significant improvements and some really great new features, but you're won't run smack into the learning curve that users of Access 2003 encountered upon upgrading to 2007 (and will still encounter if they move up to 2010 without the interim step).

If you're coming from 2003, the biggest changes are found in the interface — gone are the familiar menus and toolbars of 2003 and prior versions, replaced by a ribbon bar divided into tabs that take you to different versions of those old standbys. It's a big change, and it takes some getting used to.

In this book, however, we're going to assume you already got your feet wet with 2007 and aren't thrown by the interface anymore. We're figuring you upgraded to 2007 or have played with it enough to feel comfortable diving into 2010.

New and improved features

So what's new in Access 2010? In the order you're most likely to encounter them, here goes:

✔ The File tab and its associated Backstage View panel are new; they replace the Office button and resulting menu in Access 2007. Using the panel on the left (shown in Figure 1-6), you make your choices for opening new files, accessing recently used files, saving files, printing, and exiting the application (among other momentous decisions). It's a lot like ye olde File menu from Access 2003 in terms of what's available; Backstage view makes the commands and features that used to live on the File menu easily accessible. To get to it, just click the File tab.

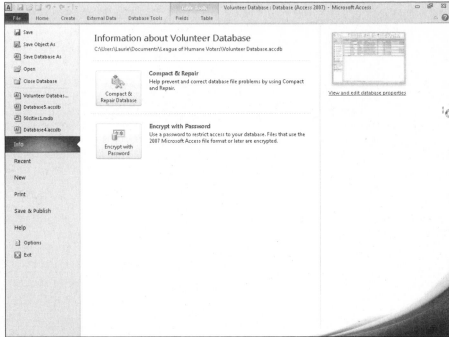

Figure 1-6:
Backstage
view —
new but
hauntingly
familiar to
those who
remember
the File
menu.

✔ Speaking of that ribbon bar that's new to Access 2003 users, the Ribbon — as Microsoft likes to refer to it — is now much more customizable. Using the Options menu, available through Backstage view, you can create new tabs, and customize existing ones by adding and reorganizing buttons on the associated Ribbon groups. (More about this feature in this very chapter — Chapter 1.)

✔ Office Themes make it easy to create visual uniformity within your database, its reports and forms. *Themes* affect colors and fonts, and apply consistent graphical elements, and are available throughout the Office 2010 suite, making it easy to give all your Office creations from Access, Word, Excel, and PowerPoint the same look.

✔ Pre-built database templates, available through Backstage view, make it easy to build a database with components that make sense for the kind of data you're dealing with. Use the Office online templates (see Figure 1-7 for the categories) and pick a template that suits your needs. The secrets to this new feature are found right here in Chapter 1.

✔ Application Parts are, in essence, different aspects of your existing databases that you can recycle for use in new ones. Already developed a great form or query? Reuse it. Learn how in Chapter 7.

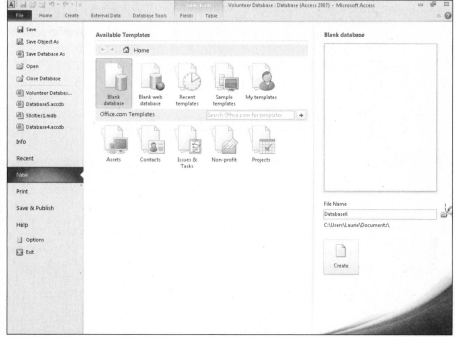

Figure 1-7:
Pick a
template
from any
category
offered with
Office online
templates
to speed
up your
database-
building
process.

✔ Publishing to the Web is even easier, including the reports you've created, your forms, and your data itself. The whole shooting match can be opened in a browser window once you publish and upload it to the Web. Look in Chapter 10 for more information on how this works.

✔ Navigation forms make it easier to organize your database components, using a simple drag-and-drop method to display desired parts of your database. (More about this feature in Chapter 21.)

✔ Table Events (also known as *triggers*) — which create new data based on the data in your tables — are new in 2010. You'll find out more about those in Chapter 6; for now, suffice to say you'll find data macros to be a very handy way to add effective automation to your database.

✔ Between Data Bars and Conditional Formatting, reports have become much more dynamic in Access 2010. Discussed in Chapter 17, you'll find out how to apply formatting based on the content of your data — based on values found in the records themselves, in other words — making your reports that much more intuitive.

So that's a lot of new features and powerful tools you've now got at your disposal. Other than the Backstage view, which you get to see by default when you start the application, however, you won't encounter most of them until and unless you want to. So for the new user, and for the early stages of your database development, you've still got the same solid and dependable tools Access always offered for building tables, setting up reports and forms, and creating the relationships between your tables that make the database everything you need it to be.

Reach out with SharePoint

What the heck is SharePoint? You may be asking that, along with lots of other people who've been seeing the product name and hearing how it provides access to your Access data from anywhere — using desktop applications, a Web browser, or even your phone. Well, it's a Microsoft software product that does all that and more, helping you manage your documents and collaborate with co-workers via the company network. Simply click the Save and Publish command in Backstage view (see Figure 1-8), and you're on your way to publishing your database to SharePoint, which means you can access it from pretty much everywhere, including that beach in Maui. (On second thought, some places should probably be declared Data-Free Zones.)

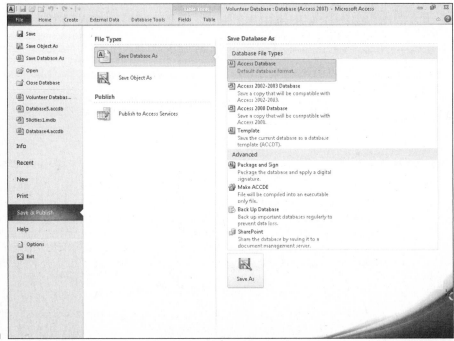

Figure 1-8:
The Save and Publish command in Backstage view offers choices for… you guessed it… saving and publishing your database.

As shown in Figure 1-8, the Save and Publish options include regular old Save Database As (to save it in some other format other than as an Access database), Save Object As (to save your database as a PDF or XPS file), and there's one more under the Publish heading: You can choose to Publish to Access Services. Figure 1-9 reveals the mysteries of Access Services, showing that you can use this command to make your database accessible via the Web or store it at a SharePoint location — which would then make it accessible to others who have the needed rights to view and snag files from that same location.

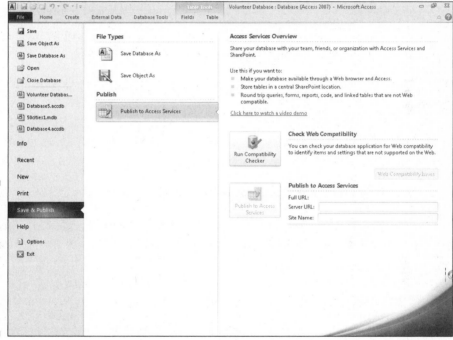

Figure 1-9: Get to know your SharePoint options by choosing to Publish to Access Services.

You must have SharePoint installed on your network or server to make full use of this feature — and of course, have other users with whom to share your files — for this process to be useful. Given that we can't delve too far into Microsoft SharePoint here (hey, this is an Access book, right?), we recommend the following resources to expand your knowledge of SharePoint:

- ✔ http://sharepoint2010.microsoft.com

- ✔ www.wiley.com: Use the Search box to find books and other learning tools that pertain to SharePoint 2010.

- ✔ http://sharepointsolutions.com: Check this site (and of course, Google for others) to find online courses in making the most of SharePoint 2010.

How Access Works and How You Work with It

When you look at all the applications in Microsoft Office — Word, Excel, PowerPoint, Outlook, and of course, Access — you'll see some features that are consistent throughout the suite. There are big differences, too — and that's where books like these come in handy, helping you deal with what's different and/or not terribly obvious to a new user.

Access has several features in common with the rest of the applications in the Microsoft Office suite. You'll find the same buttons on several of the tabs, and the Quick Access toolbar (demonstrated in Chapter 2) appears in all the applications, as do the default items on the menu itself.

If you already know how to open, save, and print in, say, Word, you're probably ready to do the same things in Access without any difficulty.

To make sure you're totally Access-ready, here's a look at the basic procedures to make sure you have a solid foundation on which to build.

Opening Access

Access opens in any one of several ways. So, like a restaurant with a very comprehensive menu, some people will love all the choices, and others will say, "I can't decide! There are just too many options to choose from!"

Now, you'll run into situations in which one of the ways is the glaringly best choice — hands down, that one will be the way to go. But what if you've never heard of it? You'll be trying to find my phone number (I'm unlisted — ha!) so you can give me a piece of your mind. So — to acquaint you with *all* your choices (so you'll be ready for any situation) — here are all the ways you can open Access:

✔ Click the Start menu button (in the lower-left corner of the screen) and choose All Programs➪Microsoft Office➪Microsoft Access 2010.

Figure 1-10 shows my Start menu. You may notice items on my menu that don't match yours — say, programs you may not have — don't worry about that. Just focus on the Microsoft Office submenu and make your choice from that.

If you've recently used Access, you'll see it in the list on the left side of the Start menu. Just choose Start➪Microsoft Access 2010, and Access opens.

✔ Double-click any existing Access database file on your Desktop or in a folder (as shown in Figure 1-11). Access opens automatically.

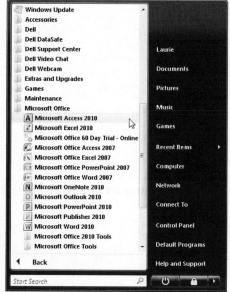

Figure 1-10:
The Windows Start menu offers all the Microsoft Office applications in one submenu.

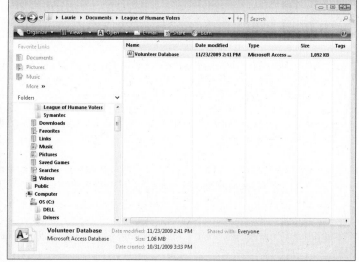

Figure 1-11:
Double-click an Access database file, and Access opens right up.

Good news: Access 2010 will open database files you created with previous versions of Access, and should support whatever features are employed within those database files. All your tables should open properly, and reports, forms, and queries should all work fine, too.

✔ If some helpful person has added Access to the Quick Launch toolbar (on the Windows Taskbar), you can click the Access 2010 icon (it looks like a pink key) and there you go. Access opens for you right then and there.

Does having an Access icon on the Quick Launch portion of the Taskbar sound extremely convenient? It is! To add the icon, follow these steps:

1. **Choose Start➪All Programs➪Microsoft Office.**

2. **When the list of Office applications appears, hold down the Ctrl key and click and drag the Access menu command down to the Quick Launch bar (that's the portion of the Taskbar immediately to the right of the Start button).**

   A black I-beam cursor, along with an icon for the application and a plus sign (indicating that the shortcut will be a duplicate of the command on the menu), appears where you point with your mouse on the bar, indicating where the new icon will go.

3. **Release the mouse button and then release the Ctrl key.**

   You've got yourself single-click access to, well, *Access.*

Don't have a Quick Launch bar on your Taskbar? Right-click the Taskbar and choose Toolbars from the pop-up menu. From the resulting submenu, choose Quick Launch. It won't have a check next to it if it's not currently part of your Taskbar — if it's already checked, you do have a Quick Launch bar displayed and just didn't realize it. If it's not checked, choose it, and you'll have a place to put the icons you want to keep handy.

If you're using Windows 7, you can also right-click on any icon in the Programs menu and choose Pin to Taskbar from the pop-up menu. Quick and easy!

Selecting a starting point

So Access is open — and (assuming you opened it from the Start menu or from the Quick Launch portion of the Taskbar) you're staring at the Access interface. You may see features whose purposes elude you or that you don't yet know how to use. Hey — don't worry — that's why you're reading this book!

You can find out more about all the tabs and buttons, panels and menus, and all that fun stuff in Chapter 2 — for now, just look at the ways Access offers you to get started with your database, be it an existing one that needs work or a new one you have all planned out and ready to go.

Opening an existing database

Well, this is the easy one. If a database already exists, you can open it by clicking the Office button (at the upper left of the workspace) and choosing Recent from the list of commands that appears. As shown in Figure 1-12, a panel opens, displaying the databases you've most recently used. Just click the database in the list and it opens — listing its current tables, queries, reports, and forms on the far left side of the window.

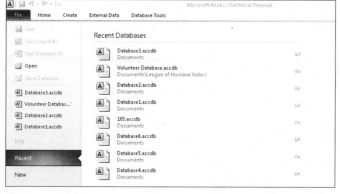

Figure 1-12: Pick your recently used database from the Recent list on the right.

When the database is open, you can open its various parts just by double-clicking them in that leftmost panel; whatever you open appears in the main, central part of the window. Figure 1-13 shows an example: a table, ready for editing.

After you open a table, you can begin entering or editing records — and you can read more about how that's done in Chapter 6, which demonstrates the different ways to edit your data and tweak your tables' setups. If you want to tinker with any existing queries, these, too, open just by clicking them in the list on the left side of the workspace. (For more information on queries, check out Chapters 11 and 12. You can do simple sorting and look for particular records with the skills you pick up in Chapters 9 and 11.)

Starting a new database from scratch

So you don't have a database to open, eh? Well, don't let that stop you. To start a new one, all you have to do is open Access — using any of the techniques listed earlier in this chapter (except the one that starts Access by opening an existing database file, which you don't have yet but will now).

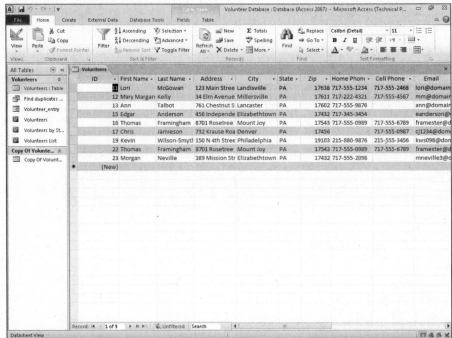

Figure 1-13:
An existing
table, ready
for records.

REMEMBER

A database file holds *all* your database components. Everything associated with the data is part of the database, including

- ✔ All the tables that house your data
- ✔ Queries that help you search and use the data
- ✔ Reports that show what your data is and what it means
- ✔ Forms that allow people to view, enter, and edit data

After Access is open, you can click the Blank Database button (shown in Figure 1-14) to get started. Actually, the assumption is that you'll start this way, so the Blank Database options already appear on the right side of the panel, also shown in Figure 1-14. If you've already clicked one of the other options (under Available Templates), you can click Blank Database to redisplay the panel shown in Figure 1-14.

At this point you can give your database a name (see the File Name box on the right), and click the Create button. To take this slowly and step-by-step (always a good idea for your first time), read on:

1. **With Access open and the Available Templates panel displayed, click the Blank Database button under the Available Templates heading.**

A panel appears on the right side of the Access window, asking you for a name for your new database. (See Figure 1-14.)

Blank Database button

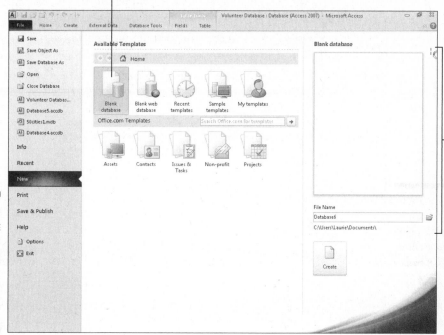

Figure 1-14:
The far-right panel lets you name and choose a home for your database.

Blank Database options

2. **Replace the default** `DatabaseX` **with whatever name you want to use.**

   The *X* in the preceding file name represents a number — Access assigns consecutive numbers to the default names, counting from any previously created databases.

   If this is your absolute first database in a fresh installation of Access, the file name offered in this panel will be `Database1`. Note that you don't need to type a file extension here — Access will add the correct one for you.

3. **As needed, choose a new location for the database file by following these steps:**

   a. *Click the little file folder (with an arrow on it) found to the right of the File Name box.*

      Doing so opens the File New Database dialog box (shown in Figure 1-15), which you can use to navigate to the drive or folder where your database should live.

b. *Use the panel on the left side of the File New Database dialog box to navigate to a folder for your database. When you're looking at a list of folders, click once to select the one in which you want to store your database.*

c. *As needed, click the New Folder button and name your new folder — click OK to return to the File New Database dialog box.*

d. *Click OK — the name you gave the file back in Step 2 is applied, and the file is saved to the location you chose.*

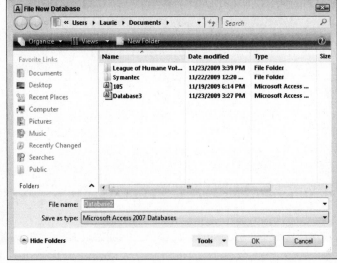

Figure 1-15:
Name and
choose a
location to
store your
database
file.

4. **Click the Create button.**

   A blank table opens. An ID column is automatically created, along with the first field of your database, with the instructions "Click to Add". The cell beneath that instruction is active, awaiting data.

At this point, you can begin entering records into your first table or begin naming your fields and setting them up. The field names go in the topmost row (the `ID` field is already created, as previously stated), and the label `Click to Add` is atop the column with the active cell. If you choose to save your table now (right-click the Table1 tab and choose Save), you can name your table something more useful than `Table1`.

Starting with a template

Access provides *templates* (prepared files that work sort of like database cookie-cutters) for your new database needs. You'll find a set of template icons in the Available Templates panel, as soon as you open Access. As shown in Figure 1-16, you can choose a template category by clicking any of the icons (which changes the displayed icons in the center of the workspace).

Click a template icon, and you see its details displayed on the right — along with the File Name box you saw when starting a new Blank Database. When you've found a template that looks like a good fit for your needs — one that starts with the tables, forms, reports, and so on that you think you'll find useful — give the new template-based database a name and choose a location for it, just as we explained in the "Starting a new database from scratch" section earlier in this chapter.

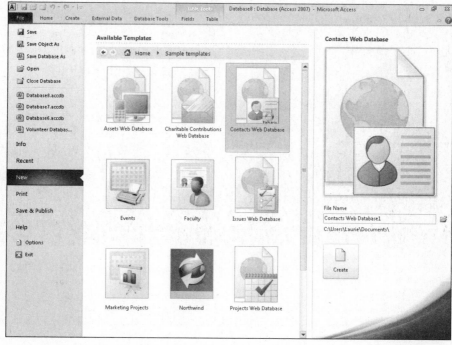

Figure 1-16:
Pick a template, any template — and then name your new template-based database.

Use the Back button at the top of the Available Templates panel to go back to the original set of template categories — and to the original set of icons, including those listed under the Office.com Templates Heading. Assuming you have an Internet connection going, you'll see the templates Microsoft has to offer. Choose one by clicking it, and then follow the on-screen instructions to utilize it for your new database. Note that you can also use the Search Office. com for Templates box to look for a particular template (just click the arrow button after you've entered your search terms). Again, you must be online to use this feature.

After you've downloaded the template (or chosen a template that was available in your installed copy of Access), you can start building data into it. There's one major difference from the previous procedure that uses this right side of the Available Templates panel to build a database from scratch (naming it, choosing a place to store it): Instead of having a blank "Table1" and nothing else, the template gives you pre-made tables, reports, queries, and forms (in various combinations and numbers, all based on the template you chose) and they're all set up — all *you* have to do is start entering records. Figure 1-17 shows the populated list of database components that comes with the Web Contacts database template.

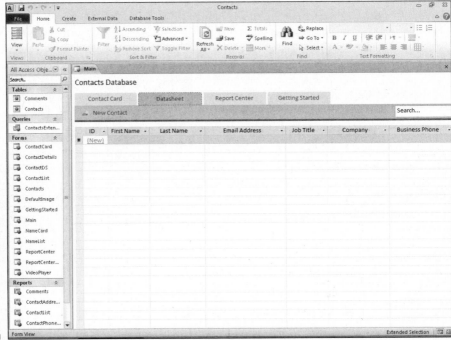

Figure 1-17: The basic fields for each table are already set up for you, along with reports based on the table's fields.

Just like a table you build from scratch, template-based tables need to be populated with data. You can change field names (see Chapter 5 for directions) and add and remove fields, too. After you tweak them until they're appropriate for *your* database, you can begin entering records, one field at a time.

Now what?

So you've got a new database started. What do you do now? You leaf on over to Chapter 2, where you can find out more about all the tools that Access offers — which tools are on-screen almost all the time, and which ones are specific to the way you chose to dig in and start that database.

In Chapter 3, you actually begin building a database, setting up tables and the fields that give them structure. And you'll figure out which tables you need to set up, putting that great plan you built in this chapter to work!

Chapter 2

Finding Your Way Around Access

• •

In This Chapter

▶ Getting started

▶ Trying out the tabs, buttons, and menus

▶ Using your mouse to get from here to there

▶ Letting your fingers do the walking

• •

*I*f you skipped Access 2007 and are coming to Access 2010 from the 2003 version, you're probably surprised by the new interface, which was introduced with Office 2007. If you did upgrade to Access (or Office) 2007 when it first came out, then the 2010 interface looks very familiar — and you'll find much of it to be the same as what you're accustomed to.

For those to whom the Office 2010 is a big change, take note of the following changes to the interface, which is strikingly different from that which you may have used in Office XP and previous versions:

✔ Menus have given way to tabs and buttons arranged in a strip across the top of the screen — known as the *Ribbon*.

✔ Toolbars are no longer made up of distinct, 3-D buttons. Instead, there are buttons and graphic examples of formatting, pictures of what the buttons create, and drop-down lists.

For users of Access 2007: Notice the new File tab and resulting Backstage View panel. Instead of spawning a square menu, the button now displays the panel shown on the right in Figure 2-1, where common tasks such as saving and printing are available.

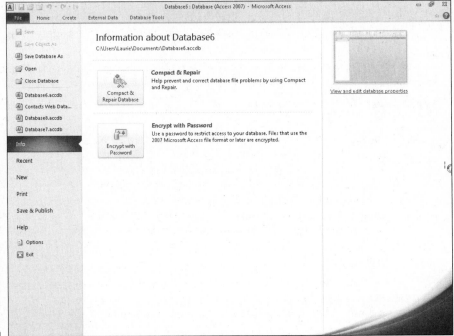

Figure 2-1:
The File tab
displays a
list of com-
mands plus
information
about the
open
database.

You also see features in the center and on the sides of the workspace, which change depending on what you're doing or which button you've clicked:

- If you're starting a new database, options for doing so appear in the center pane.

- If you're working with an existing database, its parts are listed in a panel on the left side of the workspace.

- Panels also open up along the bottom of the workspace when specific activities are taking place.

I won't go into every possible combination of on-screen features in this chapter — you get to know a lot of them in the subsequent chapters. For now, I'll show you the basic workspace in three states:

- When Access first opens up

- When a new database is being built, either from scratch or when you've started with one of Access's database templates

- When you're working on an existing database

As you read through the following sections, you can refer solely to the accompanying figures or, if you want, try to work along with the procedures — you'll find doing what you see described here boosts your confidence when you're using Access later, on your own.

Diving Right In

So you're ready to dive in. Well done, you! It's easy to start Access. You can start the application in multiple ways, accommodating nearly any situation you're in. (Chapter 1 discusses most of them.) Whether you're starting Access to view and edit an existing Access database (which gives you what you see in Figure 2-2) or are about to create your own (which opens the application and displays Backstage view and the Available Templates icons, shown in Figure 2-3), you can get to the tools you need right away. Figure 2-2 shows an existing database open to one of its tables, its other components are listed on the left side of the workspace.

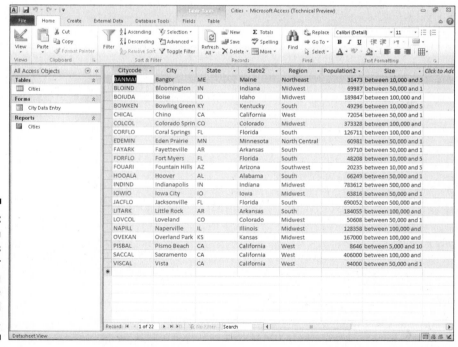

Figure 2-2: Open Access *and* your existing database in one fell swoop.

When you first open the application (as you also discover in Chapter 1), you're presented with a workspace that offers three basic ways to make that swan dive into the pool that is Access. You can pick which part of the existing database you want to work with, you can start a new, blank database from scratch, or you can start out with one of the Access templates.

Figure 2-3 shows the Available Templates icons with the Blank Database icon highlighted. Beneath that button are the Office.com Templates icons, for using various preset databases as your jumping-off point.

If you opened Access by using the Start menu or a Desktop/Taskbar icon and *now* you want to open an existing database, you can use the Recent command in the panel on the left (see Figure 2-4), or, if you haven't used the database in question for a while, you can use the Open command.

When you use the Recent command, clicking any one of the Recent Databases listed opens that sucker right up, displaying its parts on the panel on the left side of the workspace.

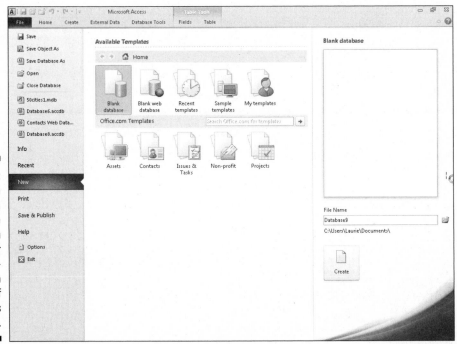

Figure 2-3:
You can build a database from nothing or from something — in the form of an Access template.

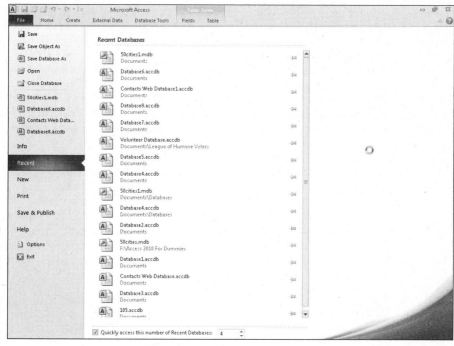

Figure 2-4:
Open an
existing or
recently
used
database.

In addition to offering commands like Save, Open, Print, and Help, Backstage view offers a list of the last four Access files you've used (they appear between Close Database and Info in that left-hand panel). If you want to see more than four files at a time here, use the field marked Quickly Access This Number of Recent Databases, found at the bottom of the workspace when you're in Recent view. Use the triangles to adjust the number up or down. The maximum you'll be able to set it to is 17. One other thing — don't confuse this with the number of files that can be viewed in the center section of the workspace in Recent view — this number affects only the File tab's Backstage View menu.

So that's it, really — any way you want to get started is represented in the (appropriately named) Getting Started window. After you get working, however, it's time to use the on-screen tools that don't appear until you open a database. Read on for a whirlwind tour of the Access workspace, including views and explanations of all the major bells, whistles, and buttons.

Working with On-Screen Tools in Access

When you open a database — be it an existing one or one you're just starting from a blank database or a template — the workspace changes, offering the Ribbon and its tabs shown in Figure 2-5 (Home, Create, External Data, Database Tools, Fields, and Table). These tabs are not to be confused with the database components' tabs, which appear in the center of the workspace for whichever tables, reports, queries, or forms you have chosen to open from the list on the left.

When the Ribbon tabs first appear, many of their buttons are dimmed — because they don't become available until you're doing something that warrants their use. For example, if you haven't opened any tables, forms, reports, or queries in your open database, the tools for editing or formatting your database will appear on the tabs, but they'll be dimmed, which indicates that they're unavailable. Tools for creating new components are available on the Create tab, but anything that works with existing data will be dimmed.

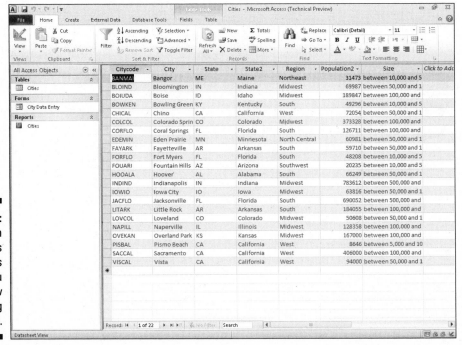

Figure 2-5:
The main Ribbon tabs appear as soon as you open a new or existing database.

After you open a table, report, query, or form, the tools for that table, report, query, or form become available. Displaying a form, for example, adds the Form Layout Tools group to the main set of five tabs, as shown in Figure 2-6.

Clicking tabs

To move from one tab on the Ribbon to another, simply click the tab's name. It's easy to see which tab is currently open — as shown in Figure 2-7, the tab is bright, and you can see all its buttons. When you mouse over another tab, a hairline border appears around it; the active tab remains bright, though, until you click a new one, making that the active tab.

When you have a table open, the Home tab is displayed, and a new label — Table Tools — appears above the Fields and Table tabs.

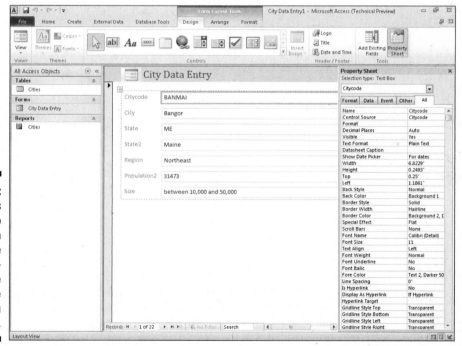

Figure 2-6:
The buttons relevant to what's open and active in your database are available when you need them.

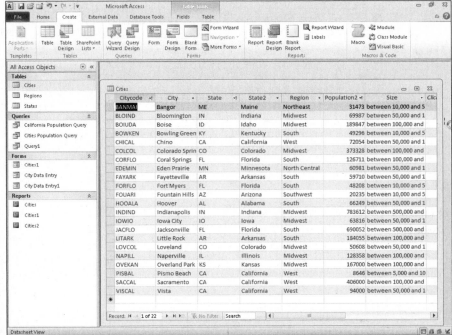

Figure 2-7:
You can
easily tell
the active
tab from
the inactive
ones.

Using buttons

Access buttons come in two varieties:

✔ **Buttons that do something when they're clicked,** either opening a
  dialog box or wizard or performing some change or task in your open
  table, report, query, or form.

✔ **Buttons that represent lists or menus of choices.** This latter variety
  comes in two flavors of its own:

  • Drop-down list buttons are accompanied by a small, down-pointing
    triangle, appearing to the button's right. When you click the tri-
    angle, a list of options appears, as shown in Figure 2-8.

  • Some buttons have a down-pointing triangle at the bottom of the
    button (as shown in Figure 2-9). Click anywhere on the button (not
    necessarily on the triangle), and a menu appears.

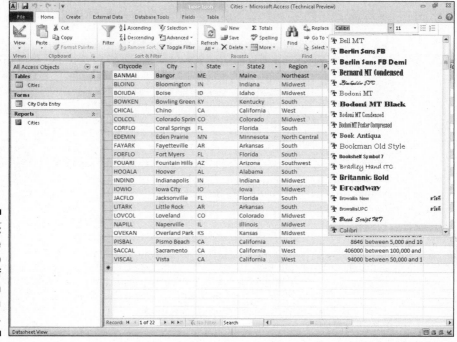

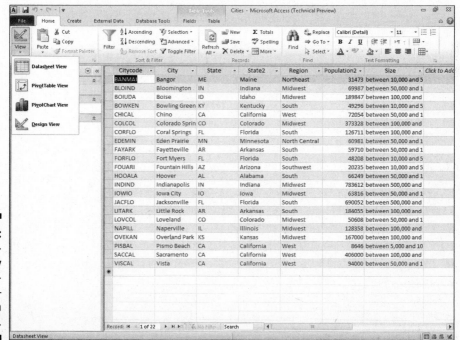

The File tab and Quick Access tools

If you've used previous versions of Office (XP and previous), you'll be relieved to see a File tab. Office 2007 users lost that familiar word in that version's interface, replaced then by an Office button, with no comforting word "File" on it. The word File is back in 2010, however, on the left-most tab that takes you to Backstage view, for opening files, saving files, starting new files, printing, sharing, and accessing Help, as shown in Figure 2-10.

Click the File tab to display the Backstage view, and all the commands it offers — from Save to Exit. As you click on the commands, you get either a dialog box (such as Save As or Open) or a large pane offering options for which files to open from the Recent files list or choices for which kind of Print task you want to perform. Choices from within these panes may or may not open a dialog box that gives you more options.

Just above the File tab is the Quick Access toolbar. Beginning with a little Access application icon (the little "A" also shown in Figure 2-10), you're offered quick(er) access to the Save button, and to Undo and Redo. It's just a handy device to save you from having to click the File tab whenever you want to use these frequently needed commands.

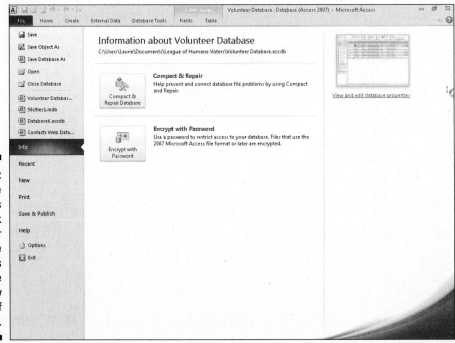

Figure 2-10: Craving the File menu's tools? Look no further than the File tab and its Backstage View panel of commands.

What's that triangle at the end of the Quick Access toolbar? It offers a pop-up menu with several choices, from Customize Quick Access Toolbar to Show Below the Ribbon. In between, you'll find some of the same commands found on the File tab's Backstage View panel, plus Print Preview.

Accessing panes, panels, and context-sensitive tools

Depending on what's going on within the workspace — that is, what you've just done as you edit your table, report, query, or form, or which button you've clicked on one of the Ribbon tabs — Access offers relevant on-screen tools and panels. As an example of this context-sensitive feature, if you open a table and click the Report button on the Create tab (see the Reports section of the Create tab), not only does a report appear, but you also get new tabs — Design (shown in Figure 2-11), Arrange, and Format.

To find out more about reporting, including the capability to group, sort, and total your data, see Chapters 17 through 19.

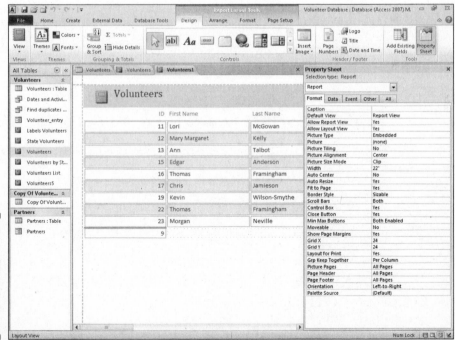

Figure 2-11: Reporting-related tools appear precisely when they're needed.

As you work with Access, you'll get a feel for what's going to appear when you do certain things. Things appear and disappear as you work because Access offers you just what you need for the task you're performing or feature you're using.

Customizing the Access Workspace

Any good application provides some capability for the user to customize the workspace — from adding and rearranging buttons on the toolbar to dragging toolbars and panes around to optimize the layout.

Access is certainly a good software application, so it does what any good application does: It allows you to customize the workspace. You can move the Quick Access toolbar, you can add buttons from the main tabs to the Quick Access toolbar, you can resize the Ribbon, you can tweak the status bar, and you can decide how (or if) your ScreenTips are displayed as you mouse over the tools.

There's no need to do any customization, really — the default settings for toolbar locations, button combinations, and on-screen help are designed with the average or most common user in mind, and they're pretty good. On the other hand, you may just want to tweak things to feel at home. (Think of the times you've fluffed the pillows on the couch before lying down — they may not have needed it, but you want to make your mark on your environment, right? Right.)

Repositioning the Quick Access toolbar

For the position of the Quick Access toolbar, you have two choices:

✔ **Above the Ribbon, which is the default location**
✔ **Below the Ribbon**

To move the Quick Access toolbar, simply right-click it and choose Show Quick Access Toolbar Below the Ribbon. Figure 2-12 shows the pop-up menu with this command available. Note that if you click the down-pointing triangle at the right end of the Quick Access toolbar, the command is Show Below the Ribbon.

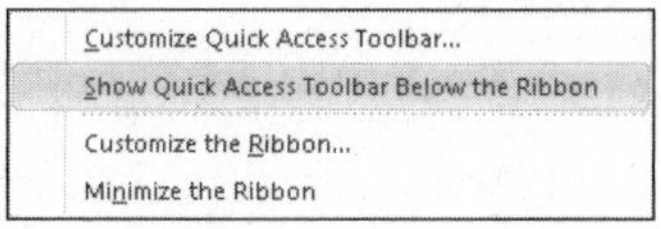

Figure 2-12:
Right-click
the Quick
Access tool-
bar to move
it above or
below the
Ribbon.

C̲ustomize Quick Access Toolbar...
S̲how Quick Access Toolbar Below the Ribbon
Customize the R̲ibbon...
Mi̲nimize the Ribbon

When you place the Quick Access toolbar below the Ribbon, you'll notice that the same command (viewed by right-clicking the toolbar in its new location) is now Show Quick Access Toolbar Above the Ribbon. So it toggles like that, switching from Above to Below, depending on its current location.

You don't have to right-click specifically the Quick Access toolbar in order to reposition it. The aforementioned command (Show . . .) is available in the pop-up menu that appears when you right-click the tabs, too.

Adding buttons to the Quick Access toolbar

Speaking of the Quick Access toolbar and all the ways you can access commands for customizing it, try this to add commands:

1. **With any database open (so that the Ribbon tabs are displayed), right-click any of the buttons on any of the tabs.**

   You can also right-click the Quick Access toolbar or any Ribbon tab.

2. **Choose Customize Quick Access Toolbar.**

   The Access Options dialog box opens (shown in Figure 2-13), with its Customization options displayed.

3. **Click the Choose Commands From drop-down list and choose a command category.**

   A list of Popular Commands appears by default.

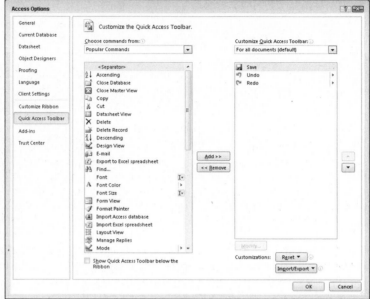

Figure 2-13:
Pick a
command
category
and a com-
mand to
add to
the Quick
Access
toolbar.

4. **From any (or each) category, choose the commands you want to see at all times in the Quick Access toolbar by clicking them one at a time and then clicking the Add>> button.**

   As you click the Add>> button, the command you chose is added to the list on the right. Note that you have up and down-pointing triangles on the right side of the list of commands you've added — with one of the commands you've chosen to add selected, use them to reorder the list, which rearranges the left-to-right order in which they'll appear on the toolbar.

5. **Continue selecting categories and commands on the left and using the Add button to add them to the list on the right.**

   Not all commands will be usable at all the times that the Quick Access toolbar is displayed. For example, if you choose to place a button from the Create tab on the Quick Access toolbar, the button won't be available until and unless a table, query, report, or form is open.

6. **When you've added all the commands you want to add, click OK to add them and close the dialog box.**

   When you click OK, the changes to the Quick Access toolbar are applied. The toolbar's space on the top of the workspace grows to accommodate all the new buttons (Close Database and Open, in this case), as shown in Figure 2-14.

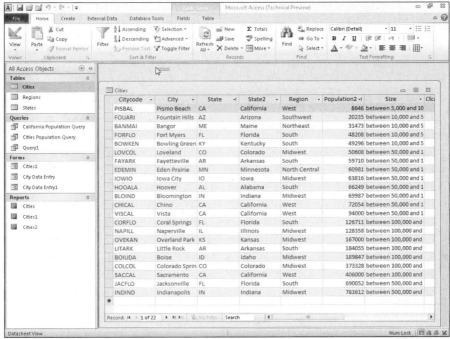

Figure 2-14:
Add as
many but-
tons as you
want — the
toolbar will
make them
all fit.

If you're in a hurry to add a specific button to the Quick Access toolbar, and you're looking right at the button you want to add, just right-click the button and choose Add to Quick Access Toolbar from the menu that appears. The button you right-clicked instantly appears on the toolbar *and* remains in the tab where it was living when you right-clicked it.

Why, then, would you use the Access Options dialog box if a simple right-click takes care of business? Because it gives you the ability to select buttons from all the various tabs in one place — no need to go hunting on the tabs for the buttons you want to add. But when there's just one you want and you can see it at the time, the right-click method can't be beat.

Removing buttons from the Quick Access toolbar

Want to remove a command from the Quick Access toolbar? It's easy:

1. **Point to the unwanted button on the Quick Access toolbar and right-click.**

2. **Choose Remove from Quick Access Toolbar from the pop-up menu (see Figure 2-15).**

   Voilà! It's gone.

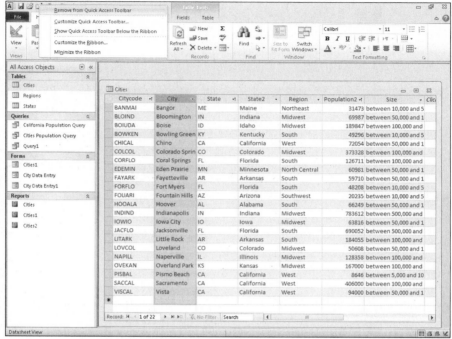

Because the button remains on the tab where it originally lived, it's not lost — it's just not taking up space at the top of the Access workspace.

Be careful *not* to remove the default buttons — Save, Undo, and Redo. Why? Because they're used so often that it's silly to remove them from such a great location. If you do remove them, you'll have to use the Quick Access menu button and select them from that menu when you want to use them. That's two steps (opening the menu and making a selection) instead of one, and who wants to increase steps by 100 percent? Not me!

Minimizing the Ribbon

Need more elbow room? If you need to spread out and want more workspace, you can make the Ribbon smaller, reducing it to just a strip of the tab titles (whichever tabs are in place at the time you choose to minimize the Ribbon). When it's minimized, you can bring it back to full size with minimum fuss.

To minimize the Ribbon, follow these steps:

1. **Right-click anywhere on the Ribbon.**

   A pop-up menu appears. Note that you can click on a button, a Ribbon tab, or a section name (such as "Reports" on the Create tab, or "Font" on the Home tab) and the appropriate pop-up menu will appear.

2. **Choose Minimize the Ribbon.**

   The Ribbon is reduced to a long bar with just the tab titles on it, as shown in Figure 2-16.

3. **To bring the Ribbon back to its full glory, right-click the reduced Ribbon and then choose Minimize the Ribbon.**

   Note that the command is now checked (as also shown in Figure 2-16), indicating that the Ribbon is currently minimized. Performing this step — reselecting the command — toggles this setting off, and the Ribbon returns to full size.

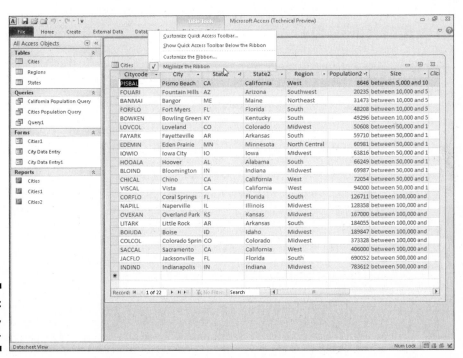

Figure 2-16:
The Ribbon, minimized.

Working with ScreenTips

ScreenTips are the little names and brief descriptions of on-screen tools that appear when you put your mouse pointer over buttons, commands, menus, and many of the other pieces of the Access workspace.

Not all on-screen features have ScreenTips, but for anything you can click to make something happen — as when a dialog box opens, Access performs some task for you, or something is created — these things typically have associated ScreenTips that you can choose to view or not view. If you choose to view them, you can choose to see very brief or more elaborate tips.

To tinker with Access' ScreenTips settings, follow these steps:

1. **Click the File tab.**

   Backstage view appears on the left side of the workspace, as shown in Figure 2-17.

2. **Click the Options command, near the bottom of the menu.**

   The Access Options dialog box appears on-screen.

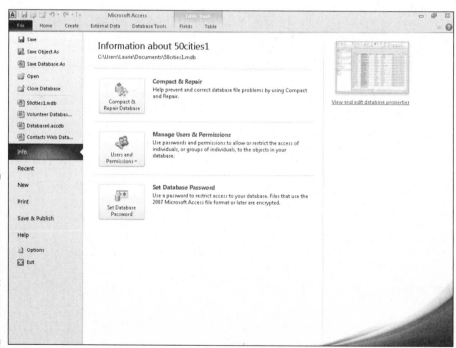

Figure 2-17: Backstage view lets you behind the scenes, where you can adjust how Access looks and works.

3. **From the list on the left side of the Access Options dialog box, select General.**

   The options in the dialog box change to show other options related to ScreenTips, file formats and folders, and how your name and initials are stored, as shown in Figure 2-18.

4. **In the first section of the dialog box, click the ScreenTip Style drop-down list.**

5. **Choose from the following options:**

   - *Show Feature Descriptions in ScreenTips:* This option displays ScreenTips with extra information, as shown in Figure 2-19. Here you see that in addition to the name of the button, a brief description of how it works (or its effect) is displayed for your benefit. It even points to more assistance and information — in this case, the ScreenTip references the use of the F1 key to open Access's Help files.

   - *Don't Show Feature Descriptions in ScreenTips:* If you want just the facts, ma'am, this is for you. ScreenTips will show just the button name with no further explanation.

   - *Don't Show ScreenTips:* Want to go it alone? Turn off ScreenTips.

6. **Click OK to close the Access Options dialog box.**

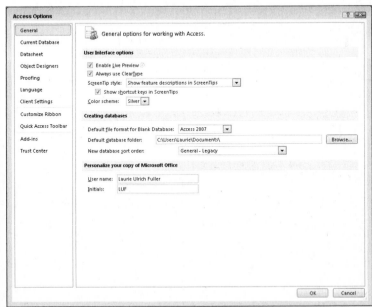

Figure 2-18: The settings for just about everything you can see and use in Access are available through the Access Options dialog box.

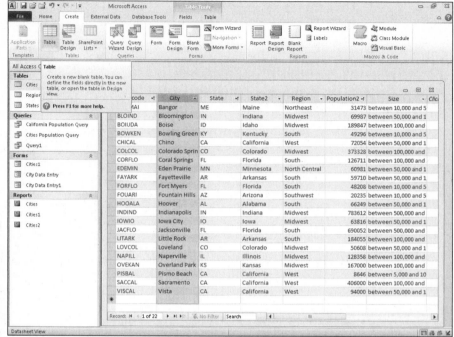

Figure 2-19:
View the
helpful but-
ton and tab
names and
information.

Establishing the level of detail included in ScreenTips isn't the end of your options. You can also choose whether or not to include keyboard shortcuts in ScreenTips. This is on by default, and it's pretty useful. You also have the ability to set the Color Scheme for your ScreenTips, choosing from Blue, Silver, and Black (Silver is the default). That's not a lot of color choices, but enough to allow you to make them blend in or stand out from the rest of your Access workspace.

Mousing Around

Access, like all Windows applications, is meant to be used with the mouse. The mouse is assumed to be your main way of communicating with the software — clicking Ribbon tabs, buttons, and drop-down lists, and making choices in dialog boxes to use things like the Report Wizard and the Access Options dialog box discussed in the previous sections of this chapter.

You can left-click to make standard choices from on-screen tools and right-click to access pop-up menus — also known as *context-sensitive* menus because the menu choices vary depending on what was right-clicked. If you right-click a Ribbon tab or button, you get choices for customizing toolbars and buttons. If you right-click a database component tab (say, the Table tab while that table is open), you get choices related to the table.

Not a big fan of the mouse? Check out the online Cheat Sheet for this book, available at `www.dummies.com/cheatsheet/access2010`. It's full of powerful keyboard shortcuts.

Navigating Access with the Alt Key

If you like to use the keyboard as much as possible when you're working with software, Access makes it somewhat easy to do that. I say *somewhat* because you need to use a special key in order to make the rest of the keyboard work as a commander.

When you want to switch tabs and issue commands with the keyboard (rather than with the mouse), press the Alt key. As shown in Figure 2-20, pressing Alt causes numbers and letters to appear in small squares on the Quick Access toolbar and the Ribbon's tabs. When the numbers and letters are visible, you can press one of those characters on your keyboard to issue a command (such as pressing 1 to Save) or to switch to a tab (such as pressing C to get to the Create tab).

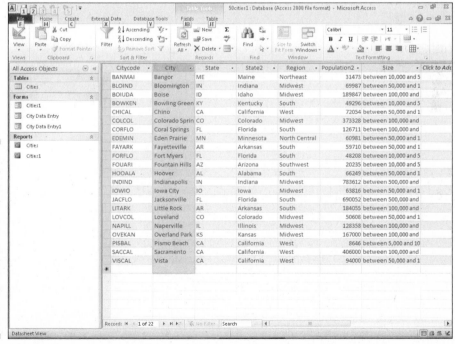

Figure 2-20:
Rather press a letter or number than click a tab or button with your mouse? The Alt key shows you how.

When you're on a tab (but only if you press its letter key to activate it), the individual buttons on that tab have their own keyboard shortcuts displayed. Instead of single numbers or letters, however, now you're looking at pressing key combinations, such as W+1 (displayed as W1 on-screen) to activate the Report Wizard. Figure 2-21 shows the keyboard shortcuts for the Create tab.

The goal is not to try to press the two keys at the exact same time. Instead, press the first one listed — and with that key still pressed, tap the second key. Voilà!

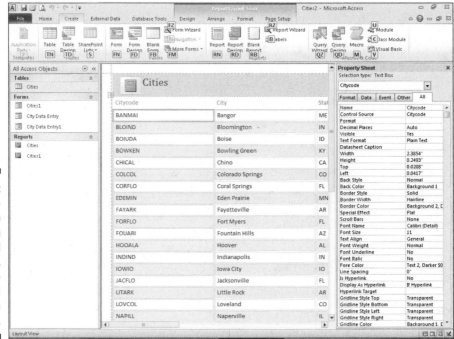

Figure 2-21: Each button on a tab has its own keyboard shortcut, often a combination of a letter and a number.

Chapter 3

Database Basics

In This Chapter

▶ Getting to know some basic terms and concepts

▶ Outstanding in your field(s)

▶ Deciding to go flat-file or relational with your database

▶ Getting a table started

This may be the single most important chapter in this book. That probably sounds like a strong statement, but it's really true. When you want to figure out how to actually *do* something, it's essential to understand not just how it works, but *why* it works that way, and what's going on behind the scenes. So after you've read about why Access is the right tool for you (in Chapter 1) and how to get around in the Access interface (Chapter 2), it's time to really nail down how Access works and how to start building your database.

Database Lingo

Now, if the section heading ("Database Lingo") is making you panic because you think I want you to memorize a bunch of database jargon, don't worry. Just relax. Breathe normally. The next section, and many throughout this chapter, simply uses some terms you need to know so you can figure out what Access is referring to in its various dialog boxes as well on the various tabs it uses to give you access to commands in the Access workspace. Knowing these terms will, therefore, help you get around and get things done in Access.

Unfortunately, you simply must know technical terms — there's no two ways about it. I'm talking about only a handful of words, though — some of which you probably already know and maybe even use in reference to information in general — words like *record* and *database*. See? Nothing high-tech, just some basic words and concepts you really need to absorb so you can move on and use Access effectively.

The terms in this section appear in size order, starting with the smallest piece of a database — the data — and advancing to the largest — the entire database itself. I've done it this way so you get the big picture, a little bit at a time, and see that the big picture is made up of smaller items. Seeing how they all fit together (and what to call each piece) is what this chapter's all about.

Data, no matter how you pronounce it

Data is the stuff that Access stores. Information you may store in your head one way will be stored in a different way in a database program like Access. For example, you may think of someone's name as *John Smith,* or you may only ever think of the guy as *John* — either because you don't know his last name or because you never use his last name. A database, however, stores his name as either *John Smith,* in a *field* called Name, or as two pieces — Last Name (Smith) and First Name (John). The latter approach is best because it gives you more freedom to use the data in more ways. You can sort the data by Last Name, for example, which is hard to do if you've just stored the entire name as one chunk.

Get the idea? As I say in Chapter 1 (where you plan out your database), it's a good idea to break down the data as much as possible. No matter how you pronounce it — "day-tah" or "dat-tuh" — it's your information, and you want to be able to get at it in the simplest, most logical way possible. As you read on in this chapter, and when you review Chapters 1 and 2, you'll see that Access gives you all the tools you need to do just that — it's just a matter of using the right tools at the right time!

Fields of dreams (or data)

Because people don't want their data to wander around homeless, the technical wizards created *fields* — places for your data to live. Each field holds one kind of data. For example, to track information about a baseball card collection, your fields might include Manufacturer, Player Name, Position, Year, Team, and Average (or ERA, for pitchers). If you have a name and address database, your fields might consist of `Last Name`, `First Name`, `Middle Initial`, `Address1`, `Address2`, `City`, `State`, `Zip`, `Phone`, `Cell`, and `Email`. When you think about it, it's pretty logical. What are all the things you can know about a baseball player? A client? A product? These *things* become *fields.*

As with the term *data,* other database programs (such as FoxPro and FileMaker) all agree on what a field is. In larger database packages, however (such as Oracle and Microsoft SQL Server), you find the term *column* replacing *field.* And to make things more exciting, Microsoft Excel stores your fields *in* columns when you use an Excel spreadsheet to store a list. The tabular structure of a database table is what leads Oracle and SQL to refer to columns rather than fields, but for heaven's sake — couldn't they have stuck to a term we all know?

Records

Having fields is a good start, but if you stop there, how do you know which last name works with which first name? Something needs to keep those unruly fields in order — something like a *record.* All the fields for one baseball card — or one client or one product — are all collectively known as a *record.* If you have two baseball cards in your collection, you have two records in your database, one for each card. Fifty clients? Fifty records.

For a little more about records, check out the following:

- ✔ FoxPro and FileMaker concur on the term *record.* Oracle and Microsoft SQL Server use the term *row* instead. Again, this comes from the tabular (table-like) structure of the tables in which their records . . . er, rows . . . are stored.

- ✔ Each record in a *table* contains the same fields but (usually) has different data in those fields. And not every record has to have data in every field. If someone doesn't have a cell phone, you can't very well have any data in the Cell field for that person, right?

- ✔ A single record contains all the information you need about a single item (accounting entry, recipe, or whatever) in your table. That's all there is to it.

Tables

A *table* is a collection of records that describe similar data. The key phrase to remember in that last sentence is *similar data.* All the records in a single table contain fields of similar data. The information about that baseball card collection may fit into a single table. So would the client or product data. However, a single table would *not* handle both baseball cards *and* clients because they're unrelated databases. You wouldn't put the records for your car's repairs in the folder where you keep your Christmas cookie recipes, right?

Why? Because if anyone else needed to know when you last had the tires rotated, they aren't going to know to look in the same place one finds the best recipe for Ginger Snaps. *You* might remember that they're stored in the same place, but it's just too confusing for anyone else. And too limiting. Access lets you write reports and queries based on your data, and if the data in your database isn't all related, it'll be chaos trying to write a report or generate a query that pulls data from that database. You could end up with a recipe that calls for motor oil or a maintenance schedule that tells you to pre-heat the car to 350 degrees. Such a report might be amusing, but it's hardly useful.

The database

An Access *database,* or *database file* (the terms are interchangeable), is a collection of everything relating to a particular set of information. The database contains all the tables, queries, reports, and forms that Access helps you create to manage and work with your stuff. Instead of storing all those items *individually* on the disk drive — where they can become lost, misplaced, or accidentally erased — Access group them into a single collective file.

Here's an important point: All those parts — the tables, the reports, queries, and forms — all cumulatively make a database. And that's before you even enter any records into the tables. The database, therefore, is more than the data; it's the tools that store, manipulate, and allow you to look at the data, too.

Field Types and Uses

A field, you remember, is where your data lives. Each field holds one piece of data, such as Last Name or Batting Average.

Because there are so many different kinds of information in the world, Access offers a variety of field types for storing it. In fact, Access puts the following field types at your disposal:

- Text
- Number
- Currency
- Date & Time
- Yes/No

✔ Lookup & Relationship

✔ Rich Text

✔ Memo

✔ Attachment

✔ Hyperlink

✔ Calculated

There's also an Autonumber field type, which is applied automatically to the first field in a new, blank database. The types just listed are those available for fields you create in addition to that first field — the ones that will contain your data. For now, suffice to say that the Autonumber field is a field that contains an automatically-generated number so that each record is unique in that it has a unique autonumber, or "ID." You get the word about the need for (and ways to create) unique fields later on, in Chapter 4.

For now, don't worry about figuring out what each field type is or what it does based on its name — I go over each one shortly. As you can see, though, the list covers just about any type of data you can imagine. And remember, each one can be customized extensively, resulting in fields that meet your needs exactly. If you absolutely cannot wait to find out about modifying all the specs for your fields, Chapter 4 should be your next stop.

The upcoming bulleted list introduces the ten field types and how they're used. You'll also find out a little bit about how you can tweak them to meet your specific needs:

✔ **Text:** Stores up to 255 characters of text — letters, numbers, punctuation, and any combination thereof.

Numbers in a text field aren't numbers to calculate with; they're just a bunch of digits hanging out together in a field. Be careful of this fact when you design the tables in your database — you don't want to enter, say, a value that you intend to use in a Calculated field or to extract some other kind of information from a report and have that value stored as text, rendering it inoperable as a number. If the data is numeric, store it that way.

Text fields have one setting you need to know about: size. When you create a text field, Access wants to know how many characters the field holds. That's the field *size*. If you create a field called First Name and make its size 6, *Joseph* fits into the field, but not *Jennifer*. This restriction can be a problem. A good general rule is to make the field a little larger than you think you need. It's easy to make the field even larger at some later point if you need to, but it's potentially dangerous to make it smaller. Surgery on fields is covered in Chapter 4.

- ✔ **Number:** Holds real, for-sure numbers. You can add, subtract, and calculate your way to fame and fortune with number fields. But if you're working with dollars and cents (or pounds and pence), use a currency field instead.

- ✔ **Currency:** Tracks money, prices, invoice amounts, and so on. In an Access database, the bucks stop here. For that matter, so do the lira, marks, and yen. If you're in the mood for some *other* kind of number, check out the number field.

- ✔ **Date/Time:** Stores time, date, or a combination of the two, depending on which format you use. Use a date/time field to track the whens of life. Pretty versatile, eh?

- ✔ **Yes/No:** Holds Yes/No, True/False, and On/Off, depending on the format you choose. When you need a simple yes or no, this is the field to use.

- ✔ **Lookup & Relationship:** If you want a field within one table to actually display content from a field in another table, choose this as the field type. A simple Lookup wizard opens as soon as this field type is chosen, through which you select the table and field to lookup through this new field in your table.

- ✔ **Rich Text:** Need the content of a particular field to be formatted just so? Choose this field type, and the formatting applied to the data in the field (using the Text Formatting tools on the Home tab) will be how it appears onscreen and in reports.

- ✔ **Memo:** Holds up to 64,000 characters of information — that's almost 18 pages of text. This is a *really big* text field. It's great for general notes, detailed descriptions, and anything else that requires a lot of space.

- ✔ **Attachment:** Use this field type to attach files — Word documents, Excel worksheets, PowerPoint presentations, or any other kind of file, including graphics (a photo of the volunteer, product, or location, perhaps?) to the record.

- ✔ **Hyperlink:** Thanks to this field type, Access understands and stores the special link language that makes the Internet such a powerful place. If you use Access on your company's network or use the Internet extensively, this field type is for you. You'll find out more about hyperlinks and other neat ways Access and the Internet play well together in Chapter 8.

- ✔ **Calculated Field:** This field type is used when you want to fill the field in question with the result of a formula that uses one or more other fields in the same table. For example, in a table that contains a list of your products, other fields might include Price and Discount. If you want to also have a field that calculates the new price (the Price, less the Discount), you'd make that a Calculated field. When you choose this as the field type, you use a submenu to choose what kind of data will house the result, and then an Expression Builder dialog box appears, through which you set up the formula.

To help you start thinking about your database and your data and to begin imagining the fields you could use for some common types of data, I present, in Table 3-1, a breakdown of field types and ways you might use them.

Table 3-1	Common Fields for Everyday Tables		
Name	*Type*	*Size*	*Contents*
Title	Text	4	Mr., Ms., Mrs., Mme., Sir, and so on.
First Name	Text	15	Person's first name.
Middle Initial	Text	4	Person's middle initial; allows for two initials and punctuation.
Last Name	Text	20	Person's last name.
Suffix	Text	10	Jr., Sr., II, Ph.D., and so on.
Job	Text	25	Job title or position.
Company	Text	25	Company name.
Address 1, Address 2	Text	30	Include two fields for the address because some corporate locations are pretty complicated these days.
City	Text	20	City name.
State, Province	Text	4	State or province; apply the name appropriately for the data you're storing.
Zip Code, Postal Code	Text	10	Zip or postal code; note that it's stored as text characters, not as a number.
Country	Text	15	Not needed if you work within a single country.
Office Phone	Text	12	Voice telephone number; increase the size to 17 for an extension.

(continued)

Table 3-1 *(continued)*

Name	Type	Size	Contents
Fax Number	Text	12	Fax number.
Home Phone	Text	12	Home telephone number.
Cellular Phone	Text	12	Cell phone (or "mobile phone" for you cosmopolitans).
E-mail Address	Text	30	Internet e-mail address.
Web Site	Hyperlink		Web-page address; Access automatically sets the field size.
Telex	Text	12	Standard Telex number; increase the size to 22 to include answerback service.
SSN	Text	11	U.S. Social Security number, including dashes.
Comments	Memo		A freeform space for notes; Access automatically chooses a field size.

All these field types listed as samples in Table 3-1 are really *text* fields, even the ones for phone numbers. This is because Access sees their content as text rather than as a number that could be used in a calculation. Of course, some of the field types (listed in the Type column) are not Text fields — you also see a Memo field and a Hyperlink field. These, too, are considered text, but these various types of text fields give you options for the specific kind of text that will be stored in such fields. If all this text versus numbers stuff is confusing you, remember that computers think there's a difference between a *number* (that you'd use in a calculation) and a string of digits, such as the digits that make up a phone number. When it comes to different kinds of text fields, it's a matter of how much text will be stored in the field, and if it needs any special formatting in order to work properly in the database.

Fun with field names

Of all the Windows database programs out there, I think Access has the simplest field-naming rules. Just remember these guidelines to make your field names perfect every time:

✔ **It's a good idea to start with a letter or a number.** Although Access won't stop you

from using certain characters at the beginning of or within your field name, it's not a good idea. It can make things confusing for other people who might use your database, and symbols are hard to read if the type is very small. They also have only limited logical use in identifying the content of the field — what would "^Address" tell you that "Address" wouldn't? Of course, after the first character you might find logical uses for symbols such as plus signs and underscores. You can include spaces in field names, too. Oh — and which symbols are no-nos? See Table 3-2.

✔ **Make the field name short and easy to understand.** You have up to 64 characters for a field name, but don't even think about using all that space. But don't get stingy

and create names like N1 or AZ773 unless they mean something particular to your company or organization.

✔ **Use letters, numbers, and an occasional space in your field names.** Although Access lets you include all kinds of crazy punctuation marks in field names, don't do it. Keep it simple so that the solution you develop with Access doesn't turn into a problem on its own.

Table 3-2	**Prohibited Symbols**		
Symbol	**Name**	**Symbol**	**Name**
/	Forward slash	?	Question mark
*	Asterisk	-	Dash
;	Semicolon	"	Double quotes
:	Colon	'	Single quote
!	Exclamation point	$	Dollar sign
#	Pound sign	%	Percent
&	Ampersand		

Choosing Between Flat and Relational Databases

Unlike ice cream, databases come in just two flavors: flat-file and relational. Also unlike ice cream, it's not really a matter of preference as to which one you choose. Some databases require a relational approach; others would be overwhelmed by it. Read on to figure out how to tell the difference.

Isolationist tables

In a *flat* system (also known as a *flat-file system*), all the data is lumped into a single table. A phone directory is a good example of a flat-file database: Names, addresses, and phone numbers (the data) are crammed into a single place (the database). Some duplication occurs — if one person has three phone lines at home, his or her name and address are listed three times in the directory — but that's not a big problem. Overall, the database works just fine.

Tables that mix and mingle

The *relational* system (or *relational database*) uses as little storage space as possible by cutting down on the duplicated (also known as *redundant*) data in the database. To accomplish this, a relational database splits your data into several tables, with each table holding some portion of the total data.

Borrowing the preceding phone book example, note that one table in a relational database can contain the customer name and address information, whereas another can hold the phone numbers. Thanks to this approach, the mythical person with three phone lines has only one entry in the "customer" table (after all, it's still just one customer) but has three distinct entries in the "phone number" table (one for each phone line).

The key to relational databases

The *key field* (or *linking field*) is the key to this advanced technology. All related tables in a relational database system contain this special field. The key field's data identifies matching records from different tables.

The key field works just like the claim stub you receive when you drop off your dry cleaning. To pick up your dry cleaning when it's finished, you present the claim check, complete with its little claim number. That number identifies (or *links*) you and your cleaning so the clerk can find it.

Likewise, in the phone book example, each customer can have a unique customer ID. The "phone number" table stores the customer ID with each phone number. To find out who owns a phone number, you look up the customer ID in the "customer name" table. Granted, it takes more steps to find someone's phone number than it does in the plain flat-file system, but the relational system saves storage space (no more duplicate names) and reduces the chance of errors at the same time.

If this process seems complicated, don't feel bad. Relational databases *are* complicated! But that's mostly behind the scenes, where Access is doing the stuff it does when you make a selection in a tab or ask it to run a wizard for you. A good deal of the complexity is invisible to you; all you see is the power it gives you. When you're ready to find out more about all that behind-the-scenes stuff, check out Chapter 4.

But do your tables need to relate?

Now you at least have an idea of the difference between flat-file and relational databases. But do you care? Yes, you do. Each approach has its unique pluses and minuses for your database:

- **Flat-file systems are easy to build and maintain.** A Microsoft Excel spreadsheet is a good example of a flat-file database. A list of records is stored, one record per row, and you have as many records as can fit on the worksheet. Simple, easy, and in many cases the way to go — if your database is simple and easy, too.

- **Relational systems shine in big business applications such as invoicing, accounting, or inventory.** They're also a big help if you have a small business — your customer data, for example, could require several tables to store customer names and addresses, purchase history, and credit information. Storing everything you need to store about customers could be too big a job for a single, flat-file database.

I don't recommend that you set off to build a relational database system all by yourself after reading just some (or even all) of this book. It's a big job; you'll likely just end up discouraged if you dive in too quickly. If you're sure that you need a relational database, enlist some help in the form of a friend or colleague who's had some experience building databases. He or she can walk you through it the first time, and then, with this book (and Access help files) at your side, you can try it on your own later.

Although Access is a relational database program, it does flat-file systems quite nicely because even though it lets you set up several tables and set up relationships between them, it's also quite happy to set up a single flat-file table if you want one. Whether you choose flat-file or relational for your database project, Access is the right program.

Building a Database

So you've read a few chapters here at the beginning of the book, maybe you've leafed ahead where I've referred to other chapters, and now you feel ready. You want to dive in and start building a database. Keeping in mind my previous advice to take it slowly, you can take a whack at it here.

In the following procedure, you set up a new database and then use the Table Wizard to build the first table in the database. Ready? Here we go . . .

1. **If Access is not already running, take a moment to start it.**

   I show you how to do this in Chapter 2.

   In the Access workspace, the words *Available Templates* appear across the central section of the window, with a Blank Database button (among others) beneath it.

2. **Click Blank Database.**

   A Blank Database panel appears on the right, as shown in Figure 3-1.

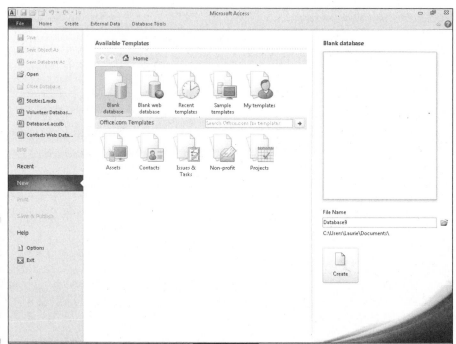

Figure 3-1: New blank databases need names. Give yours one here.

3. **Type a name to replace the generic** DatabaseX. **(where X is the number assigned chronologically to the database).**

   You don't need to type a file extension (.accdb); Windows Vista or Windows 7 display your extensions automatically. And if you accidentally delete the file extension while changing the file name, don't worry — Access adds it to the file name you type.

Just beneath the File Name text box you can find the contents of the currently selected folder into which your database will be saved when you click Create.

4. **If you don't like the folder that Access picked out for you, click the little folder icon and choose where to store the new database.**

As shown in Figure 3-2, when you click that little folder icon, the File New Database dialog box opens. From here, you can navigate to anywhere on your local system or on a network to which you're connected and select the drive and folder on which to store your new database. When you've finished selecting a spot for your new database, click OK to return to the workspace.

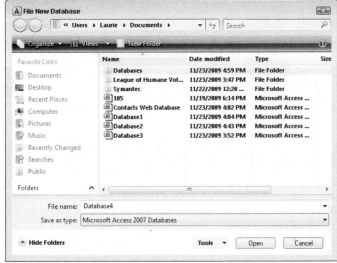

Figure 3-2:
Select a home for your new database.

5. **Click the Create button.**

A blank table, called Table1, appears in the central section of the workspace, and on the left, a panel lists the parts of your database (there's just one part so far). Figure 3-3 shows your new table and the left-hand panel.

When you click Create, if a dialog box pops up and asks whether you want to replace an existing file, Access is saying that a database with the name you entered is already on the disk.

• If this is news to you, click No and then come up with a different name for your new database.

• If you *intended* to replace that old database with a new one, click Yes and proceed.

Click to Add

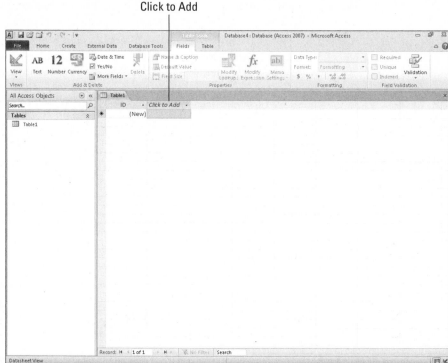

Figure 3-3:
New table,
new
database.

6. **Create and name your fields in the table by double-clicking where it says Click to Add at the top of the second column in the table.**

7. **Click the arrow to the right of the words Click to Add and choose the type of field you want to add.**

   The many choices are discussed earlier in this chapter. For most fields, Text will be the type, but your data and its nature (and your desired uses for it) will dictate what's best to choose here.

   What's that ID field in the first column? It's there by default and will contain a unique number for each record you create (when you start entering records, later). This provides the unique field that each table requires, especially if you're going to relate your tables. You can change its name by double-clicking the name "ID" and changing it to, for example, Customer Number.

   Later on, after you've set up your tables and established relationships between them, you can reassign what's known as the *primary key* (another name for a unique field in a table), and at that point, the ID field can go bye-bye.

8. **Type a new field name (to replace the highlighted placeholder name), and press Enter to save the new field name.**

As soon as you press Enter, a new field appears, with a blank at the top, awaiting a name.

Repeat these Steps 7 and Step 8 until you have all the fields you think you'll need in this table. You can always rename them later (by double-clicking the current names), so don't worry about perfection at this point. Just start setting up fields so you can start entering data. Figure 3-4 shows a new field name in place and a new one awaiting the Enter key to confirm it.

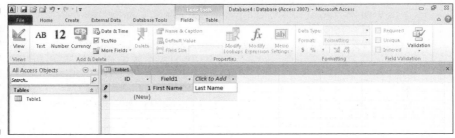

Figure 3-4: Create new fields by pressing Enter after naming each one.

9. **To save your new table and the entire database, press Ctrl+S or click the Save button on the Quick Access toolbar.**

   It's a good idea to save each time you've done something important — building a table, updating some fields, adding records, and so on — essentially after anything you'd hate to have to do over again.

Rarely is "Table1" a really useful name for a table. Before or after saving your database, renaming a table is easy. Just follow these steps:

1. **Right-click the Table tab.**

2. **Choose Save from the pop-up menu that appears.**

3. **Type a name for the table in the resulting Save As dialog box.**

4. **Click OK to keep the name.**

5. **Resave your database to include this change.**

Adding and Removing Tables

Nobody's expecting perfection at this stage of the game. Certainly not in your first foray into database creation, and not even on your second or third attempt. Even seasoned experts forget things now and then, realizing after they've built a table that they didn't need it, or after they've started setting up reports and queries that they've forgotten a table that they needed. It can happen to anyone.

What to do? Use Access's simple interface to add the tables you want and delete the tables you don't.

One more, please

If, after you start building your database, you decide that your database warrants more than one table — in other words, if you realize you need a *relational* database — then you need to add another table. If you already knew that your database was going to need multiple tables, then — after building the first one — the only thing to do is build the rest, one by one.

To add new tables to an existing database, repeat the following steps for each new table:

1. Click the Create tab on the Ribbon.

The Create tab's buttons appear, as shown in Figure 3-5.

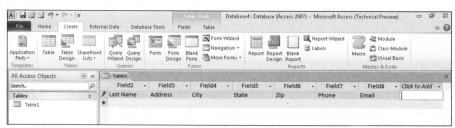

2. Click the Table button on the Ribbon.

A new table, blank and awaiting the name for the first field, appears, as shown in Figure 3-6.

3. Build and name the fields for this new table as shown in the previous procedure.

Save your database periodically as you work.

4. Continue adding tables, using Steps 1 through 3 for as many tables as you need in the database.

You don't have to do this perfectly from the start — you can always go back to rename fields and add or remove tables (more on how to do that in a second). The goal here is to just *do it* — just get started and get the database going, so you can see what you have and start working with it.

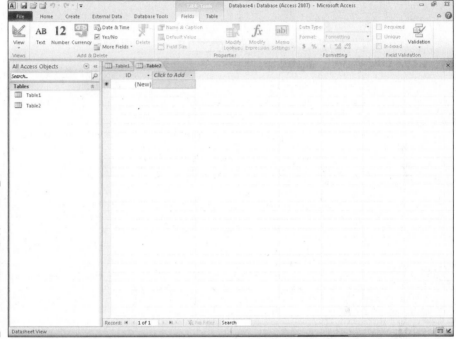

Figure 3-6:
Looks familiar, doesn't it? A new table awaits fields and field names, not to mention records.

Naming tables is important — because you're going to need to know, at a glance at that left-hand panel, what's in Table1 or Table 2 or Table3, right? Better to name them Volunteers, Events, and Groups, so you don't have to remember each one by a generic number. To name a table, you can do so when you first close it and are prompted to save it. As shown in Figure 3-7, the Save As dialog box gives you a Table Name box. Enter the name and press Enter. If you decide you don't like the name later on, simply right-click the name it currently has, as displayed in the left-hand panel, and the current name is highlighted. Type the new name, and press Enter to confirm it. You can also choose Rename from the menu that appears if you right-click the table's name in the left-hand panel listing your database components. This also gives you the opportunity to type a replacement name.

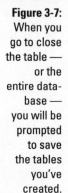

Figure 3-7:
When you
go to close
the table —
or the
entire data-
base —
you will be
prompted
to save
the tables
you've
created.

Oops, I didn't mean to do that

So you have a table you didn't want. Maybe you realize after building Table C that you really only need Tables A and B — or that Table D, which you've also created, really makes Table C unnecessary. Whatever the reason, tables, even ones with records in them, are easy to get rid of.

Let me state that again: Tables are easy to get rid of. Perhaps too easy. Before you delete a table, check and recheck your database to make sure you aren't deleting information that you need to keep. When a table is deleted, *all connections to it* — including all relationships and references in queries and reports — are deleted too. A prompt appears when you choose to delete a table, reminding you of this.

Still committed to ditching the table? Here's how it's done:

1. **With your database open, look at the panel on the left side of the workspace.**

   You should see a list of your tables in that panel, each one represented by a long, horizontal button, as shown in Figure 3-8.

Figure 3-8:
Each table
has its own
button,
emblazoned
with the
name you
gave the
table.

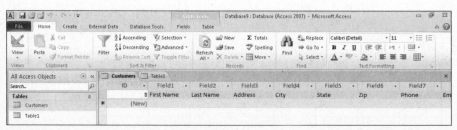

2. **Right-click the table name in the panel on the left side of the work-space, and choose Delete from the pop-up menu, as shown in Figure 3-9.**

3. **Click Yes in response to the resulting prompt if, in fact, you do want to delete the table.**

All gone!

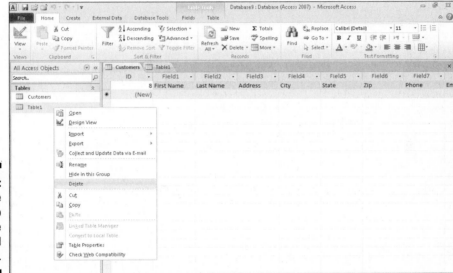

Figure 3-9:
Choose
Delete to
get rid of the
unwanted
table.

Now, you probably think it's time to start entering records, but no, I don't advise doing that yet. Before you start populating your tables with data, it's a better idea to set up your table relationships, establish the key fields that will connect your relational tables, and define the specs for each of your fields — taking advantage of those field options I mention earlier in this chapter.

Even if your database will be a (relatively simple) flat-file database, you need to iron out the settings for your fields before you start entering data — establishing the rules for entering names, numbers, dates, and so forth — so that what you enter is graciously accepted by the fields you've set up.

Chapter 4 helps you prepare your database for its relational duties. In Chapter 5 and Chapter 6, you get a handle on customizing your fields to suit your needs. After that's done, you can enter your data and begin taking advantage of Access's forms, queries, and reports — all the stuff covered in the *rest* of the book!

Part II
Getting It All on the Table

The 5th Wave   By Rich Tennant

"My girlfriend ran a spreadsheet of my life, and generated this chart. My best hope is that she'll change her major from 'Computer Sciences' to 'Rehabilitative Services.'"

In this part . . .

So by now you've started your database (or at least you've read about how that's done) and you're ready to start setting up your tables and filling them with data. Or maybe you just kept turning pages in Part I and you ended up here. Hey — you're on a roll and you might as well keep reading, right?

If you decide to keep turning pages (and reading, hopefully), this part of the book will show you how the tables that make up a database are built, how they work together, and how you can customize them to become perfect homes for your very important data.

From Chapter 4's explanation of how tables relate to each other to Chapters 5 and 6 that show you what's going on (and how to control what's happening behind the scenes with your tables and their data), Part II will help you start building your database, one table at a time.

Chapter 4

Keys, Relationships, and Indexes

....

In This Chapter

▶ Identifying your records uniquely with a primary key

▶ Understanding relationships

▶ Building relationships between your tables

▶ Indexing for faster queries

....

*L*ife in today's world is all about doing things faster and more efficiently to increase productivity. Isn't that what your life is about? Oh, you have a life outside the office, too? (What a concept.) Maybe you have a relationship? This chapter is about making your databases faster and about building good relationships (the database kind, not the human kind!).

As with any good relationship, the end result is often harmony and happiness. Making your Access tables work well together will make things so much easier in so many ways as you move on to build your queries, forms, and reports. The good news is that building relationships in Access takes a lot less time than building human relationships.

How can you make Access work faster and more efficiently? With key fields and indexes, that's how! Each table should have that one special field assigned as a *primary key*. A primary key prevents duplicate records from being entered into a table — hence more efficient data entry. (I love the word *hence!*) To retrieve your data faster, you need to create the proper balance of indexes for each table. Not enough indexes, and querying 100,000 records will take forever; too many, and the same could be true. So assigning indexes to the correct fields is an art form. You find out all about the art of indexes in this chapter.

The Primary Key to Success

A table's primary key is a special field in your table. You use this field to uniquely identify each record in the table.

Usually the primary key is a single field. In *very* special circumstances, *two or more* fields can share the job. The technical term for this type of key is a *multi-field key.*

The lowdown on primary keys

Before we discuss how to create a primary key, you'll need to know some rules and guidelines for using one. This section contains the when, where, and why of the primary key.

Uses

Almost every table you create should have a primary key. Here's why:

- **A primary key organizes your data by *uniquely* identifying each record.**

  That's one reason why a primary key makes your database work a little faster. For an explanation of indexes and their creation, see the section "Indexing for Faster Queries" later in this chapter.

  For example, a Customer table typically contains a `Customer Number` field. This field would be the primary key. If your Customer table contains a dozen Jane Smiths, you need a way to tell them apart. The `Customer Number` field for each record *uniquely* identifies each Jane Smith — and every other customer, too.

- **Tables by default are sorted by primary key.**

  This helps Access find a particular record much faster.

- **Your database could freak out if you don't have a primary key.**

  Without a primary key, finding the requested records can be difficult for Access. Think of the Jane Smith example we used earlier. How does Access know which Jane Smith you want if there are multiple Jane Smith customers in your database? Well, by the primary key. It is unique for each customer and therefore can be used to uniquely identify each Jane Smith. Problem solved!

Rules

Before you create a primary key, you need to know a few guidelines. Here's our handy listing:

- **Location:** Access doesn't care where the primary key field appears in the table design. The key can be the first field, the last field, or buried in the middle.

Even if Access doesn't care where you put things, I always recommend that you make the primary key field the first field in your table. It makes relationships easier to build (as you see later in this chapter).

✔ **Defaults:** Access tries to save you time and trouble with the default actions it gives to the primary key:

Access really, really wants you to have a primary key in your table.

If you create a new table in table design mode without a primary key, Access suggests adding a primary key field when you save the table.

Access gives this automatic primary key field a wildly creative name — ID — with an AutoNumber data type.

If the first field you add in a table is an AutoNumber type, Access automatically makes that AutoNumber field the primary key.

Access indexes the primary key field automatically.

✔ **Restrictions:** You can't just create primary keys willy-nilly. Access imposes these limits:

A table can have only one primary key.

You can't use the Calculated, Attachment, Memo, Hyperlink, or OLE Object data types for a primary key.

Avoid using the yes/no field type in a primary key. You can have only two records in such a table: Yes and No.

All primary key indexes must have a name (just as all fields must have a name).

Access automatically names all primary key indexes PrimaryKey.

Creating a primary key

To create a primary key, follow these steps:

1. **Open the table in Design view.**

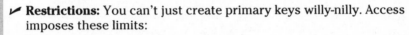

   If you just asked yourself "how do I do that?" then it might not be time for you to create a primary key. Chapter 3 shows you the table basics you need before you can create a primary key.

2. **Click the field name for the primary key.**

   Don't know which field to select for your primary key? See the sidebar, "The key to table happiness." The preceding section, "Rules," relates the guidelines for selecting a primary key.

The key to table happiness

What makes a good key field? How do you find the right one? Good questions! In fact, they're the two most important questions to ask about a primary key.

Primary key values must be unique for each record. Leaving a primary key field blank is not an option. So start by looking at some sample data that will go into your table. Is there something like a phone number, customer number, or Social Security Number that will be unique for each record? If so, you've just found your primary key field. If not, then an `AutoNumber`

field is the way to go. When you designate a field's data type as `AutoNumber`, Access assigns sequential numbers to each record entered into the table. (Isn't our good pal Access a peach?)

`AutoNumber` fields always create a unique identifier for each record. When you delete a record with an `AutoNumber` field, Access even keeps track of those numbers and will not use them again. (Access, you are quite a pal indeed!)

---

3. **On the Ribbon, click the giant button with the key on it (shown in Figure 4-1).**

   A key symbol appears on the button next to the field name you selected.

   The primary key is set!

Click to set the primary key field.

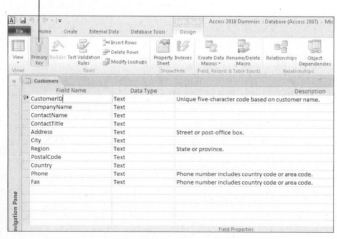

Figure 4-1: The completed primary key.

Making Tables Get Along

Relational databases split data among two or more tables. Access uses a linking field, called a *foreign key,* to tie related tables together. For example, one table may contain customer names and addresses while another table tracks the customer order history. The order information is tied to the customer information with a linking field, which (in this example) is probably a Customer number.

Why is this important? Well, suppose you need to print an invoice for customer Anita Cash's latest order. By placing the Customer number in the Orders table and relating the Orders table to the Customer table via the Customer number, you can pull Anita Cash's name and address information for the invoice without having to put that information in the Orders table.

Rules of relationships

Keep this in mind when relating tables:

- ✔ Tables you want to relate must have at least one field in common. While the field name need not be identical, its data type must be the same in each table. For example, you can't relate a text field to a number field.

  Keep key field names consistent between your tables. If you don't, that ball of confusion will roll your way at some point down the road.

- ✔ Usually, the linking field is one table's primary key but rarely the primary key in the other table.

  The Customer table, for example, is probably arranged by Customer number, while order data is likely organized by Order number.

- ✔ After the two tables have been created and share a common field, you're not done. You still have to build that relationship. (You'll find out how to actually do that in the later section, "Building Table Relationships.")

Relationship types

There is more than one type of table relationship in Access. When you relate two tables, you can choose one of three possible relationship types.

Unless you want to be an Access expert, you only need to understand the one-to-many table relationship. It's the most common.

One-to-many

One-to-many relationships connect one record in the first table to *many* records in the second table. This is the default — and by far the most common — relationship type.

Typical example: One customer may make many purchases at the store, so one customer record is linked to many sales records in the Transaction table.

One-to-one

One-to-one relationships link one record in the first table to *exactly* one record in the second table.

One-to-one relationships aren't common. Tables that have a one-to-one relationship can be combined into one table, which usually happens.

Many-to-many

Many-to-many relationships link *many* records in one table to *many* records in another table.

Here's a common example of a many-to-many relationship:

- ✔ A customer-order database contains separate tables for
  - Customers
  - Individual products
- ✔ Every individual product needs to be available to every customer.

  In other words, *many* customers need to be able to order *many* of the same products. The database needs to satisfy queries that look for *both* of these:
  - Every customer who ordered the same product
  - Every product that one customer ordered

In Access 2010, there are two ways to link *many* customers to *many* of the same products: *multivalued fields* and *junction tables*.

Multivalued fields

Access 2010 allows the creation of many-to-many relationships between two tables via *multivalued* fields.

Multivalued fields were a new capability in Access 2007. Prior to Access 2007, many-to-many relationships between two tables were bad — so bad that Access didn't allow them. Older versions of Access required a third table called a junction table (more on junction tables in a minute) to accomplish a many-to-many relationship.

A multivalued field can store many similar data items. Adding a multivalued field ends the need for creating multiple records to record multiple products ordered on one customer order. For example, you can add a multivalued field called `ProductID` to the Order Detail table. All products ordered can be stored in one field, so only one record per order is required.

Multivalued fields are not all peaches and cream. Use a junction table if you need to query or sort the data stored in the multivalued field as sorting and querying these fields is quite cumbersome.

A many-to-many relationship created with a junction table gives you much more data-retrieval flexibility than one created via a multivalued field. Microsoft created multivalue fields as an "easy" alternative to junction tables — and to make Access more compatible with SharePoint. Unless you're certain you'll never need to query or sort the field, avoid multivalued fields.

Junction tables

A *junction table* is a special table that keeps track of related records in two other tables:

- ✔ The junction table has a *one-to-many* relationship with both tables.
- ✔ The result works like a direct *many-to-many* relationship between both tables.

For example, a junction table called Orders can connect the customers to the order details for a particular order. The junction table has a one-to-many relationship with *both* the Customer and Order Details tables.

Building Table Relationships

If you can drag and drop, you can build a table relationship.

Keep these three limitations in mind:

- ✔ **You can only relate tables that are in the same database.**
- ✔ **You can relate queries to tables, but that's unusual.**
- ✔ **You need to tell Access specifically how your tables are related.**

When you're ready to play the matchmaker between your amorous tables, here's how to do it.

The Relationships window

To build a table relationship, first open the Relationships window. Follow these steps:

1. **Open the table in Design view.**

   The Design tab appears on the Ribbon. (See Figure 4-2.)

2. **From the Relationships group, click the Relationships button.**

   The Relationships window appears.

   If some tables are already listed in the window, someone (or some wizard) has already defined relationships for this database. If you're not sure how they got there and if more than one person is working on your database, stop and consult all database developers before changing the relationships. What might work for you could be disastrous for your colleagues.

When the Relationships window is open, you can select and relate tables.

Set Relationships

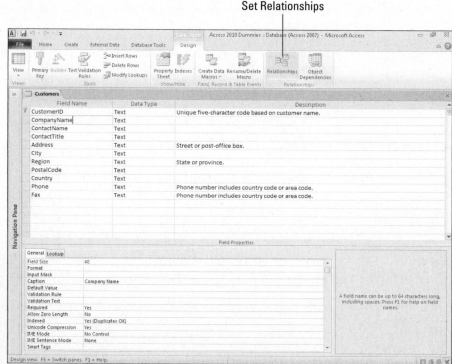

Figure 4-2: The Relationships button on the table Design tab.

Table relationships

For each pair of tables you relate, you must select the tables then join their common fields. The following sections show you how.

Selecting tables

To select tables to relate, open the Relationships window (find out how in the preceding section) and follow these steps:

1. **Choose Show Table from the Ribbon's Relationships group. (If you don't see the Relationships group, select the Design tab from the Ribbon.)**

   The Show Table dialog box appears, listing the tables in the current database file.

2. **For each pair of tables you want in the relationship, follow these steps:**

   a. Click the table.

   b. Click Add.

   In the big Relationships workspace, a little window lists the fields in the selected table. As you add tables to the layout, a separate window appears for each table. You can see these windows to the left of the Show Table dialog box in Figure 4-3.

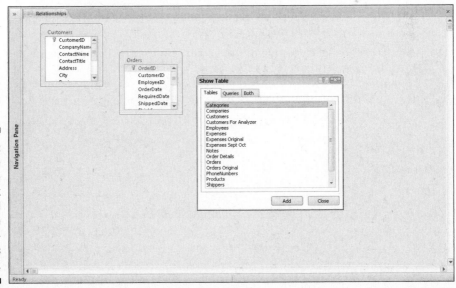

Figure 4-3: Use the Show Table dialog box to add tables to the Relationships diagram.

Repeat Step 2 for each pair of tables you want to relate. If one of the tables in the pair is already present (due to an existing relationship it has with another table), you don't have to add it again.

3. **After you finish adding tables, click the Close button.**

When you have all the tables present, you're ready for these tables to get to know each other. The following sections show how to relate the tables.

Managing relationships

This section contains all the information you'll need to create, edit, and delete your table relationships.

Creating relationships

After you select the tables (as shown in the preceding instructions), follow these steps to create a relationship between two tables:

1. **Decide which two tables you want to relate.**

   Since the one-to-many relationship is the most common, these instructions pertain to it. The two tables in a one-to-many relationship are designated as fulfilling one of two roles:

   - *Parent:* In the parent table, the related field is the primary key. Each record in the parent table is uniquely identified by this related field.

   - *Child:* In the child table, the related field contains the same information as the field in the parent table. Typically it has the same name as the corresponding field in the parent table — although this is not a requirement.

   To make relating tables easier, put related fields near the beginning of the field list. In Access, you must see the related fields on the screen before you can make a relationship. If the related fields are not at the beginning of the field list, you have to do a lot of scrolling to find them.

2. **Follow these steps to select the parent field from the list:**

   a. *Put the mouse pointer on the field you want to relate in the parent table.*

   Usually the field you want to relate in the parent table is the primary key.

   b. *Hold down the left mouse button.*

3. **While holding down the left mouse button, follow these steps to join the parent field to the child field:**

a. *Drag the mouse pointer from the parent field to the child table.*

A plus sign appears at the base of the mouse pointer.

b. *Point to the related field in the child table.*

c. *Release the mouse button.*

The Edit Relationships dialog box appears, detailing the soon-to-be relationship, as shown in Figure 4-4.

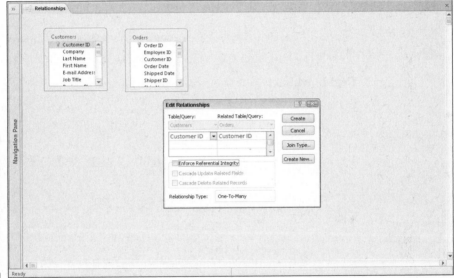

Figure 4-4:
The Edit Relationships dialog box details how Access connects two tables.

Be very careful before releasing the mouse button. Put the tip of the mouse pointer *directly* on the child field before you let go.

• If you drag between the two fields correctly, the Edit Relationships dialog box displays the parent and child fields side by side, as shown in Figure 4-4.

• If you miss, click Cancel in the Edit Relationships dialog box and try Step 3 again.

4. **In the Edit Relationships dialog box, select the Enforce Referential Integrity option.**

Child Tables' Protective Services?

Enforce Referential Integrity sounds harsh, doesn't it? It simply means that Access makes sure that a record is present in the parent table before you can add one to its child table. (Shouldn't every child have a parent watching?)

For example, with Referential Integrity enforced, Access won't let you enter an order in the Orders table for a customer that is not present in the Customers table.

5. Double-check that your field names are the correct ones and then click Create.

Access illustrates the new relationship in the Relationships window:

- A line between the related fields shows you that the tables are related.

- If you checked the Enforce Referential Integrity option in the pre-ceding step, Access places a 1 next to the parent in the relation-ship and an infinity symbol next to the child, as shown in the full set of relationships in Figure 4-5.

To relate another pair of selected tables, repeat Steps 1 through 5.

Figure 4-5:
A one-to-many relationship between two tables.

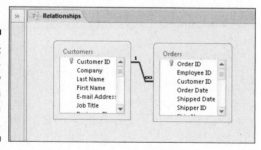

Access also provides tools for modifying and removing relationships. The fol-lowing section shows how to use them.

Modifying relationships

After you relate tables, you can see, organize, and remove the relationships.

If you create a relationship you don't want, open the Relationships window and follow these steps to delete the relationship:

1. **Click the Relationship line connecting the two tables.**

   If you were successful, the line will thicken. That means the line is selected.

2. **Tap the Delete key on your keyboard.**

   Voilà! The relationship is gone.

If you are relating many tables together, the Relationships window may look a little messy because Relationship lines will cross each other. This makes it difficult to determine which tables are related to each other. To rectify this situation, click and drag the title bar of a table window to another part of the screen. It's good practice — although not always possible — to show parents either *above* or to the *left* of their children. Try to arrange the parent and child tables so the lines between the parent and child tables don't cross over any lines that illustrate other table relationships.

Having trouble understanding your relationships? (Who isn't?) Are you scrolling all over the place in the Relationships window to see everything? If so, the Relationship Report is just for you. To preview this report, click the Relationship Report button in the Ribbon's Tools group. All the related tables in your database will display in an easy-to-read report. (Okay, *easier* to read!)

Indexing for Faster Queries

You may find yourself sitting for a minute or two waiting for a query or report to run. (I've sat longer than that for some reports during the development stage.) So what can be done to speed up your queries? Add *indexes* to your tables, that's what.

A table index in Access works just like the index in a book. It helps Access find a record in a table just as a book index helps you find a topic in a book.

The benefit of an index depends on the number of records in the table:

- If you have 100 customers, an index won't improve performance much.
- If you have tens of thousands of customers, an index will make a significant performance improvement.

How an index works

An index is essentially a copy of the table that's already *sorted* on the indexed field.

When a table is indexed properly, queries run faster because the indexes help Access locate the data faster.

Here's an example. Suppose you need to produce a list of all your Pennsylvania customers, and you often query your customer table by state:

✔ If you index the State field in your Customers table, all the Pennsylvania customers will be in one place. When Access reaches the Pennsylvania customers, it can stop there and return them to you in your query.

✔ Without the index, Access must scan every record in the table to return the desired results.

Create your own index

Here's the skinny on indexes:

✔ Each field in a table can be indexed if it isn't one of these data types: *calculated, attachment, hyperlink,* or *OLE object.*

✔ As with the primary key, an index may have a unique name that's different from the field name. It can also have the same name as the field name. Access won't balk either way.

✔ You don't have to name your index; Access does that for you.

✔ Indexes either *allow* or *prevent* duplicate entries in your table.

Here are some guidelines to help you decide which fields to index, presented in their recommended order:

1. Start by querying the table whose query performance you'd like to improve. Make note of the time it took to run the query.

2. Next, index each field that you know you'll query frequently. For example, in a Contacts table, you might query by Contact ID, Contact Last Name, and Contact State.

3. Finally, query the newly indexed table. If the query time improves, your indexes are correct. If your query time worsens, try removing one index at a time, starting with the field you think you'll query the least. Rerun your query and note performance.

   When you've optimized performance, your indexing is complete.

4. Apply an index type.

   The sidebar "To duplicate or not to duplicate" shows which index type to apply.

To list a table's indexes, follow these steps:

1. **Open the table in Design view.**

2. **On the Design tab, click the Indexes button in the Ribbon's Show/Hide group. (See Figure 4-6.)**

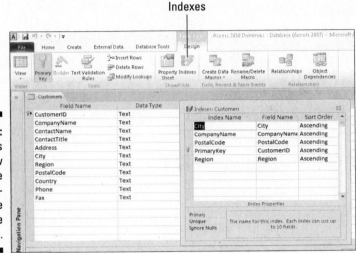

Figure 4-6:
The Indexes window with the Indexes button above it on the Ribbon.

Building too many indexes in a table slows down some tasks. Adding records to a table with several indexes takes a little longer than adding records to an un-indexed table. Access spends extra time updating all those indexes behind the scenes. The trick is to get the right number of indexes assigned to the right fields. Sometimes it comes down to trial and error when you're optimizing query performance via indexes.

Adding and removing indexes

After you decide on the correct fields to index (as outlined previously in this section), creating an index is a snap.

In the following instructions, Step 4 can *delete* an existing field index. You may decide to delete a field index if it's hindering data input more than it's enhancing query performance.

To duplicate or not to duplicate

When you create an index, you have two options for handling duplicate values:

✔ If records can have the same value in this field, click *Yes (Duplicates OK)*.

Yes (Duplicates OK) is the most common choice.

✔ If every record needs a unique value in this field (such as customer numbers in your

Customer table), click *Yes (No Duplicates)*, as shown in the figure included here.

The No Duplicates setting tells Access to make sure that no two records have the same value in the indexed field.

Access indexes primary key fields automatically as No Duplicates when you designate the primary key.

No Duplicates Index

To add or remove field indexes, open the table in Design view and follow these steps:

1. Click the name of the field you want to index.

The blinking cursor lands in the field name.

2. In the General tab of the Field Properties section, click the Indexed box.

Now the cursor moves into the Indexed box, and a down arrow appears on the right end of the box.

If the Indexed display has no entry, this field type doesn't work with indexes. You can't index `Calculated`, `Attachment`, `Hyperlink` or `OLE Object` fields.

3. Click the down arrow at the end of the Indexed box.

A list of index options appears:

- *Yes (Duplicates OK)*
- *Yes (No Duplicates)*
- *No*

The previous sidebar "To duplicate or not to duplicate" shows how to decide the correct index setting.

4. **Select the index type you want from the list.**

   To *remove* an existing index from the selected field, click *No*.

5. **To make the change permanent, click the Save button on the Quick Access toolbar.**

   If your table contains thousands of records, Access may take a few moments to create the index.

Chapter 5

Remodeling Your Data

In This Chapter

▶ Opening an existing table or database

▶ Adding new records to your table

▶ Changing an existing record

▶ Renaming fields and tables

▶ Deleting unwanted records

▶ Turning back time — to before your mistake was made

From remembering to change your car's oil every 3,000 miles to cleaning out your rain gutters, everything in your surroundings needs a little maintenance now and then. Most of that maintenance involves tidying up, getting rid of old or unwanted things, or making improvements. Sometimes *all* these things are part of the maintenance process.

Well, it's no different for your database — an Access database needs a tune-up now and then, just to keep things running right. This can be as simple as checking for blank fields where you need to plug in missing data, as common as purging old or inaccurate records, or a practical matter such as changing the names of tables and fields so your database makes more sense to those who use it.

Unlike getting your car serviced or cleaning out your gutters, however, maintaining your database isn't expensive or difficult. Of course, *not* keeping your database in good working order *can* get expensive — it can cost you in terms of your time, the potential impact of inaccurate records on your organization, more time (and paper) wasted printing reports that include obsolete data, and the confusion that plagues those who use a database that has incorrect (or vague) field and table names.

Don't worry, though — for all those doomsday potentialities, the solution is as simple as a few clicks, a couple double-clicks, and a little bit of typing — and it's free!

Opening a Table for Editing

When you open Access 2010 (as discussed in Chapters 1 and 2), the workspace shows you several features to help you get started — templates you can call upon to help you build a new database, a list of recently opened databases, and one-click access to the Backstage View panel, which offers you commands to use such as Save, Print, and Open. All these options are visible in Figure 5-1.

Of course, to open a database (and then the table or tables you've targeted for editing), you'll need that Open command I just mentioned. But you have other choices, which you can use depending on the situation.

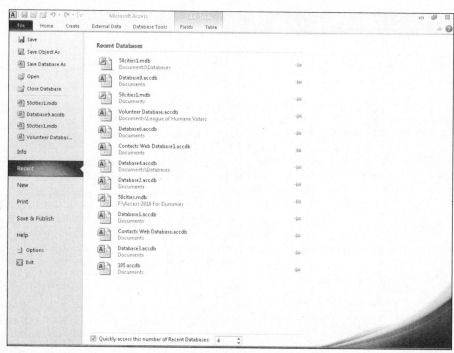

Figure 5-1:
The Access 2010 workspace makes opening a database easy.

To explore these options a bit, check out the following list and repeat after me: "I can open a database in any of the following ways . . . ."

➤ **If you've recently used the database,** choose your database from the list displayed when you click the word Recent in the Backstage View panel. Don't see Backstage view? Click the tab to the left of the Ribbon's Home tab, and the panel (on the far left) appears.

To open a database from the Recent Databases list, just point to it and click once.

✔ **If you don't remember where your database is stored,** click the Windows Start button and click in the field at the bottom of the menu, where the words "Start Search" appear. After typing the name of the database you're looking for, click the magnifying-glass icon or press Enter. You may even notice files appearing in the menu as you type, because Windows starts looking for files matching your text as soon as you begin to type.

As shown in Figure 5-2, if you don't see the file you want, you can click the Search Everywhere link in the Start menu, and use the resulting window to search your entire computer — all drives, folders, and even other computers to which you're attached via a network.

When the name of the file you want appears in the right side of the window, double-click the name to open the file.

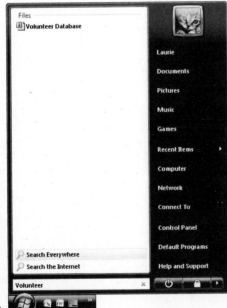

Figure 5-2:
Use the Start menu's Search field to find the database file you seek.

✔ **If you remember where your database is stored, but it isn't in the Recent Databases list,** use the following procedure to use the Open dialog box to navigate to and open your database:

File

1. Click the File tab to the left of the Home tab, and choose Open from the list of commands.

The Open dialog box pops onto the screen, as shown in Figure 5-3.

By default, the Open dialog box goes to the My Documents folder, which may contain your database.

2. *If the database isn't in the My Documents folder, use the links on the left side to check your Desktop, local hard drive, or network drives.*

3. *When you find the database, open it by double-clicking its name.*

The database file opens immediately, as shown in Figure 5-4.

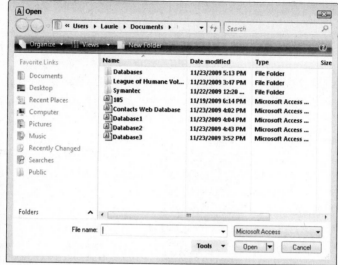

Figure 5-3:
Use the Open dialog box to open your database.

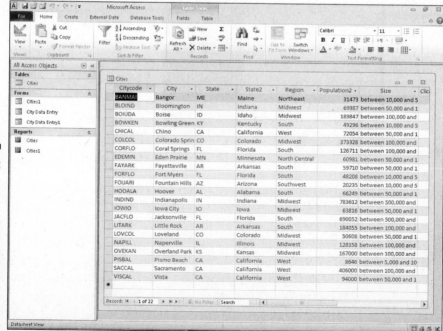

Figure 5-4:
The database file opens, and the database window displays all the tables, queries, and so on.

An introductory screen known as a *switchboard* (or, perhaps — utilizing a new feature in Access 2010 — a *Navigation form*) may appear instead of the tabbed dialog box. Access is telling you that your database either contains some custom programming or was created by the Database Wizard. You probably have some special forms that help you interact with the information in your database. If you want to find out how to create your own switchboard, check out Chapter 22.

4. *Below the All Tables heading (or All Access Objects heading, which you'll see if your database was created with a prior version of Access) on the left side of the workspace, look for the table you want to open.*

   Each table has its own listing, accompanied by a table icon.

5. *Double-click the table you want to edit.*

   The table opens in Table view, and you can begin your maintenance of the data. You can add or remove fields or change the names of your fields — topics I discuss later on in this information-packed chapter.

Inserting Records and Fields

Ever gone on vacation and forgotten your toothpaste? Sure, you can probably just pick up a tube at a drugstore in the place you're visiting, but it's still a pain. The same "Darn!" feeling overcomes you when you realize you've left something out of your database suitcase. (Okay, you might use a different four-letter word in that case, but this is a family publication.)

Luckily, adding a forgotten record or field to your table is about as easy as making a quick trip to the drugstore for that forgotten toothpaste — so easy that you may forget to say "Darn!" (or any other word expressing regret) when you discover a missing field. Instead, you'll calmly launch into the following steps — one set for inserting a missing record and one set for inserting a missing field.

Adding a record

To add a record, follow these steps:

1. **In the Table view of the table that's missing a record, click inside the first empty cell at the bottom of the table — below the last displayed record in the table.**

   Your cursor blinks in the first field in that record, as shown in Figure 5-5.

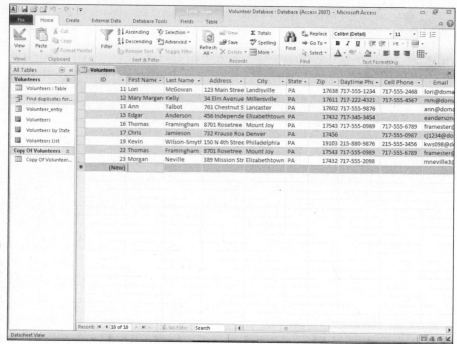

Figure 5-5:
A new
record
awaits its
data.

2. **Type your information for the first field.**

   If the first field is an AutoNumber type, then you're automatically placed in the second field when you click the row. In the second field, you can begin typing the data for that field. As soon as you start typing, the AutoNumber field generates a new number and displays it in the field.

   Don't panic if the AutoNumber field seems to skip a number when it creates an entry for your new record. When an AutoNumber field skips a number, it means you probably entered (or at least started to enter) a record at some point during this (or a previous) data-entry session and then deleted it.

3. **Press Tab to move through the fields and enter all the data for this new record.**

4. **When you finish entering data into the last field for the new record, you're finished!**

   Because Access saves the new record automatically while you're typing it, you have nothing more to do. Pretty neat, eh?

   If you want to add another record, press Tab and type away, filling in yet another new record.

If you change your mind and want to kill the new addition, you have a couple of options:

- ✔ While the new record is in progress, press Ctrl+Z to undo whatever work you've done thus far on the new record.

- ✔ Right-click the cell to the far left of the record (the empty cell to the left of the first field). From the resulting pop-up menu, choose Delete Record. Click Yes when asked whether you're sure about the deletion.

Inserting a field

With the field-challenged table open, follow these steps to add the field you're missing:

1. **In Table view, find the field heading aptly called *Click to Add* (see Figure 5-6).**

   The column will be found at the very end of your existing fields — so be prepared to scroll all the way to the end to see it.

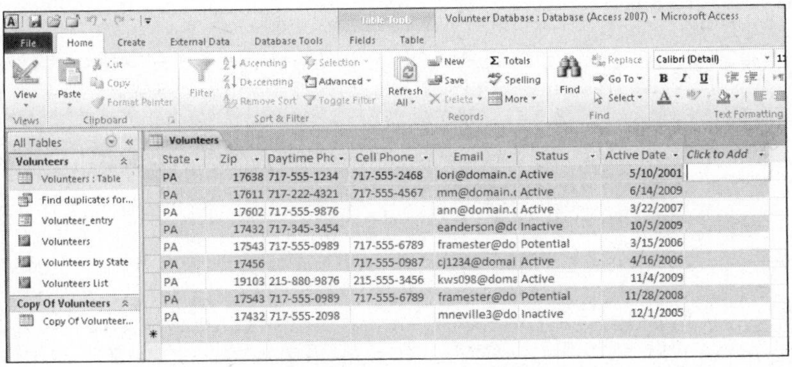

Figure 5-6: Right there in the table is a new field, awaiting creation.

2. **Click the instructional Click to Add heading you found in Step 1.**

   A pop-up menu appears, from which you can choose the type of field this new field will be, as shown in Figure 5-7.

3. **Choose a field type from the list.**

   The new field appears, entitled `Field1`, and the Click to Add column moves over one column. `Field1` is highlighted and awaiting your new name for it, as shown in Figure 5-8.

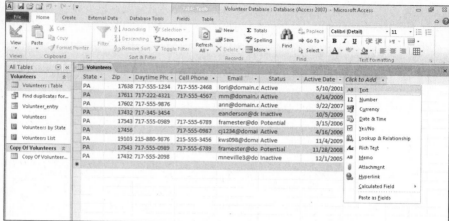

Figure 5-7:
Not sure
what field
type to
choose? Text
is a good
choice, as
it was the
default for
new fields
when you
built the table
originally.

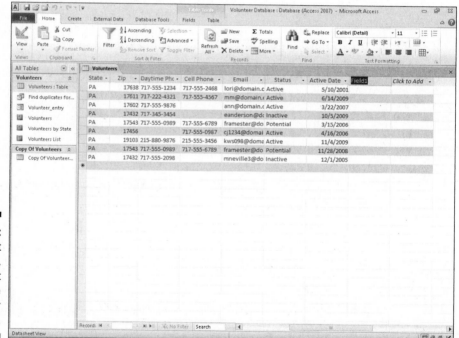

Figure 5-8:
Name that
new field,
and make it
feel at home
in your
table.

4. Type the name of your new field and press Enter.

Your new field is created.

5. **To rearrange your fields so the new field is where you want it to be among the existing fields, click the heading of the field column you just created — and then click again.**

   On the first click, the entire column is highlighted, and the black down-pointing arrow changes to a left-pointing white arrow. On the second click, the arrow acquires a small box just below it, indicating that you're ready to move the column.

6. **Drag to the left or right depending on where you want to drop your new field.**

   A thick vertical line follows you, indicating where the field will appear as soon as you release the mouse button, as shown in Figure 5-9.

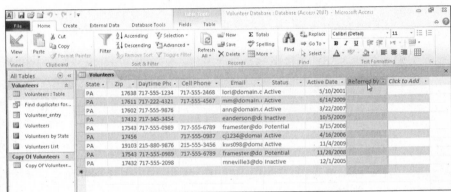

Figure 5-9: Drag and drop your field to reposition it among the other fields in the table.

7. **When you're happy with the intended location of the field, release the mouse button.**

   Your field is relocated.

By default, all fields created in Table view are Text fields. If this isn't the type of field you want, you can change the Data Type (as well as other settings) for the new field by doing the following:

1. **With the field selected, click the Ribbon's Fields tab from the Table Tools group, as shown in Figure 5-10.**

2. **In the Formatting section of the tab, click the Data Type drop-down arrow.**

3. **Choose a format — Memo, Currency, Hyperlink, whatever — from the resulting list, as shown in Figure 5-10.**

You can also tinker with settings that go with the data type you choose — for example, if you choose a Number format, you can use the buttons in the Formatting section to determine how many decimal places will appear on-screen.

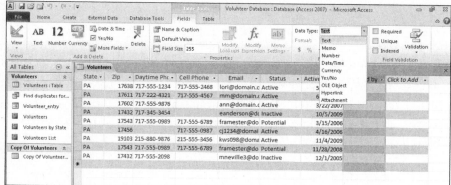

Figure 5-10:
Need a type
of field other
than the
default Text
data type?
The Data
Type drop-
down menu
gives you
options.

Deleting a field

Getting rid of a field is no big deal — in fact, it might be too easy. Access does, at least, give you a little nudge (in the form of a dialog box) to make sure you're *positive* you want to get rid of the field in question.

To get rid of an existing field that you no longer need, follow these steps:

1. **Right-click the heading for that field column.**

2. **From the resulting pop-up menu, shown in Figure 5-11, choose Delete Field.**

3. **When prompted, click Yes to confirm your desire to complete the deletion.**

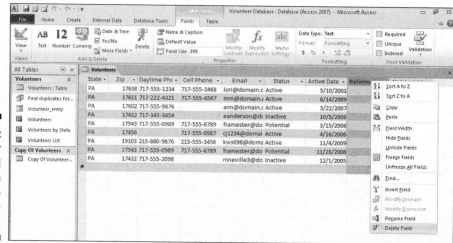

Figure 5-11:
Bid your
field a fond
adieu with
just two
clicks of the
mouse.

Modifying Field Content

Although your stuff is safely tucked away inside a table, you can reach in and make changes easily. In fact, editing your data is so easy that I'm not sure whether this is a good feature or a bad one.

Whenever you're browsing through a table, please be careful! Access doesn't warn you before saving changes to a record — even if the changes are accidental. (If I were one of those preachy authors, I'd probably make a big, guilt-laden point about how this "feature" of Access makes regular backups all the more important, but that's not my style.)

To change something inside a record, follow these steps:

1. **Scroll through the table until you find the record that needs some adjusting.**

2. **Click the field (the individual cell in the table) that you want to change.**

   The blinking line cursor pops into the field.

   If your mouse has a wheel button, use the wheel to take a quick spin through the table. (For such a small innovation, that wheel is a big timesaver!)

3. **Change the field.**

   What you change and how you change it is up to you:

   - *Replace the entire field:* Press F2 to highlight the data and then type the new information. The new entry replaces the old one.

   - *Repair a portion of the data in a field:* Click the field and then use the right and left arrow keys to position the cursor exactly where you want to make the change.

   - *Remove or add characters:* Press Backspace to remove characters to the left of the cursor; press Delete to remove characters to the right. Insert new characters by typing.

     If you're in a time/date field and want to insert the current date, press Ctrl+; (semicolon). To insert the current time, press Ctrl+Shift+; (semicolon).

     If you change your mind and want to restore the original data, press Esc or Ctrl+Z to cancel your edits.

4. **When you're finished with the record, press Enter to save your changes.**

Don't press Enter until you're positive about the changes you typed. After you save them, the old data is gone — you can't go back.

Name-Calling

You've built your table, and maybe you've done a stellar job from the get-go — you didn't forget any fields, you put the fields in the right order, and you set up the fields to house the right kind of data. Well done, you!

Okay, back to reality. (Of course nothing in life is that simple, is it?) It's not uncommon to realize, after building your table (and accepting my previous "Well done, you!") that you need to make a few changes. You may need to change the table's name or you might need to change one or more of the field names in the table. Or both! If this happens, it doesn't mean you messed up or anything, it just means you're a human being who, with even the most scrupulous planning and preparation, can make a mistake or change your mind — or perhaps the terminology has changed since the table was first created, and now it needs updating. Luckily, regardless of the reason you need to do it, Access makes it easy to make either kind of change.

Renaming fields

Uh-oh. The field name you used when you first built the table has been the source of some confusion. People don't know what "Status" means — does it mean has the member paid their dues or does it refer to whether or not they're active in the organization? It's clear enough to you, but it's important that any other folks who use the data feel confident that they understand what's in it.

This sort of field-naming dilemma is common when you're setting up a table for the first time, and can even crop up later on, when you're working with a table that's been around and in use for a while. The need to edit field names can arise for any reason, at any time; it's never too early or too late to edit them.

So, for whatever reason, you find you have to edit a field name. What to do?

Access makes it incredibly easy to rename a field — to keep it simple, do it first in Table view. The simplicity doesn't end with how the actual renaming takes place, either — as soon as you rename a field; Access updates a whole slew of things automatically:

> ✔ All connections from that field to other tables (if you've already set up your table relationships, as discussed in Chapter 4)
>
> ✔ All queries, reports, and other goodies that already use the field

What could be easier than that?

Working in Table view

So when you're ready, follow these steps:

1. **Double-click the field name, as shown in Figure 5-12.**

   The current name is highlighted in place, atop the column.

Figure 5-12: A selected field name is ripe for editing.

2. **Edit the name as needed:**

   • *To replace the current name entirely,* type the new name while the current name is still highlighted.

   While the field name is highlighted, the very next thing you type will replace the current name — so don't start typing at that point unless you want to replace the entire field name.

   • *To edit the name (leaving some of the current name in place),* click inside the existing, selected name and then insert or remove characters as needed.

3. **When you like the name you see, click in any cell in the table.**

   The new name appears at the top of the column, and you're ready to do whatever you need:

   • Enter new records.

   • Edit another field.

   • Save the table and close it (if you've finished working).

Using the Modify Fields tab

To rename a field in the Fields tab in Table view, follow these steps:

1. **Click the field name that you want to edit.**

   You can also click in any cell in that column — just give Access some way of knowing which field you want to rename.

2. **Click the Fields tab, in the Table Tools section of the Ribbon.**

3. **In the Properties section, click Name & Caption.**

   A dialog box opens (as shown in Figure 5-13), through which you can rename the field.

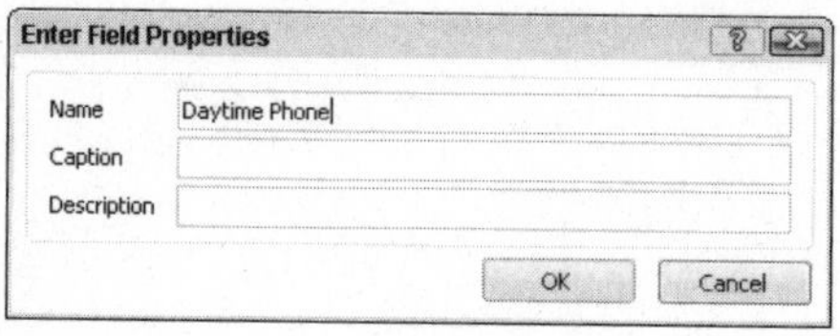

Figure 5-13:
Rename your field Enter Field Properties dialog box.

Enter Field Properties	?
Name	Daytime Phone
Caption	
Description	
	OK Cancel

4. **Type the new name in the Name field in the dialog box.**

5. **Press Enter or click OK to change the name.**

   This tells Access to accept your change, and you return to the table, with your field's new name in place.

If you prefer the quick and easy way to change a field name (and have no other changes you need to make, such as editing the Field Size, via the Fields tab in the Data Tools section of the ribbon), you can always double-click the existing field name, and when it highlights, type the new name. Press Enter to confirm your change.

Renaming a table

Renaming an entire table is not as common as needing to rename a field, but it can happen. Maybe you misspelled the name. Maybe the name you gave it is too long, too short, or is misleading to people who have to guess which table to open when they're looking for something in particular.

To edit the name of a table, follow these steps:

1. **Open the database that contains the table you want to rename.**

   With the chosen database listed on the left side of your Access workspace, be sure all its tables are listed, too.

Don't open the table itself. It can't be open during the renaming process if you want those steps to work.

2. **Right-click the table name.**

3. **Choose Rename from the menu that appears, as shown in Figure 5-14.**

   The name is highlighted.

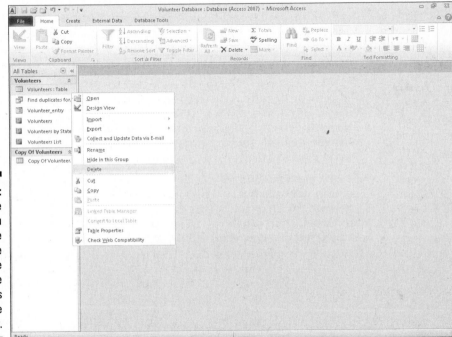

Figure 5-14:
To rename a table, you have to be able to see its name listed in the All Tables panel on the left.

4. **Change the table name.**

   You can make the change in one of two ways:

   • Type the new name.

   • Modify the current name (use your arrow keys to move within the name and your Backspace and/or Delete keys to edit).

After you've renamed your table, all the items that link to or use it within your database will be updated to use the same table with the new name. You don't need to re-create any of your queries, reports, forms, or relationships.

Turn Uh-Oh! into Yee-Hah!

Okay, none of the following three methods for cleaning up after a bad edit are magical or really high-tech, but they are helpful. What's a "bad" edit? An Access session in which the wrong data was entered, a change was made to field or table names in error, or other changes were made to data or table structure that are now regretted. Here goes:

- ✔ **You can recover from one addition or edit with the Undo command.** Unfortunately, you cannot Undo the deletion of a record. Access will warn you, though, if you attempt to delete one or more records; you can choose not to proceed if you're not absolutely sure.

- ✔ **Double-check any change you make before saving it.** This sounds painfully obvious, but really — just do it. And if the change is important, triple-check it. When you're sure it's right, press Enter and commit the change to the table. If you're not sure about the data, don't save the changes. Instead, get your questions answered first — and then feel free to edit the record.

- ✔ **Keep a good backup so you can quickly recover missing data and get on with your work.** Good backups have no substitute. If you make good backups, the chance of losing data is greatly reduced, your boss promotes you, your significant other unswervingly devotes his or her life to you, and you may even win the lottery. At the very least, you'll sleep better, knowing that your data is safe.

Chapter 6

What's Happening Under the Table?

In This Chapter

▶ Locating your table settings (and I don't mean flatware!)

▶ Changing how data displays

▶ Keeping bad data out with input masks

▶ Understanding required fields

▶ Performing detailed testing through validation

▶ Adding data automatically with default values

*I*f you have a sound table structure but poor data collection, your database won't report anything of interest to its intended audience. You know the old saying "garbage in, garbage out"? This chapter helps you limit the garbage that is put into your tables by detailing five tools Access puts at your disposal. (Access doesn't call them tools; it calls them *properties*.)

You don't want the task of going back and cleaning up your data after it has all been typed. Better to type it correctly the first time. This chapter shows you how to use formatting, input masks, required fields, and validation to keep your data nice and tidy.

Access Table Settings

This chapter shows how to use the following five properties to help keep incorrect data out of your database:

- ✔ **Format:** Control how your data appears without changing the way it is stored.

- ✔ **Input mask:** Force data entry to follow the correct structure, such as typing phone numbers in the (###) ###-#### format.

✔ **Required:** Force the entry of data in the field before the record can be saved.

✔ **Validation Rule:** Require that data be typed in a field following a specific set of rules, such as a number between 0 and 100.

✔ **Default Value:** Auto enter data when a new record is inserted.

All five properties are in the same place: in Table Design view on the General tab in the Field Properties section. Use the following steps to access and modify the four properties:

1. **Open the database file that contains the data you want to keep clean. From the Navigation pane, right-click the table you want to modify.**

   The shortcut menu appears.

2. **Choose Design View from the menu, as shown in Figure 6-1.**

   The table flips into Design view, showing its fields and field properties.

   If the table you want is already on the screen in Datasheet view, just click the View button from the Home tab of the Ribbon. This toggles between Design and Datasheet views.

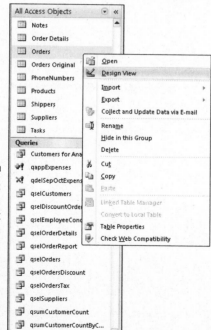

Figure 6-1:
You can
see and edit
a table's
structure,
including
its field
properties,
in Design
view.

3. Repeat these steps for each field whose properties you want to alter:

a. *Click the name of the field.*

The General tab in the Field Properties section (the bottom half of the window) displays the details of the current field, as shown in Figure 6-2. You're ready to do your thing!

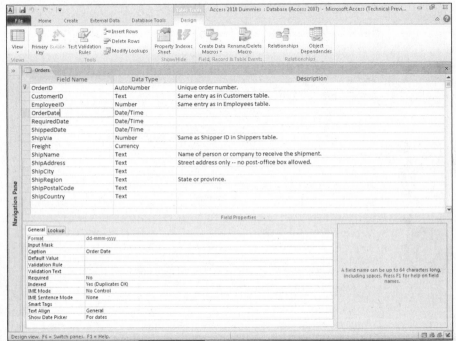

b. *In the Field Properties section, click in the Format, Input Mask, Validation Rule, Required, or Default Value boxes and type your changes.*

In the remainder of this chapter, I delve into these properties in more detail to show you what they do and how to modify them to suit your needs.

The Format, Required, Validation, and Default Value properties can be modified in Datasheet view. Just click the Fields tab on the Ribbon and check out the Formatting, Properties, and Field Validation groups.

Validation Text has a box, too. It goes with the Validation Rule box (kind of like coffee and cream). The "Making your data toe the line with validation" section, later in this chapter, explains how these two properties work together to prevent the entry of unwanted data.

4. **When you've made all necessary property changes, click the Save button on the Quick Access toolbar to keep your changes.**

   To *reject* your changes, close the table (click the x in its upper-right corner) and click No in the resulting dialog box.

Using formats, masks, required fields, validations, and default values involves many more details, but use the preceding steps to get started. These steps are the same regardless of which property you apply.

The following sections tackle each property individually.

Field Data Formats

Formatting helps you see data in a recognizable, clear arrangement. Formats only change the way you *see* your data on the screen, not how your data is *stored* in the table.

Some field data types require different formatting codes than others. For example, text formatting uses different codes than numeric formatting. The following sections cover formats for the most common field data types.

If your format command doesn't work the first time, follow these steps to troubleshoot it:

1. **Double-check the data type.**

   For example, if you see left aligned numbers without a standard number of decimal places, you may have selected the Text data type for a numeric field. Just change the data type to Number or Currency and like magic, you have beautiful numbers!

2. **Review the format commands and make any necessary changes.**

   For example, if you see percent signs and your intention was dollar signs, just flip the format from Percent to Currency by using the Format Property drop-down list.

Text and memo fields

Text and memo fields can be formatted in four ways that affect *capitalization,* *spacing,* and *punctuation.*

Apply formatting, minimize data-entry errors

Although formatting won't stop inaccurate data entry, it can make data-entry errors more recognizable. Here's how formatting can cut down on errors:

✔ **Make errors more visible.**

For example, suppose you need to type the number *one million* into a numeric field. Without formatting, you see this: 1000000. (Uh, how many zeros are in that?) With standard formatting, you see this: 1,000,000.

✔ **Cut down on typing during data entry.**

For example, phone numbers are often seen as (111) 222-3333. With text formatting applied to a phone number field, simply type **1112223333**. Access displays the phone number with the parentheses and the dash. (Can you say "fewer keystrokes"?)

Access does not have predesigned formats for text and memo fields, but you can make your own. Just string together some special characters to construct a formatting string that Access can use to display the text in a standardized way.

Table 6-1 lists the special characters that you can use to build your text and memo formats.

Table 6-1	Formatting Codes for Text and Memo Fields
Character	*Display Option*
>	Show whole field as uppercase (capital letters).
<	Show whole field as lowercase.
@	Show a space in this position if there isn't a data character.
&	Display a character if there is one; otherwise don't do anything.

Here's what you need to know about the formatting codes in Table 6-1.

Capitalization

By default, Access displays text and memo fields with the actual capitalization of the stored data. However, Access can automatically display a field in all *uppercase* (capital) or *lowercase* letters, regardless of how the data is stored.

Set the Format property of a text or memo field to the greater-than or less-than symbol to affect the capitalization of the whole field.

Uppercase

The *greater-than* symbol (>) makes all the text in that field appear in uppercase (capital) letters, regardless of how the text was typed. To use this option, type a single greater-than symbol in the Format text box.

This format is great for abbreviating the names of U.S. states, whose abbreviations are normally seen as uppercase.

Lowercase

The *less-than* symbol (<) makes all the text in that field appear in lowercase, regardless of how the text was typed. To use this option, type a single less-than symbol in the Format text box.

Spacing and punctuation

Access allows you to format the spacing and punctuation of typed text. Through formatting, you can add extra spaces or special characters like dashes.

When using the @ or & character in a format, always include one @ or & to represent *each typed character* in the field.

Show filler spaces

The *at sign* (@) forces Access to display either a character or a space in the field. If the typed field data is shorter than the formatting code, Access adds extra spaces to fill the format.

For example, if a field uses @@@@@@ as its format, but the field's data is only three characters long (such as *Tim* or *now*), Access displays three spaces and *then* the data. If the field data is four characters long, the format pads the beginning of the entry with two spaces.

Don't show filler spaces

The *ampersand* (&) means "display a character if there's one to display; otherwise don't do anything."

This is the default format.

You can use this to create special formats. For example, a Social Security Number can use this format: &&&- &&- &&&&

If someone types **123456789** in that field, Access applies the format and displays 123-45-6789, adding the dashes in the middle of the numbers by itself.

Make Access see red so you don't

Here's a great tip for highlighting missing text data in a record: When you're typing data, sometimes you need to skip a text field because you don't have that particular information at hand. Wouldn't it be great if Access automatically marked the field as blank as a reminder for you to fill in the info later?

Access can create such a custom text format. For example, the following character string displays the word *Unknown* in red if the field doesn't contain a value. Type the following command in the field's Format text box exactly like this (there are no spaces between the characters in the string) and punctuation:

```
@;"Unknown"[Red]
```

It's easy to customize the above formatting example to suit your needs:

- ✔ **Text:** Between the quotes, substitute any display text you want instead of Unknown.

- ✔ **Color:** Between the square brackets, substitute any display color you want instead of Red.

Formatting changes only the appearance of data, not the data itself. Therefore, if you intend to export the data to another program (such as Excel), the formatting won't necessarily come with it. So if you type **pa** in a State field and apply the > formatting code to that field, the data will appear as PA in Access but will export to Excel as pa.

Number and currency fields

Microsoft makes it easy for you to apply numeric formats to your numeric fields. They built the seven most common formats into a pull-down menu right in the Format text box.

To set a number or currency field format, follow these steps:

1. **With your table in Design view, click the Format text box for the field you'd like to format.**

2. **Click the down arrow that appears at the right side of the box and select a format for your field.**

   Figure 6-3 shows the drop-down menu, which is divided in half:

   - The left side shows each format's given name.

   - The right side shows a sample of how each format looks.

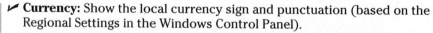

Figure 6-3:
The number
format list.

Numeric formats change only the appearance of the number, not the number as it is stored. So if you choose Standard to format a field that contains the number 1.235678, you see 1.24 on the screen — but Access *stores* 1.235678 in the field. Any calculations done with the numbers in that field will use the actual typed-in number, not the formatted number seen on-screen.

The following sections describe the numeric formats built into Access.

General Number format

The General Number format is the Access default. It merely displays whatever you put in the field without making any editorial adjustments to it.

Currency formats

The currency formats make a standard number field look like a currency field.

Some numeric fields store decimal characters, and others do not — it all depends on the field size you select. So decimal formatting is irrelevant if you select a field size that doesn't store decimal places (the long-integer size, for example). Chapter 3 covers number fields and field sizes in more detail.

These two formats show the data with two decimal places (the "cents" part of a dollar amount), substituting zeros if decimals aren't already present:

✔ **Currency:** Show the local currency sign and punctuation (based on the Regional Settings in the Windows Control Panel).

Don't assume that the Currency formats automatically perform an exchange-rate conversion for the selected currency. They don't. They merely display the selected currency symbol in front of the value typed in the field.

✔ **Euro:** Use the Euro symbol (ε) regardless of the Regional Settings.

Scientific, Percent, and Decimal formats

The remaining built-in formats are used for a variety of purposes, from displaying a large number in scientific notation to showing decimals as percents:

- ✔ **Fixed:** Shows the decimal value without a comma as a thousands separator.

- ✔ **Standard:** Shows the decimal value with a thousands separator.

  For either Fixed or Standard format, you can adjust the number of decimal places that appear:

  - By default, Fixed and Standard round the display to two decimal places.

  - To specify a different number of decimal places, type a number between 0 and 15 in the Decimal Places setting right below the Format setting.

- ✔ **Percent:** This format turns a simple decimal like .97 into the much prettier 97%.

  Type the data as a decimal (for example, type **.97** for 97 percent). Otherwise Access displays some awesomely *wrong* percentages!

  If your percentages are displayed only as 0.00% or 1.00%, the sidebar "What happened to my percentages?" has a solution.

- ✔ **Scientific:** Displays numbers in *scientific notation* (the first *significant digits* plus the number of places where the digits belong on the left or right side of the decimal point).

  Scientific notation is mostly for very *big* numbers (like the distance light travels in a year) and very *small* numbers (like the distance light travels in a trillionth of a second) that are hard to measure precisely or read at a glance.

Date/time fields

Microsoft provides you with a pull-down menu full of ready-to-use date and time formats. Here's how to apply a date/time format to a field:

1. **With your table in Design view, click the Format text box for the field you'd like to format.**

2. **Click the down arrow that appears on the text box's right side.**

   The menu shown in Figure 6-4 pops down to serve you.

3. **Select the format you want to use.**

What happened to my percentages?

When you create a field with the Number data type, Access assigns the Long Integer field size by default. Because integers are by definition whole numbers, Access rounds any decimal number entered in such a field. So if you enter **0.25** in a field with the Percent format, and Access displays your entry as 0.00%, your entry

✔ Automatically rounds to the nearest whole number (in my example, 0)

✔ Always displays zeros in the decimal places

The solution? Change the Field Size setting (pictured in the following figure) from Long Integer to Single. This setting tells Access to remember the decimal part of the number.

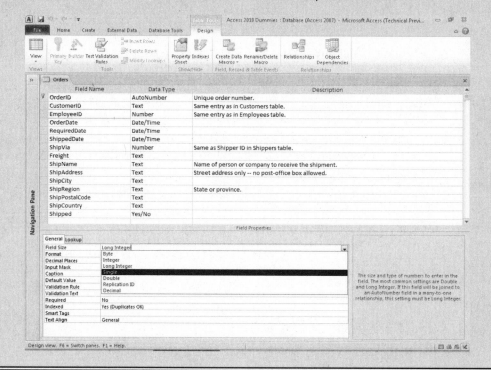

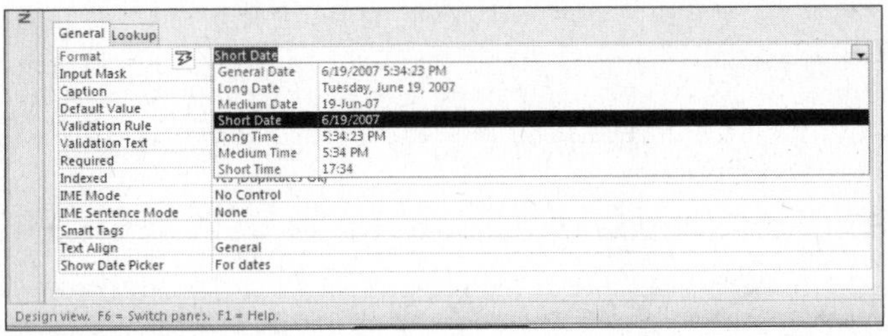

Figure 6-4:
The ever-
popular
date/time
format list.

Keep these tips in mind when you apply a date/time format:

✔ When you use one of the longer formats, such as General Date or Long
Date, make sure that the datasheet column is wide enough to display all
the information. Otherwise you'll see a wacky date that makes no sense.

✔ If more than one person uses the database, choose a format that
provides *more* information, not *less* information.

My clients often ask me to provide a date in the *m/d/yy* format with a two-digit
year (such as 1/1/09 instead of 1/1/2009). To display a date with a two-digit
year, type the following in the format box: **m/d/yy**.

Yes/No fields

You can say only so much about a field with three options. Oddly, Yes/No
fields are set to the Yes/No formatting by default.

If you want the ability to type Yes/No, True/False, or On/Off in the field, make
sure that Display Control in the Lookup tab (next to the General tab) is set to
Text Box. Otherwise you'll have check boxes in your field (because Check Box
is the default display for a Yes/No field).

Allowable Yes/No field entries

Here's what you can type in a Yes/No field (see Figure 6-5):

✔ Yes and No (this is the default)

✔ On and Off

✔ True and False

Yes and No is the default, but you can change how a Yes/No field formats its content. Here's how:

1. **With your table in Design view, click the Format text box for the field you'd like to format.**

2. **Click the down arrow that appears on the text box's right side.**

   The menu of three Yes/No formats pops down for your inspection.

3. **Select the format you want to use.**

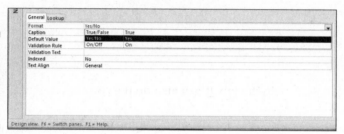

Figure 6-5:
Not much to talk about with Yes/No formatting.

General	Lookup		
Format	Yes/No		
Caption	True/False	True	
Default Value	Yes/No	Yes	
Validation Rule	On/Off	On	
Validation Text			
Indexed	No		
Text Align	General		

Design view. F6 = Switch panes. F1 = Help.

Create your own Yes/No format

To display your *own* choices instead of a boring *Yes* and *No,* type a customized entry in the Format box. A good example format looks something like this:

```
"REORDER"[Red]; "In stock"[Green]
```

The No and Yes parts of the format are separated by a semicolon (;)

- ✔ The part on the left appears if the field is equal to No.
- ✔ The part on the right appears if the field is equal to Yes.

With the preceding example, type **Yes** in the field and the text *In stock* appears in green. Type **No** in the field and *REORDER* screams a warning in bright red.

A custom Yes/No format simply changes the way the typed data appears. A Yes/No field will still only accept the entries as outlined in the previous section "Allowable Yes/No field entries" regardless of what custom format is applied to it.

You can type any words between the quotes and any Access-allowed color names between the square brackets. Who knew that formatting could be so much fun!

Gaining Control of Data Entry

The remaining sections in this chapter explore Access field properties that allow you to control what data is entered in a field. The more you control the data that goes into your tables, the less you'll need to clean it up after it has been entered.

You really need to put a mask on those fields

An *input mask* is a series of characters that tells Access what data to expect in a particular field — and actually prevents users from typing data that does not fit the mask.. If you want a field to contain all numbers and no letters, an input mask can do the job. It can also do the reverse (all letters and no numbers) and almost any combination in between.

Formatting (shown previously in this chapter) can make some data entry errors *visible,* but formatting doesn't *block* errors. Input masks, on the other hand, keep that bad data out.

Input masks are stored in the Input Mask property box of the field's General tab. (The beginning of this chapter shows the steps to follow to access the General tab.)

Add these masks to fields that contain dates, times, phone numbers, Social Security Numbers, and Zip codes, among other things. You'll be so glad you did. If you don't, expect to see plenty of phone numbers like 111-123 and Zip codes like 0854.

Input masks work best with *short, consistent* data. Numbers and number-and-letter combinations that follow a consistent pattern are excellent candidates. Phone numbers, dates, and Zip codes are common examples of data items that follow a consistent pattern.

You create an input mask in one of two ways:

  ✔ **Ask the Input Mask Wizard for help.**

  The Input Mask Wizard can't possibly contain every mask for every situation. It only knows about text and date fields, and offers just a few options.

  Always start with the wizard. If it doesn't have your solution, then you need to manually build the mask.

✔ **Type the mask manually.**

Create the mask manually if your data follows a consistent pattern (such as a six-digit part number) yet is not a choice offered by the Input Mask Wizard.

Using the Input Mask Wizard

The Input Mask Wizard gladly helps if you're making a mask for text fields (such as those containing phone numbers, Social Security Numbers, and United States Zip codes) or simple date and time fields.

If your data doesn't fit one of the masks that the wizard provides yet follows a consistent pattern, the next section shows how to create a mask manually.

To ask for the wizard's help, follow these steps:

1. **Open the database file that contains the data you want to mask. From the Navigation pane, right-click the table you want to modify and choose Design View.**

   The table flips into Design view.

2. **Click the name of the field that will receive the input mask.**

   You can use the wizard only with text and date/time fields.

   The General tab in the Field Properties section (the bottom half of the window) displays the details of the current field.

3. **Click the Input Mask box.**

   The cursor monotonously blinks away in the Input Mask box. To the right of the box, a small button with three dots appears. That's the Builder button, which comes into play in the next step.

4. **Click the Builder button.**

   The wizard appears, offering a choice of input masks, as shown in Figure 6-6.

Figure 6-6:
The Input
Mask
Wizard.

Input Mask Wizard

Which input mask matches how you want data to look?

To see how a selected mask works, use the Try It box.
To change the Input Mask list, click the Edit List button.

Input Mask:	Data Look:
Long Time	1:12:00 PM
Short Date	9/27/1969
Short Time	13:12
Medium Time	01:12 PM
Medium Date	27-Sep-69

Try It: _____

Edit List   Cancel   < Back   Next >   Finish

The rest of the Input Mask Wizard

This sidebar shows my recommendations for the last two steps of the Input Mask Wizard. If you click Next instead of Finish at the end of my steps, the Input Mask Wizard continues asking you about changing some obscure settings that are best left at the defaults:

✔ **The placeholder character for the input mask.**

The *placeholder* character in the mask represents the actual typed character by the user. The default is a dash. You can change from the default to a # or %.

✔ **Storing the data with the symbols included within the input mask.**

For example, a Social Security Number could be stored with or without the dashes.

The default is No (for *don't store the symbols)*. I recommend you keep it that way. The mask takes care of the data display. Why store extra characters in your database?

---

5. **Scroll through the list of input masks to find what you want.**

6. **Click the input mask you want.**

   To play with the mask a bit and see how it works, click the Try It area at the bottom of the dialog box and then type a sample entry.

7. **Click Finish to close the wizard and use the mask with your field.**

   If you click Next instead of Finish, the wizard gives you more options, but we recommend avoiding them. (The sidebar "The rest of the Input Mask Wizard" has the details.)

   The chosen mask appears in the Input Mask text box in the table's Field Properties section, as shown in Figure 6-7.

Figure 6-7:
The Input
Mask
Wizard
completes
its master-
piece.

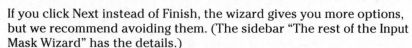

General	Lookup
Format	Short Date
Input Mask	99/99/0000;0;_
Caption	Order Date
Default Value	
Validation Rule	
Validation Text	
Required	No
Indexed	Yes (Duplicates OK)
IME Mode	No Control
IME Sentence Mode	None
Smart Tags	
Text Align	General
Show Date Picker	For dates

Design view. F6 = Switch panes. F1 = Help.

Making a mask by hand

It's not uncommon to need a mask that the Input Mask Wizard doesn't provide. If your fingers can string together a seemingly nonsensical string of characters on the keyboard, then you can make your own input masks. The trick is making sense out of all the nonsensical characters.

Table 6-2 shows the codes you can use in an input mask; each code has an explanation of the character(s) that it represents:

- ✔ **Required Code:** User must type that type of character (whether they actually want to or not).

- ✔ **Optional Code:** User can type or not type the kind of character mentioned in the first column.

Table 6-2	Codes for Input Masks	
Kind of Characters	*Required Code*	*Optional Code*
Digits (0 to 9) only	0 (zero)	9
Digits and + and -	(not available)	# (U.S. pound sign)
Letters (A to Z) only	L	? (question mark)
Letters or digits only	A	a (must be lowercase)
Any character or space	& (ampersand)	C
Any character typed into the mask fills it from right to left	!	None
Any literal character	\ (for example, * displays as just *)	None
All characters typed into the mask are forced to lower case	<	None
All characters typed into the mask are forced to upper case	>	None

You must use the input mask codes to design an input mask.

Designing an input mask

Before you can create a mask, you must determine what mask codes you'll need to build the mask. Here's how:

1. **On a piece of paper, write several examples of the data that the mask should let into the table.**

If the information you're storing has subtle variations (such as part numbers that end in either a letter/number or letter/letter combination), include examples of the various possibilities so that your input mask accepts them all. You can't build a mask if you don't know your data.

2. **Write a simple description of the data, including which elements are required and which are optional.**

   For example, if your sample is a part number that looks like 728816ABC7, write *six numbers, three letters, one number; all parts are required.*

   Remember to allow for the variations, if you have any. The difference between *one number* and *one letter or number* can be crucial.

   If you need to include a special character in your mask, like a dash or parentheses or a combination of static characters, use this list for guidance:

   - **Dash, slash, or parenthesis characters:** Put a backslash (\) in front of it, like \- for a dash.

   - **Multiple characters:** Put quotation marks around them.

     For example, an area code may be separated from the rest of the number by *both* a parenthesis and a space, like this:

     (567) 555-2345

     The corresponding mask has quotes around the parenthesis and the space, like this: `!\(999"-)  "000\-0000`

   The phone-number mask also begins with an exclamation point. The exclamation point forces the typed data to fill the mask from right to left instead of left to right (the default). What's the big deal about that? Some phone numbers don't require an area code; others do. Suppose you had to type a seven-digit phone number. If not for the right-to-left entry, you'd have to move the cursor past the area code (___) placeholder part of the mask to get to the beginning of the seven-digit part.

   If your field includes letters and you want them to be stored as all-uppercase, add a greater-than symbol (>) to the beginning of your mask To store the letters as all-lowercase, use a less-than symbol (<) instead.

3. **Write the mask codes that represent the elements you've written in Step 2.**

   If (for example), you wrote "six numbers, three letters, one number; all parts are required" in Step 2, then you need the mask codes `000000LLL0`. Refer to Table 6-2.

Putting on your input mask

Now that you have your mask written on paper, it's time to enter it in Access. Here's how:

   1. **With the database file open, right-click the table you want to work with and then choose Design View from the shortcut menu.**

      The table flips into Design view.

   2. **Click the name of the field you want to adjust.**

   3. **Click the Input Mask box.**

      The cursor blinks in the Input Mask box.

   4. **Carefully type your finished mask into the Input Mask area of the Field Properties (as shown in Figure 6-8).**

      If you don't know what to type here, see the preceding section.

Figure 6-8:
Manually
adding a
capitaliza-
tion mask.

   5. **At the end of the mask, add ; ; _ (two semicolons and an underscore character).**

      These three characters tell Access to display an underscore where you want each character to appear. The placeholder is not required, but it does make the mask easier to understand for the data-entry person.

   6. **Click the View button on the Ribbon to switch to Datasheet view and place the cursor in the masked field to check out your new mask.**

      When prompted to Save, click Yes so you don't lose your work.

      When you've entered the mask and have saved the table, try these tests:

      a. *Type something unacceptable into the masked field.*

         The input mask should prevent you from typing an incorrect value (see Figure 6-9).

      b. *Try an acceptable entry.*

         The mask should accept your entry.

      c. *Try all the variations you identified in the mask-planning process.*

         All should be accepted by the mask. If they are not, switch back to Design view and tweak your mask until all possible variations of your entry are acceptable to the mask.

Figure 6-9:
I have
violated the
input mask.

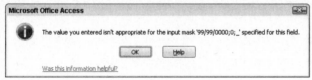

Microsoft Office Access

The value you entered isn't appropriate for the input mask '99/99/0000;0;_' specified for this field.

[OK]   [Help]

Was this information helpful?

If you're adding a mask to an existing table with data, Access doesn't report to you on existing records that fail the mask; it gives that data a free pass to exist as typed. To enforce the mask on existing records, you'll need to repeat these steps for each record:

1. **Click the field in the record.**

2. **Edit the data.**

   You can delete the last character and then retype it.

   When you move the cursor out of the field, you'll see the warning if the data doesn't comply with the mask.

To require or not to require

There are many occasions when you won't want a record typed until all the facts are in. For example, you certainly wouldn't want an order typed without an order date, customer, and product information. The Required property prevents records that are missing essential data from being saved to a table.

The Required property has two settings:

- ✔ **Yes:** The user cannot leave the record without putting something in the field.
- ✔ **No:** Anything goes. (This is the default.)

To require data entry in a field, follow these simple steps:

1. **While in a table's Design view, click the field in which you want to require data entry.**

2. **Click in the Required box on the General tab in the Field Properties section.**

   An arrow appears at the end of the box. By default, the box reads No.

3. **Click the arrow and select Yes from the list that appears, as shown in Figure 6-10.**

   Watch out, the field is now required!

4. **Click the View button on the Ribbon to switch to Datasheet view and then test your work.**

   Type a new record, omitting data entry in the required field. You should see a message box admonishing you for forgetting the required data.

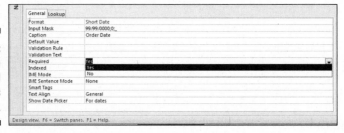

Figure 6-10:
The
Required
property is
set to Yes.

Don't get overzealous with the Required property and set it to Yes for nonessential fields. For example, a contact without a fax number and job title is usually better than no contact at all.

Making your data toe the line with validation

With a *validation,* Access tests the incoming data to make sure that it's what you want in the table. If the data isn't right, the validation displays an error message (you get to choose what it says) and makes the user try the entry again.

Like the other options in this chapter, validations are stored in the General tab of the Field Properties area. Two options relate to validations:

✔ **Validation Rule:** This rule is the validation itself.

✔ **Validation Text:** The text is the error message you want Access to display when some data that violates the validation rule is typed.

Validations work best with number, currency, and date fields. Creating a validation for a text field is possible, but the validations tend to get very complicated very fast.

Tables 6-3 and 6-4 contain some ready-to-use validations that cover the most common needs. These are ready for you to type into the General tab of the Field Properties area.

Table 6-3	Common Number-Field Validations
Validation Rule	*What It Means*
> 0	Must be greater than zero
<> 0	Cannot be zero
> 0 AND < 100	Must be between 0 and 100 (non-inclusive)
>= 0 AND <= 100	Must be between 0 and 100 (inclusive)
<= 0 OR >= 100	Must be less than 0 or greater than 100 (inclusive)

Table 6-4	Common Date-Field Validations
Validation Rule	*What It Means*
>= Date ()	Must be today's date or later
>= Date () OR Is Null	Must be today's date, later, or blank
< Date ()	Must be earlier than today's date
>= #1/1/2000# AND <= Date ()	Must be between January 1, 2000 and today (inclusive)

Here's how to enter a validation rule:

1. **With the database file open, right-click the table you want to work with and choose Design View from the shortcut menu.**

   The table flips into Design view.

2. **Click the name of the field you want to adjust.**

3. **Click the Validation Rule box.**

   The cursor blinks in the Validation Rule box.

4. **Type the validation rule that matches your data.**

   For example, if you want to allow only numbers between 0 and 1,000 into the field, type **>0 AND <1000**.

5. **Click in the Validation Text field.**

   The cursor blinks in the Validation Text box.

6. **Type the message you'd like the user to see if he breaks the validation rule.**

Keep it short and simple. For my example in Step 4, you might type **Please enter a number greater than 0 and less than 1,000.**

When you apply a validation rule to a field, watch out for these gotchas:

- ✔ When using AND, both sides of the validation rule must be true before the rule is met.
- ✔ With OR, only one side of the rule needs to be true for the entire rule to be true.
- ✔ Be careful when combining >= and <=. Accidentally coming up with one that can't be true (such as <= 0 AND >= 100) is too easy!

Give your fingers a mini vacation by default

Wouldn't it be a dream come true if every time you entered an order, you didn't have to type the current date in the Order Date field? Well, guess what? Access is all about making your dreams come true! (Your data-entry dreams, anyway.) It accomplishes this feat through the Default Value property. The Default Value property places the data that you specify for a field into that field every time a new record is inserted into the field's table. Yes, it sounds too good to be true — but I assure you it is not!

Here's how to enter a default value:

1. **With the database file open, right-click the table you want to work with and choose Design View from the shortcut menu.**

   The table flips into Design view.

2. **Click the name of the field you want to adjust.**

3. **Click the Default Value box.**

   The cursor blinks in the Default Value box. The Build button appears.

4. **Type the data that you'd like to appear for that field when a new record is inserted.**

   For example, if you want the current date to appear in an Order Date field for each new record, type **Date()** in the Default Value text box. (See Figure 6-11.)

5. **Click the View button on the Ribbon to switch to Datasheet view and then test your work.**

   Here's a quick test: Add a new record; then scroll to the field that contains the default value you just set. Note the contents of the field.

Figure 6-11:
The Default
Value
property set
to return the
current date
with the
Date()
function.

General	Lookup	
Format	Short Date	
Input Mask	99/99/0000;0;	
Caption	Order Date	
Default Value	Date()	
Validation Rule		
Validation Text		
Required	Yes	
Indexed	Yes (Duplicates OK)	
IME Mode	No Control	
IME Sentence Mode	None	
Smart Tags		
Text Align	General	
Show Date Picker	For dates	

Design view. F6 = Switch panes. F1 = Help.

Part III
Data Mania and Management

The 5th Wave   By Rich Tennant

"Hold your horses! It takes time to build a database for someone with as many parts as you have."

In this part . . .

Okay, so the word "mania" was added just to make this section sound more exciting. You're probably not fooled, but how motivated would you be to read this section if it were simply entitled "Data Management"? Maybe not so much.

Of course, if you really want to understand how to use and control your Access database, that's all the motivation you need, and the four chapters in this section deliver — if not the mania, certainly the management.

First you find out about some really powerful features — in particular, forms, which can be used for building, editing, and viewing your database. Next you discover ways to import and export data (making the building of a table full of records go much faster), and then you get a look at how to edit your database automatically, ferreting out duplicate records, misspellings, and other data atrocities. Last but not least, you also find out — drum roll, please — how your Access data can find a home on the Web.

Chapter 7

Creating Data Forms

• •

In This Chapter

▶ Creating forms the easy way with AutoForm

▶ Building a form with the Form Wizard

▶ Adding the finishing touches

• •

Access forms are similar to paper forms in their function — they're used in part to collect data — but Access forms go beyond paper forms by having a direct connection to the database tables that store the collected information. In the "old days," after you completed a paper form, some poor soul had to manually organize and file each form in a file cabinet or tabulate results by hand. With the advent of electronic databases such as Access, the data typed into an electronic form is simultaneously placed in the "file cabinet" (the table) connected to that form.

Like reports and queries, forms are named and stored in the database file. Forms are full-fledged Access objects, so you can custom-tailor them easily to meet the needs of your business.

This chapter shows what forms can do for you, shows you how to make forms, and provides tips for customizing forms so they're exactly what you need.

Generating Forms

Depending on your needs, you can create forms in three ways:

✔ The AutoForm tools make attractive forms with a click of the mouse.

✔ The Form Wizard asks some questions and then produces an attractive form based on your answers.

✔ Form Design view lets you start with a blank form and build from the ground up. In addition, you can use this view to spruce up forms that have been created with the AutoForm and Form Wizard tools.

Why use forms?

Access forms have all kinds of advantages over old-fashioned paper forms — and they'll spoil you if you're used to wandering through your data in Datasheet view (where the data appears in a spreadsheet format).

Here are the most important reasons for using Access forms to manage your data:

✔ **Say goodbye to Datasheet view:** Maintaining your data in Datasheet view isn't much fun. The constant scrolling back and forth and up and down can make you dizzy. With a form, you focus on one record at a time with all of its data laid out on a single screen. Maintaining your data becomes a snap, and you can watch those datasheet-induced headaches disappear.

✔ **Modify at will:** When your needs change, update the form in Design view. When you need to collect a new piece of data, just add a field to the appropriate table and to the form associated with that table.

✔ **See your data any way you want:** Access lets you take one set of data and maintain it with as many different forms as you want. Create a special form for the data-entry department, another for your manager, and a third for yourself. Each form can display just the fields that those people need to see. Well-designed forms give the right information to the right people without revealing unnecessary data.

✔ **View the entries in a table or as the results of a query:** Forms pull information from tables or queries with equal ease.

✔ **Combine data from multiple tables:** One form can display data from several related tables. Forms automatically use the relationships built into your database. So you can (for example) see a list of customers and their corresponding orders all on one form.

The AutoForm tools and the Form Wizard make it easy to create a form. We focus on using these two methods to build forms. Building forms from scratch in Design view is beyond the scope of this book.

The Form Wizard and AutoForm tools are a time-saving gift from your friends at Microsoft. Use them to create your forms. They happily do the hard stuff so all you have to do is provide the finishing touches. Some people (especially computer geeks) think wizards are for sissies, as if *real men* (and *real women*) always build everything from scratch. Well, I don't; life is short. If I am given a gift, I accept it with a "thank you" and a smile. So: *Thanks, Microsoft!*

Use these criteria to determine which form-building tool to use:

✔ Use AutoForm if

- You want all fields in the selected table or query to appear on the report.
- You don't want control over the type of style that is applied to the form.

✔ Use the Form Wizard (covered later in this chapter) if

- You want to select specific fields for your form.
- You want to select fields from more than one table or query.
- You want choose from a list of layouts for your form.

Keeping it simple: AutoForm

I have good and bad news about the AutoForm tools:

✔ **Good news:** They're fast, and they don't ask any questions or talk back!

✔ **Bad news:** They're extremely inflexible little fellas.

You want a larger font and a different background color? Keep it to yourself. AutoForm tools decide what font, colors, and layout you get.

After you create a form with an AutoForm tool, you can *modify* the form. In this chapter, the "Rearranging the Parts" section gives you the straight scoop.

To use AutoForms, open your database and follow these steps:

1. **From the Navigation pane, select the table or query that contains the data your new form should display.**

2. **Click the Create tab on the Ribbon.**

   Several tool groups appear on the Ribbon, including the Forms group. (See Figure 7-1.)

Figure 7-1:
The Create tab of the Ribbon holds the Forms tools.

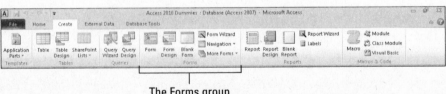

The Forms group

Meet the AutoForms

There are three kinds of AutoForms:

- **A simple form** displays one record at a time. If the data source you select for the form has a related child table, the Simple Form tool shows that data as well.

  Suppose you have a Customers table and an Orders table related by a `Customer ID` field (see Chapter 4 for an explanation of table relationships). If you select the Customers table before you click the Simple Form tool, you get a form that displays not only customer data but also order data for that customer.

- **Split forms** display one record on the top half of the form and its related records on the bottom half — think a single customer record on the top half with that customer's related orders on the bottom half.

  Use a split form if you want to browse and edit multiple records in a user-friendly fashion. The split-screen format lets you easily browse records in the datasheet portion (top half) of the form and see and edit each record's detail in the currently selected record portion (bottom half) of the form.

- **Multiple Items** shows all records from the data source in a beautiful datasheet-like format.

  Create a Multiple Items form if you'd like to see all records at a glance. This usually works best with tables that contain only a small number of fields; each field translates into a column on your screen.

3. **Click the AutoForm tool of your choice from the Forms tools.**

   The Simple Form tool is labeled Form. The Multiple Items and Split Form tools are on the More Forms drop-down list.

   The sidebar "Meet the AutoForms" shows the best AutoForm tool for your data.

   A beautiful form appears before your eyes! (And in Figure 7-2!)

4. **To finish your form, follow these steps:**

   a. *Click the Save button on the Quick Access toolbar.*

   The Save As dialog box appears.

   b. *Type a name for the form in the dialog box, and click OK.*

   Your form name appears on the Navigation pane.

Granting most wishes: The Form Wizard

When you want to control field selection and the style of form design, use the Form Wizard.

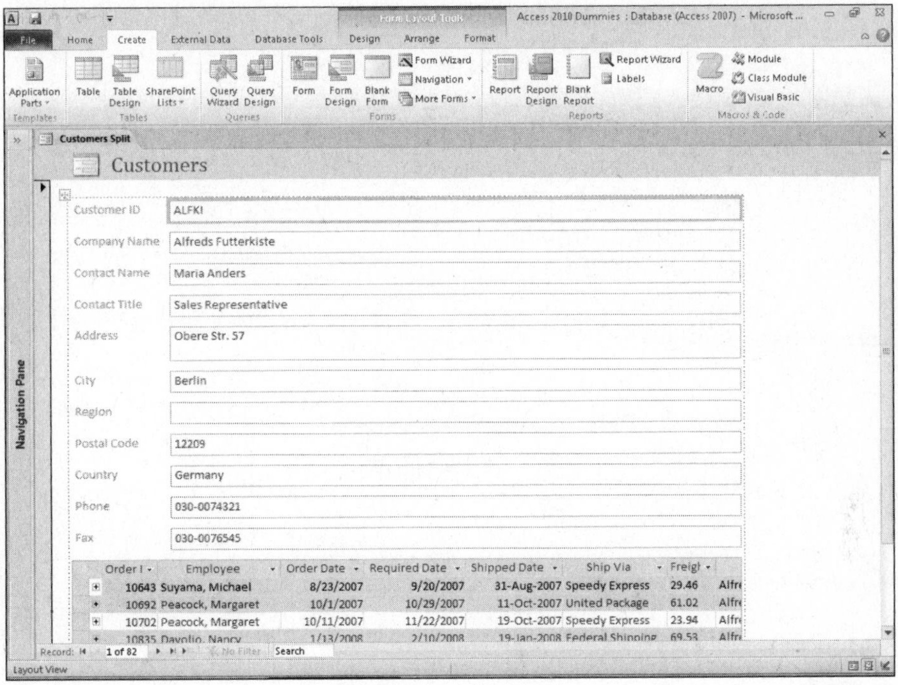

Figure 7-2:
Form based
on the
Customers
table using
the Split
Form tool.

As with all Access wizards, the Form Wizard steps you through the creation process. To use the Form Wizard, follow these steps:

1. **Open your database file.**

2. **Click the Create tab on the Ribbon.**

   Several tool groups appear on the Ribbon, including the Forms group.

3. **Click the Form Wizard tool. (Refer to Figure 7-1.)**

   The Form Wizard springs into action, as shown in Figure 7-3.

4. **Using the Tables/Queries drop-down menu, select the source of the form's fields:**

   a. *Click the down arrow to list the database's tables and queries.*

   b. *Select the table or query that contains the fields you want to view with this form.*

   The Form Wizard lists the available fields.

5. **Select the fields you want.**

   - To select *individual* fields, double-click each field you want in the Available Fields list. (Again, see Figure 7-3.)

- If you want to add *all* the fields from your table or query to your form, click the >> button in the middle of the screen.

TIP

Feel free to select fields from different tables, provided the tables are related properly. The wizard will not let you select fields from unrelated tables.

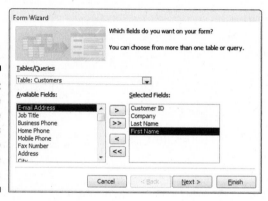

Figure 7-3:
Select the
data source
and fields
you want to
see on the
form.

TIP

To remove a field that you accidentally chose, double-click its name in the Selected Fields list. The field jumps back to the Available Fields side of the dialog box.

6. **After you've selected all the fields you want to include on your form, click Next.**

TECHNICAL STUFF

If you selected fields from more than one table, the Form Wizard takes a moment to ask how you want to organize the data in your form. If you choose to organize your data by the parent table (Chapter 4 shows how), you'll be asked to show the child table data as either

- *Subform:* Shows all data from both tables on one form.

- *Linked form:* Creates a button that, when clicked, will take you to a new form that displays the child table data.

7. **When the wizard asks about the form layout, choose one of the following layouts and then click Next:**

- *Columnar:* Records are shown one at a time.

- *Tabular:* Multiple records are shown at one time with an attractive style applied to the form.

- *Datasheet:* Multiple records are shown at one time in a rather unattractive spreadsheet-like way.

- *Justified:* Arranges the fields on the form in a tidy block of rows that have pronounced left and right margins.

Don't know which layout is best? Check out the "Giving forms the right look" sidebar.

8. **Enter a descriptive title in the What Title Do You Want for Your Form? box at the top of the Form Wizard screen.**

   There are good reasons to give your form a descriptive title instead of the default name (which is the name of the data source):

   • Tables and forms that share the same name can become confusing.

   • The name you type is used to save your form. Letters and numbers are allowed in form names. It's a great opportunity to impose some order.

9. **Click Finish.**

   Your new form appears on-screen, as shown in Figure 7-4.

   The Form Wizard automatically saves the form as part of the creation process. You don't need to manually save and name it. All saved forms display in the Forms section of the Navigation pane.

The rest of this chapter shows how to customize forms you've created with the Form Wizard and AutoForm tools.

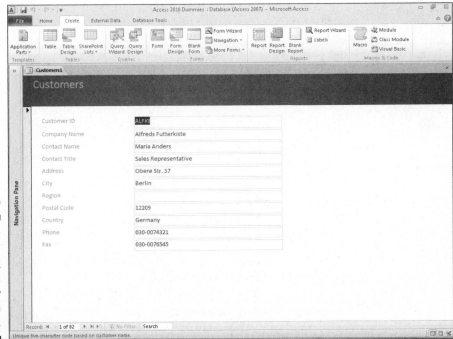

Figure 7-4: Lookin' good. A form created by the Form Wizard.

Giving forms the right look

Depending on the data you select for your form (for example, whether you use more than one table), you have different options for displaying your data:

✔ **Columnar:** A classic, one-record-per-page form.

   Most data-entry forms are Columnar.

✔ **Tabular:** A multiple-records-per-page form.

   This layout is best for tables with few fields, like the form based on the Shippers table (shown on the left side in the following figure). For tables with a larger number of

fields, be prepared to scroll back and forth if you select Tabular.

✔ **Datasheet:** A spreadsheet-like grid.

   Essentially, this is an Access Datasheet view embedded in a form. It's appropriate when an Excel-style presentation suits your needs.

✔ **Justified:** The data is laid out across the whole form over multiple rows (shown on the right side in the figure below).

   This layout may be especially useful when you have memo fields.

Customizing Form Parts

The Access 2010 AutoForm tools and Form Wizard do a great job building forms. In fact, for the typical user, they do just about everything — but they don't always do it all. So you may need to do some form-tweaking.

If you know some form-design basics, you can clean up most of the ills left behind by the AutoForm tools and Form Wizard.

The rest of this chapter shows how to change the overall look of the form. In particular, you get a handle on moving, sizing, labeling, and formatting *controls* on your forms. (A *control* is any design element on a form — say, a line, label, or data-entry box — that affects how data is displayed on the form. More about that later in the chapter.)

A form with a view

Access forms have multiple personalities, all useful: They can be displayed in several ways, called *views*. Each view serves a purpose in using or maintaining the form.

Use the view buttons on the right side of the status bar to switch between these views. (The following figure shows the Form View tools on the status bar.)

Here are the most common views:

- **Design:** Sound familiar? Every Access object has its Design view.

  In this view, you can modify the layout and appearance of the objects (called *controls*) on the form.

- **Layout:** Use this view to see data on the form and edit its layout and appearance simultaneously. Now if that isn't fun, I don't know what is!

  This view is very helpful for stuff like sizing controls properly and choosing fonts.

- **Form:** Yes, a form has a Form view. Bizarre but true.

This view displays the data connected to the form, but unlike Layout view, the design of the form cannot be altered. End users of the database typically see all forms in Form view.

- **Datasheet:** A spreadsheet-like grid.

  Essentially, this is an Access Datasheet view embedded in a form. It's appropriate when an Excel-style presentation suits your needs.

- **Pivot Chart:** A graphical analysis of data that lets you drag and drop items.

Taking the Layout view

You can make form design changes in either Design or Layout view.

The sidebar "A form with a view" explains these views.

These instructions concentrate on Layout view because it's easier to use.

To enter Layout view, follow these steps:

1. **On the Navigation pane, right-click the form you'd like to modify.**

   The shortcut menu appears.

2. **Select Layout View from the shortcut menu.**

How can you tell whether you're in Layout view or Form view? Look at the status bar in the lower-left corner of your screen. It tells you the current view for an open form.

The theme's the thing

After building your new form with the Form Wizard or AutoForm tools, you may not like the appearance that the tools have chosen for your form. Fear not! It is easy to change the look of the form by using the Theme group of tools. Here's how:

1. **From the Navigation pane, right-click the form that needs a new look and choose Layout View from the menu that appears.**

   The form opens in Layout view.

2. **Click the Design tab on the Ribbon.**

   Several tool groups appear on the Ribbon, including the Themes group. (See Figure 7-5.)

Figure 7-5: The Themes group on the Ribbon

The Themes group

3. **Click the Themes tool.**

   An illustrated list (called a Gallery) of themes drops down.

4. **Roll the mouse pointer slowly over each theme.**

   The form in the background changes to match the highlighted theme.

5. **When you've found the theme you like, click it to select it from the drop-down list and apply it to the form.**

Choose a theme with fonts and colors that are easy on the eyes. Form users will thank you for it!

Managing form controls

A *control* is any design element (such as a line, label or data-entry box) that appears on a form. The Form Wizard and AutoForm tools do a fine job of constructing forms but often don't place or size them just right. This section discusses how to take charge of your controls.

Control types

The two most common control types serve to display data plucked from an underlying table or query (as with a text box) or supply a design element to keep the data organized on the form (as with a line).

Here are the most common form controls:

- **Text box:** The box where you type your data.

  Text boxes are either *bound* (a way of saying *linked*) to a table field or *unbound* (containing a calculation derived from other fields in a table).

- **Label:** The descriptive text next to the text box or the title of the form.

- **Combo box:** A drop-down list of choices.

- **List box:** A box that contains a list of choices, from which the user can choose more than one item.

- **Check box:** A square box attached to a field that can store only true/ false, on/off, or yes/no answers. For example, a personnel table may have a field called Married. Either you are or you aren't.

- **Subform:** A form inside another form.

  Subforms usually display the "many" records of the "one" record when tables are in a one-to-many relationship. (For details on table relationships, see Chapter 4.)

If your form is *columnar* (most are) and you've created it with the Form Wizard or AutoForm tools, all text boxes and labels on the form are *anchored*. Anchored controls behave as a group when you size them. Additionally, you can move anchored controls as long as they're among the other controls in a group; you can't move them if they're outside the group.

Moving controls

To move a control, enter Layout view (as shown previously in this chapter) and then follow these steps:

1. **Put the mouse pointer anywhere on the control that you want to move.**

   The mouse pointer changes to a four-headed arrow.

2. **Hold down the left mouse button.**

   The control is *selected*, so a thick border appears around it. See Figure 7-6 for an example of a selected control.

   To select additional controls such as a label corresponding to a text box, press and hold the Ctrl key while clicking the additional control. A thick border will appear around all selected controls.

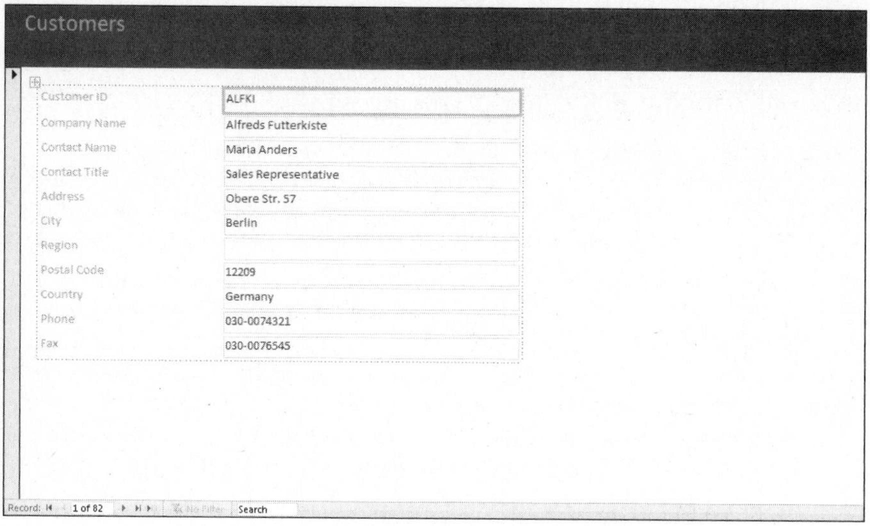

Customers

Customer ID	ALFKI
Company Name	Alfreds Futterkiste
Contact Name	Maria Anders
Contact Title	Sales Representative
Address	Obere Str. 57
City	Berlin
Region	
Postal Code	12209
Country	Germany
Phone	030-0074321
Fax	030-0076545

Record: 1 of 82   No Filter   Search

Figure 7-6:
A selected
control
on the
customers
form.

3. **Drag the control to its new location.**

   A line follows the mouse pointer as you drag up, down, left, or right.

   If the form's controls are anchored and your form is arranged in a single column, you can move the control up or down, not left or right. (Sorry!)

4. **When the control is in position, release the mouse button.**

   The control drops smoothly into place.

   If you don't like an adjustment you've made, press Ctrl+Z to undo the change and start over from scratch. Access has multiple undo levels, so play to your heart's content; you can always undo any mistakes.

Sizing controls

Sometimes the Form Wizard and AutoForm tools fall a bit short (literally) when they're sizing your text boxes and labels. A common problem is that the last part of the information displayed in a label or text box is cut off.

To size a control, enter Layout view (as shown previously in this chapter) and then follow these steps:

1. **Put the mouse pointer on the control that you want to size.**

   The mouse pointer changes to a four-headed arrow. If the controls are anchored, it doesn't matter which control you roll the mouse pointer over.

2. **Click to select the control.**

   A thick border appears around the control to indicate that the control is selected.

3. Move the mouse pointer to the edge of the selected control.

A double-arrow pointer shape appears.

4. Click and drag to resize the control.

Anchored controls size together horizontally within the same column and vertically within the same row. So when you change the width of one control in a column, all are changed to that same width. When you change the height of one control in a row, all in that row are changed to the same height.

Editing labels

The Form Wizard and AutoForm tools use field names as control labels when they build your forms. If you abbreviated a field name (say, FName for First Name) when creating a table, that abbreviation will become the label for the control created by the Form Wizard and AutoForm tools. So if a label doesn't quite say what it should, you'll need to know how to edit the text in it.

To edit a label, enter Layout view (as shown previously in this chapter) and try this:

1. Put the mouse pointer anywhere on the label that you want to edit.

The mouse pointer changes to a four-headed arrow.

2. Click to select the label control.

A thick border indicates that the control is selected.

3. Click the word you'd like to edit.

A blinking cursor appears on the word.

4. Edit the word.

5. Click outside of the label control.

The label is deselected and the edit is preserved.

Deleting controls

Sometimes an Access form contains an unneeded or unwanted control:

✔ Maybe you selected an unwanted field while using the Form Wizard.

✔ Maybe you added a control (such as a line) and in retrospect decided it wasn't needed.

✔ Maybe you're just tired of looking at that control.

Here's how you remove the control:

1. In Layout view, put the mouse pointer anywhere on the control that you want to delete.

The arrow mouse pointer changes to a four-headed arrow.

2. **Click to select the control.**

   A thick border appears around the control, indicating that it is selected.

3. **Tap the Delete key on your keyboard.**

   The unwanted control disappears into digital oblivion.

When you delete a text box, its corresponding label will also be deleted. When you delete a label, however, its corresponding text box (if there is one) won't be deleted. Go figure!

Chapter 8

Importing and Exporting Data

. . . .

In This Chapter

▶ Pulling data into Access

▶ Deciding when to import and when to link data

▶ Speaking in foreign data tongues

▶ Pushing your comfortable data into the cold, cruel world

. . . .

*I*t would be nice if all computer software spoke the same language, but unfortunately this is not the case. Software applications have proprietary "languages" called *file formats*. Just as a person who speaks only English can't easily communicate with one who speaks only Spanish, software of one file format cannot directly communicate with software of another file format.

If you're a typical business user, you'll come across a situation in which you need some data in your Access database, but it happens to be in another file format. Or you'll get the question, "Can you put that data in a spreadsheet for me so I can play around with it?"

Do you limber up your fingers in preparation for hours of data re-entry? Not with Access! Access provides tools that speak the languages of other software applications. This chapter looks at these *import* and *export* capabilities of Access. If you work with Access and almost any other program, you need this chapter — because sometime soon, some data *will* be in the wrong place.

If you'd like to try the import and export techniques described in this chapter for yourself, download the sample files used in the chapter at http://www.dummies.com/go/access2010. There you'll find two Access sample databases you can link together, as well as a sample spreadsheet to import.

If you're using databases of your own as guinea pigs, make copies of your databases *before* trying the techniques in this chapter.

Retrieving Data from Other Sources

Access includes two ways of grabbing data from other applications:

- **Importing:** This capability translates the data from a foreign format into the Access database file format— and then adds the translated data to an Access table. You can import in one of two ways:

    - *Create a new table in an Access database for the data.* You might do this if you're creating a new database and some of your data is already in spreadsheets.

    - *Append the data as new records at the end of an existing table.* Perhaps you need to import monthly expense data into your expense reporting database from your credit card company and that data can only be provided in spreadsheet format.

- **Linking:** Build a temporary bridge between the external data and Access. The data remains at its original source — yet Access can manipulate it just as if it were residing in the source (usually an Access database). When a link is established, it remains until the link is deleted or the source file is moved or deleted.

When you link tables between two Access databases, you can't edit the source table's structure in the destination database (the database that contains the links). You must open the source database to edit the structure of a table linked to a destination database.

Translating file formats

Regardless of whether you import or link the data, Access understands only certain data formats.

Always back up your data before importing, exporting, or mowing the lawn — er, trying anything that could do serious damage to the data. The "I should have backed up" lesson is one of the most painful to learn — and one of the most common. Make a copy of your database *before* trying the techniques in this chapter.

Tables 8-1 (spreadsheets), 8-2 (other file types), and 8-3 (databases) list the file formats that Access can understand. These tables cover the vast majority of data formats used on PCs all over the world.

Table 8-1		Compatible Spreadsheet File Formats	
Program	*File Extension*	*Versions*	*Comments*
Excel	.XLS, .XLSX, XLSB	3.0, 4.0, 5.0, 7.0/95, 8.0/97, 9.0/2000, 10.0/2002, 2003, 2007, 2010	Although Excel is a spreadsheet program, many people use it as a simple flat-file database manager. See Chapter 3 for more on flat-file databases.

Table 8-2		Other Compatible File Formats	
Program	*File Extension*	*Versions*	*Comments*
Text	.TXT	n/a	Plain text, the "if all else fails" format; Access understands both delimited and fixed-width text files.
XML	.XML	All	XML (eXtensible Markup Language) stores and describes data.
HTML	.HTM, .HTML	1.0 (lists), 2.0 (tables), 3.x (tables)	The descriptive codes that make a Web page a Web page.
Web Service	n/a	n/a	Connects Web-based applications over the Internet.
SharePoint list	n/a	n/a	Collaborative software using Web-based data. Replaces data-access pages in previous versions of Access.

Table 8-3		Compatible Database File Formats	
Program	*File Extension*	*Versions*	*Comments*
Access	.MDB, .ADP, .MDA, .MDE., .ADE, .ACCDB, ACCDA, .ACCDE	2.0, 7.0/95, 8.0/97, 9.0/2000, 10.0/2002, 2003, 2007, 2010	Although they share the same name, these versions use different file formats.
ODBC	n/a	n/a	Use ODBC (Open DataBase Connectivity) to connect to other databases, such as Oracle and SQL Server.
Outlook/ Exchange	n/a	n/a	Link your Outlook or Exchange folder straight to an Access database.
dBASE	.DBF	III, IV, 5	Many programs use the dBASE format.

Here is some additional information on how to prepare the most common import file formats so that your import will go smoothly. I don't mention prepping other database file formats because typically, there is no preparation needed. I'll get to the step by step instructions on importing and exporting later in this chapter.

Spreadsheets

When you import a spreadsheet file each spreadsheet *column* becomes an Access table *field:*

✔ **The first row in the spreadsheet (the *column headings*) becomes the *names* of the fields.**

If you want to use the first row for field names, you must check the First Row Contains Column Headings check box during the import process.

An ideal spreadsheet for import will have field names in Row 1.

✔ **Each following row becomes a *record* in the Access table.**

An ideal spreadsheet for import will have data starting in Row 2.

When you import data from spreadsheets, watch for these quirks:

✔ **Double-check spreadsheet data to be sure that it's *consistent* and *complete*.**

✔ **Make sure that all entries in each spreadsheet column (field) are the same *data type* (numbers, text, or whatever).**

✔ **Remove *titles* and *blank rows* from the top of the spreadsheet.**

✔ **Make your spreadsheet column headings *short* and *unique*.**

I usually shorten my spreadsheet column headings to the field names I'd like Access to use so I don't get scolded during import about field name issues.

✔ **If you're adding data to an *existing Access table,* make sure the spreadsheet columns are of the same number and in the same order as the Access table fields. Your spreadsheet columns and table fields must line up exactly.**

Text files

If you have difficulty importing a format (such as a Lotus 1-2-3 spreadsheet) into Access, you may be able to import the data as text. Text is the most widely recognized form of data known to man (or computer). Try these steps to import the data as text:

1. **Open the file with the old software product.**

2. **Use the old product's exporting tools to export your data into a text file.**

   Computer geeks use a text file's formal name: ASCII.

   A *delimited* text file is preferred if the old product supports this type of text file. A delimited file contains a marker character (such as a comma) to separate each field from the next so Access can easily understand where one field ends and another begins.

3. **Import the text file into Access (as shown later in this chapter).**

Importing and linking

Because Access offers two ways to get existing data in — linking and importing — a logical question comes up: Which method should you use? The method depends on the situation:

✔ **Link:** If the data in the other program must remain in that program, link to the source.

If the data is in a SQL Server database that's a permanent business fixture, it's not going anywhere; link to the source.

✔ **Import:** If you want the database in which you're placing the data to *replace* the source, then import. This is the option for you if you're creating an Access database to replace an old spreadsheet that no longer meets your needs. You should also import if the source data is supplied by an outside vendor in a format other than an Access format. For example, suppose you receive cash-register sales data from an outside vendor on a monthly basis in spreadsheet format. Access is a great tool for reporting so you can import the data into Access and use its reporting tools to generate your reports.

The following section shows how to link and import data from the file formats discussed in the previous sections of this chapter.

Steps for importing

Here are the steps for importing or linking data sources to your Access database:

1. **Open the Access database that will hold the imported data.**

2. **Click the External Data tab on the Ribbon.**

   The Import and Link group of tools appears on the Ribbon (see Figure 8-1).

   Each tool is connected to a wizard that walks you through the process:

   • Common file formats such as Excel or Text (labeled as Text File) have their own specific buttons.

   • You can find the less common file formats on the More button.

Figure 8-1:
Make sure that you choose the correct button for your file format.

The Import & Link group

3. **Click the tool that matches your file format.**

   A Get External Data dialog box specific to the selected file format appears on-screen. (See Figure 8-2.)

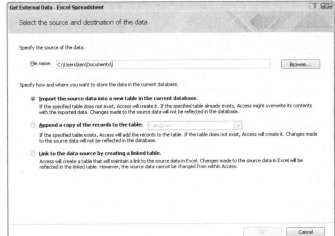

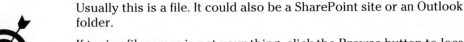

Figure 8-2:
The Get
External
Data – Excel
Spreadsheet
dialog box.

4. **Select the data source that you want to import or link to Access.**

   Usually this is a file. It could also be a SharePoint site or an Outlook folder.

   If typing filenames is not your thing, click the Browse button to locate the file.

5. **Select the method of data storage.**

   This is where you tell Access whether to *import* or *link* the data.

   The sidebar "Storing data from external data sources" shows the common data storage options.

6. **Follow the remaining steps in the Get External Data dialog box.**

   From this point forward, the steps depend on which data format you're importing. Follow the prompts carefully. The worst that can happen is that you get an imported (or linked) table full of gibberish. If you do, check the format of the source file. For example, if the source is a text file and you get gibberish, you may need to confirm that the text file was saved as a *delimited* file (with a character — a comma, for example — placed between fields). It's also possible that the source file isn't in the correct format (for example, you may think it's an Excel spreadsheet but it's not).

   If you expect to import or link to this type of file often, click the Save Import Steps check box. (The check box will be located on the last screen of the wizard.) After you check the box, you'll be prompted for a name for your import, as shown in Figure 8-3.

Storing data from external data sources

When you select a method of data storage, most of the Get External Data dialog boxes ask you to select from the following storage methods:

Import the source data into a new table in the current database. This means creating a new table from the imported data.

Access warns you that this choice could over-write an existing table with the same name as the imported data's filename. However, Access usually just creates another table with the number 1 after it. For example, if you have a Contacts table and you import a file called `Contacts.dbf`, Access creates a new table called Contacts1.

Append a copy of the records to the table. This choice adds the imported data to the end of existing records in an existing table.

When you append, make sure that the import file and the existing table have

✔ The same number of columns

✔ The same order of columns

✔ The same data types

Link to the data source by creating a linked table. Access creates a table that manages the data in the external file. Depending on the source, the link may be either of the following:

✔ *Two-way link.* Edits in *either* file (the internal Access file or the external file) automatically appear in *both* files.

A link to another Access data source is an example of a two-way link.

✔ *One-way link.* You can change the data in the external source but not in Access.

A spreadsheet link is a one-way link. You can change the data in the spreadsheet but not in the Access table linked to the spreadsheet.

Figure 8-3: Saving the Customers import steps.

The External Data tab's Import group on the Ribbon contains a button called Saved Imports. (Refer to Figure 8-1.) You can use this button to call up saved imports and run them as often as you like. (See Figure 8-4.)

Figure 8-4:
The Saved Imports tab of the Manage Data Tasks dialog box.

Troubleshooting

During the import or linking process, Access may have difficulties. If it does, you'll know — because the import or linking process takes noticeably longer time or Access displays an error message. This section describes some common problems that crop up during import and linking — and how to resolve such problems.

Slow imports and links

If importing is taking forever, Access is probably struggling with errors in the inbound data. Follow these steps to troubleshoot the problem:

1. **Press Ctrl+Break to stop the import process.**

2. **Open the source file in its native application and check the data that's being imported for problems, such as**

   • Corrupt data: The file you are attempting to import may be unusable.

   • Badly organized spreadsheet data.

   • An invalid index: Sometimes database indexes become corrupt, making the data within the table with the corrupt index unusable. Access will usually holler at you when you open the source table that contains the invalid index. For more on indexes see Chapter 4.

- Too much data (in which case, break the file into several smaller files).

3. **Make any necessary changes and then save the corrected source file.**

4. **Start the import or linking process again, as outlined in the previous section of the chapter.**

Bad data

If the imported table barely resembles the source, open the source file in its native program and clean up the data before importing again.

Follow the tips in the preceding section ("Translating file formats") to clean up your data.

Get This Data Out of Here

Every Access object can be exported; the most common export task is exporting data in a table or query to another program (such as a spreadsheet). Therefore this chapter concentrates on exporting table and query data to other file formats.

Exporting a table or query involves reorganizing the data it contains into a different format. As with importing, Access can translate the data into a variety of file formats, depending on your needs.

Because every Access object can be exported, the External Data tab on the Ribbon presents you with all the file formats in which the object can be exported.

Export formats

Access exports to the same formats that it imports (as listed earlier in the chapter). Access also exports to PDF (Adobe Acrobat files), Microsoft Word, Snapshot Viewer, and to an e-mail attachment.

When you're exporting the main problem to keep an eye out for is *data loss*. A fabulous Access table doesn't always translate into a fabulous Dbase table. Not all databases share the same rules for the following:

✔ **Data types:** Special Access data types such as AutoNumber, Yes/No, Memo, and OLE may cause problems in other programs not equipped to handle them. You may need some creative problem-solving to make the data work just the way you want it to work.

✔ **Field names:** Each database program has its own set of rules governing field names, such as their length and the special characters you're allowed to use in them (such as dollar or percent signs).

To avoid field-name problems during export, keep your Access field names short and use only letters and numbers in them. If your Access table's field names break the rules of the program you're exporting to, the export won't work properly.

Be ready to spend time fine-tuning the export so it works just the way you want. If you have a problem during export, consult the documentation of the software whose file format you're exporting to; pay special attention to any rules governing field names and data types.

Exporting table or query data

The steps to exporting a table or query are simple:

1. **With the database open, click the table or query that you want to export. All database objects are located in the Navigation pane.**

   The table name is highlighted.

2. **Click the External Data tab on the Ribbon.**

   The Export tool group appears on the Ribbon. (See Figure 8-5.) Note the following features of the Export tool group:

   • The common exporting tasks have their own buttons.

   • The seldom-used formats are lumped together; you can get at them with the More button.

Figure 8-5:
The Export tool group.

The Export group

3. **Click the tool that matches the program to which you'll export your data.**

   An Export dialog box (see Figure 8-6), customized to your format of choice, appears.

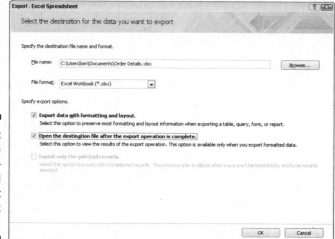

Figure 8-6:
Step 1 of the
Export –
Excel
Spreadsheet
dialog box
completed.

4. Follow the steps in the Export dialog box to complete the export.

The Export dialog box displays the choices for your export file's format:

- Every choice asks for a filename (including path) for your exported data.

- Some export processes also ask whether you want to open your new file after the export is complete.

    This latter feature can prevent a frustrating search after you save the file.

5. Select the Save Export Steps check box if you know you'll do this export again.

The check box is located on the last screen of the Export Wizard. After you check the box, you'll be prompted for a name for your export.

The Ribbon contains a button called Saved Exports. (Refer to Figure 8-5.) Use this button if you want to make the frequent export of a table or query easier. Figure 8-7 shows a table exported from Access as it appears in Excel.

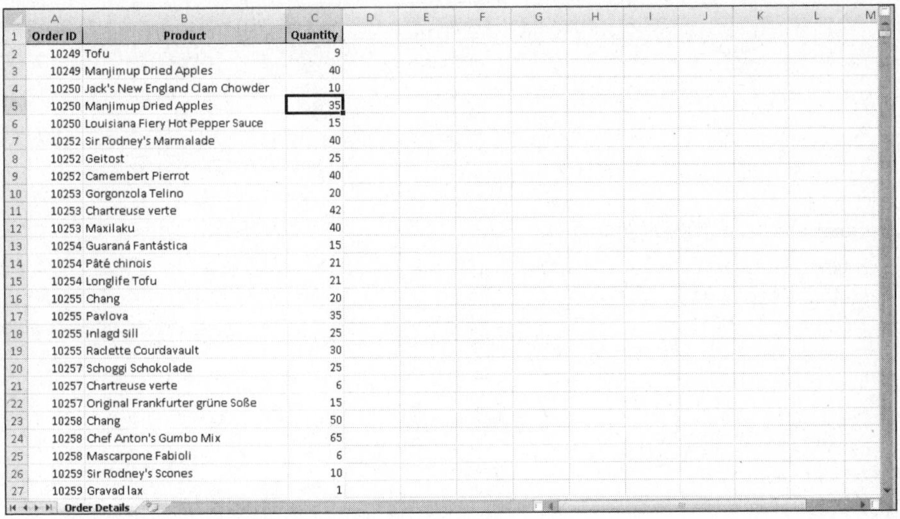

	A	B	C
1	Order ID	Product	Quantity
2	10249	Tofu	9
3	10249	Manjimup Dried Apples	40
4	10250	Jack's New England Clam Chowder	10
5	10250	Manjimup Dried Apples	35
6	10250	Louisiana Fiery Hot Pepper Sauce	15
7	10252	Sir Rodney's Marmalade	40
8	10252	Geitost	25
9	10252	Camembert Pierrot	40
10	10253	Gorgonzola Telino	20
11	10253	Chartreuse verte	42
12	10253	Maxilaku	40
13	10254	Guaraná Fantástica	15
14	10254	Pâté chinois	21
15	10254	Longlife Tofu	21
16	10255	Chang	20
17	10255	Pavlova	35
18	10255	Inlagd Sill	25
19	10255	Raclette Courdavault	30
20	10257	Schoggi Schokolade	25
21	10257	Chartreuse verte	6
22	10257	Original Frankfurter grüne Soße	15
23	10258	Chang	50
24	10258	Chef Anton's Gumbo Mix	65
25	10258	Mascarpone Fabioli	6
26	10259	Sir Rodney's Scones	10
27	10259	Gravad lax	1

Order Details

Figure 8-7:
The exported OrderDetails table in Excel, ready for some crazy calculations.

Chapter 9

Editing Data Automatically

In This Chapter

▶ Fixing your mistakes

▶ Replacing data automatically

▶ Finding unwanted duplications in your data

Correcting an incorrect entry in an Access table is pretty easy: A few clicks, some typing, and voilá — the problem is gone. But what if you need to correct 26,281 records? Manually editing so many records would involve a whole bunch of clicking and typing and clicking and typing. (Editing an entire table by hand doesn't sound like an opportunity for a triumphant "Voilá!")

Fortunately, Access offers some handy, large-scale housekeeping and editing tools you can use to make big changes to your database — all without wearing out your keyboard, mouse, or fingertips.

Please Read This First!

If you're following my not-terribly-subtle suggestion to *not* skip this section, you're well on your way to successful database maintenance. Why? Because the fact that you're reading this tells me you're a careful sort who follows suggestions and instructions. These traits are the key to managing thousands of records, keeping them accurate and up to date, and making the types of corrections I talk about in this chapter.

Why do I sound so serious, all of the sudden? Well, when you're making large-scale changes to a database, things can go wrong and mistakes can be made. If you're going to do anything major to your database — especially if you're editing and/or deleting a whole lot of records— you want a backup there behind you; if you do make a mistake and wipe out the wrong records, or edit something that should have been left alone, you can easily go back to the original version of the database and start over.

Careful people make backups of their work before starting any task that involves a margin for error. Here's how you back up the table you want to edit:

1. **Open the database file that contains the table you want to edit.**

   The list of tables in the database appears on the left side of the window.

2. **Right-click the table name in the list on the left.**

3. **Choose Copy from the pop-up menu that appears (see Figure 9-1).**

   Access places a copy of the table on the Windows Clipboard.

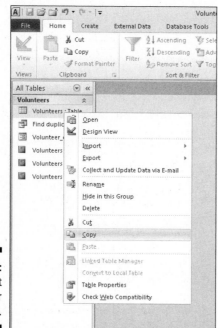

Figure 9-1:
Copy that table for safekeeping.

4. **Right-click anywhere below the list of tables, reports, and so forth in the left side panel (as shown in Figure 9-2).**

   A pop-up menu appears.

5. **Choose Paste from the pop-up menu.**

   The Paste Table As dialog box appears, as shown in Figure 9-3. It offers choices for how to paste your copied table data, but you don't really need to worry about them at this point.

Figure 9-2:
Choose
Paste from
the pop-up
menu to
make a
backup
version of
the table.

Figure 9-3:
The Paste
Table As
dialog box.

6. **Type a name for the new table into the dialog box's Table Name field.**

   Access suggests "Copy of _____" where the blank is the current table name (which might be a good choice).

7. **Click OK.**

   Don't worry about the options in the dialog box. The default setting (Structure and Data) works just fine.

   The dialog box closes, and you now have a copy of the original table.

With your table copy there to support you, you now have a backup — something to go back to should any of the steps in the rest of this chapter go awry when you apply them to your data.

Backup at the ready, it's time to move on and start editing your database — automatically.

Creating Consistent Corrections

Automated editing queries have a lot of power. But before you haul out the *really* big guns, here's a technique for small-scale editing. The technique may seem simplistic, but don't be fooled; it's quite handy.

You can practice small-scale editing by using the Replace command as follows:

1. **Open a table in Datasheet view.**

2. **Click in the field you want to edit.**

3. **On the Home tab, click the Replace button in the Find section.**

   The Find and Replace dialog box appears, as shown in Figure 9-4.

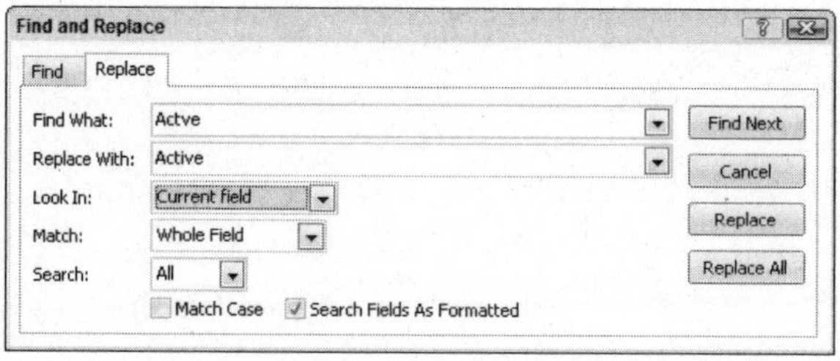

Figure 9-4:
The Find and Replace dialog box.

4. **In the Find What box, type the value you want to change. In the Replace With box, type a new value.**

   With this information in place, you're ready to start making changes.

5. **(Optional) Click the Look In drop-down list to choose a different field in which to search.**

   The Find and Replace dialog box assumes you want to search and make changes to the active table (or form, report, or query, whatever's the open and active part of your database). The Look In field, therefore, offers options for searching the current field (the one you clicked in while in Table view, back in Step 2). Alternatively, you can search the Current Document, which means to search all fields in the active table, form, report, or query.

6. **Click one of the buttons on the right side of the dialog box to apply the changes to your table.**

   • **To find the next record to change, click Find Next.** The cursor jumps to the next record in the table that contains the text you entered in the Find What box. No changes get made at this point — Access only finds a matching candidate. To make a change, click the Replace button, explained next.

   • **To apply your change to the current record, click Replace.** This makes the change *and* moves the cursor to the next matching record in the database. Click Replace again to continue the process. To skip a record without changing it, click Find Next.

   • **To make the change *everywhere* in your table, click the Replace All button.** Access won't ask about each individual change. The program assumes that it has your permission to correct everything it finds. Don't choose this option unless you are *absolutely certain* that you want the change made everywhere.

The moment you click either the Replace or Replace All button, Access *permanently* changes the data in your table. Access lets you undo only the last change you made; so if you clicked Replace All and updated 12,528 records, Access lets you undo only the very last record that you changed — the other 12,527 records stay in their new form.

7. **When you finish, click Cancel or the X button in the top-right corner of the dialog box.**

   The Find and Replace dialog box closes.

One of the most common reasons to use Find and Replace is to correct a misspelling. We all hate it when we make such a mistake, but we hate it less when the solution is as simple as making Access go look for the error and replace it with the correction, utilizing the very powerful Find tools we've been discussing in this section. SO . . . if you misspell a word, any word, throughout your data and need to change all its occurrences to the proper spelling, follow these steps:

1. **Open the Find and Replace dialog box.**

   Clicking the Replace button in the Find section of the Home tab will do the trick.

2. **Type the incorrect spelling in the Find What box.**

3. **Type the proper spelling in Replace With box.**

4. **Click the Replace All button.**

   Your computer goes off and does your bidding, changing each instance of the word in the Find What box to the word in the Replace With box.

Access gives you a lot of control over the process. In addition to the options of the Find command (discussed in Chapter 11), Replace offers additional options:

- ✔ **Match Whole Field:** Selected by default, Whole Field (in the Match drop-down list) makes Access look only for cases in which the information in the Find What box *completely matches* an entry in the table. That is, if the data in your table includes any additional characters in the field — even a single letter — Match Whole Field tells Access to skip it.

- ✔ **Match Any Part of Field:** If you select Any Part of Field from the Match drop-down list, Access performs the replace action whenever it finds the text in *any portion* of the matching text in the field. For instance, this setting picks the area code out of a phone number. Unfortunately, it also replaces those same three numbers if they appear anywhere else in the phone number, too.

- ✔ **Match Start of Field:** If you choose Start of Field from the Match drop-down list, Access replaces the matching text only if it appears at the beginning of the field. This option could replace only the area code in a series of phone numbers without touching the rest of the numbers.

If your editing goes awry, remember that the wonderful Undo option corrects only the *very last record* that Access changed. Just click the Undo button on the Quick Access toolbar or press Ctrl+Z.

Using Queries to Automate the Editing Process

Queries — especially those created through the Query Wizard — are exceptionally easy to create (as you discover in Chapter 12). In this chapter, you create a very simple and specific query not created elsewhere in the book — a query designed solely to look for duplicate records.

So what about correcting those 26,281 records? If Find and Replace doesn't solve the problem, you're looking at some serious querying — a topic covered in Chapters 11 through 14 — and you may find that creating the exact query you need is not within the skills imparted in those chapters. Be prepared to do some editing of individual records, maybe combined with a Find and Replace procedure to locate consistent errors and replace them with something you can spot easily (such as a big "X" in a particular field) and then replace the placeholders with the correct data. This is kind of a twist on using Find and Replace to fix spelling errors (covered previously in this chapter), but instead of fixing an error, you're using Replace to flag certain records for editing.

Generally, however, Find and Replace will do what you need because a universal misspelling, a bunch of Zip codes entered accidentally into the wrong numeric field — or any repeated error of that sort — can be fixed pretty quickly by searching for the erroneous content and replacing it with what should be there instead. With a backup copy of your table preserved for safekeeping (you *did* read the "Please Read This First!" section, didn't you?), feel free to experiment with Find and Replace and even some queries that you make on your own.

Looking for duplicate records

What, exactly, *is* a duplicate record? You will have duplicated data in your database — people who live in the same city, for example, will have the same city in their records in the City field. Products that have the same price, or that come in the same colors, will have the same data in some or nearly all of their fields. What we mean here by a duplicate *record* is an entire record that is an exact duplicate — every field is the same in one record as it is in another record (or in several others, as the case may be).

How do duplicate records get made? It can happen quite easily:

✔ It happens a lot when more than one person is doing data entry; two or more people might have the same list or stack of cards or other source of data that's being keyed into your Access table.

✔ If you're relying on an Excel worksheet as the source of the table data, or if some other electronic source is providing the records, accidental duplication is still a common risk; it's just as easy to paste the same rows of data into the table twice as it is to enter the same records twice manually. Maybe easier.

Duplicate records waste time and money. If you think that it's no big deal to have the same person entered into your database three times, or that the record for your Green Widget with the Deluxe Carrying Case is in the database twice, consider the extra postage you would spend mailing a catalog more than once to the people who appear in the database multiple times, or the confusion when only one instance of a product is updated to reflect a price increase. Which record is correct after they're no longer identical? So it's a good idea not only to be vigilant about avoiding duplicates from the beginning, but also to ferret them out and get rid of them whenever they're found.

Running the Find Duplicates Query Wizard

The Find Duplicates Query Wizard can help you spot that common curse of the database — duplicate records. Duplicates waste time and money, especially when the database is used for mailings or some similar business activities. This wizard can help your database clean up its act.

To run the Find Duplicates Query Wizard, follow these simple steps:

1. **Open the table with possible duplicates you want to check and click the Ribbon's Create tab.**

   The Create tab's five sections — Templates, Tables, Forms, Reports, and Macros & Code — appear.

2. **Click the Query Wizard button, found in the Macros & Code section.**

   The New Query dialog box opens, as shown in Figure 9-5.

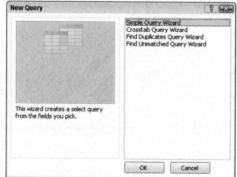

Figure 9-5: The Query Wizard is here to help you.

3. **Choose the Find Duplicates Query Wizard from the list of available wizards.**

   A description of the wizard's function appears on the left side of the dialog box.

4. **Click OK.**

   The original Query Wizard dialog box closes and is replaced by the Find Duplicates Query Wizard dialog box, shown in Figure 9-6.

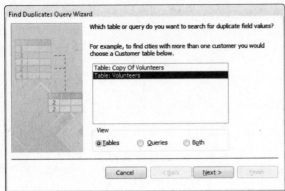

Figure 9-6:
The Find
Duplicates
Query
Wizard
takes you
through
duplicate-
finding
steps.

5. **Choose the table in which you want to search for duplicates.**

   • Notice that in the View area you can choose to see Tables, Queries, or Both, so if this isn't your first query or if another user has created one for you, you can certainly search a query for duplicates, too.

   • If this is your first query, and your data is only in tables that you or someone else made, simply leave Tables selected in the View area.

   You'll also see your backup copy of the table in this list, so be sure you pick the right table and don't start operating on your backup!

6. **Click Next.**

   In the Available Fields list (see Figure 9-7), double-click those fields you're worried could have duplicate entries in them. Skip fields that are supposed to have duplicates anyway or where duplicates, however unlikely, are no problem — such as cities, states, Zip codes, or last names.

Figure 9-7:
Pick the
fields that
might have
unwanted
duplicate
entries.

7. **When the Duplicate-Value Fields list is populated with those fields that you want the query to look in, click Next.**

   The next step in the wizard appears, as shown in Figure 9-8.

8. **From the Available Fields list, double-click those fields you want to include in the query's results in addition to those with duplicate values.**

   Such fields typically include those that help you identify records that are harboring duplicate data — such as First Name if you're looking for records that might have identical Last Names, or Product Numbers if you're looking for products that have the same description or price. In our example, we're looking for duplicate records in a volunteer database — which will prevent mailings going out to anyone more than once (or at an old and a new address for the same person), or overestimating the number of people who could be called upon to help with a project or make donations.

9. **Click Next.**

   The last step in the Find Duplicates Query Wizard appears, as shown in Figure 9-9. Here's where you decide on a name for your new query.

10. **If you don't like the default name Access gave your query, just enter a new name into the text field.**

    Preferably, the name should be short but should identify the query's purpose — "Duplicate Names Query" is a good name for this example. The default query name that Access offers will be "Find duplicates for _____," where the blank is the name of the table searched for duplicates.

11. **Click Finish.**

    The results of your query appear on-screen, as shown in Figure 9-10. You can print the results as needed using the Quick Access menu's Print button.

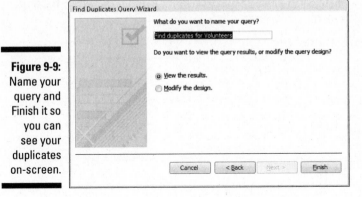

Figure 9-9:
Name your
query and
Finish it so
you can
see your
duplicates
on-screen.

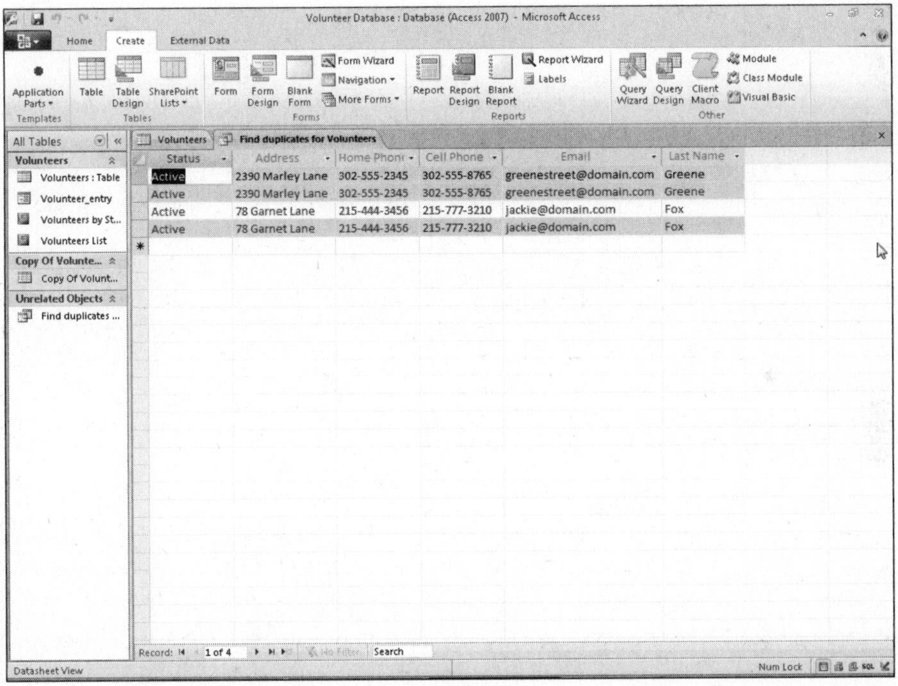

Figure 9-10:
All these
records
have
duplicate
entries in
one or more
fields.

Now that you know which records have duplicate data within them, you can

- ✔ **Edit them individually,** by clicking within the records shown as
  duplicates and making changes to names, addresses, or whatever else
  might be incorrect, if an error is the cause of the duplication.

- ✔ **Use Find and Replace** to make more targeted changes, such as taking all
  records with a particular word in a particular field and either

  - Changing that word to something else, or

- Appending a character or digit to that entry to make it different from the others.

✔ **Delete the unwanted records.** To do so, simply click the left-most cell in the row for the unwanted record (the entire record/row will be selected) and then press the Delete key.

You'll be asked to confirm your deletion, and you can choose Yes if you do want to get rid of the extra record.

Chapter 10

Gather Locally, Share Globally

....

In This Chapter

▶ Getting a look at how Access works with the Web

▶ Creating and using hyperlinks

▶ Embedding Web content into your Access forms

▶ Publishing your database and tables to the Web

....

Access can be a great resource for Internet *and* intranet information. If the data you're working with really needs global exposure — or if you simply want to be able to reach your data from anywhere you might be — Access 2010 (and the entire Office 2010 suite, for that matter) is ready to get you started. In fact, a connection to all things Web-related has been a priority for Microsoft as each new version of Office has been released over the years.

In this chapter, you take a quick look at the online capabilities of Access and uncover some of the details of hyperlinks, Web content within your database, and online database publishing. It may seem a bit daunting to think of putting your data online for all to see, but it's really a simple process with some very straightforward tools and procedures — and some real benefits to those who have a far-flung client list or a workforce who doesn't necessarily work in one office together.

Access and the Web

It's almost a requirement these days that software be Web-ready, if not at least Web-friendly. Even word processors — which should never be used to create a Web page — contain "Save for Web" commands and tools (and Word is no exception on either count, despite improvements since the command first appeared). Graphics software has evolved to help you create Web-ready images — leaving (in some cases) print formats in the dust in terms of support and new gadgets when the new software releases come out.

Unlike its Office sibling Word, however, Access is a natural fit for the Web — because data is something we've all come to expect to find online. Unlike graphics software, Access hasn't left any of its features behind just to support Web-readiness. The data, not the application, is what you put on the Web, and Access makes that easy — it doesn't assume you're building any database exclusively for the Web, but once the data's there, putting it online is quite simple.

As I said, databases are a perfect complement to the Web, where people turn for nearly everything these days — from phone numbers to driving directions to music to job searches. The Web offers lots of interactivity and a flexible presentation medium, which makes it ideal for ever-changing, ever-growing databases. In previous years, publishing a database on the Web was a complex process that required a great deal of time and effort (and a willingness to cheerfully rip your hair out by the roots). This is not the case anymore, though, because Microsoft makes it relatively simple to bring the Web right into Access.

To make Access do its Internet tricks, you must have

- ✔ **A version of your browser that's no more than a year old (so it will be compatible with the current version of Office)**
- ✔ **A connection to the Internet (or to your company's intranet)**

Click! Using Hyperlinks in Your Access Database

If you've ever looked into or done any Web page design, the term *link* is probably quite familiar — it's the text or pictures that serve as jumping-off points to other data. Click a link and you go to another Web page. Click an image that's set up as a link (your mouse pointer turns to a pointing finger), and you go to a larger version of the image — or to another Web site where information pertaining to the subject of the image can be found. Underlined text (or text in a different color or that changes color when you point to it) is the typical sign of the existence of a link; another term, *tag*, is what's added to the Web-page code to make the text or image perform as a link.

So what's this *hyperlink* stuff? Although *hyperlink* makes it sound like a link that's had way too much coffee, within the context of Microsoft Office (of which Access is a part), it's actually a special storage compartment for storing the address of a resource on either the Internet or your local corporate network (or a file stored on your local computer). Hyperlinks start with a special identification code that explains to the computer what kind of resource it's pointing to.

Table 10-1 lists the most common *protocol codes* (a harmless but scary-sounding term that simply refers to portions of the programming code that allow a browser to use a hyperlink). You'll find, along with the code itself, an explanation of the kind of resource the code refers to.

Table 10-1	Types of Hyperlink Protocol Codes in Access
Protocol Code	*What It Does*
`file://`	Opens a local or network-based file
`ftp://`	File Transfer Protocol; links to an FTP server
`http://`	Hypertext Transfer Protocol; links to a Web page
`mailto:`	Sends e-mail to a network or Internet address
`news://`	Opens an Internet newsgroup

For more information on links and how Access understands and uses them, press F1 or click the handy Help icon (blue circle with a question mark in it, upper-right corner of the workspace) to open the Access Help system and then search for the term *hyperlink*.

If you surf the Web regularly, many of these terms and concepts should be familiar. Although most of them are geared to Internet or intranet applications, Access can also use hyperlinks to identify locally stored Microsoft Office documents (that's what `file://` does). This enables you, for example, to create a hyperlink in your Access table that opens a Word document, or a hyperlink in an Excel worksheet that opens an Access table. Links can be placed in PowerPoint slides, Outlook e-mail messages, anywhere within any file created by — or for use with — Office. This technology is so flexible that the sky's literally (thanks to wireless and satellites) the limit.

Adding a hyperlink field to your table

Access provides a handy field type specifically designed for this special type of data. As you probably guessed, this type is called the *Hyperlink field*.

Adding a Hyperlink field to a table doesn't require special steps. Just use the same steps for adding *any* field to a table — get to Design view for your table and use the Data Type column to choose the Hyperlink Field type, as shown in Figure 10-1, where the Web addresses for various organizations will be stored in a Web Address field.

The Hyperlink Field type is no different from the other Field types in terms of applying it. When you hop back to Table view, you'll see that your entries (if any) in the Hyperlink field are underlined, looking just like link text on a Web page.

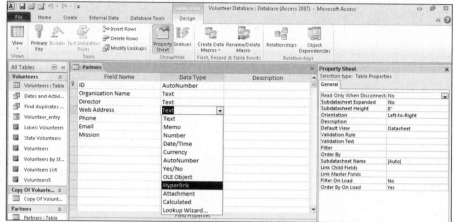

Figure 10-1:
In Design
view,
choose
Hyperlink
from the
list of data
types.

To switch between Design and Table views of your data, click the View button on the Ribbon's Home tab or its Design tab. It's the first button, and either appears as

- A table icon (a small grid), as it appears in Figure 10-1
- An icon combining images of pencil, ruler, and angle

A few words about the Web (and why you care)

Although hyperlinks may seem like just so much technohype, they really are important. Nearly all businesses have a Web presence, and many (if not most) are moving information to the Web. Companies are also creating in-house *intranets* (custom servers offering information to networked employees on private, in-house networks, often with connections to the Web).

The capabilities of Access put it in the middle of the Web-and-intranet excitement — and that presents a great opportunity for you. Duties that used to belong exclusively to *those computer people* are landing in graphic arts, marketing, and almost everywhere else. New jobs are born overnight as companies wrestle with the Web's powerful communication features.

If you're looking for a new career path in your corporate life, knowledge of the Web may be just the ticket. Whether you move into Web-site development, information management, or even your own Web-oriented consulting business, this is an exciting time full of new possibilities. Dive in and discover what's waiting for you — certainly in the current economy, any business with the low overhead of a Web storefront, eliminating expensive printed materials, expensive real estate, and salespersons' travel expense accounts can be a real advantage for the people who create the tools to run such a business — or who run one themselves.

Typing your hyperlinks

Hyperlinks in Access can have up to four parts, all separated by pound signs (#). In order, the parts of the hyperlink look like this:

```
display text#address#subaddress#screen tip
```

Table 10-2 lists these four parts individually and tells a little about what each one does. Most of the parts are optional, as the table shows.

Table 10-2		Formatting Hyperlinks in Access
Hyperlink Part	*Requirement*	*What It Is*
Display text	Optional	The text that's displayed. If omitted, Access displays the URL
Address	Required	The URL (Uniform Resource Locator), such as a Web page
Subaddress	Optional	A link on the same page or document
Screen tip	Optional	Text that pops up if the user pauses his or her mouse cursor over the address

Here are some examples of formatted hyperlinks and the obscure commands required to create them. (But don't fret about the complexity. The following section shows an easier way to make complex hyperlinks.)

✔ `www.microsoft.com` displays the URL `http://www.microsoft.com` in the field.

✔ `Microsoft Corporation# http://www.microsoft.com#` displays the words *Microsoft Corporation* in your Access table instead of showing the hyperlink itself.

✔ `Microsoft Corporation# http://www.microsoft.com# Information#` displays *Microsoft Corporation* and links to a topic called Information on the Microsoft home page.

✔ `Microsoft Corporation# http://www.microsoft.com# Information#Bill Gates#` displays *Microsoft Corporation* and links to a topic called Information on the Microsoft home page. When the user pauses the mouse pointer over the link, the words *Bill Gates* pop up.

This works well when referring to documentation on an in-house Web site — for example, you can set up a link that appears as "Vacation Request" and have it link to a document that lives in a folder on a network drive, the actual address of which would tell no one what the document is or is used for.

Here's a variant on the Bill Gates screen tip: `Microsoft Corporation#` `http://www.microsoft.com##Bill Gates#` displays *Microsoft Corporation* but does not link to a more specific topic. When the user pauses the mouse pointer over the link, the name *Bill Gates* pops up.

Because this hyperlink doesn't include a subaddress, it uses two pound signs (##) between the URL and the tip (`Bill Gates`).

Fine tuning your hyperlinks

If all of those pound signs seem a little complicated, or you're afraid you'll forget where and how to use them, fear not. You can format your hyperlinks the easy way with the Edit Hyperlink menu. Follow these steps:

1. **Right-click the hyperlink field you want to change in your table.**

2. **Choose Hyperlink⇨Edit Hyperlink from the pop-up menu.**

   The nifty little dialog box shown in Figure 10-2 appears.

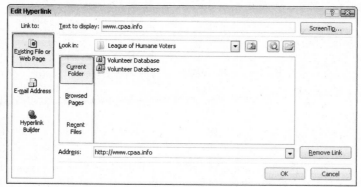

Figure 10-2: The Edit Hyperlink dialog box.

3. **Use the dialog box to fill in the following information:**

   • The text that's displayed.

   • The screen tip (the little text that pops up when your mouse pointer hovers over a Web address). To create one, click the ScreenTip button and use the resulting Set Hyperlink ScreenTip dialog box to create your tip — then click OK to return to the Edit Hyperlink dialog box.

   • Links for documents, spreadsheets, graphics, or even e-mail addresses in an Access database.

   • The site address.

4. **Click OK.**

Your hyperlink is edited, showing the text you chose to display and pointing to the Web address (document or other file) that you designated. If you chose to create a ScreenTip, you can test the new tip by mousing over your hyperlink and seeing what appears.

Pretty neat, huh? Experiment with the dialog box a little to find out how everything works. It takes only a moment.

Although most hyperlinks store Web or other Internet addresses, they can point to just about anything in the known world. Thanks to their flexible tags, hyperlinks understand Web pages, intranet servers, database objects (reports, forms, and such), and even Microsoft Office documents on your computer or another networked PC.

Testing links

Hyperlinks in your table work just like the ones you find on the Web — just point and click. You can double-check for yourself by doing the following:

1. **Either log on to your network or start your Internet connection.**

   Although Internet Explorer (or whichever browser you're using) will open whenever a hyperlink that points to a Web site is clicked, if you're not online at the time, it won't go where the hyperlink points.

2. **Open the Access database you want to use.**

3. **Open the table containing hyperlinks.**

   The fun is about to begin!

4. **Click the hyperlink of your choice.**

   • If the hyperlink leads to a Web page, Internet Explorer leaps onto the screen, displaying the Web site from the link.

   • If the link leads to something other than a Web site, Windows automatically fires up the right program to handle whatever the link has to offer.

Embedding Web Content into Your Access Forms

Forms make it easier to enter and edit your database content — populating one or more tables quickly, in an orderly fashion. It only makes sense, then, to be able to bring the power of the Web to your forms — to access Web pages from within the form and to embed links within the form (through fields that contain Web addresses) and within the header and other display sections of the form.

As shown in Figure 10-3, both text (*Subscribe to our blog!*) and an image (the organization's logo) can be added to the header section. Fields from the database table itself also serve as links, as you can see by the underlined data in the Web Address and Email fields. Of course, the hyperlink fields within the database portion of the form were established as such through Design view of the table(s) in question, a process covered earlier in this chapter.

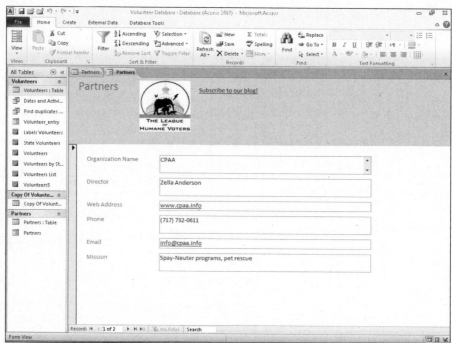

Figure 10-3: Images and text can serve as links to Web addresses, giving your form real depth and usefulness.

Adding hyperlinks to your form

To add a hyperlink — be it an image or a line of text that links to somewhere else (a Web page, local or network document, or e-mail address) — you need to have a form to which the link will be added. If you're not sure how to create a form, check out Chapter 7, where you find out how to use the Form Wizard.

So, assuming you have that form created, here's a look at some places where you might need (or want) to put some Web content:

✔ A link to a Web site where information pertinent to the database can be found would enable someone using the form to enter or edit records to find needed information. Need a Zip code for a mailing list database? A link to a Web site that lists Zip codes (or postal codes outside the U.S.) would be really handy.

✔ Does the data pertain to a particular company, organization, or person? It can be useful to be able to jump to the Web site for that entity with a simple click. Doing so opens a browser window, where the Web site (or any page within it, if you want the link to be that specific) appears on-screen. The form remains open in the Access workspace; a quick toggle of Alt + Tab allows the user to hop between the Web site and the database form.

✔ If you're publishing the form to the Web for people to use in entering data online, having an e-mail link for asking questions or reporting problems with the form would be very useful.

Inserting an image to serve as a link

So you've come up with a Web address that would be useful for someone using your form, but you'd really like to use a picture as a link, rather than (or in addition to) a text link. It's simple to add the image to the form and then turn it into a link — and now you'll know how to add images to your forms or reports, too, because that part of the procedure is the same, no matter which application part you're creating/editing in Design view.

1. **Open the form to which you want to add the image/link.**

2. **Switch to Design view.**

3. **On the Ribbon's Design tab, click the Insert Image button found nestled in the Form Design Tools group, as shown in Figure 10-4.**

   Any images added recently appear in the drop-down list, along with a Browse button. If you want one of the recently used pictures, simply click it, or use the Browse button to navigate to and then select your image.

4. **In the resulting Insert Picture dialog box (shown in Figure 10-5), navigate to the folder containing the image you want to use.**

5. **After you've found the image you want to use, double-click it or click once on it and then click the Open button.**

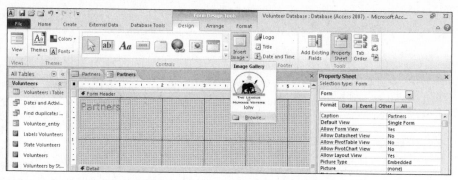

Figure 10-4:
Click
Browse
to find the
image you
want to
insert.

Figure 10-5:
The organi-
zation's logo
serves as
a link to its
Web site.

6. **Note that, back in Design view, your mouse pointer now appears as a picture icon with a small plus sign. Click and drag to draw a box for the image you've just selected.**

   As soon as you release the mouse button after drawing the box, the image appears in it, as shown in Figure 10-6.

7. **Turn that image into a hyperlink by clicking it to select it.**

   An orange border and little box handles appear around the image.

8. **Display the Properties sheet for this form element (if the panel's not already visible), as shown in Figure 10-7.**

   To display Properties for the image, right-click it and choose Properties from the pop-up menu.

Figure 10-6:
Draw a box,
and voilá!
Your image
appears.

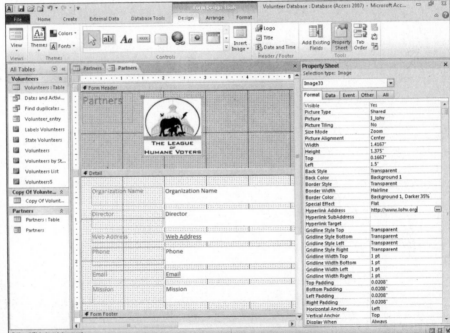

Figure 10-7:
Enter
the Web
address
that the
hyperlink
image
should
point to.

9. **Edit the Hyperlink Address field in the Properties sheet, typing the full Web address (including the `http://`).**

   The Hyperlink Address field is found on both the Format and All tabs within the Property sheet. Note that you can also click the ellipsis (three little dots) to open and use the Edit Hyperlink dialog box, which you saw back in Figure 10-2.

10. **Using the first button on the Ribbon, switch from Design to Form view to check your form and make sure the link works properly.**

    Figure 10-8 shows the finished form, with the image in place.

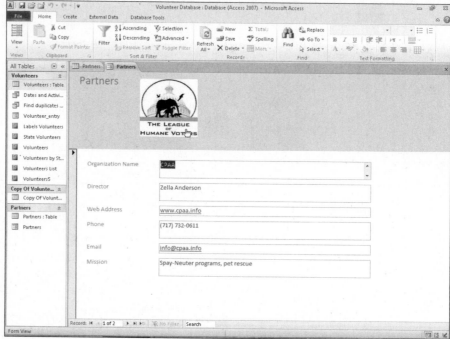

Figure 10-8:
Click the
logo to open
a browser
window on
the Web site
you desig-
nated for
this image
link.

Using text links

Adding a text hyperlink is even easier than adding an image that serves as a link. In Design view of your form, follow these steps:

1. **Locate the spot where the text should appear.**

   The Form Header area (where we added the image in Figure 10-8) is a good spot, although you can also add it to the Form Footer.

2. **Click the Hyperlink button, found on the Design tab in the Controls section of the Ribbon.**

   The big globe-and-chain button opens the Insert Hyperlink dialog box, which is shown in Figure 10-9.

3. **Using the Text to Display field in the dialog box, type the text that you want to appear as the link.**

   Here we typed Visit Our Blog!.

4. **Click in the Address field in the dialog box, and then type the Web address that this text should point to.**

   Here we typed the address of the blog, as shown in Figure 10-9.

5. **Click OK to create the link and return to Design view.**

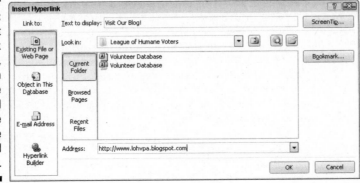

Figure 10-9:
In the Insert Hyperlink dialog box, you can both create the text and decide where the link should point.

You may (probably will) have to drag the new text object to the desired location on the Form Header or Form Footer, and may also need to resize it to accommodate a long string of text.

Want your text link to stand out? Use the Form Design tool's Format tab to change the font and size of the link text.

6. **Click the Form View button (you're currently in Design view) to see the form with the new text link in place and then test it, as shown in Figure 10-10.**

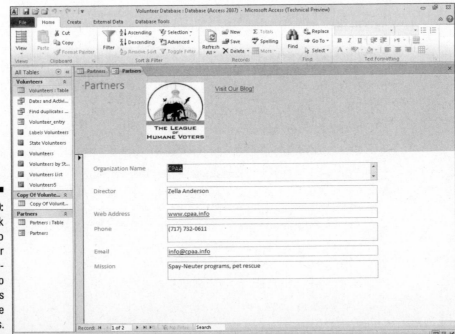

Figure 10-10:
The text link points to a blog for the organization to which this database pertains.

Publishing Your Data to the Web

If Access contains your most desirable and important information, why not share your stuff with others in your company — or even publish it for the world? Whether you're building a commercial site geared toward fame and online fortune or an interdepartmental intranet to infuse your company with valuable information, Access contains all the tools you need to whip your data into Web-ready shape in no time.

Although you don't need to know anything about HTML (*HyperText Markup Language*, the scripting language that is used to build Web pages) if you want to create Web pages with Access, you probably *will* need to know some HTML before your project is finished:

- For a painless introduction to HTML, check out *HTML, XHTML, and CSS For Dummies,* 6th Edition, by Ed Tittel and Jeff Noble (published by Wiley Publishing, Inc.).

- You can find out quite a bit online, specifically at the World Wide Web Consortium's Web site: www.w3c.org. From their home page, you can pursue any of their links to the scoop on Web-related technologies.

- To focus solely on HTML, visit the W3C's markup page, which tells you all about HTML and other such languages. Check this out at www.w3c.org/markup.

- If you want to sample the information at other Web sites, type **HTML** at the Google search box (or use any other search engine you prefer). While the W3C's site offers the most accurate and up-to-date information, you can also learn a lot from Web developers who maintain Web sites designed to showcase their knowledge and experience with HTML.

Microsoft provides two ways to take your data to the world (or to the next cubicle) with Access 2010:

- **Publish your tables individually as HTML documents.**

  The rest of this chapter shows how to publish HTML tables.

- **Publish your whole database with Office's SharePoint services.**

  SharePoint is beyond the scope of this book. To find out more about SharePoint, check out *Office 2010 and SharePoint Productivity For Dummies* by Vanessa Williams (Wiley; due out in January 2010).

Publishing your Access tables

Just sticking Web content into your tables and forms (or reports, for that matter) isn't the end of the connection between Access and the Internet. You can publish your Access tables as HTML documents, which enables you to upload them to a Web server and make them available to the world online. Visitors can view the data in a grid (as they do when a table or form is published as an HTML document) or as a screenful of data if you publish a report.

Follow these steps to make your tables and their data available with a Web browser:

1. **Open the database containing the table (or data within a table) destined for your intranet or the Web.**

   The database window hops to the screen.

2. **In the All Tables list on the left side of your window, select the table that you want to save as an HTML document.**

   Your desired table opens in the central part of the Access window. Note that you can also simply right-click the table in the left panel (which lists the parts of your database) without opening the table. If you want to publish only certain records, however, you have to open the table so you can perform Step 3.

3. **As needed, select the records you want to make part of the HTML document.**

   Drag through a series of records to select them.

   You don't need to select individual records if you want to publish the entire table. The idea here is to select a range of records if you want only those records to appear in the HTML document.

4. **In the External Data tab, locate the Export section and click the More button.**

   The available Export types, in addition to the standards, appear in a list, as shown in Figure 10-11. Note that you can also right-click the table in the database list at the left of the screen, and choose HTML Document from the Export command submenu.

5. **Select HTML Document from the list.**

   The Export – HTML Document dialog box opens (see Figure 10-12). The current table's location and filename appear in the File Name field, with the table's file extension changed to `.html`.

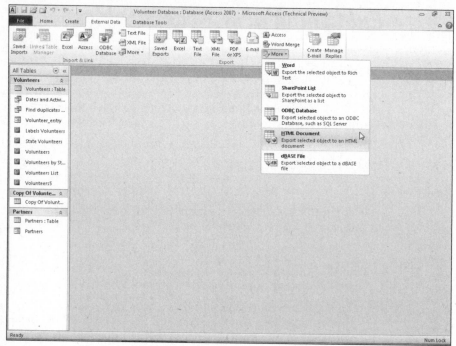

Figure 10-11:
Choose to
export your
table as an
HTML
document.

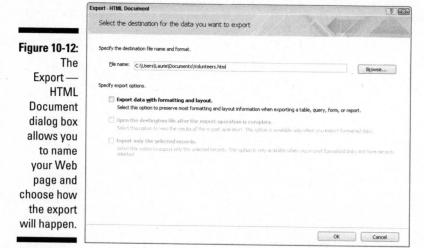

Figure 10-12:
The
Export —
HTML
Document
dialog box
allows you
to name
your Web
page and
choose how
the export
will happen.

6. If needed, click the Browse button to establish the folder location and file name of the file you're about to publish.

You're better off having selected the table within the Access workspace (as described in Steps 1 through 5) than trying to change horses at this point. You can also type a new name for the HTML document by editing the last segment of the File Name field content. The last segment is the actual file name, ending in .html — just edit the name, which appears to the left of the period.

7. Click the box next to the Export Data with Formatting and Layout option to place a check mark there.

The remaining two options are now available:

- Open the Destination File after Export Operation is Complete
- Export Only Selected Records (this is only available if you selected one or more records in the table before beginning this process)

8. Click the Open the Destination File after Export Operation is Complete option to select it.

If you don't want to publish all your available records — that is, if you selected specific records back in Step 3 — be sure you check Export Only Selected Records as well.

9. Click OK.

Assuming you performed Step 8 and chose to Open the Destination File, a second dialog box opens, entitled HTML Output Options (see Figure 10-13). The HTML document is created, and an Internet Explorer window with your HTML document name is opened, represented by a button on your taskbar.

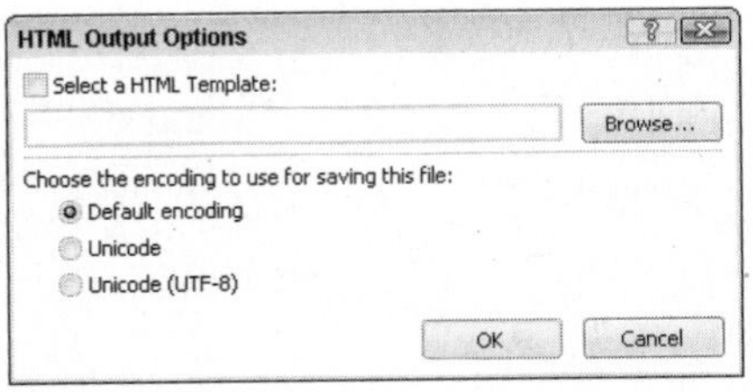

Figure 10-13:
Choose
an HTML
template or
click OK to
accept the
defaults.

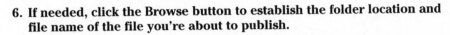

10. **Select an HTML output option and click OK:**

    • If you don't have an HTML template and simply want a table to appear in a browser window, just click OK.

    • If you do have a template — in the form of an existing HTML document — click in the Select a HTML Template check box and then click the Browse button to navigate to the template, telling Access where to find it. In the resulting HTML Template to Use dialog box, you can return to the Export HTML Document dialog box by selecting the template file you want and clicking OK.

    • You don't have to worry about the encoding method (unless a knowledgeable geek in your IT department has advised you of such a need), so accept the Default Encoding option.

11. **Click Close.**

    The Export HTML Document dialog box closes.

Access asks you whether you want to save your Export settings. Leave the Save Export Steps option unchecked and click Close. There's no need to save the steps. The procedure is simple; there really aren't any unique steps taken that you'd want or need to skip next time.

12. **Open Internet Explorer (or the Web browser of your choice) and view your new HTML document.**

    As shown in Figure 10-14, your table (or the records you chose from within it) appears in a simple grid right within the browser window. Note that if you chose Open the Destination File after Export Operation is Complete in Step 8 of this procedure, you don't need to fire up a browser — a browser window opens automatically, displaying your new HTML document.

If you didn't choose the Open the Destination File after Export Operation is Complete option (in Step 8), you will have to remember where you chose to save the file back in Step 6.

Now all that's left to do is upload your HTML document to one of two locations:

✔ Your in-house intranet server

✔ A Web server for global accessibility

You'll need some FTP software (FTP stands for *File Transfer Protocol* and the software simply ensures that what you upload conforms to the rules for uploading documents to servers) and login information for the server where your document will be stored. After the file is uploaded, you can view it online by typing the URL (Web address) for the Web site that contains your HTML document into any browser's address bar.

Volunteers - Mozilla Firefox

File Edit View History Bookmarks Tools Help

file:///C:/Users/Laurie/Documents/Volunteers.html

Most Visited Getting Started Latest Headlines

Norton - | Norton Safe Search | Search | Cards & Log-ins -

Volunteers

Volunteers

ID	First Name	Last Name	Address	City	State	Zip	Daytime Phone	Cell Phone	Email	Status	Active Date
11	Lori	McGowan	123 Main Street	Landisville	PA	17638	717-555-1234	717-555-2468	lori@domain.com	Active	5/10/2001
12	Mary Margaret	Kelly	34 Elm Avenue	Millersville	PA	17611	717-222-4321	717-555-4567	mm@domain.com	Active	6/14/2009
13	Ann	Talbot	761 Chestnut Street	Lancaster	PA	17602	717-555-9876		ann@domain.com	Active	3/22/2007
15	Edgar	Anderson	456 Independence Court	Elizabethtown	PA	17432	717-345-3454		eanderson@domain.com	Inactive	10/5/2009
16	Thomas	Framingham	8701 Rosetree Boulevard	Mount Joy	PA	17543	717-555-0989	717-555-6789	framester@domain.com	Potential	3/15/2006
17	Chris	Jamieson	732 Krause Road	Denver	PA	17456		717-555-0987	cj1234@domain.com	Active	4/16/2006
19	Kevin	Wilson-Smythe	150 N 4th Street, Apt 3B	Philadelphia	PA	19103	215-880-9876	215-555-3456	kws098@domain.com	Active	11/4/2009
22	Thomas	Framingham	8701 Rosetree Boulevard	Mount Joy	PA	17543	717-555-0989	717-555-6789	framester@domain.com	Potential	11/28/2008
23	Morgan	Neville	389 Mission	Elizabethtown	PA	17432	717-555-2098		mneville3@domain.com	Inactive	12/1/2005

Done

Figure 10-14:
Congrat-
ulations!
You've just
created an
HTML
document!

You can find plenty of shareware and freeware versions of FTP software. Just search at Google or Yahoo! (or the search site of your choice) for **FTP software**. If you're uploading files to your company's intranet or Web server, you'll probably be given IT-approved software and instructions for how and where to upload your files.

Part IV

Ask Your Data, and Ye Shall Receive Answers

The 5th Wave   By Rich Tennant

"Your database is beyond repair, but before I tell you our backup recommendation, let me ask you a question. How many index cards do you think will fit on the walls of your computer room?"

In this part . . .

Data isn't very useful if you can't get at it — if you can't look for the one record you need and actually *find* it quickly, without undue hassle. Why would you spend hours building tables and entering data into them if you weren't going to be able to use what you've built?

Part IV is all about the return on your database-building investment — getting the information you need out of the data you're storing. You find out about putting your records in a particular order and then distilling them down to just the one or two that you need to see. You also discover cool ways to ask your tables questions — the database version of playing "Go Fish" — except instead of saying "Gimme all your eights," you'll be saying, "Show me everyone who lives in Pennsylvania" or "Gimme all the gizmos that cost more than $5.00 but don't come from the Chicago warehouse."

This part covers all the various ways Access provides for getting at your data — from the painfully simple to the breathtakingly powerful — from Chapter 11's coverage of basic sorting and filtering to Chapter 15's study of queries that perform calculations. And if that's not enough, stick around for Chapter 16, where you get the lowdown on Action Queries. (If that sounds good, you're really a geek. But that's why we like you!)

Chapter 11

Fast Finding, Filtering, and Sorting Data

In This Chapter

▶ Locating data with the Find command

▶ Sorting your database

▶ Filtering by selection

▶ Filtering by form

*Y*ou probably already know what databases do. They help you store, organize, view, and document the information that's important to you — your personal information, your business-related information, any kind of information you need to keep track of.

Of course, this is not a new concept. People have been storing information for as long as there've been people. From making scratches in the dirt to keep count of the number of sheep in the flock to handwritten census information kept in huge ledgers to metal filing cabinets filled with typed lists and reports, man has been using some form of database for a long, long time.

Of course, things are a lot easier now. You can store millions of records in a single computer — and people all over the world can access them, assuming they have permission. Farmers can keep track of their sheep, countries can keep track of their populations, and you can keep track of your friends, family, employees, products, and holiday card lists — anything your little data-driven heart desires.

But what is all this "keeping track" of which I speak? It's not just storing the data — it's getting at it when you need it. Thanks to the magic of the Find, Sort, and Filter commands, Access tracks and reorganizes the stuff in your tables faster than ever, putting it literally at your fingertips whenever you need to locate one or more of the pieces of information you're storing. When you need a quick answer to a simple question, these three commands are ready to help. This chapter covers the commands in order, starting with the speedy Find, moving along to the organizational Sort, and ending with the flexible Filter.

Find, Sort, and Filter do a great job with *small* questions (such as "How many people are active volunteers but didn't give us a cell phone number?"). Answering big, complex questions (such as "How many people attended Major League Baseball games in July and also bought a team hat?") still takes a full-fledged Access query (in this case, querying a database of baseball-game attendees and the database of items sold in the team store). Don't let that complexity worry you, though, because you can flip back to Chapter 10, which explains queries in delightful detail.

Using the Find Command

When you want to track down a particular record *right now*, creating a query for the job is overkill. Fortunately, Access has a very simple way to find one specific piece of data in your project's tables and forms — the Find command.

Find is found — big surprise here — in the Find section of the Home tab, accompanied by a binoculars icon. You can also get to Find by pressing Ctrl+F to open the Find dialog box.

Although the Find command is pretty easy to use, knowing a few tricks makes it even more powerful. And if you're a Word or Excel user, you'll find the tricks helpful in those applications, too — the Find command is an Office-wide feature. After you get through the Find basics (covered in the next section), check the tips for fine tuning the Find command in the "Shifting Find into high gear" section, later in the chapter.

Finding anything fast

Using the Find command is a very straightforward task. Here's how it works:

1. **Open the table or form you want to search.**

   Note that the Find command works in both Datasheet view and with Access forms, and becomes available as soon as a table or form is opened.

   If you want to dive into forms right now, flip to Chapter 7.

2. **Click in the field that you want to search.**

   The Find command searches the *current* field in all the records of the table, so be sure to click the right field before starting the Find process. Access doesn't care which record you click — as long as you're on a record in the right field, Access knows exactly which field you want to Find in.

3. **Start the Find command.**

   You can either click the Find button in the Find section of the Home tab or press Ctrl+F.

   The Find and Replace dialog box opens, ready to serve you.

4. **Type the text you're looking for into the Find What box, as shown in Figure 11-1.**

   Take a moment to check your spelling before starting the search. Access is pretty smart, but it isn't bright enough to figure out that you actually meant *plumber* when you typed *plumer*.

Figure 11-1:
The Find
and Replace
dialog box.

Find and Replace	?

Find | Replace

Find What: Denver | ▾ | Find Next |
| | Cancel |

Look In: Current field ▾
Match: Whole Field ▾
Search: All ▾
☐ Match Case ☑ Search Fields As Formatted

5. **Click Find Next to run your search.**

   • If the data you seek is in the active field, the Find command immediately tracks down the record you want.

   The cell containing the data you seek is highlighted.

   What if the first record that Access finds isn't the one you're looking for? Suppose you want the second, third, or the fourteenth *John Smith* in the table? No problem — that's why the Find and Replace dialog box has a Find Next button. Keep clicking Find Next until Access either works its way down to the record you want or tells you that it's giving up the search.

   • If Find doesn't locate anything, it laments its failure in a small dialog box, accompanied by the sad statement,

   ```
   Microsoft Access finished searching the records. The search item was not
                        found.
   ```

   If Find didn't find what you were looking for, you have a couple of options:

   ✔ You can give up by clicking OK in the small dialog box to make it go away.

✔ You can check the search and try again (you'll still have to click OK to get rid of the prompt dialog box), Things to look for once you're back in the Find and Replace dialog box:

a. Make sure that you clicked in the correct field and spelled everything correctly in the Find What box.

You can also check the special Find options covered in the following section to see whether one of them is messing up your search.

b. If you ended up changing the spelling or options, click Find Next again.

Shifting Find into high gear

Sometimes just typing the data you need in the Find What box doesn't produce the results you need:

✔ You find too many records (and end up clicking the Find Next button endlessly to get to the one record you want).

✔ The records that match aren't the ones you want.

The best way to reduce the number of wrong matches is to add more details to your search, which will reduce the number of matches and maybe give you just that one record you need to find.

Access offers several tools for fine-tuning a Find. To use them, open the Find and Replace dialog box by either

✔ Clicking the Find button on the Home tab

✔ Pressing Ctrl+F

The following sections describe how to use the options in the Find and Replace dialog box.

If your Find command isn't working the way you think it should, check the following options. Odds are that at least one of these options is set to *exclude* what you're looking for.

Look In

By default, Access looks for matches only in the *current* field — whichever field you clicked in before starting the Find command. To tell Access to search the entire table instead, choose Current Document from the Look In drop-down list, as shown in Figure 11-2.

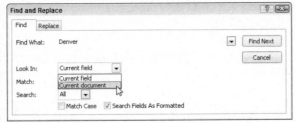

Figure 11-2:
To search
the entire
table,
change
Look In.

Match

Access makes a few silly assumptions, and this setting is a good example.

By default, Match is set to Whole Field, which assumes that you want to find only fields that *completely match* your search text. The Whole Field setting means that searching for *Rich* doesn't find fields containing *Richard, Richelieu,* or *Ulrich.* Not terribly intuitive, eh? Well, you can turn up the intuition level in Access by changing the Match setting to either

> ✔ **Any Part of Field:** Allows a match anywhere in a field (finding *Richard, Ulrich,* and *Lifestyles of the Rich and Famous*).

> ✔ **Start of Field:** Recognizes only those matches that start from the beginning of the field.
>
> This option allows you to put in just part of a name, too — especially if you only know the beginning of a name or the start of an address.

To change the Match setting, click the down arrow next to the Match field (see Figure 11-3) and then make your choice from the drop-down menu that appears.

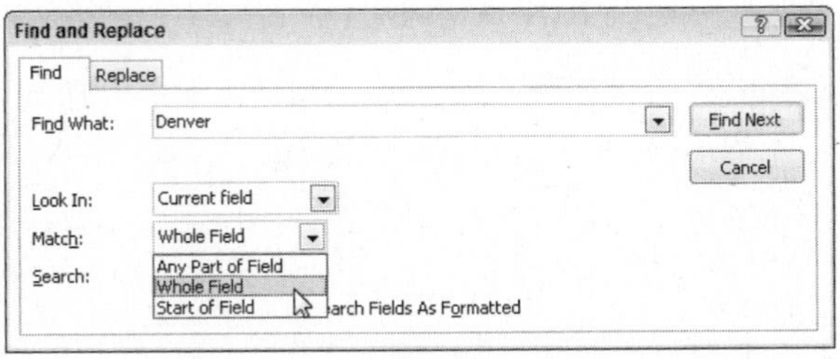

Figure 11-3:
Using the
Match
option.

Search

If you're finding too many matches, try limiting your search to one particular portion of the table with the help of the Search option. Search tells the Find command to look either

✔ At all the records in the table (the default setting)

✔ Up or down from the current record

Clicking a record halfway through the table and then telling Access to search Down from there confines your search to the bottom part of the table.

Fine-tune your Search settings by clicking the down arrow next to the Search box and choosing the appropriate offering from the drop-down menu.

Match Case

Checking the Match Case check box makes sure that the term you search for is *exactly* the same as the value stored in the database, including the same upper- and lowercase characters.

This works really well if you're searching for a name, rather than just a word, so that *rich custard topping* is not found when you search for (capital-*R*) *Rich* in the entire table.

Search Fields as Formatted

This option instructs Access to look at the formatted version of the field instead of the actual data you typed.

Limiting the search in this way is handy when you're searching for dates, stock-keeping unit IDs, or any other field with quite a bit of specialized formatting.

Turn on Search Fields as Formatted by clicking the check box next to it.

This setting doesn't work with Match Case, so if Match Case is checked, Search Fields as Formatted appears dimmed. In that case, uncheck Match Case to bring back the Search Fields as Formatted check box.

Most of the time, this option doesn't make much difference. In fact, the only time you probably care about this particular Find option is when (or if) you search many highly formatted fields.

Sorting from A to Z or Z to A

Very few databases are organized into nice, convenient alphabetical lists. You don't enter your records alphabetically; you enter them in the order they come to you. So what do you do when you need a list of products in product-number order — or a list of addresses in Zip code order — right now?

Sorting by a single field

The solution lies in the sort commands, which are incredibly easy to use. The sort commands are on the Ribbon's Home tab, in the Sort & Filter section. The two buttons (Ascending and Descending) do the job quite well:

✔ Sort Ascending sorts your records from top to bottom:

- Records that begin with *A* are at the beginning, and records that begin with *Z* are at the end.

- If your field contains numeric data (such as Zip codes and prices), an Ascending sort puts them in order from lowest number to highest.

✔ Sort Descending sorts your records from bottom to top:

- Records that begin with *Z* are at the top, and records that begin with *A* are at the bottom of the list.

- If your field contains numeric data, a Descending sort puts the records in order from highest number to lowest.

Sorting on more than one field

What if you want to sort by Zip code, and then within that sort you want all the people with the same Zip code to appear in Last Name order?

You can sort by more than one column at a time like this:

1. **Click the heading of the first column to sort by.**

   The entire column is highlighted.

2. **Hold down the Shift key and click the heading of the last column to sort by.**

   All columns from the first one to the last one are highlighted.

3. **Choose either Sort Ascending or Sort Descending.**

   The sort is always performed from left to right.

   In other words, you can't sort by the contents of the fourth column and within that by the contents of the third column.

Sorting has its own peculiarity when working with numbers in a text field. When sorting a field that has numbers mixed in with spaces and letters (such as street addresses), Access ranks the numbers as if they were *letters,* not numbers. This behavior means that Access puts (say) "1065 W. Orange Street" before "129 Mulberry Street." (Thanks to the peculiar way that your computer sorts information, the 0 in the second position of 1065 comes before the 2 in the second position of 129.)

Fast and Furious Filtering

Sometimes you need to see a group of records that share a common value in one field — perhaps they all list a particular city, a certain job title, or they're all products that have the same cost. Always willing to help, Access includes a special tool for this very purpose — the Filter command.

Filter uses your criteria and displays all matching records, creating a mini-table of only the records that meet your requirements. It's like an instant query without all the work and planning. Of course, it's not as flexible or powerful as a query, but it's all you need when you're looking for a fairly simple answer.

The Filter tool appears in the Sort & Filter section of the Ribbon's Home tab, and you have the following choices for a simple filter:

- ✔ Filter
- ✔ Selection
- ✔ Advanced, Filter by Form
- ✔ Advanced Filter/Sort
- ✔ Toggle Filter

Each type of filter performs the same basic function, but in a slightly different way. The following sections cover the first three options. The Advanced Filter/Sort option, found by clicking the Advanced button, opens a window that actually has you building a query — selecting tables and fields to filter, setting up criteria for the filter to use while it's finding specific records, that sort of thing. You can read about queries and familiarize yourself with the Advanced Filter/Sort tool by reading Chapter 12.

Filters work in tables, forms, and queries. Although you can apply a filter to a report, filtering reports can be a daunting task — one that we're not going to get involved with here. Of course, what you read here can be applied to that process, should you want to try it on your own. And in the following sections, what you learn to apply to a table can also be applied when you're working with queries and forms.

Filtering by a field's content

The main Filter command enables you to filter your records so you view only records that meet specific criteria. Suppose, for example, that you wanted to see all records where employees work in the Sales Department. Here's how to do it:

1. **In your table of interest, click the small triangle on the field name for the field you want to filter (City in this case).**

   Access displays a pop-up menu like the one in Figure 11-4.

   Don't right-click the header at the top of the column (where it says *City* in the figure). Right-clicking there displays a different pop-up menu filled with wonderful things you can do to that column of your table.

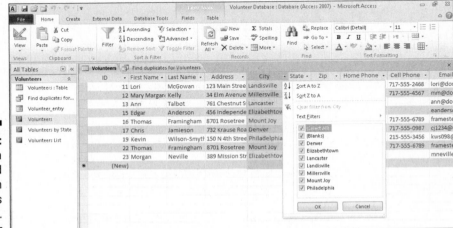

Figure 11-4: Filtering a single field based on that field's entries.

2. **If you want to omit some entries from your filter, remove their check marks in the pop-up menu.**

   You can either

   - Remove check marks from individual entries.
   - Remove the Select All check mark to uncheck all the items.

   Uncheck everything so you can easily check only those entries whose matching records you want to see. With all the entries checked, you see all the records.

3. **Place check marks next to those entries you want to use in constructing your filter for the field.**

   Access searches the selected field and displays only those records that meet your Filter criteria.

4. **Click OK.**

   All the records meeting the criteria set (by virtue of the items you checked) are displayed. This might be several records, a whole lot of records, or just one.

To jump back and see all of the original (unfiltered) records, you can either

✔ Click the Toggle Filter button in the Sort & Filter section of the Ribbon.

✔ Click the field name's tiny triangle again and choose Clear Filter From *Field Name*.

The entire table, full of records, returns to view.

Filter by selection

The Selection command is the easiest of the Sort & Filter commands to use. It assumes that you've found one record that matches your criteria. Using the Selection filter is a lot like grabbing someone in a crowd and shouting: "Okay, everybody who's like this guy here, line up over there."

For example, imagine you want to find all the volunteers who live in Elizabethtown. You can use Selection filter in this manner:

1. **Click the field that has the information you want to match.**

   In this case, it's the `City` field.

2. **Scroll through the list until you find the field entry that will serve as an appropriate example for your filter.**

3. **Click to select the value you're searching for, right-click the cell containing the selection, and then choose Equals *Whatever*. (In this instance, it would be "Equals Elizabethtown," as shown in Figure 11-5.)**

   Access immediately displays a table containing only the records matching your selection. (Again, check out Figure 11-5, where our City filter has been applied.)

Figure 11-5: Access shows only those records matching the Filter by Selection criterion.

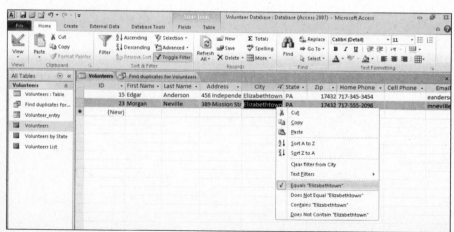

4. **Click the Toggle Filter button on the toolbar after you finish using the filter.**

   Your table or form returns to its regular display.

At this stage of the game, you may want to save a list of everything that matches your filter. Unfortunately, the Filter's simplicity and ease of use now come back to haunt you: To permanently record your filtered search, you have to create a query. (See Chapter 12 for details about creating queries.)

Filter by Form

You can tighten a search by using additional filters to weed out undesirable matches, but that takes a ton of extra effort. For an easier way to isolate a group of records according to the values in more than one field, try Filter by Form.

Filter by Form uses more than one criterion to sift through records. In some ways, it's like a simple query. (What's a query? See Chapter 12.) It's so similar to a query that you can even save your Filter by Form criteria *as* a full-fledged query!

Suppose, for example, that you need a list of all the employees at your c ompany who work in a certain department and have a particular title. You can perform two Selection filters (on the Department and Job Title fields, using our employee database as an example), and write down the results of each to get your list, or you can do just *one* search with Filter by Form and see all the records that meet your criteria (based on their entries in multiple tables) in a single step.

To use Filter by Form, follow these steps:

1. **On the Ribbon's Home tab, click the Advanced button in the Sort & Filter section.**

   A menu appears.

2. **Choose Filter by Form from the menu.**

   The table is replaced by a single row of cells, one under each field header in your table, as shown in Figure 11-6.

3. **Click the first column that you want to filter.**

   Use the scroll bars to bring the column on-screen if it's off to the right and can't be seen.

   The down arrow jumps to the column you click.

   • Normally Access shows a down-arrow button next to the first field in the table.

- If you previously used a Filter command with the table, Access puts the down-arrow button in the last field you filtered. (Again, see Figure 11-6.)

Figure 11-6:
Filter by
Form offers
a grid and
drop-down
lists to set
criteria for
each field.

4. **Click the down arrow to see a list of values that the field contains, as shown in Figure 11-7.**

Figure 11-7:
The drop-
down list
shows all
unique
values in
this field.

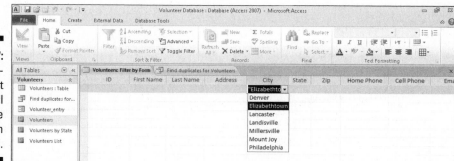

5. **In the list of values, click the value that you want to use in this Filter.**

   For instance, if you select Elizabethtown from the drop-down list in the `City` field, `"Elizabethtown"` moves into the City column (or in this case, as shown in Figure 11-7, the town of Denver was eventually selected). Access adds the quotes automatically — one less detail that you have to remember!

6. **To add another filter option for the chosen field, click the Or tab in the lower-left corner of the table.**

   A new Filter by Form window appears, letting you add an alternate search condition. In addition, Access adds another Or tab to the lower-left corner of the display, as shown in Figure 11-8.

The Filter by Form command likes to answer simple questions, such as "Show me all the records containing 'Inactive' in the `Status` field." It also provides answers to more complex questions like "Show me all the records containing 'Active' or 'Potential' in the `Status` field and who have 'Lancaster' in the `City` field," and it performs both tasks easily.

Asking a more complex question (such as "Show me all the volunteers in either Lancaster or Denver who are Active and have been members since before the year 2000") requires a query. To find out about queries, flip ahead to Chapter 12.

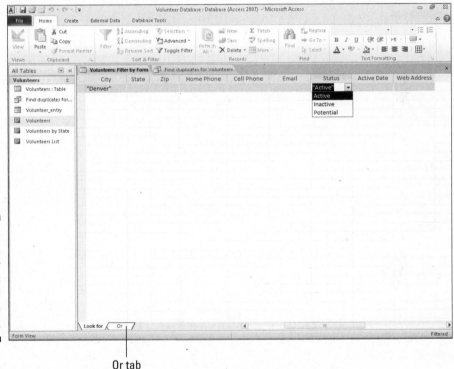

Figure 11-8:
Use as many Or statements as you need to define the criteria.

Or tab

7. **For each additional field you want to filter, repeat Steps 3 through 6.**

   In this example, the second field to be filtered is `Status`, and Active is selected from the drop-down list.

8. **When you finish entering all the criteria for the filter, click the Toggle Filter button.**

   Figure 11-9 shows the results.

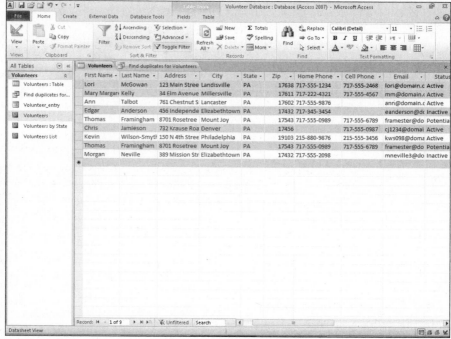

Figure 11-9:
Access
finds all
Active
volunteers
from the
cities of
Lancaster
Or Denver.

A final thought about Filter by Form:

✔ Although you can get fancy by adding Or searches to your heart's
content, keeping track of your creation gets tough in no time at all.
Before you go too far, remind yourself that queries work better than
filters when the questions get complex. Flip to Chapter 12 for the
lowdown on queries.

When you finish fiddling with your filter, click the Toggle Filter button. At
that point, your table returns to normal (or at least as normal as data tables
ever get).

Unfiltering in a form

What do you do when you enter criteria by mistake? Or when you decide that
you really don't want to include Ohio in your filter right after you click OH?
No problem — the Clear Grid command comes to the rescue!

When you click the Clear Grid command (found in the Sort & Filter section's
Advanced menu), Access clears all the entries in the Filter by Form grid and
gives you a nice, clean place to start over again.

Filter by excluding selection

The Selection filter can also be used to exclude certain records. This works great for times when you want to briefly hide a bunch of records that all share a unique attribute (a particular Zip code, a certain state, a particular price, and so on).

Here's how to make the Selection filter exclude records for you:

1. **Scroll through the table until you find the value you want to exclude.**

2. **Right-click the field containing the value and then choose Does Not Equal _____ (where the blank represents the value you've right-clicked) from the menu that appears, as shown in Figure 11-10.**

   Those records matching the value you've chosen get out of the way so you can concentrate on those records that really interest you.

Figure 11-10:
With one click, Access hides all records for volunteers who are from Mount Joy.

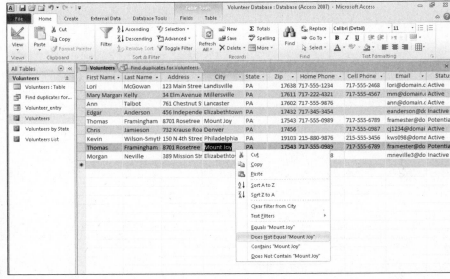

You can also click the Selection button (in the Sort & Filter section of the Home tab) and choose Does Not Equal from the menu there. You'll also notice the Contains and Does Not Contain commands — these are handy for culling records that have something in common, such as a particular word or number within them.

Chapter 12

I Was Just Asking . . . for Answers

In This Chapter

▶ Defining what queries are and what they can do

▶ Posing questions (and getting answers) with filter and sort queries

▶ Asking deep questions with queries

▶ Making query magic with the Query Wizard

You know the old saying, "The only stupid question is the one you didn't ask." It's supposed to mean that if you have a question, ask it — because if you don't, you'll be operating in the dark, and that's far sillier than your question could ever have been. Although you don't ask "meaning of life" questions of a database, you do pose questions such as, "How many active volunteers do we have?" or "What's the phone number of that guy who works for Acme Explosives?" Either of those questions, if you didn't ask it, would require you to scroll through rows and rows of data to find the information. (That's the silly approach, obviously.)

This chapter introduces you to the art of asking questions about the information in your database, using *queries*. You discover how to use the Query Wizard to pose simple questions, and then you find out about creating your own simple-yet-customized queries by using the bizarrely and inaccurately named Advanced Filter/Sort tool. After that, you get the lowdown on combining multiple tables (from the same database) — which can yield interesting answers to the questions you have about your data. Suffice it to say that by the end of this chapter you'll be a veritable quizmaster, capable of finding any record or group of records you need.

Don't worry if your first few queries produce odd or unexpected results. As with anything new, queries (along with their inherent procedures and concepts) take a little getting used to. Because they're so powerful, they can be a little complicated, but it's worth taking the time to figure things out (with the help of this book!). Take your time, be patient with yourself, and remember that old saying: "The only stupid question is the one you didn't ask."

Simple (Yet Potent) Filter and Sort Tools

Wait a minute. We were just talking about queries, and the heading above says something about *filter* and *sort*. What happened to querying? Well, sorting and filtering are queries unto themselves — using them, you can more easily find a record — say, for a particular person if your list is in alphabetical order by the Last Name field. Filtering, on the other hand, says "Give me all the records that have *this* in common" (*this* being the criterion you set your filter to look for). It's kind of like playing Go Fish with your database.

It's all related, and it's all about asking questions. There are really two ways to find a particular record:

- ✔ *Queries* use a *set* of criteria — conditions that eliminate many, if not all but one, of your records — that you present to the database and that says, "Look here, here, and here, and find THIS for me!"

- ✔ *Filters* use one criterion, saying (in effect), "Sift through all these records and find the one(s) with THIS!"

Of course, the exclamation point is optional (depending on your level of excitement about the data involved) — and so is the method you use. You can query *or* filter for any record or group of records you want. And you can sort the results of your filter. But it's still all about asking questions.

Filter things first

We begin by explaining filters because they're more straightforward, procedurally, than queries. By starting with filters, too, you can get your feet wet with them while preparing for the deeper waters of querying.

How filters work

Filters quickly scan a single table for whatever data you seek. Filters examine all records in the table and then hide those that do not match the criteria you seek.

The filtering options are virtually unlimited, but simple:

- ✔ Want every volunteer in Pennsylvania? Filter the State field for **PA**.

- ✔ Want every plumber in Hollywood? Filter for City (**Hollywood**) and Occupation (**Plumber**), and there you go.

- ✔ Want to make sure you have only the plumbers from Hollywood, California, and not the ones in Hollywood, Florida? Filter for State, too.

Fast filing with Access

Back before computers, people filed information in *file folders* and stored them in *file cabinets.*

✔ The file folders had useful information on their tabs — such as letters of the alphabet, dates, or names — indicating what kind of information could be found inside.

✔ The file-cabinet drawers had information on them, too — little cards with names, numbers, or letters on them, indicating which folders were stored inside the drawers.

The figures on the file drawers and file folders helped people find information:

✔ Need an invoice from April 10, 2009? Go to the Invoice cabinet, open the drawer for April, and pull out the folder with invoices from the week of April 10. Leaf through a few sheets of paper, and voilà!

✔ Need to know how much a given donor gave to your cause in the last quarter of 2008? Go to the 2008 cabinet, open the drawer of donor folders, and pull the folder for the donor you're interested in.

In a sans-computer environment, you'd also need a calculator, abacus, or scrap paper and a pencil to tally the expenditures racked up by that particular customer.

Querying in Access is a lot like the process of opening a file drawer, looking at folder tabs to figure out which folder is needed, and then leafing through the pages in the folder. The process just happens a lot faster, and you don't get any paper cuts!

✔ The data stored in an Access table can be found by using a query that goes to a particular table, looks in particular fields, and pulls out certain records, based on the criterion set for the query, such as "Show me all the volunteers with *Active* in the Status field."

✔ You can even perform calculations with queries (such as tallying the donations for a particular donor). Chapter 15 shows you how.

There's a price to pay for ease and simplicity. Filters aren't *smart* or *flexible:*

✔ You cannot filter multiple tables without first writing a query that contains — *brings together* — the tables.

✔ A filter cannot be the basis for the records seen on a report or form.

Chapter 11 covers filters in their limited-but-useful glory.

What about queries?

Queries go far beyond filters. But to get to that great "beyond," queries require more complexity. After all, a bicycle may be easy to ride, but a bike won't go as fast as a motorcycle. And so it goes with queries. Queries work with one or more tables, let you search one or more fields, and even offer the option to save your results for further analysis, but you can't just hop on and ride a query with no lessons.

For all the differences between filters and queries, the most advanced filter is, in reality, a simple query — which makes some bizarre sense: Your first step into the world of queries is also your last step out of the domain of filters. Welcome to Advanced Filter/Sort, the super-filter of Access, masquerading as a mild-mannered query.

Advanced Filter/Sort

Advanced Filter/Sort is more powerful than a run-of-the-mill filter. It's so powerful that it's like a simple query:

✔ You use the same steps to build an Advanced Filter/Sort as you do to create a query.

✔ The results look quite a bit alike, too.

Advanced Filter/Sort looks, acts, and behaves like a query, but it's still a filter at heart and is constrained by a filter's limits, including these:

✔ Advanced Filter/Sort works with only one table or form in your database at a time, so you can't use it on a bunch of linked tables.

✔ You can ask only simple questions with the filter.

Real, honest-to-goodness queries do a lot more than that.

✔ The filter always displays all the columns for every matching record.

With a query, *you* choose the columns that you want to appear in the results. If you don't want a particular column, leave it out of the query. Filters aren't bright enough to do that.

Even with those limitations, Advanced Filter/Sort makes a great training ground to practice your query-building skills (that's why we're starting with this feature, despite the word "Advanced" in its name).

Although this section talks about applying filters only to tables, you can also filter a query. There's a good reason to filter queries: Some queries take a long time to run, so it's faster to *filter* the query results than to *rewrite and rerun* the query. Suppose (for example) that you run a complicated sales-report query and notice it includes data from *every* state instead of the individual state you wanted. Rather than modify the query and run it again, you can apply a filter to your query's results. *Poof!* You get the results you're after in a fraction of the time.

Fact-finding with fun, fast filtering

Before you use the Filter window, you need to take a quick look at its components and what they do. In the section that follows this one, you find out how to access and use the Filter window.

The Filter window is split into two distinct sections, as shown in Figure 12-1:

- ✔ **Field list** (the "Cities" box in Figure 12-1). The Field list displays all the fields in the *current table or form* (the table or form that's open at the time). Not sure about forms? Check out Chapter 7!

  At this point, don't worry about the upper half of the window. The Field list comes more into play when you start working with full queries. The table you were working on is already shown in the upper half of the window, so you don't have to do anything with this part of the window now.

- ✔ **Query grid** (the lower half of the screen). When you use the Advanced Filter/Sort command, you are presented with a blank *query grid* for the details of your filter.

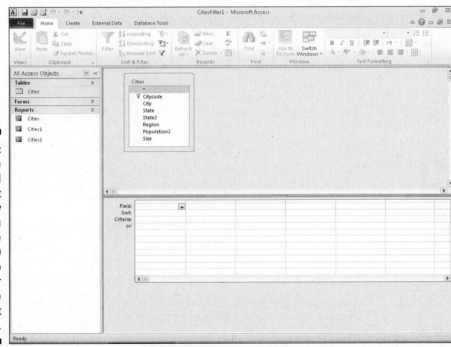

Figure 12-1: The Advanced Filter/Sort window allows you to choose the Field(s) on which to filter your data in the current table.

You're building a filter, but Access calls the area at the bottom of the screen a query grid because you use the same grid for queries. (You also see it later in the chapter, in the section about building real queries.)

To build the filter, you simply fill in the spaces of the query grid at the bottom of the window you see in Figure 12-1. Access even helps you along the way with pull-down menus and rows that do specific tasks. The procedure for filling in these spaces appears in the next section, along with details about each part of the grid and how it all works.

Here's the "advanced" part

The Advanced Filter/Sort tool also works on *forms*. If you feel particularly adventuresome (or if you mainly work with your data through some ready-made forms), try the filter with your form. Filtering a form works like filtering a table, so you can follow the same steps.

The following sections show how to design and use filters.

Starting the process

Start your filter adventure by firing up Access's basic query tool, the Advanced Filter/Sort.

1. **Decide what question you need to ask and which fields the question involves.**

   Because it's your data, only you know what information you need and which fields would help you get it. You may want (for example) a list of volunteers who live in a particular state, donors who've donated in excess of a certain amount to your organization, cities in a particular state, books by your favorite author, or people whose birthdays fall in the next month (if you're painfully organized, in which case I commend you).

   Whatever you want, decide on your question first and then get ready to find the fields in your table or form that contain the answer.

   Don't worry if your question includes more than one field or multiple options. Both filters and queries can handle multiple-field and multiple-option questions.

2. **Open the table (or form) that you want to interrogate.**

   Assuming you have the right database open, your table or form pops into view.

3. **Click the Ribbon's Home tab at the top of the Access workspace.**

4. **In the Sort & Filter section of the Ribbon's Home tab (see Figure 12-2), choose Advanced ⇨ Advanced Filter/Sort.**

   The Filter window appears, ready to accept your command. What you see depends on the following considerations:

   • If you previously used a filter of any kind with this table, Access puts that most recently used filter information into the new window.

   • If no filter was done previously, the Filter/Sort window looks pretty blank — for now.

   The Filter window is nothing but a simplified query window. The filter looks, acts, and behaves a lot like a real query. More information about full queries comes later in the chapter, so flip ahead to the next section if that's what you need.

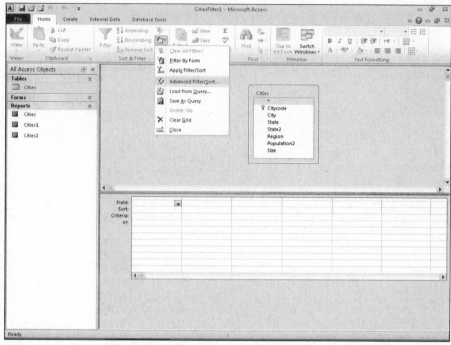

Figure 12-2:
Click the
Advanced
button to
choose
Advanced
Filter/Sort.

After you open the Filter window, you're ready to select fields and criteria for your filter. The following section shows you how.

Selecting fields and criteria

As you begin selecting the fields you want to use in your filter and set up the criteria against which your fields' content will be compared, be sure to follow these steps carefully:

1. **Click the first box in the Field row and then click the down arrow that appears to the right of the box.**

   The drop-down menu lists all the fields in your table (or form).

2. **Click the field (as identified in the preceding section) that you want to query.**

   Access helpfully puts the field name in the Field box on the query grid. So far, so good.

   If you want to see the results of your filter in the same order that your data always appears in, skip to Step 4.

3. **If you want to sort your filter results by this particular field, follow these steps:**

   a. *Click the Sort box.*

b. Click the down arrow that appears.

      c. Select Ascending or Descending from the drop-down menu.

      Ascending order is lowest to highest (for example, *A, B, C . . .*). *Descending* order is highest to lowest (for example, *Z, Y, X . . .*). If you don't want to stop and click the drop arrow to choose a sort method, just type an "a" or a "d" and Access fills it in for you, and you can move on to the Criteria field to specify what you're looking for.

4. Set up your criteria for the field.

  Follow these steps:

      a. Click the Criteria box under your field.

      *b. Type each criterion (such as =***value***, where "value" refers to a specific word or number that is represented within your data or < or > followed by a value).*

      Setting criteria is the most complex part of building a query — it's the most important part of the entire process. The criteria are your actual questions, formatted in a way that Access understands. Table 12-1 gives you a quick introduction to the different ways you can express your criteria.

Table 12-1		Basic Comparison Operators	
Name	*Symbol*	*What It Means*	*Example*
Equals	=	Displays all records that exactly match whatever you type.	To find all items from customer 37, type **37** into the Criteria row.
Less Than	<	Lists all values that are less than your criterion.	Typing **<50000** in the `Salary` field finds all employees who earn less than $50K.
Greater Than	>	Lists all values in the field that are greater than the criterion.	Typing **>50000** in the `Salary` field finds all employees I'll be hitting up for a loan because they earn more than $50K.
Greater Than or Equal To	>=	Works just like Greater Than, except it also includes all entries that exactly match the criterion.	**>=50,000** finds all values from 50,000 to infinity.

Name	Symbol	What It Means	Example
Less Than or Equal To	<=	If you add = to Less Than, your query includes all records that have values below or equal to the criterion value.	**<=50000** includes not only those records with values less than 50,000, but also those with a value of 50,000.
Not Equal To	<>	Finds all entries that don't match the criterion.	If you want a list of all records except those with a value of 50,000, enter **<>50000**.

If you're making comparisons with logical operators, flip to Chapter 13 for everything you need to know about Boolean logic, the language of Access criteria.

   c. *If your question includes more than one possible value for this field, click the Or box and type your next criterion in the box to the right of the word Or.*

If you move on to a new box, the criterion you entered is automatically placed in quotes. Don't worry. This is just Access acknowledging that you've given it a specific value to look for, to

   • Make an exact match.

   • Use the value with a greater-than or less-than symbol for comparison.

If your question involves more than one field, repeat the preceding Steps 1–4 for each field. Just use the next block in the grid for the additional field or fields you want to use in your filter.

With all the fields and criteria in place, it's time to take your filter for a test drive. Figure 12-3 shows an example that uses two criteria: the Cities table filtered for cities in the database that are in California and have a population of less than 100,000 people.

Running the filter

After completing the process of choosing fields and setting criteria, you're ready to run the filter. Click the Toggle Filter button in the Sort & Filter section of the Ribbon.

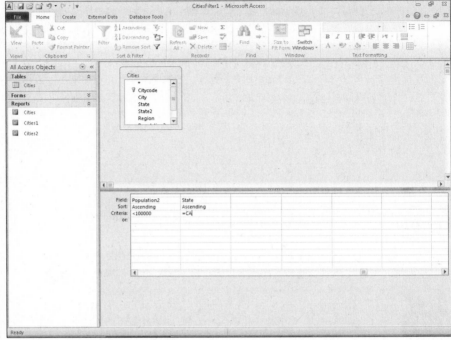

Figure 12-3:
Two fields
are que-
ried in this
example —
Population2
and State.

Access thinks about it for a moment, and then the record or records that met your criteria appear. This is shown in Figure 12-4. Pretty cool, eh? Note the little Filter symbols on the Field Name headers for the two fields by which this particular table was filtered — a tiny arrow and a Filter icon — to remind you which fields your filter used.

There are two ways to see all the data again:

✔ Click the Toggle Filter button, found in the Sort & Filter section of the Ribbon's Home tab.

The filtered records join their unfiltered brethren in a touching moment of digital homecoming.

✔ Click the Filtered button.

This button appears at the bottom of the Access window (next to the Record buttons that you use to move through your records one at a time, and you can see it in Figure 12-4). When you click the Filtered button, your entire table comes back, and the button changes so its label says *Unfiltered*. Click again? The results of your query return. It's a quick toggle, perhaps even toggle-ier than the Toggle Filter button!

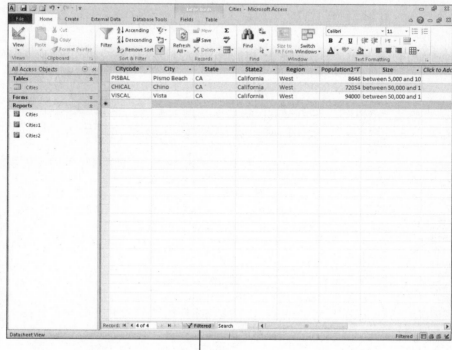

Figure 12-4:
Voilà! Your
filtered data
appears;
no abra-
cadabra
needed.

Filtered button

Select Queries

The basic query tool, created to make your life easier, is the *Select query* —
so named because it *selects* matching records from your database and
displays the results according to your instructions.

The sidebar "Secrets of the Select query" summarizes the differences that
make Select queries more powerful than lesser filters. If upon reading these
secrets, you suspect that the Select query sounds like the right tool for the job
you have in mind, you may be able to use a filter instead of a query.

The best process for creating a Select query depends on the following:

✔ If you're new to writing queries, the Query Wizard is a fast, easy way
to get started. It walks you through the process of selecting tables and
fields for your query — and can even add some summary calculations
(such as counting records) to your query.

✔ If you've already written some queries and are comfortable with the Query Design window, you'll probably want to bypass the Query Wizard and build your queries from scratch. Later in this chapter, "Getting Your Feet Wet with Ad Hoc Queries" guides you through the process.

Solid relationships are the key to getting it all (from your tables)

In life, solid relationships make for a happier person; in Access, solid relationships make for a happier query experience.

To query your database effectively, you need to know the following about its table structure:

✔ Which tables do you need to use?

✔ How are the tables you need to use related to each other?

✔ Which fields contain the data you want to know about?

✔ Which fields do you need in the solution?

Access maintains relationships between the tables in your database. Usually you (or your Information Systems department) create these relationships when you first design the database. When you build the tables and organize them with special key fields, you actually prepare the tables to work with a query.

Key fields relate your Access tables to each other. Queries use key fields to match records in one table with their related records in another table. You can pull data for the item you seek from the various tables that hold this data in your database — provided they're properly related before you launch the query.

Want to refresh your memory on creating relationships between the tables in your database? Check out Chapter 4, where all those secrets are revealed.

If you don't relate your tables via the Relationships window, you'll have to do so for each multiple-table query you build in Access. As a general rule, put in the time to properly design and relate your tables. With proper table design and relationships, you'll get the results you want in a shorter amount of time.

Secrets of the Select query

Unlike its simplified little brother Advanced Filter/Sort (shown previously in this chapter), a Select query offers all kinds of helpful and powerful options, including these:

✔ **Use more than one table in a query.** Because a Select query understands the relational side of Access, this query can pull together data from more than one table.

✔ **Show only the fields you want in your results.** Select queries include the ever-popular Show setting, which tells Access which fields you really care about seeing.

✔ Put the fields into any order you want in the results. Organize your answer fields where

you want them without changing the order of the fields in your original table(s).

✔ **List only as many matching entries as you need.** If you need only the top 5, 25, or 100 records, or a percentage, such as 5% or 25%, use the *Top Value setting*. (This and other query options are covered in Chapter 14).

✔ **You can save your query for future use.** Unlike the Advanced Filter/Sort query, which lives only as long as you keep that window open, a Select query can be given a name and run over and over, whenever you need it.

Running the Query Wizard

You can rely on the Query Wizard — and the Simple Query Wizard found within it — for a real dose of hands-free filtering. With the Simple Query Wizard, you enter *table and field information.* The wizard takes care of the behind-the-scenes work for you.

Access isn't psychic (that's scheduled for the next version); it needs *some* input from you!

To create a query with the Query Wizard's Simple Query Wizard, follow these steps:

1. **On a piece of paper, lay out the data you'd like in your query results.**

   A query returns a datasheet (column headings followed by rows of data), so make your layout in that format. All you really need are the column headings so you'll know what data to pull from the database.

2. **Determine the table location of each piece of data (column heading) from your paper.**

   Write down the table and field name that contains the data matching the column heading on the paper above the column heading.

3. **In the Database window, click the Create tab on the Ribbon and then click the Query Wizard button from the Macros & Code section.**

   The New Query Wizard dialog box appears, asking you what kind of Query Wizard you'd like to run. Choose Simple Query Wizard and click OK.

4. **Choose the first table you want to include in the query (see Figure 12-5).**

   You'll use the Tables/Queries drop-down menu, which shows all the tables (and any existing queries) in your database. Here are the specifics.

   a. *Click the down arrow next to the Tables/Queries drop-down menu (as shown in Figure 12-6).*

   b. *Click the name of the table or query to include in this query.*

Figure 12-5:
The Simple
Query
Wizard
starts and
asks which
table(s) you
want to
query.

5. **Select the fields from that table for your query.**

   Repeat these steps to select each field you want included in your query:

   a. *Click the name of the table or query to include in this query.*

      The Available Fields list changes and displays the fields available in the table.

   b. *In the Available Fields list, double-click each field from this table or query that you want to include in the query you're creating.*

   If you add the wrong field, just double-click it in the Selected Fields list. It will go back home. If you just want to start all over, click the double-left chevron (that's what you call the symbol that looks like a less-than sign) and all the selected fields go away.

Figure 12-6:
The Tables/
Queries
drop-down
list.

6. After you select all the fields, click Next.

If the wizard can determine the relationships between the tables you selected, the window in Figure 12-7 appears.

If you don't see the window, not to worry. Access just wants you to name the query instead. Skip to Step 8.

Figure 12-7:
The Query
Wizard may
give you the
chance to
summarize
your data.

If you include fields from two tables that aren't related, a warning dialog box appears. The dialog box reminds you that all the selected tables must be related before you can run your query — and suggests that you correct the problem before continuing. In fact, it won't let you go any further until you appease it in one of two ways:

- Remove all the fields selected for your query from the unrelated tables.

- Fix the relationships so that all tables you've selected in your query are related.

7. **If the wizard asks you to choose between a Detail and a Summary query, click the radio button next to your choice and then click Next.**

   • *Detail* creates a datasheet that lists all records that match the query. As the name implies, you get all the details from those records.

   • *Summary* tells the wizard that you aren't interested in seeing every single record; you want to see a summary of the information instead.

   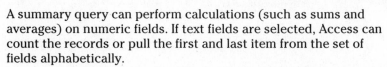

   A summary query can perform calculations (such as sums and averages) on numeric fields. If text fields are selected, Access can count the records or pull the first and last item from the set of fields alphabetically.

   If you want to make any special adjustments to the summary, click Summary Options to display the Summary Options dialog box shown in Figure 12-8. Select your summary options from the check boxes for the available functions — Sum, Avg, Min, and Max — and then click OK.

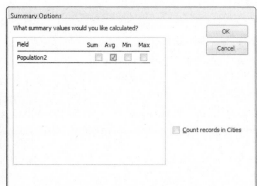

Figure 12-8:
Access
offers differ-
ent ways of
summarizing
the data.

If you're curious about how the wizard decides whether to display the Detail or Summary step, the sidebar "To summarize or not to summarize" tells the story.

8. **In the wizard page that appears, select a radio button for what you want to do next:**

   • *If you want to make your query snazzy:* Select the Modify the Query Design option.

   The wizard sends your newly created query to the salon for some sprucing up, such as the inclusion of sorting and totals.

   • *If you want to skip the fancy stuff:* Select the Open the Query to View Information option to see the Datasheet view.

   The wizard runs the query and presents the results in a typical Access datasheet.

To summarize or not to summarize

How does the wizard choose whether it feels like summarizing things? Well, computers are a lot like people that way: Choices that seem arbitrary usually have reasons behind them.

The wizard displays the Detail or Summary step (shown previously in Figure 12-7) if *either* of these statements is true:

✔ Fields for your query are selected from two tables that have a *one-to-many* relationship with each other. (Chapter 4 explains one-to-many relationships.)

✔ A selected field contains numeric data.

9. Type a title for your query in the text box and then click Finish.

The wizard builds your query and saves it with the title you entered; then Access displays the results, as shown in Figure 12-9.

Congratulations! You've given birth to a query.

When you finish the steps in this section, the Query Wizard saves your query automatically with the name you typed in.

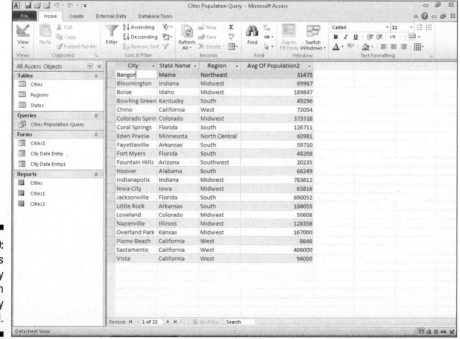

Figure 12-9: The results of a query built with the Query Wizard.

But what about the other query wizards?

Besides the Simple Query Wizard, Access offers three other query wizards.

✔ *Crosstab Query Wizard* summarizes multiple rows of data into a spreadsheet-like format.

A Crosstab is similar to an Excel PivotTable.

✔ *Find Duplicates Query Wizard* helps you locate duplicate records in a table or query.

This wizard locates all records in the customer table that have the exact same content in the fields specified during the query's creation. After it finds the duplicates, you can decide whether the records in question are truly redundant or simply have a lot in common.

✔ *Unmatched Query Wizard* finds unrelated records in two tables that share a common field.

If an Orders table contains orders for a customer who isn't in the Customers table, you have yourself a problem — orders in the system and no one to bill. Sounds like a recipe for the unemployment line! How can such a thing happen? *Referential integrity* prevents a child table from containing a record that has no corresponding record in the parent table. (Chapter 4 covers referential integrity.) If you don't turn Referential Integrity on, it's quite possible to put in an order for a nonexistent customer. The Find Unmatched Query Wizard can find records with reference problems and help you get to the bottom of such a dilemma.

Use the following list to modify or use a query created with the Query Wizard:

✔ To write complex AND and OR criteria, see Chapter 13.

✔ To add calculations like sums and averages, see Chapter 14.

✔ To add custom formulas (like a sales tax calculation), see Chapter 15.

✔ To attach the query to a report, see Chapter 17.

Getting Your Feet Wet with Ad Hoc Queries

If you use Access regularly, you need to know how to build a query from scratch. This is where Design view comes into play. Design view may look daunting — check out Figure 12-10, if you don't believe me — but it's really not that bad. I promise!

✔ The top half of the view is where you place the tables or previously-created queries you want to include in this new query.

✔ The bottom half is called the Design Grid; it contains the Field, Table, Sort, Show, Criteria, and Or rows used to generate the results.

You'll notice that a new tab appears on the Ribbon as soon as you enter a Design task. The Design tab appears under a Query Tools heading, as shown at the top of the window in Figure 12-10.

To build a multiple-table query by hand in Design view, follow these steps:

1. **Click the Create tab from the Ribbon.**

   A series of buttons organized by object type appears on the Ribbon.

2. **From the Macros & Code section, click the Query Design button.**

   The Show Table dialog box appears, listing all tables and queries available for your new query.

   Yes, you can query a query.

3. **Add the tables you want in your query:**

   a. *In the Show Table dialog box (see Figure 12-11), double-click the names of each table or query you want.*

      After you double-click a table, a small window for that table appears in the Query Design window. (To see the three tables chosen for the query in this example, each in such a window, refer to Figure 12-10.)

   b. *After you add the last table you want, click Close.*

      The Show Table dialog box is dismissed.

In the Query Design window, lines between your tables (as shown in Figure 12-12) show *relationships* between the tables. The following sidebar, "Get the right tables," explains how these relationships are essential to the proper building and execution of your query.

4. **In the table/s that now appear(s) in the top half of the Query window, double-click each field you want in the list at the top of the Query Design window.**

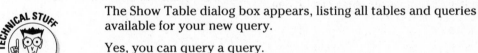

Consider the following while choosing fields:

• Choose your fields in the order you want them to appear in the query results.

• You can include fields from any or all of the tables at the top of the query window (the tables you selected in the preceding step).

Figure 12-13 shows fields selected from multiple tables in Query Design view.

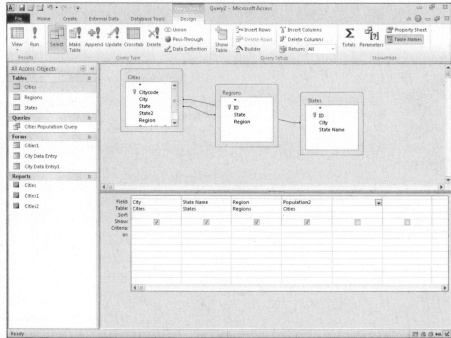

Figure 12-10:
A query showing City, State, Region, and Population fields from three related tables in Design view.

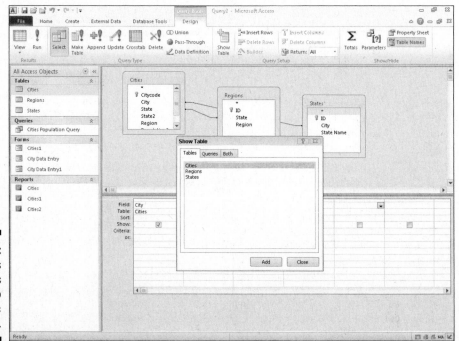

Figure 12-11:
The Cities table is added to the ad hoc query.

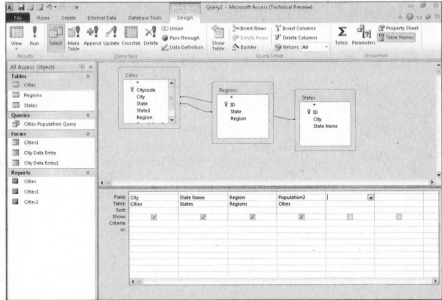

Figure 12-12:
Access
knows how
the Cities,
Regions,
and States
tables are
related.

Get the right tables

If you've been a faithful reader from Page 1 of this book, you've probably established relationships between your selected tables together and saved yourself an extra step when building a query.

That's one reason table relationships are important. Each time you create a new query and select multiple tables, the relationship lines will already be in place for your queries. Database geeks call these relationship lines *join lines* or just plain old *joins*. Without those relationships, you'll have to join the tables manually for each new query.

What happens if you create a query but no line appears between the tables? Access is telling you that it doesn't have a clue how to relate the tables. It's possible that you selected the wrong tables — that is, tables that don't share a common field and therefore cannot be related. If you've selected the wrong tables, follow these steps to delete the unwanted tables and add the correct tables to your query:

1. **Click the title bar of the table that doesn't belong.**

   The little * at the top of the table's Field list will highlight, indicating that the entire Table List window is selected.

2. **Tap the Delete key on your keyboard to remove the table.**

   Repeat Steps 1 and 2 for each table you'd like to remove from the query.

   The Show Table dialog box should appear. If it doesn't, click the Show Table button, found in the Query Setup section of the Ribbon.

3. **Select the correct table or tables for your query.**

If you select the right tables and still get no join lines, then you can go back to the Relationships window and relate the tables correctly. Chapter 4 shows you how. (You can also join tables in Query Design view, but I don't recommend it.)

If you accidentally choose the wrong field, you can easily correct your mistake:

    a. Click the field name's entry in the Query grid.

    b. Select the Delete Columns button from the Ribbon's Query Tools Design tab.

    The field is removed from the Query grid.

Now you're ready to put the finishing touches to your query by adding functionality such as sorting. The following section shows you how.

Adding the finishing touches

To sort your query results in Design view (as shown here), follow these steps:

  1. Repeat these steps for each field you want to use for sorting:

    a. In the Query grid, click the Sort box under the field name.

    b. Click the down arrow that appears at the edge of the Sort box.

    c. Click either Ascending or Descending (as shown in Figure 12-14).

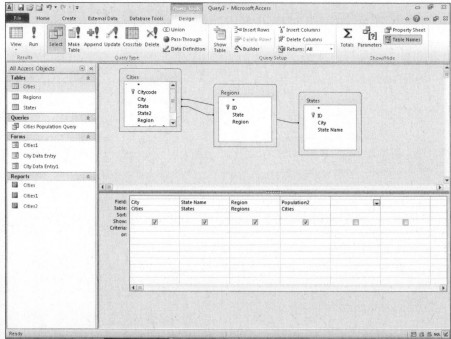

Figure 12-13: This query will grab data from two fields from the Cities table, and one each from the States and Region tables.

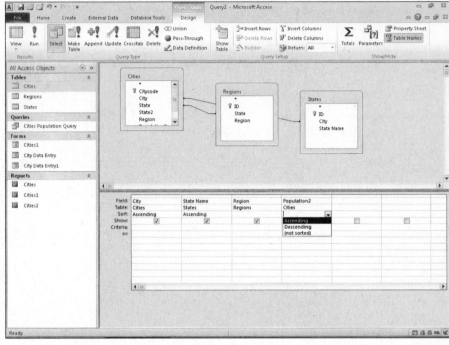

Figure 12-14:
Sorting on
the Cities'
City field,
the States'
State
Name and
the Cities'
Population2
fields.

The sidebar "Just these, and in this order" shows how to arrange sort fields. For all you need to know about sorting, see Chapter 11.

2. **In the Criteria row for each field you want to use as criterion, type the criterion appropriate to that field.**

   For example, to show cities with a population greater than 100,000, you would type >**100,000** in the Criteria row under the Population2 field column heading, as shown in Figure 12-15. Table 12-1, earlier in the chapter, shows some criteria examples.

3. **If you don't want that field to appear in the final results, deselect the check box in the Show row for that field.**

   The Show setting really stands out in your Query grid. There's only one check box in there — the Show option.

After you tell the query how to sort and select data, you're ready to see your query results by running the query.

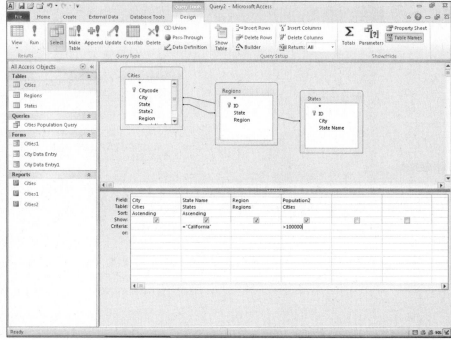

Figure 12-15:
Here the
criteria are
set to show
only cities
in California
with a
population
in excess of
100,000.

Saving the query

After you create your query, you're ready to save it. Follow these steps:

1. **Review your work one more time. When you're sure it looks good, click the Save button on the Quick Access toolbar to save your query.**

   The Save As dialog box appears.

2. **In the Save As dialog box, type a name for the query and then click OK.**

   You're saving the design of the query and not the results returned by the query. So as records are added, edited, and deleted from your data tables, the query always returns the data *as it is at the moment the query is run.*

Running your query

After you create your query and save it, you're ready to run it. Follow these steps:

Just these, and in this order

Access has a nice tool for sorting the results from a query. After all, queries don't get much easier than clicking a little box labeled *Sort* and then telling the program whether Ascending or Descending is your choice for sort-flavor-of-the-moment.

The only problem with this little arrangement is that Access automatically sorts the results from *left* to *right*. If you only request one sort, this order is no big deal. But if you request *two* sorts, the column that's closest to the *left* side of the query automatically becomes the primary sort, with any other field playing second (or third) fiddle.

Taking control of the sort order isn't hard, but it also isn't obvious. Because Access looks at the Query grid and performs the sorts from left to right, the trick is to move the column for the main sorting instruction to the left side of the grid. Follow these steps to move a column in the grid:

1. **Put the tip of the mouse pointer in the thin gray box just above the field name on the Query grid.**

2. **When the mouse pointer turns into a black downward-pointing arrow, click *once*.**

   All of a sudden the chosen field is highlighted; the mouse pointer changes from a downward-pointing black arrow to an upward-pointing white arrow.

3. **While still pointing at the thin gray box just above the field name, hold down the mouse button and drag the field to its new position on the grid.**

   As you move the mouse (which includes a gray outline of a box, along with the white arrow) a black bar moves through the grid, showing you where the field will land when you let up on the mouse button.

4. **When the black bar is in the right place, release the mouse button.**

   The field information pops into view, safe and happy in its new home.

This moving trick also changes the order in which the fields appear in your query results. Feel free to move fields here, there, or anywhere, depending on your needs.

Is this some great flexibility or what?

Run

1. **Take one last look to make sure it's correct.**

   Inspect the fields you've chosen and your other settings in the query grid. The sidebar, "Query troubleshooting," lists common query problems.

2. **Click the Run button (the huge red exclamation point, shown second from left in the Ribbon's Design tab in Figure 12-15).**

   Did you get the answer you hoped for? If not, take your query back into Design view for some more work. To do so, click the Design View button on the Quick Access toolbar.

Query troubleshooting

If your query results *aren't* exactly what you thought you asked for (isn't that just like a computer?), double-check your query design for errors. Common design errors include

✔ Mixing up the greater-than (>) and less-than (<) signs

✔ Leaving out an equals sign (=) in your greater-than-or-equal-to statements

✔ Misspelling criteria such as region name, state, or postal code

✔ Entering criteria in the wrong field

Chapter 13

I'll Take These AND Those OR Them

In This Chapter

▶ Setting criteria for your queries

▶ Working with the AND and OR operators

▶ Including AND and OR in the same query

As you build larger and more complex databases with Access, your questions about the data they contain become larger and more complex. Changing the order of your records — sorting from A to Z and then from Z to A and filtering it from one or more perspectives — just isn't enough for you or your database anymore. You want more — or (to be more accurate) you *need* more — from your database, and you need it quickly.

What to do? You can use queries that ask questions (present criteria to the database to see which records meet them) to help you ferret out the records you need to *access* (pardon the expression) right now.

This chapter shows how to set more specific criteria for your queries, controlling the answers to your database questions with ease and speed. You find out about two very powerful Access operators: AND and OR. what the operators do, how they do it, and (most important) when and why to use them.

If AND and OR are not the solutions to your query-building needs, Chapter 12 takes a more detailed stroll through the basics of querying, and may help point you in the right direction. You can create queries automatically, or you can build them from scratch. Chapter 12 gives you some more advanced ideas about queries and helps you craft specialized queries for your specific needs.

Working with AND and/or OR

AND and OR are the most powerful and popular of the *Boolean* terms.

In written language, you probably know when to use *and* versus *or*. If you're not sure how this knowledge can be transferred to your use of Access, read on:

- ✔ AND is used when all the items in a list are to be chosen. For example, "bring a salad, side dish, and a dessert to the potluck dinner" would tell the person to bring all three items to the dinner.

- ✔ OR creates a list wherein each item is a choice — "bring a salad, side dish, or a dessert to the potluck dinner." In this example, the person reading the instruction would know that only one item need be brought, but it's okay to bring one or more (or all) of the items.

  With the OR example, you'll be spending less time in the kitchen, and with OR in your query, you'll be making it possible for more of the records to meet your criteria. Using our employee database as an example, your query might say, "Give me all the people who work in Accounting AND Operations" — and none of the employee records would meet that criterion, because nobody works in two departments at the same time. However, using OR would work: "Give me all the people who work in Accounting OR Operations" would provide a list of all the employees in the two departments.

Boolean logic (named for the guy who invented it) allows you to use words like AND, OR, NOT, LESS THAN, GREATER THAN, and EQUAL TO to search a database. In Access, these terms are called *operators*.

If you're not sure you can remember when to use AND versus OR, think of it this way:

- ✔ AND **narrows your query.** Fewer records match.

  In normal usage, *and* gives you no options. You do *everything* in the list.

- ✔ OR **widens your query.** More records match.

  In normal usage, *or* gives you more options because you can pick and choose which items from the list you want to do.

As an example, in Access, if you're searching a customer database and you say you want customers who live in a particular city *and* who live in an area with a particular Zip code *and* who have purchased more than $50,000 worth of items in the past year, you're probably going to end up with a short list of customers — you'll have fewer options. On the other hand, if you want customers who are in a particular city *or* have a particular Zip code *or* who have purchased more than $50,000 in goods this year, you'll get many more choices — everyone from the city, with the Zip code, and over that purchasing level — probably many more customers than the *and* query will give you.

Data from here to there

One of the most common Access queries involves listing items that are between two values.

Here's an example. You may want to find all the volunteers who joined your organization between June 1, 2006 and January 1, 2009. For this list of records, you use AND criteria to establish the range. Here's how:

- ✔ Put the two conditions (on or after June 1, 2006 and before January 1, 2009) together on the same line.
- ✔ Separate the conditions with an AND operator.

Figure 13-1 shows the query window for this range of Active Date field's dates.

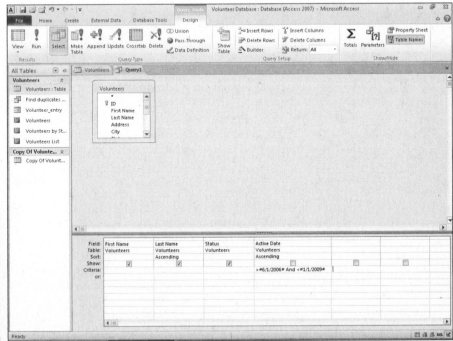

Figure 13-1:
Find data that falls within a range of dates by using AND.

Don't worry about the pound signs (#) — Access puts those in automatically for you.

Here's what's going on in the query window:

1. Access begins processing the query by looking through the records in the table and asking the first question in the criteria:

   Did this volunteer join after June 1, 2006?

   • If the volunteer joined before this date, Access ignores the record and goes on to the next record.

   • If the volunteer joined on or after the date, Access goes to Step 2.

2. If the record was entered on or after June 1, 2006, Access asks the second question:

   Was the record entered before January 1, 2009?

   • If yes, Access includes the record in the results.

   • If no, the record is rejected, and Access moves on to the next record.

   Access repeats Step 1 and Step 2 for all records in the table.

3. When Access hits the last record in the database, the query's results appear.

Note that using the less-than sign (<) for the first date would allow the query to include only records for those volunteers who joined after June 1, 2006 — the omission of the equal sign (=) eliminates those records with a June 1, 2006 (6/1/2006) date in the Active Date field.

This type of "between" instruction works for any type of data. You can list numeric values that fall between two other numbers, names that fall within a range of letters, or dates that fall within a given area of the calendar.

You could also search for dates by using the BETWEEN operator (see Figure 13-2 for an example of BETWEEN in action). The criteria BETWEEN #6/1/2006# AND #6/30/2006# selects records if the dates land on or between June 1, 2006, and June 30, 2006, a span of thirty (30) days.

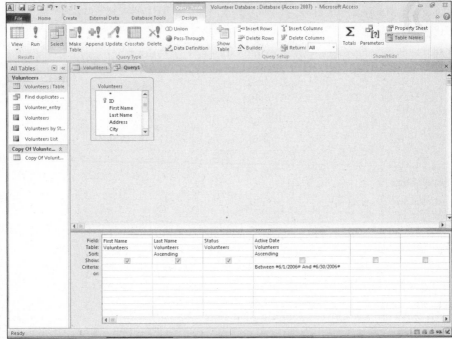

Figure 13-2:
The
BETWEEN
operator is
the
ultimate
range
finder.

Using multiple levels of AND

Overall, Access lets you do whatever you want in a query — and for that reason, flexibility really adds to the application's power.

Access doesn't limit you to just *one* criterion in each line of a query — you can include as many criteria as you want, even if by adding more and more criteria you end up whittling your results down to one record, or even no records. When you add multiple criteria, Access treats the criteria as if you typed an AND between each one and the next.

All that power can backfire on you. Each AND criterion that you add must sit with the others on the same row. When you run the query, Access checks each record to make sure it matches *all* the expressions in the given Criteria row of the query before putting that record into the result table. Figure 13-3 shows a query that uses three criteria: Because they all sit together on a single row, Access treats the three criteria as if they were part of a big AND statement. This query returns only employees who joined before January 1, 2008, AND who are Active (in the Status field), AND live in Pennsylvania (PA in the State field)

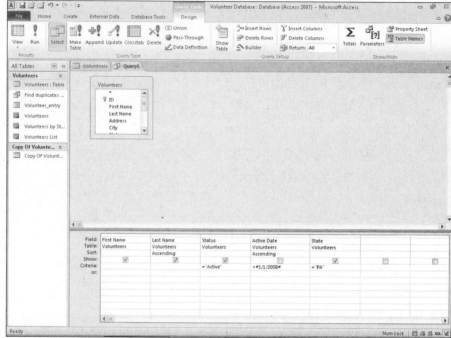

When you have a very large database and want to restrict your results to a minimum of records, combining a few criteria is the most useful way to go.

Really want to whittle that list of records down? Because Access displays the query results in Datasheet view, all the tools available in Datasheet view work with the query — including filters! Just use any of the filter commands (use the Filter tool group's buttons to filter by Selection, for example) to limit your query results. (If you need a quick refresher on filters, flip back to Chapter 11.)

Establishing criteria with OR

When you want to find a group of records that match one of several possibili-ties (such as volunteers who live in *either* PA *or* DE) you need the OR operator when you choose your criteria. It's the master of multiple options.

Access makes using OR easy. Because the OR option is built right into the Access query dialog box, you can just

- ✔ Choose the field on which to query the data.
- ✔ Indicate which values to look for.

To make a group of criteria work together as a big OR statement, list each criterion on its own line at the bottom of the query, as shown in Figure 13-4. Here you see that volunteer records for those people in the Pennsylvania OR Delaware will meet the query's criteria.

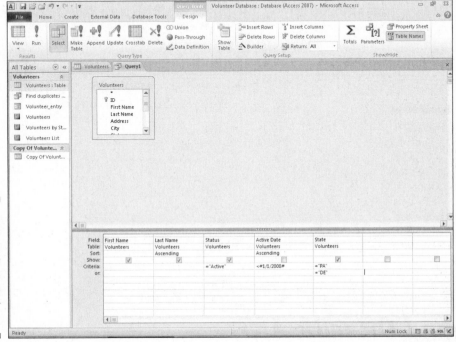

Figure 13-4: OR allows more (yet very specific) records to meet your criteria.

Each line can include criterion for whichever fields you want, even if another line in the query *already* has a criterion in that field. (This is easier than it sounds.)

Of course, you can list the criteria in different columns, as shown in Figure 13-5. Here we see a query that searches for volunteers who are Active (Status field) OR who joined before June 1, 2009. Such a search would let the organization know how active their members are, especially those who may turn up as Inactive (and make it into the query result by meeting the date criteria) even though they've been in the database for some time. This could trigger some outreach to remind those volunteers to pitch in, and let the Active volunteers receive some sort of thank you.

Each OR criterion is on a separate line. If the criteria are on the same line, you are performing an AND operation — only records that match both rules appear.

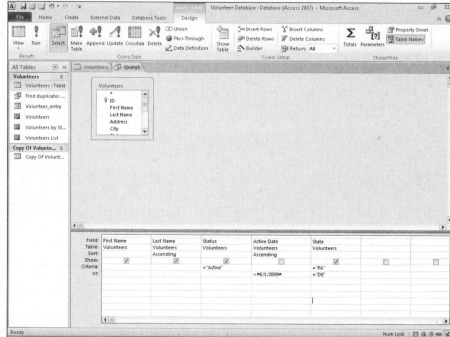

Figure 13-5:
The OR operator can be used to set criteria for data from different fields.

Combining AND with OR and OR with AND

When it comes to combining the use of AND and OR operators, Access can bend like a contortionist (how do they *do* that?). When the AND and OR operators by themselves aren't enough, you can combine them within a single field — or in multiple fields in one or more tables.

These logically complex queries get really complex, really fast. You can end up confused as to why certain records came back in your results — or worse, why certain records didn't make the cut. If a query grows to the point that you're losing track of which AND the last OR affected, you're in over your head, and it's time to start over again.

Instead of adding layer upon layer of conditions into a single query, you can break down your question into a series of smaller queries that build on each other:

1. **Begin with a simple query with one or two criteria.**

2. **Build another query that starts with the first query's results.**

3. **If you need more refining, create a third query that chews on the second query's answers.**

   Each successive query whittles down your results until the final set of records appears.

   This procedure lets you double-check every step of your logic, so it minimizes the chance of any errors accidentally slipping into your results. You can also use it to build on an existing query, adding more criteria and including more (or different) fields in the query — just open the previously-created query and begin working on it as though it was a new query in progress.

Each OR line (each line within the query) is evaluated separately, so that all the records that are returned by a single line will appear in the final results. If you want to combine several different criteria, make sure that each OR line represents one aspect of what you're searching.

For example, in the Volunteers database, querying which people joined before June 1, 2009 and after December 31, 2007 requires the OR condition, and using an OR condition means that the criteria go on separate lines.

Imagine, however, that you want to find only the people who joined within that range of dates but who also live in a particular state or are considered Active. For such a query to work, you need to repeat the date-range information on each OR line.

To set up this query, you need criteria on separate lines:

- ✔ One line asks for people who joined within a range of dates (Active Date).
- ✔ The other Criteria line gives you people by State or Status field.

Because the criteria are on different lines, Access treats them as a big OR statement. Figure 13-6 shows this combination of AND and OR operators in action.

When reviewing your query criteria, keep these points in mind:

- ✔ Separately, make sure each line represents a group that you want included in the final answer.
- ✔ Check to be sure that the individual lines work together to give you the answer you're seeking:
  - • AND criteria all go on the same line and are evaluated together.
  - • OR criteria go on separate lines. Each line is evaluated separately.
  - • Criteria that you want to use in each OR statement must be repeated on each separate line in the query grid.

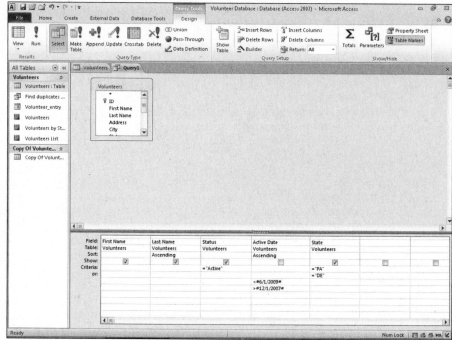

Figure 13-6:
Any criteria
placed on
separate
lines are
seen as OR
statements.

Chapter 14

Queries That Think Faster Than You

In This Chapter

▶ Doing more with the Total row

▶ Uncovering the Total row in your query grid

▶ Organizing with Group By

▶ Summing your results

▶ Counting everything at one time

▶ Exploring the ins and outs of `Where`

*E*ver need to know how many orders were placed in the past month? Or total dollar sales for last year? How about the top ten best-selling products for the current year? If you answered yes to any of these questions (or have similar questions that need answering), then this chapter is for you. Here I discuss the ever-wonderful Total row. The Total row slices, dices, and makes julienne fries out of your data! Well, actually, it summarizes your data via the select query. (If you don't know what a select query is or how to create one, I suggest you go back and read Chapter 12 before beginning the material in this chapter.)

Kissing That Calculator Goodbye via the Total Row

In Chapter 12, I show you how simple select queries can fetch data, such as a list of customers who reside in California or all the details of tofu sales. The Total row takes the select query one step further and summarizes the selected data. The Total row can answer questions such as, "How many of our customers reside in California?" and "How much money did we make in tofu sales last month?" It can also do statistical calculations, such as standard deviations, variances, and maximum and minimum values. For a complete list of what the Total row can do, see Table 14-1.

To compel Access to perform these calculations, you must first group your records together by using the Total row's Group By function. (The Total row makes an appearance in Figure 14-1.) As you might imagine, Group By treats multiple repeated instances of information as one. It puts all the Californians together on one row so you can count the number of Californians in your database. Typically you apply Group By to a text or ID field and the remaining functions in the Total row on numeric fields.

Totals button

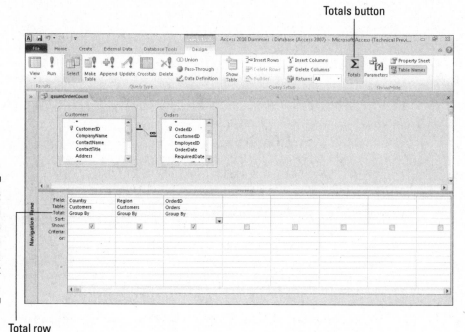

Figure 14-1:
The Total row appears between the Table and the Sort rows.

Total row

Table 14-1	Total Row Functions
Function	*What It Does*
Group By	Groups the query results by the field's values.
Sum	Totals all the values from this field in the query results.
Avg	Averages the values in this field in your query results.
Min	Tells you the lowest value found in the field.

Function	What It Does
Max	Reports the highest value found in the field.
Count	Counts the number of records that match the query criteria.
StDev	Figures the statistical standard deviation of the values in the field.
Var	Calculates the statistical variance of the values in the field.
First	Displays the first record that meets the query criteria.
Last	Displays the last record that meets the query criteria.
Expression	Tells Access that you want a calculated field. (See Chapter 15 for the different calculations Access can perform.)
Where	Uses this field for record-selection criteria but doesn't summarize anything with it.

The most commonly used items among the Total row's offerings are Group By, Sum, Avg, Count, and the odd-sounding option Where. Later sections in this chapter go into more depth about these items — explaining what they do, how to use them, and why you really *do* care about all this stuff.

Adding the Total Row to Your Queries

By default, Access always assumes you want a simple select query. You must tell it specifically that you want to summarize your data; adding the Total row to your query does the trick.

Okay, enough chatter about the Total row; it's time to get busy. Make sure you're in Design view, and then follow these steps to create summary queries with the Total row:

1. **Create a new select query or open an existing select query that contains the data you want to summarize.**

   If you're scratching your head at this point, go to Chapter 12 for an explanation of creating select queries.

2. **Turn on the Total row by clicking the Totals button in the Show/Hide group of the Ribbon's Query Tools tab.**

   The Total row appears between the Table and Sort rows on the query grid. For every field already in your query, Access automatically fills the Total row with its default entry, Group By.

   The Totals button displays the Greek letter sigma (Σ). Mathematicians, engineers, and others with questionable communication skills use this symbol when they mean "give me a total."

3. **To change a field's Total entry from Group By to something else, click that field's Total row.**

   The blinking-line cursor appears in the Total row, right next to a down-arrow button.

4. **Click the down-arrow button in the field's Total row and then select the new Total entry you want from the drop-down menu that appears.**

   The new entry appears in the Total row.

5. **Make any other changes you want and then run the query.**

   With the Total line in action, the query results automatically include the summary (or summaries) you selected. How about that?

The following section shows how to use the most popular and useful Total row options.

Giving the Total Row a Workout

This section focuses on the most commonly used options in the Total row's toolbox: Group By, Sum, Count, and Where.

Unless you're a statistician or scientist, the information in this chapter should suffice for all your Total row needs. Even though we don't discuss standard deviations or variances, however, they work the same way as Sum or Count. Check the Access help system (press F1 on your keyboard) for more about the less popular Total row functions.

Most Total row options perform well by themselves, but they also work well with others. When you run multiple queries, try using several different options together to save yourself time. It takes some practice to ensure that everything works the way you want, but the benefits (more information with less effort) make up for the investment.

Organizing things with Group By

The Group By instruction has two functions:

- To organize your query results into groups based on the values in one or more fields.
- To eliminate duplicate entries in your results.

When you turn on the Total row in your query grid, Access automatically puts in a Group By for every field on the grid. Group By combines like records so that the other Total row instructions (such as Sum and Count) can do their thing. So to make effective use of the Total row, your query must return one or more fields that contain duplicate information across records.

✔ Putting a single Group By instruction in a query tells Access to total your results by each unique value in that field (by each customer number or product name, for instance). Each unique item appears only once in the results, on a single line with its summary info.

✔ If you include more than one Group By instruction in a single query (such as the one shown in Figure 14-2), Access uses the Group By instruction to build a summary line for every unique combination of the fields.

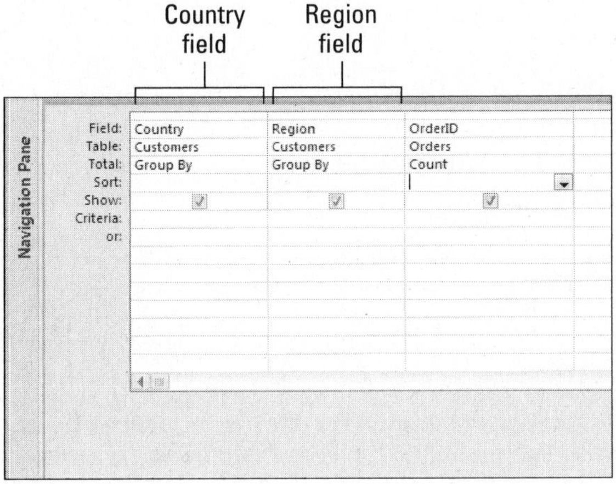

Country field   Region field

Figure 14-2: This query counts the number of orders for every combination of data in the Country and Region fields.

Put the Group By instruction into the field you want to summarize — the one that answers the question, "What do you want to count *by?*" or "What needs totaling?" To count California customers (for example), group by state the `State` field in your table. To produce a list of total dollar sales by product within each state or province you need to group by the `State` and `Product` fields.

When you use Group By, Access sorts the results automatically, in an order based on the field you specified with the Group By instruction. If you put Group By in the `State/Province` field, for example, Access sorts your results alphabetically by the contents of that field. To override this behavior and choose a different sorting order, just use the Sort row in your query grid. Here's how:

1. **Choose the field that you want to sort everything by.**

2. **Put the appropriate sorting command (ascending or descending, depending on your needs) in that field's Sort row, as shown in Figure 14-3.**

   Access automatically organizes the query results in the right order.

Figure 14-3: Make Access sort your results the way you want with a quick click in the query grid's Sort row.

Field:	Country	Region	OrderID
Table:	Customers	Customers	Orders
Total:	Group By	Group By	Group By
Sort:			Descending
Show:	☑	☑	☑
Criteria:			
or:			

Performing sums

Sum finds the total value of numeric fields:

- ✔ When you put the Sum instruction in a field, Access totals the values in that field.

- ✔ If you use the Sum instruction all by itself in a query grid, Access calculates a grand total of the values in that field for the entire table.

- ✔ When you pair a Sum instruction with a Group By instruction (as shown in Figure 14-4), your results display a sum for each unique entry in the Group By field.

- ✔ Pair the Sum instruction with any other Total row option to get more than one summary for each line of your results. Count and Sum naturally go together, as do Sum and Avg (Average), Min (Minimum value) and Max (Maximum value).

To limit the range of the records totaled in Sum, use the Where instruction (described later in this chapter).

Don't see what you expect in your results?

Sometimes, when I run a summary query, a few lines are "missing." I expect to see them but they just aren't there. That begs the question "Why?" Usually it's because of the type of *join* between tables in my query. The default join is called an *inner join*, in which a row can only appear in the query if matching records exist in both tables. So for a customer to show up on an orders-count query that joins the Customer and Order tables, every customer must have at least one order in the Orders table. If I want a query to show customers who haven't placed an order yet, I have to change the type of join to an *outer* join, which will accommodate that condition.

To change join types between any two tables in a query (in my example above, the Customers and Orders tables), display the Join Properties dialog box by double-clicking the line that connects the two tables. You have to be good with the mouse on this one. If you miss the join line, nothing will happen. This can be one of those throw-a-brick-at-your-computer moments. However, don't despair. Just point to the line once again and double-click. If the tip of the mouse pointer is on the line, the Join Properties dialog box will pop up.

Read options 2 and 3 carefully and select whichever one is appropriate for your situation. Each option will create an outer join. In the example given previously, the option that reads "2: Include ALL records from 'Customers' and only those records from 'Orders' where the joined fields are equal" would be correct. This option displays all customers, regardless of their order situation. So I'll see 0 next to each customer who has yet to order — plus an order count next to those who have ordered.

Adding a sum instruction

Field:	CustomerID	CompanyName	ProductID	Quantity
Table:	Customers	Customers	Order Details	Order Details
Total:	Group By	Group By	Group By	Sum
Sort:				Descending
Show:	✓	✓	✓	✓
Criteria:				
or:				

Figure 14-4: Put the Sum instruction in a numeric field so it has something to work with.

Counting, the easy way

Use the Count instruction in the query when you want to know how many entries are in the group, instead of performing mathematical calculations on numeric fields for the group.

Because Count doesn't attempt any math on a field's data, it works on a field of any data type in your tables.

When used by itself in a query (as shown in Figure 14-5), Count tallies the number of entries in a particular field across every record in the entire table and then displays the answer. By using Count with one or more Group By instructions in other fields, Access counts the number of items relating to each unique entry in the Group By field.

Figure 14-5:
Use Count on a single field to easily count the records in a table.

For a quick and accurate count of the number of records in a group, point the Group By and Count instructions at the same field in your query grid, as shown in Figure 14-6. To be part of the group, the records need matching data in a certain field. Because you *know* that the field for your Group By instruction contains something (namely, the data that defines groups for the query results), that field is a perfect candidate for the Count instruction as well. Add the field to your query grid a second time by choosing the same field name again — in a new column — and then selecting Count in the Total row.

Apply a calculation to a field and Access tacks on a newfangled word such as *SumOf* or *CountOf* or *<insert calculation name here>Of* to the beginning of the field name in Datasheet view. To insert your own (more meaningful) column heading, type the heading followed by a colon (as in `Order Count:`) in front of the field name on the query grid (see Figure 14-7).

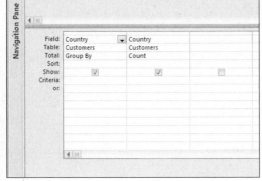

Figure 14-6:
This query counts the customers in each country.

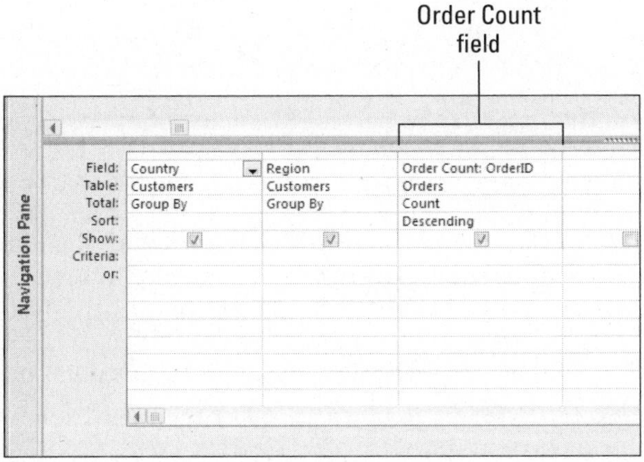

Order Count field

Figure 14-7:
The Order Count column heading is added to the count of the OrderID field.

Narrowing the results with Where

The Where instruction works a bit differently from the other options in the Total row. The Where instruction lets you add criteria to the query (such as showing customers from certain states, or including orders placed only after a certain date) without including additional fields in your results. In fact, Access won't allow you to show a field in your query results that contains the Where instruction.

The query in Figure 14-8 uses a Where instruction to limit which records appear in the query results. Normally that query would count orders by customer, using every record in the table. Adding a Where instruction to the Country field tells the query that it must test the data before including it in the results. In this case, the Where instruction's criteria include records for those people living in the United States or Great Britain. (The data in Country matches either USA or UK.)

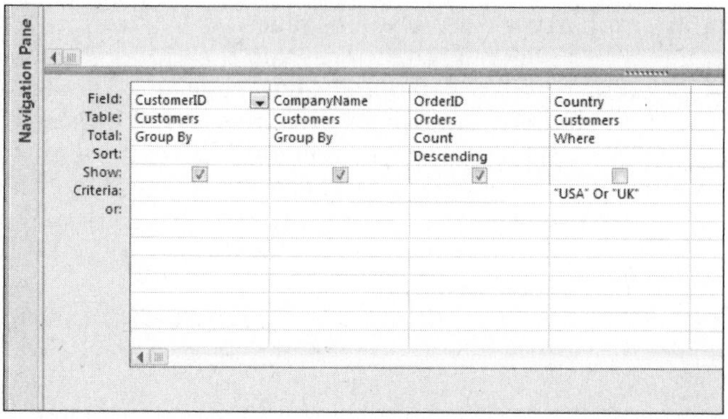

Figure 14-8:
This Where instruction counts the number of USA and UK orders by customer.

Creating Your Own Top-Ten List

Here's a problem that is a snap to solve with Access: Suppose you need a list of your top ten customers, ranked by dollar sales. Or a list of the top five best-selling products last year. Or a list of the top whatever. The query property Top Values takes all the dirty work out of this chore. Simply set it and forget it — the dirty work that is! You can return the top values (for instance, the top 5 out of a list of 40) or top percentage of values (say, the top 5% which returns the top 2 out of 40) with the Top Values properly.

Follow these instructions to make a top-ten (or whatever number you choose) list:

1. **Open the query containing the data for your top-values list in Design view.**

   The query must contain at least one numerical field so that a set of top values can be selected. Usually it's a summary query, such as total dollar sales by customer. The query must be sorted on the numerical field.

2. **From the Design tab on the Ribbon, locate the Return tool in the Query Setup group of tools.**

3. **Click the drop-down list arrow next to the Return tool and select a choice from the list or type your own number in the box.**

   Because 10 isn't on the list, you'll have to type **10** in the box to generate a top-ten list. (See Figure 14-9.)

4. **Switch to Datasheet view.**

   The list is limited to the range of top values determined by the number or percentage you entered in the box.

The Top Values property returns the top values for whatever column is sorted first in the query. If you tell Access to show you the top ten customers in dollar sales based on a field called DolAmount, you won't get them unless you sort on the DolAmount field. Choose Descending in the Sort row of the DolAmount field to have Access order them for you from highest to lowest.

Return tool

Figure 14-9:
Setting the
Top Values
property
to 10.

Choosing the Right Field for the Summary Instruction

Deciding which field gets a Sum, Count, or other Total row instruction *greatly* affects your query results. If you choose the wrong field, Access fails to tally things correctly.

Follow these guidelines when choosing fields for your summary queries:

✔ Don't apply summary functions that require numbers to calculate (such as Sum and Avg) to a text field. You'll get the ever-popular `Data type mismatch` error message if you do.

✔ Fields with repetitive information (such as order date or customer ID) make excellent Group By fields. For example, if you group by order date and count the customer ID field, you get a count of orders per day.

✔ When counting records, choose a field that contains data for each record. If you don't, Access excludes the blank fields in its count.

To see the kinds of miscues that can happen, check out Figure 14-10. There you'll see a summary query that has been written to count customers. The Count instruction has been applied to both the `Region` and `CustomerID` fields of the Customers table. The `Region` field returns 29, while the `CustomerID` field returns 82. Which is right? The latter is correct because each record in the table has a customer ID. Not every record has a region specified. Therefore Access counts only the records for which a value appears in the `Region` field for a customer. Choose your fields wisely to avoid this problem.

Figure 14-10:
The Region
and
CustomerID
fields
counted.
Huh?

The Totals row takes some getting used to. But in no time, you'll master the power of this tool in your queries. When that day comes, say goodbye to your old friends, Mr. Spreadsheet and Mr. Calculator, forever!

Chapter 15

Calculating with Your Data

. . . .

In This Chapter

▶ Developing an expression

▶ Performing complex calculations

▶ Calculating text fields

▶ Using the Expression Builder

. . . .

*E*fficient database design requires that tables contain only necessary fields. Too many fields can cause a table to load slowly — you won't notice the difference with a few hundred records, but you certainly will with a few hundred thousand. Too many fields can also eat up precious disk space. So what fields are often added unnecessarily to a table's design? The short answer: Fields that could be generated from calculations on data stored in other fields.

For example, suppose you have a Products table with a `Unit Price` field and an Orders table with `Number of Units Ordered` field. You may be tempted to add an `Amount` field to your Orders table that stores the result of multiplying unit price times quantity ordered. This is unnecessary because Access can perform these calculations on the fly — in what's called a calculated field.

A *calculated field* takes information from another field in the database and performs some arithmetic to come up with new information. Access calls the arithmetic formula used to perform the calculation an *expression*. In fact, a calculated field can take data from more than one field and combine information to create an entirely new field if that's what you want. You can perform simple arithmetic (such as addition and multiplication) or use Access's built-in functions, such as Sum and Avg (average), for more difficult calculations. (For more on using the built-in functions, see Chapter 14.)

In this chapter, you build all kinds of calculations into your queries. From simple sums to complex equations, the information you need is right here.

Although the examples in this chapter deal with calculated fields in queries, the same concept applies to calculated fields in forms and reports.

A Simple Calculation

The first step in creating a calculated field in a query is to include the tables that contain the fields you need for your calculation. In the preceding example, the product unit price was in the Products table; the quantity ordered was in the Orders table. Therefore a query to calculate unit price multiplied by product price must include information from both the Products and Orders tables. Access can't pull the numbers out of thin air for the calculation; you must make sure the fields that contain the numbers you need are present in your query.

Access uses a special syntax for building calculated fields. Here's how to create a calculated field:

1. **Click an empty column in the Field row of the query grid.**

   The good old cursor will blink in the row. Access puts the results of the calculation in the same grid position as the calculation itself, so if the calculation sits in the third column of your query grid, the calculation's result will be in the third column, too.

2. **Enter a name for your calculation, followed by a colon (:).**

   Access will refer to this calculation from now on by whatever name you enter before the colon. Keep it short and sweet (say, **Amount** or **Tax**) so it's easier to refer to later on. If you don't name your calculation, Access will put the generic `Expr` (followed by a number) as its name. It has to be called something, so why not `Expr1` or `Expr2`, right?

3. **Enter your calculation, substituting field names for the actual numbers where necessary.**

   My `Amount` calculated field would look something like (well, *exactly* like) the calculation in Figure 15-1.

You don't have to use only field names in your calculations. You can also enter formulas with numbers, like this:

```
Tax: Quantity * UnitPrice * .06
```

 If a field name contains more than one word, put square brackets around it. Access treats anything else it finds in the calculation as a constant (which is the math term for *it is what it is and it never changes*). If the field name contains no spaces, Access will put the square brackets in for you after you enter the field name. That's why I always use one-word field names — so I don't have to type those irritating square brackets.

Amount calculation

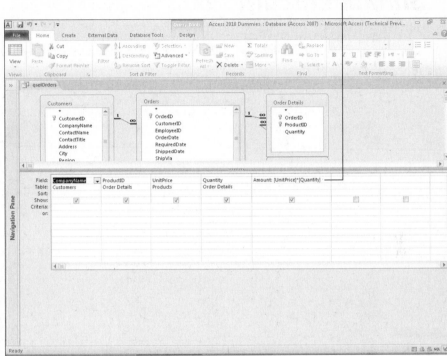

Figure 15-1:
The Amount
calculation.

When you create formulas, keep these general guidelines in mind:

✔ **You must type the field names and constants into your formula.** You can't just drag and drop stuff from the table list.

✔ **Don't worry if your calculation grows past the edge of the Field box.** Access still remembers everything in your formula, even if it doesn't appear on-screen.

To make the query column wider, aim the mouse pointer at the line on the right side of the thin bar above the calculation entry. When you get it right over the line, the pointer changes into a line with a horizontal arrow through it. When that happens, click and drag the mouse to the right. As you do, the column expands according to your movements. To fit the width to just the right size, position the mouse to size the column as described earlier — and then double-click!

✔ **If it's a really, really, really long calculation, press Shift+F2 while the cursor is somewhere on the calculation.**

This opens the Zoom dialog box so you can easily see and edit everything in a pop-up window.

When you run a query containing a calculation, Access

✔ Produces a datasheet showing the fields you specified.

✔ Adds a new column for each calculated field.

In Figure 15-2, the datasheet shows the Company Name, Product, Unit Price, Quantity, and the calculated field Amount for each item ordered.

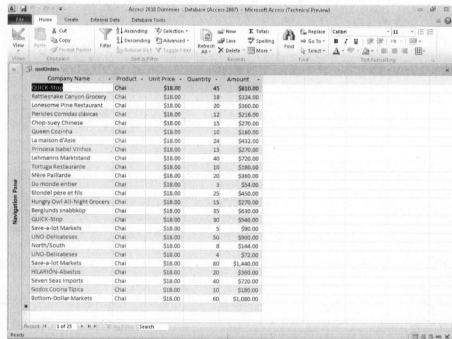

Figure 15-2:
The results
of the
amount
calculation
in Datasheet
view.

Complex Calculations

After getting the hang of simple calculations, you can easily expand your repertoire into more powerful operations, such as using multiple calculations and building expressions that use values from other calculations in the same query. This stuff really adds to the flexibility and power of queries.

Keep your calculations in order

You've written your formula and don't see the answer you expect to see. You double check the formula and it seems correct. How can the formula be correct yet the result wrong? If you have more than one mathematical operation in a calculated expression, Access will follow these rules (called the *order of operations*) when determining the results of your expression.

✔ All operations in parentheses are calculated first.

✔ Exponents (^) are calculated second.

✔ Multiplication (*) and division (/) are calculated third.

✔ Addition (+) and subtraction (−) are calculated fourth.

For example, you might expect the formula 2+3*6 to equal 30. However, due to the order of operations (multiplication before addition), Access will return 20. To make Access generate the expected result, the formula must be entered as (2+3)*6.

Calculate until you need calculate no more!

Access makes it easy to put multiple separate calculations into a single query. After building the first calculation, just repeat the process in the next empty Field box. Keep inserting calculations across the query grid until you've calculated everything you need.

You can use the same field in several calculations. Access doesn't mind at all.

Using one calculation in another

One of the most powerful calculated-field tricks involves using the solution from one calculated field as part of another calculation *in the same query*. This is sometimes called a *nested* calculation, and it can do two useful tricks:

✔ It creates a field in the query results.

✔ It supplies data to other calculations in the same query, just as if it were a real field in the table.

Figure 15-3 shows an example of a nested calculation in Design view.

Tax calculation

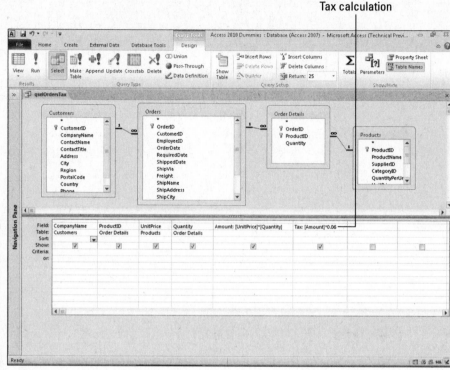

Figure 15-3:
The Amount
Calculated
column is
referred to
in the Tax
Calculated
column.

Figure 15-4 shows the actual results of the calculations.

Although this technique seems simple, tread carefully. A small error in one calculation can quickly trickle down to other calculations that are based on it, compounding a simple error into a huge mistake.

To use the results from one calculation as part of another, just use the name of the first calculation as if it were a field name. In short, treat the first calculation like a field in your table.

Using parameter queries to ask for help

At times, you may want to include a value in a formula that doesn't exist anywhere in your database (for example, the number .06 for a 6 percent tax rate in the calculation example earlier in this chapter). If you know the value, you can type it directly into the formula.

Figure 15-4:
The results
of the
Amount
Calculated
and Tax
Calculated
columns.

Company Name	Product	Unit Price	Quantity	Amount	Tax
QUICK-Stop	Chai	$18.00	45	$810.00	$48.60
Rattlesnake Canyon Grocery	Chai	$18.00	18	$324.00	$19.44
Lonesome Pine Restaurant	Chai	$18.00	20	$360.00	$21.60
Pericles Comidas clásicas	Chai	$18.00	12	$216.00	$12.96
Chop-suey Chinese	Chai	$18.00	15	$270.00	$16.20
Queen Cozinha	Chai	$18.00	10	$180.00	$10.80
La maison d'Asie	Chai	$18.00	24	$432.00	$25.92
Princesa Isabel Vinhos	Chai	$18.00	15	$270.00	$16.20
Lehmanns Marktstand	Chai	$18.00	40	$720.00	$43.20
Tortuga Restaurante	Chai	$18.00	10	$180.00	$10.80
Mère Paillarde	Chai	$18.00	20	$360.00	$21.60
Du monde entier	Chai	$18.00	3	$54.00	$3.24
Blondel père et fils	Chai	$18.00	25	$450.00	$27.00
Hungry Owl All-Night Grocers	Chai	$18.00	15	$270.00	$16.20
Berglunds snabbköp	Chai	$18.00	35	$630.00	$37.80
QUICK-Stop	Chai	$18.00	30	$540.00	$32.40
Save-a-lot Markets	Chai	$18.00	5	$90.00	$5.40
LINO-Delicateses	Chai	$18.00	50	$900.00	$54.00
North/South	Chai	$18.00	8	$144.00	$8.64
LINO-Delicateses	Chai	$18.00	4	$72.00	$4.32
Save-a-lot Markets	Chai	$18.00	80	$1,440.00	$86.40
HILARIÓN-Abastos	Chai	$18.00	20	$360.00	$21.60
Seven Seas Imports	Chai	$18.00	40	$720.00	$43.20
Godos Cocina Típica	Chai	$18.00	10	$180.00	$10.80
Bottom-Dollar Markets	Chai	$18.00	60	$1,080.00	$64.80

But what if the number changes all the time? You don't want to constantly alter a query; that's a big waste of time and effort. Instead of building the ever-changing number into your formula, why not make Access *ask* you for the number (called a *parameter*) when you run the query? This is an easy one:

1. **Think of an appropriate name for the value (such as Tax Rate, Last Price, or Discount).**

   When choosing a name for your parameter, don't use the name of an existing field in your table — Access will ignore the parameter if you do. Instead, go with something that describes the number or value itself. As you can see in the query grid shown in Figure 15-5, entering something like [Enter discount percentage as decimal] makes it very clear what is required from the user. When you look at this query months (or even years) from now, you can easily recognize that something called [Enter discount percentage as decimal] probably is a value that Access asks for when the query runs, not a normal field.

2. **Use the name in your formula as if it were a regular field.**

   Put square brackets around it and place it into your calculation, just as you did with the other fields.

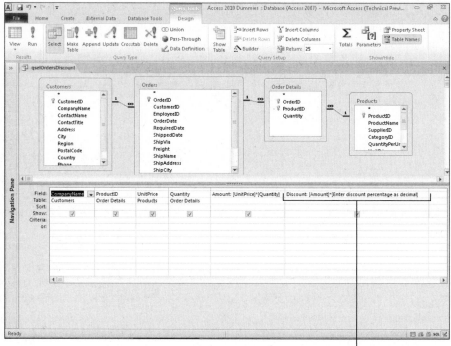

Figure 15-5: The discount parameter in the Discount Amount calculated field.

Discount Parameter

3. Run the query.

Access displays a dialog box like the one shown in Figure 15-6.

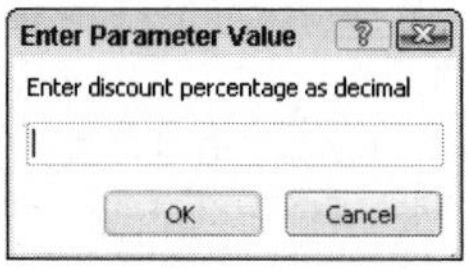

Figure 15-6: Access asks for a discount.

Enter Parameter Value

Enter discount percentage as decimal

[OK]   [Cancel]

4. Enter the prompted information.

For this example, just enter the value of your discount (as a decimal value). Access does the rest.

This option means you can use the same query with different values to see how changing that value affects your results.

Daisy-chaining your words with text formulas

Number fields aren't the only fields you can use in formulas. Access can also use the *words stored in text fields.*

A classic formula comes from working with names. If you have a Contacts table with `FirstName` and `LastName` fields, you will at some point want to string those names together on a form or report. A text formula can do this for you. It can add the first name to the last name; the result is the person's full name in one column.

The syntax for text-field formulas is similar to the syntax for number-field formulas — the field name is still surrounded by square brackets and must be carefully entered by hand. Include literal text in the formula (such as spaces or punctuation) by surrounding it with quotation marks (for example, you'd type `","` to insert a comma).

You connect text fields with the ampersand character (`&`). Microsoft calls the ampersand the *concatenation operator,* which is a fancy way to say that it connects things.

Figure 15-7 shows a text-field formula. This example solves the problem I describe earlier in this section: making one name out of the pieces in two separate fields. The formula shown in the figure combines the `FirstName` and `LastName` fields into a single full name, ready to appear on a mailing label, report, or some other useful purpose you devise.

This formula consists of the `FirstName` field, an ampersand (`&`), a single space inside quotation marks, followed by another ampersand, and then the `LastName` field. Here's what it looks like:

```
[FirstName]&" "&[LastName]
```

When you run this query, Access takes the information from the two fields and puts them together, inserting the space between them so they don't run straight into each other. Figure 15-8 shows the results of this query.

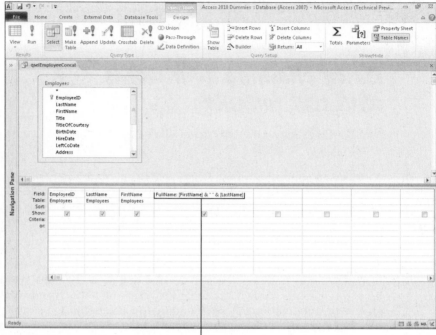

Figure 15-7:
Turning two
names into
a single
calculated
field.

FullName calculation

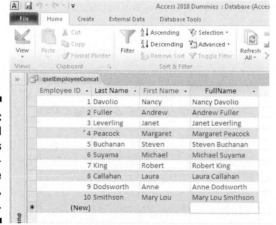

Figure 15-8:
First and
last names
are com-
bined to the
single field,
FullName.

Expression Builder (Somewhat) to the Rescue

Creating calculated fields presents you with two basic challenges:

- ✔ Figuring out what the formula should say
- ✔ Entering the formula in a way that Access recognizes

Although Access can't help you with the first problem, it tries hard to offer some assistance with the second. When all else fails, and you just can't assemble a calculated field exactly the way Access wants it, click the Builder button on the Design tab of the Ribbon to open the Expression Builder (see Figure 15-9).

Figure 15-9:
The Builder button launches our good friend the Expression Builder.

Launch the Expression Builder.

The Expression Builder has several parts, as shown in Figure 15-10.

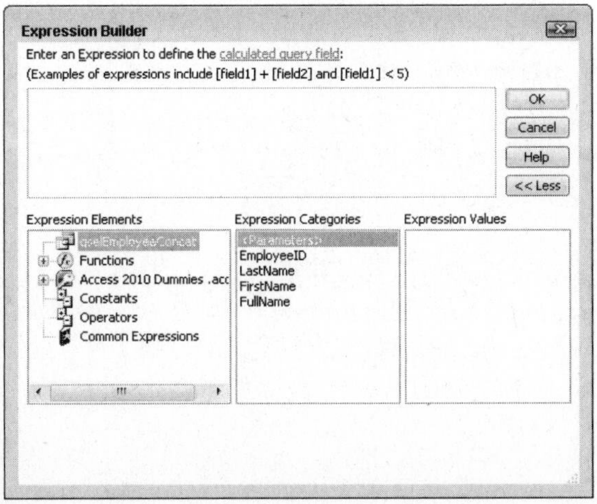

Figure 15-10:
Expression Builder in all its easy-to-use glory.

✔ You create the expression in the big window at the top.

✔ The lower half of the dialog box contains three lists that work as a team:

- The Expression Elements list provides a navigational tree containing all the items that are at your disposal to build an expression such as tables, queries, forms, reports, constants, functions, and operators.

  You'll find the tables, queries, forms and report objects within your database under an Expression Element with the same name as the name of your database. For example, if you want to select an Orders table field and you're in a database named Access 2010 Dummies.accdb, you'll see an item with that name on the Expression Elements list. Expand that item by clicking the plus sign (+) next to it to see the Tables item. Expand the Tables item to see the list of tables. Click the Orders table to see the fields in the Expression Categories list. Double-click the desired field to add it to the expression.

- When you click something in the Expression Elements list (such as Operators), the Expression Categories list populates with the categories within the selected element.

- When you click a category in the Expression Categories list (such as Comparison), the Expression Values list populates with the items within the selected category that finally (whew!), you can use in your expression.

✔ Near the bottom of the Expression Elements list, Access also includes a few items for the Truly Technical Person — including these:

- Constants (values that never change, such as *true* and *false*).

- Operators that are available for comparisons and formulas:

  The Arithmetic category contains operators for addition, subtraction, division, and multiplication.

  The Comparison category contains operators such as =, >, <, <>

  Use comparisons to develop expressions for the Criteria section of your queries, when you need a response of *True* or *False*.

  The Logical category contains logical operators such as And, Or, and Not.

  The String category contains the Ampersand (&) operator that is used to combine two text fields.

- A folder called Common Expressions, which contains stuff that makes sense only when you're building a report.

Don't rely on Expression Builder

In theory, Expression Builder walks you through the frustrating syntax of building a calculation (what Access calls an *expression*) that meets all the nitpicky requirements Access puts in place. Although Microsoft gave Expression Builder a facelift for Access 2010, its functionality is essentially the same as in previous versions of Access: It does present you with the tools to build the formula, but you have to wade through lists of every object, field, control, and function in the database to find what you need. What would be helpful is limiting each list to just those items that will work for the current situation. (Just show me fields and functions I can use in my current query. Don't show me fields from unrelated tables, queries, forms, and reports that will just generate an error if used.)

I find Expression Builder helpful for locating a list of built-in Access functions or for referring to a field properly in an expression — but beyond that, it isn't much help. For me, it's faster to type my numerical operators instead of clicking those operators from a list in Expression Builder.

Before resorting to Expression Builder, try a little troubleshooting on your own. If your formulas don't work the way you think they should, double-check the spelling of every field. Most problems come from simple field-name spelling errors. If all else fails and you're feeling adventurous, then give Expression Builder a try. With any luck, it might actually solve your problem.

Expression Builder works like a big calculator crossed with a word processor:

- ✔ At the bottom, double-click items in the Expression Categories or Expression Values lists (depending on the situation) to include them in your expression at the top.
- ✔ Click anywhere in the big pane on top; then type whatever you feel like typing.

Expression Builder can refer to controls on a form in your query so you can easily control the criteria used to run the query. Figure 15-11, for example, shows a simple form called Order Report with one combo box called Customer that lists all customers in the Customers table.

Figure 15-12 shows how the Expression Builder finds and uses the combo box on the form.

Finally, Figure 15-13 shows the expression in the Criteria row of the Order Report query. So how does all this work? Open the form and select a customer. Run the query and the query will be limited to just the orders for the customer selected on the form. Cool, huh?

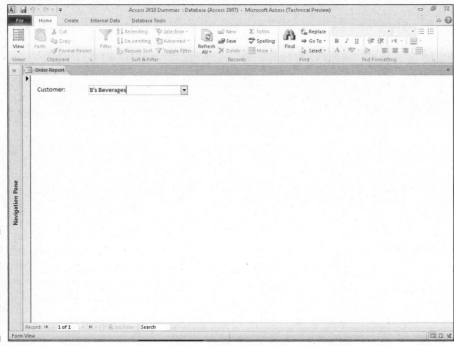

Figure 15-11:
The Order
Report form
with the
Customer
combo box.

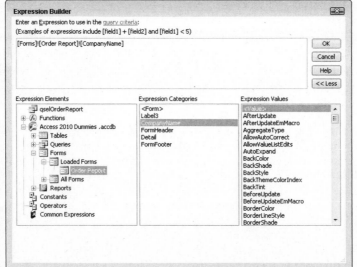

Figure 15-12:
The
Expression
Builder is
used to
select the
Company
Name
combo
box from
the Order
Report form.

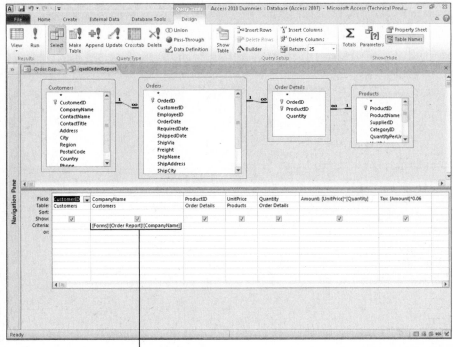

Figure 15-13: The expression as it appears in the Criteria row of the Order Report query.

Criteria expression

Chapter 16

Flying into Action Queries

In This Chapter

▶ Updating multiple records that match specific criteria

▶ Adding records from one table into another table

▶ Deleting multiple records that match specific criteria

*E*ver have to change data the same way on multiple records in a table? How about moving data from a linked spreadsheet into an existing Access table? What about deleting a certain group of records from a table? If you answered yes to any of these questions, then this chapter is for you. *Action queries* perform a specific task on a group of records in a table, all in one fell swoop, so you don't have to add or update each record manually. (Now, try to control your excitement! If you ever get into the situation where an action query is needed, I know you'll thank me for writing this.)

The three most common action queries are

▸ **Update:** This query updates the value in a field for the records you select via the Criteria row. For example, if an employee keyed in the wrong order date of 11/2/2009 on 25 orders, an update query would allow you to easily update all 25 order dates to the correct date of 11/3/2009.

▸ **Append:** Use this query type to add records from one table to another. For example, your credit card company gives you monthly expense transactions in an Excel spreadsheet and you need to input the expenses into your Access database Expense table. You can link or import (See Chapter 8 for details) the spreadsheet into your Access database then use an append query to add the records to your Expense table.

▸ **Delete:** If you are in a destructive mood, use this query to delete groups of records from a table. Suppose you work for a company that has discontinued a product as of 12/1/09 — and customers were notified that any order dated after 12/1 for delivery of the discontinued product would be deleted. Okay, they were warned; you can use a Delete query to eliminate all orders for the discontinued product that have delivery dates after 12/1/09.

The action queries described in this chapter will alter data in your database PERMANENTLY. Although they're beneficial when used correctly, they can wreak havoc if used incorrectly. The results of running an action query cannot be undone. Therefore you'd be wise to back up your data before you run *any* action query!

Easy Update

The *Update query* can replace the value in a field in a group of records with another value. To create an Update query, first you need to determine the table (and the field within it) in need of updating — and decide how you want to update that field. When you've figured that out, do this:

1. **Select the Create tab on the Ribbon.**

   The Create tools appear on-screen. Notice the Queries group toward the left side of the Ribbon.

2. **Click the Query Design tool from the Queries group (see Figure 16-1).**

   A new query opens in Design view and the Show Table dialog box pops up.

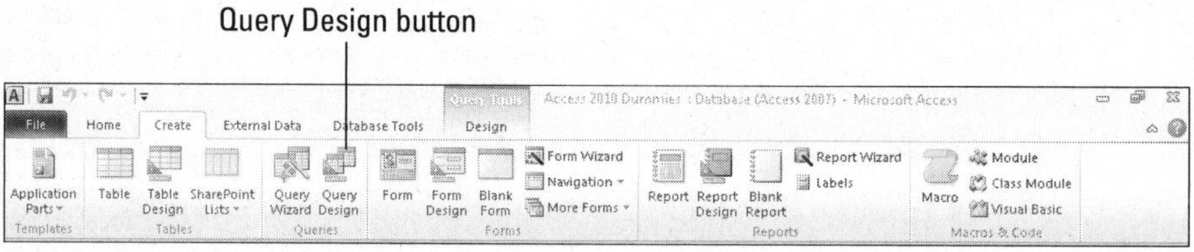

Query Design button

Figure 16-1:
Click the
Query
Design
button from
the Ribbon.

3. **Select the table that contains the field you'd like to update; then click the Add button.**

   The selected table is added to the top half of the Query Design window, as Figure 16-2 illustrates.

4. **Click the Close button in the Show Table window.**

   The Show Table window closes.

5. **From the Table field list, double-click the field name that the query will update along with any fields you'll need to write criteria.**

   The fields are added to the bottom half of the Query Design window (see Figure 16-3).

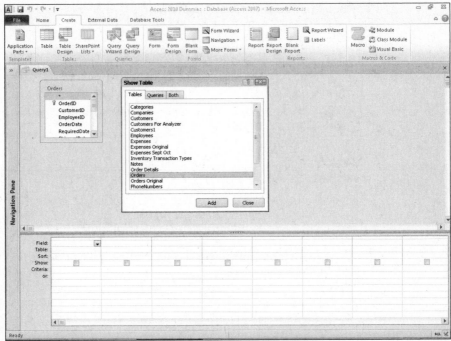

Figure 16-2:
Click the
Add button
to add the
Orders table
to the query.

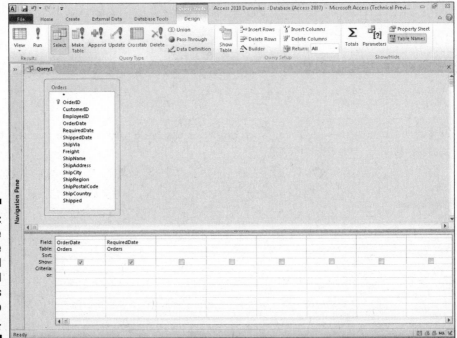

Figure 16-3:
The
OrderDate
and
Required
Date fields
as added to
the query.

6. **Click the Design tab on the Ribbon.**

   The Ribbon displays the design tools, including the Query Type group.

7. **Select the Update tool from the Query Type group.**

   The Update To row appears on the query grid, as Figure 16-4 illustrates.

8. **In the Update To row of the field you want updated, enter a value or expression to update the field.**

   The Update To row can contain a static value such as a date (12/1/2009), an expression such as Date()+10, or the name of a field such as [RequiredDate].

   If you're not sure what you can enter in the Update To row, make sure the cursor is in the row and click the Builder button from the Design Tab of the Ribbon. Expression Builder shows you your options and helps with syntax.

9. **In the Criteria row, enter the criteria that will select the records you'd like updated.**

   The query in Figure 16-5 puts the required date in the ShippedDate field for those orders required on 5/30/2008 or 5/31/2008.

Update button

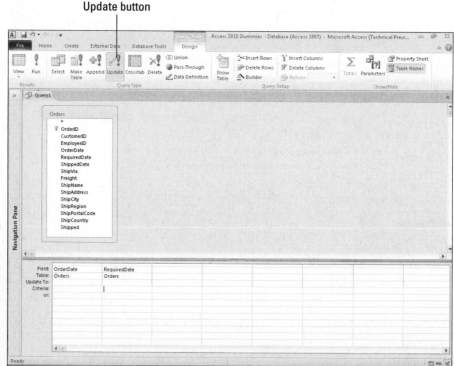

Figure 16-4: Select the Update tool on the Ribbon and the Update To row appears.

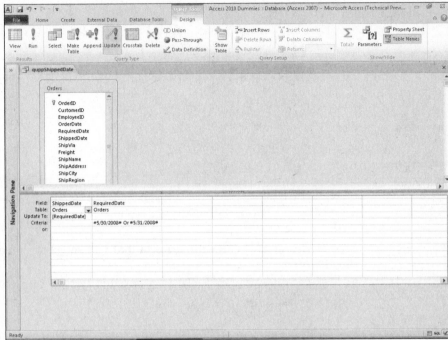

Figure 16-5:
This query
will update
the Shipped
Date field.

10. **Click the Run from the Ribbon's Results Group to run the query and update the records.**

    A message box (see Figure 16-6) appears, telling you how many records will be updated.

Figure 16-6:
Click Yes to
update your
data.

11. **Click Yes in the message box window to run the query and update your data.**

    Figure 16-7 shows the state of things before you run an update and Figure 16-8 shows what changes an update has wrought.

Update queries will update the data you specify — but the update can't be undone. Back up your data before you run Update queries — and use them with caution! Don't say I didn't warn you!

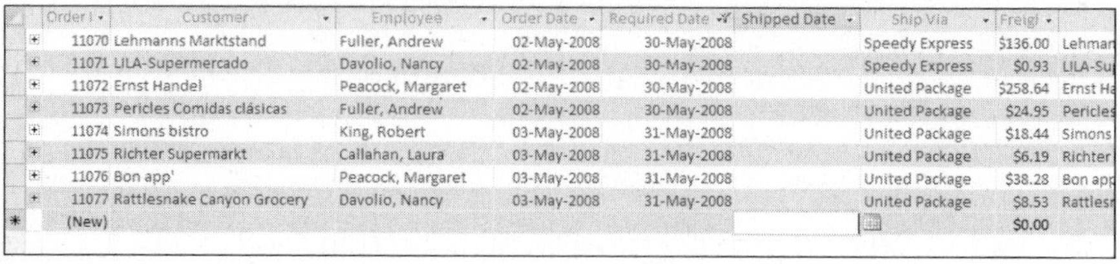

Figure 16-7:
The Shipped
Date field
before run-
ning the
Update
query.

Figure 16-7:
The Shipped
Date field
before run-
ning the
Update
query.

Order I	Customer	Employee	Order Date	Required Date	Shipped Date	Ship Via	Freigl	
11070	Lehmanns Marktstand	Fuller, Andrew	02-May-2008	30-May-2008		Speedy Express	$136.00	Lehman
11071	LILA-Supermercado	Davolio, Nancy	02-May-2008	30-May-2008		Speedy Express	$0.93	LILA-Su
11072	Ernst Handel	Peacock, Margaret	02-May-2008	30-May-2008		United Package	$258.64	Ernst Ha
11073	Pericles Comidas clásicas	Fuller, Andrew	02-May-2008	30-May-2008		United Package	$24.95	Pericles
11074	Simons bistro	King, Robert	03-May-2008	31-May-2008		United Package	$18.44	Simons
11075	Richter Supermarkt	Callahan, Laura	03-May-2008	31-May-2008		United Package	$6.19	Richter
11076	Bon app'	Peacock, Margaret	03-May-2008	31-May-2008		United Package	$38.28	Bon app
11077	Rattlesnake Canyon Grocery	Davolio, Nancy	03-May-2008	31-May-2008		United Package	$8.53	Rattles
(New)							$0.00	

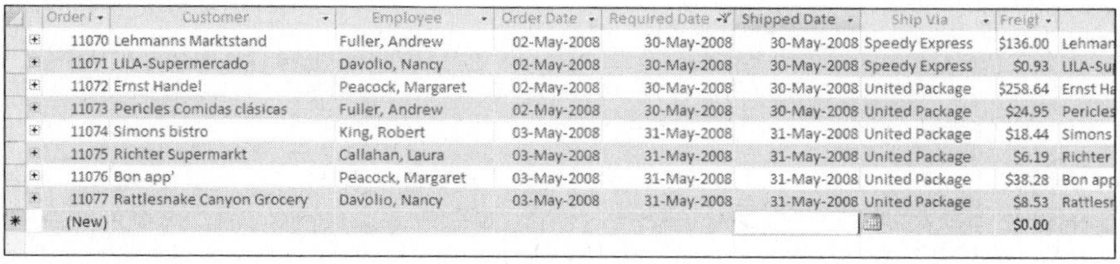

Figure 16-8:
The Shipped
Date field
after run-
ning the
update
query.

Order I	Customer	Employee	Order Date	Required Date	Shipped Date	Ship Via	Freigl	
11070	Lehmanns Marktstand	Fuller, Andrew	02-May-2008	30-May-2008	30-May-2008	Speedy Express	$136.00	Lehman
11071	LILA-Supermercado	Davolio, Nancy	02-May-2008	30-May-2008	30-May-2008	Speedy Express	$0.93	LILA-Su
11072	Ernst Handel	Peacock, Margaret	02-May-2008	30-May-2008	30-May-2008	United Package	$258.64	Ernst Ha
11073	Pericles Comidas clásicas	Fuller, Andrew	02-May-2008	30-May-2008	30-May-2008	United Package	$24.95	Pericles
11074	Simons bistro	King, Robert	03-May-2008	31-May-2008	31-May-2008	United Package	$18.44	Simons
11075	Richter Supermarkt	Callahan, Laura	03-May-2008	31-May-2008	31-May-2008	United Package	$6.19	Richter
11076	Bon app'	Peacock, Margaret	03-May-2008	31-May-2008	31-May-2008	United Package	$38.28	Bon app
11077	Rattlesnake Canyon Grocery	Davolio, Nancy	03-May-2008	31-May-2008	31-May-2008	United Package	$8.53	Rattlesr
(New)							$0.00	

Add Records in a Flash

Append queries add records from one table (called the *source table*) to another table (called the *destination*). A common use for an Append query is to add data from an external file (such as an imported or linked spreadsheet) to an existing Access table. To create an Append query, follow these steps:

1. **Select the Create tab on the Ribbon.**

   The Create tools appear on-screen. Notice the Queries group toward the left side of the Ribbon.

2. **Click the Query Design tool from the** Queries **group (as shown earlier in Figure 16-1).**

   A new query opens in Design view and the Show Table dialog box pops up.

3. **Select the table that contains the source data to be appended; then click the Add button.**

   The selected table is added to the top half of the Query Design window.

4. **Click the Close button in the Show Table window.**

   The Show Table window closes.

5. **From the Table field list double-click the field names that contain the data to be added to the destination table.**

   The fields are added to the bottom half of the Query Design window (see Figure 16-9).

6. **Click the Design tab on the Ribbon.**

   The Ribbon displays the Design tools, including the Query Type group.

7. **Select the Append tool from the Query Type group.**

   The Append dialog box appears, as Figure 16-10 illustrates.

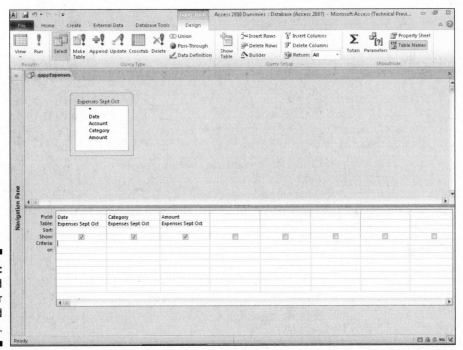

Figure 16-9: Selected fields for an Append query.

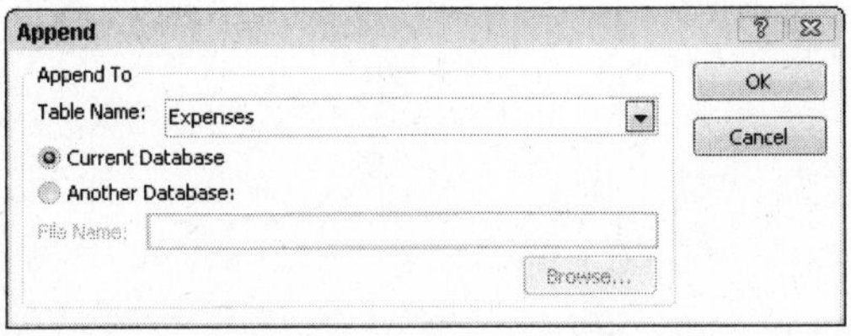

Figure 16-10: Say hello to the Append dialog box.

8. **Select the destination table from the Table Name drop-down list; then click OK to close the Append dialog box.**

   The Append To row appears in the query just above the Criteria row. If a source field name matches exactly a destination field name, the Append To row will pre-populate with each matching field name from the destination table.

   If the source and destination field names do not match for a specific field, the Append To row will not pre-populate with a field name from the destination table. To fix this, click in the Append To row with a missing destination field name. A drop-down arrow appears to the right. Select the matching destination field from the drop-down list.

9. **Write criteria if necessary to select just those records you want from the source table.**

   See Figure 16-11 for the completed Append query.

   In most cases, the source and destination fields must be of the same data type. For example, you cannot append data from a text field to a number field.

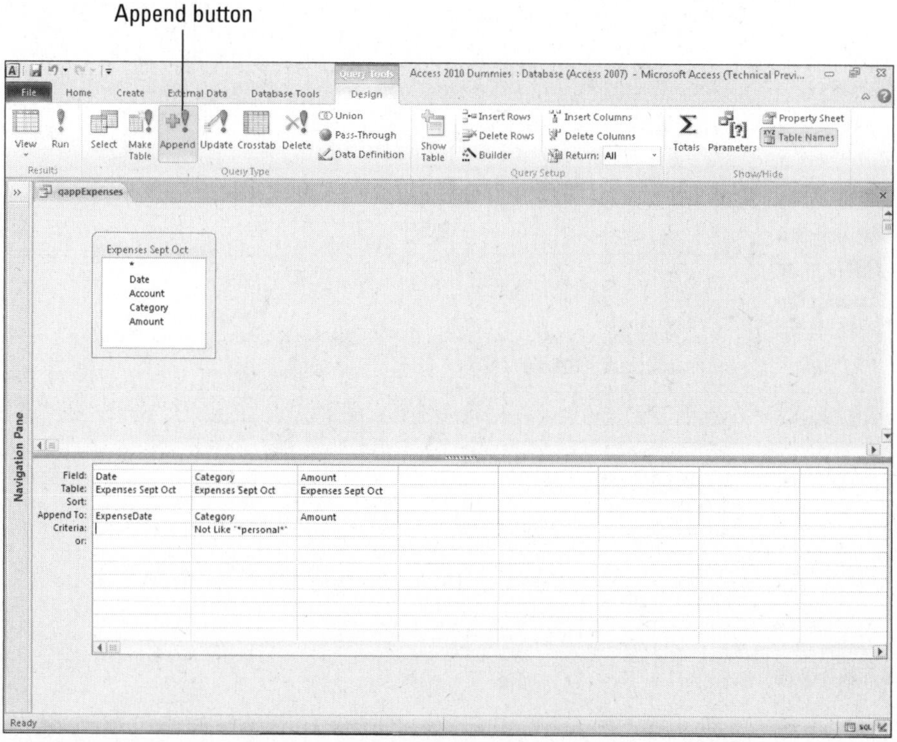

Append button

Figure 16-11:
This query
appends
all records
that don't
contain
"personal"
in the
Category
field.

10. **Click the Run button from the Ribbon's Results Group to run the query and append the records from the source table to the destination table.**

    A message box appears, telling you how many records will be added.

    When Append queries add records to the destination table, you cannot undo the results. Be sure to back up your database file before you run an Append query.

11. **Click Yes in the message-box window to run the query and add the records.**

    If you run an Append query in error, you can take one of two actions:

    ✔ Delete the appended records from the destination table manually (they will be near the bottom) or via a Delete query (see next section).

    ✔ Revert to your backup file, correct the problem, and try again.

Quick Cleanup

The *Delete* query can clean up unwanted records in a hurry. Of the three action queries that have been discussed in this chapter, the Delete query is the most dangerous: It can wipe out all the data in your table in an instant. Pay special attention to the selection criteria you write for a Delete query so you're sure you'll delete only the correct records. To build a Delete query, follow these steps:

1. **Select the Create tab on the Ribbon.**

    The Create tools appear on-screen. Notice the Queries group toward the left side of the Ribbon.

2. **Click the Query Design tool from the** Queries **group (as shown previously in Figure 16-1).**

    A new query opens in Design view and the Show Table dialog box pops up.

3. **Select the table that contains the source data to be deleted; then click the Add button.**

    The selected table is added to the top half of the Query Design window.

4. **Click the Close button in the Show Table window.**

    The Show Table window closes.

5. **From the Table field list double-click the asterisk (*) at the top of the list and any individual field names you intend to use for criteria.**

The fields will be added to the bottom half of the Query Design window.

6. **Click the Design tab on the Ribbon.**

The Ribbon displays the Design tools, including the Query Type group.

7. **Select the Delete tool from the Query Type group.**

The Delete row appears in the query grid, as pictured in Figure 16-12.

8. **Write criteria if necessary to select just those records you want to delete from the table.**

See Figure 16-13 for the completed Delete query.

If you don't write any criteria, every record in the selected table will be deleted!

Delete button

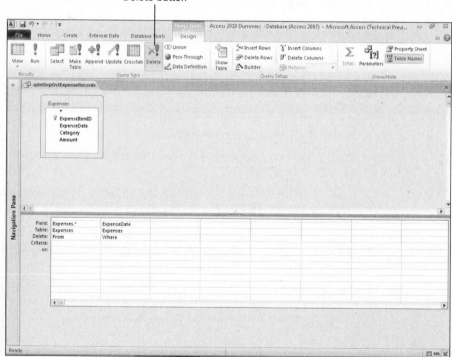

Figure 16-12:
The Delete
query
designed.

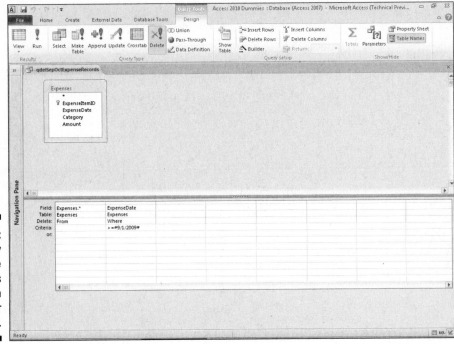

Figure 16-13:
This query
will delete
all records
dated on
or after
9/1/2009.

9. **Click the Run button from the Ribbon's Results Group to run the query and delete the records from the selected table.**

   A message box will appear, telling you how many records will be deleted.

   Delete queries delete records permanently from the selected table. You cannot undo the results of this query type. Back up your database file before running a Delete query!

10. **Click Yes in the message box window to run the query and delete the records.**

Part V
Plain and Fancy Reporting

The 5th Wave   By Rich Tennant

"Our automated response policy to a large company- wide data crash is to notify management, back up existing data and sell 90% of my shares in the company."

In this part . . .

"How can something be both plain *and* fancy?" Good question. When it comes to Access 2010, the "plain" is easy to find: It's in the simplicity of creating a report with a single click of a button. The "fancy" comes from all the bells and whistles you can add to your reports if you need or want to.

As you discover in the chapters of Part V, you can create a quick report that's a simple display of every record in a single table, or craft beautiful reports that use multiple tables and specific records from within them. You can also create reports that fall somewhere in between — call them "fain" or "plancy" — and by using a stress-preventing tool called the Report Wizard.

In Chapters 17 through 20, you find out about the simple and powerful ways that Access provides for generating reports — and even ways to do a mass mailing from your database of names and addresses, or to create product labels from your database of . . . um . . . *products*.

Anyway, you get the idea — or you will, after you read the next four chapters!

Chapter 17

Quick and Not-So-Dirty Automatic Reporting

· ·

In This Chapter

▶ Creating an instant report from a single table

▶ Making minor modifications to your instant report

▶ Setting up a report step by step with the Report Wizard

▶ Getting a sneak peak at your report-to-be

▶ Choosing the perfect layout

· ·

*T*he fact that you're reading this chapter right now tells me that either you've already been asked to create a report or you're afraid that might happen. Yes, if you're like the rest of us, *afraid* applies now and then — the idea of reporting on a database seems daunting to many users. You might be wondering, "Do I have to learn some really complex Access features? Do I have to master some word-processing program so I can make the report look like more than just a list of records?"

The answers to those questions are no and no. You don't have to learn anything other than a couple of quick mouse clicks in the Access workspace in order to whip up a snazzy report on the currently-open table, in just seconds. And you don't have to master Word or any other word-processing program to dress up your report and make it look serious and important. No, you have all you need to make a quick, simple, yet professional-looking report, right here in Access 2010.

"But what if I have to report on more than one table?" you're asking. What if your boss/customer/partner needs a report on data from Table A and Table B, and you know he or she does *not* want to see certain pieces of data from those tables anywhere on the report? In situations such as these, the Report Wizard comes in handy; using it, you can choose multiple tables as the sources for your report — and even pick and choose which fields to include from those tables.

Knowing that there are two very simple paths to follow, depending on the report you're looking for (or that someone else is hounding you for), it's time to take a look at the two paths and figure out which one is right for you.

Chances are you'll need both of Access's simple reporting tools (the Access Report and the Report Wizard) over time — so it's worth checking them both out now. I start with an analysis of them both and then get into the procedural specifics of the simplest one first.

Fast and Furious Automatic Reporting

The Access Report and Report Wizard tools make reporting on your database extremely simple. If you use the Access Report tool, Access uses your table (the open and active one at the time you click the tool's Report button) to generate a report instantly. You can then go in and tweak margins, fonts, and other formatting so the result looks more like what you'd imagined and/or fits on the number of pages you prefer.

If you use the Report Wizard, you're taken step by step through the process of choosing which fields (and which tables) to include in your report, how the report will look, and how the content will flow over one or more pages.

Each method has its merits in different situations:

- ✔ **If you want every field in your single table included in your report,** and you don't mind if your report looks a lot like a worksheet or the way your table looks on-screen while you're in Table view, then the Report tool is for you. It's quick, and it gives you a report without any formatting or other fanfare required.

- ✔ **If you want to choose which fields to include in your report,** and maybe want your report to include fields from more than one table, the Report Wizard is for you. It takes a little longer than the Report tool, but the flexibility and ability to customize the report's appearance through a series of dialog boxes (rather than using multiple tabs and buttons) is a real plus.

Creating a quick, one-table report

To generate a report on an open table, all you really have to do is click your mouse twice:

1. **Open the table that you want to report on.**

2. **Click the Ribbon's Create tab and then click the Report button (see Figure 17-1).**

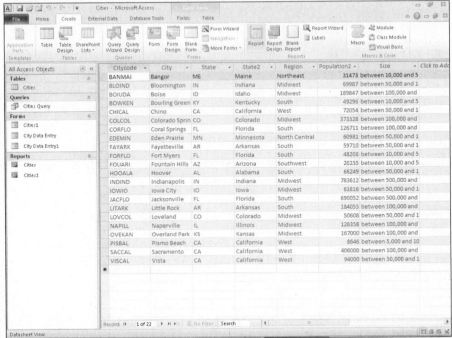

Figure 17-1:
You can find
the Report
button on
the Create
tab.

The open table is now a report, laid out exactly as it appeared in Table view — as a series of rows and columns. It has a heading and a small graphic in the upper-left corner, and some color has been added — using a default template — to the field names and the report's title (which is the same as the table name).

That big Property Sheet panel (on the far-right side of the workspace) that appears along with your report can be closed at this point. Although it comes up by default when you create a report with the Report button, it's not necessary for you to use this panel at all to run, print, or save a report as part of your database. You can make changes to the settings displayed in the panel, however, and you learn more about how to do that in Chapter 19.

3. **Use the File tab to access the Print command (or press Ctrl+P) if you want to print the report you see on-screen.**

   You can also display the report on-screen, now and in the future; there's no requirement that you print the report immediately.

If you save your database right now, the report (now with its own tab in the All Access Objects pane, as shown in Figure 17-2) becomes part of the database and will be there the next time you open it.

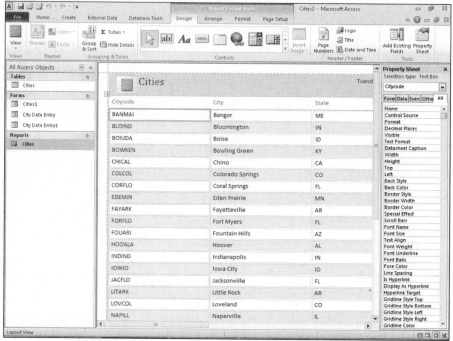

Figure 17-2:
Now your
single-table
report can
be saved as
part of the
database.

Your instant report formatting options

Although the Report tool works with only one table or query at a time, it still offers some choices for the way the report looks and how the fields appear in the report.

Did I say something about reporting on queries? Yes, I did! Check out Chapters 12, 13, and 14 for all the basics — and then some on queries. When you have your own queries put together and run, you can use the Report button to document them!

In the Report Layout Tools section of the Ribbon (the section is displayed after you use the Create tab to generate the quick, one-table report) you can choose from a variety of options for the tabular layout of your report. You can have each record listed on its own row, as a series of columns, or you can stack your fields so that (for example) when you click the Tabular button in the Table section of the Ribbon's Arrange tab, you pair up the City and State fields vertically, as shown in Figure 17-3.

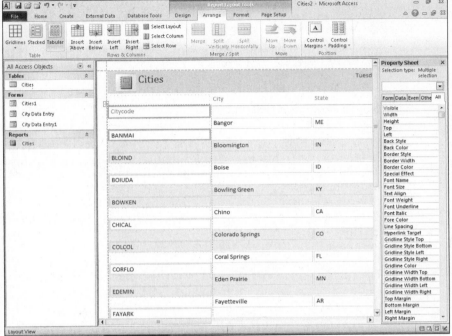

Hey, where is it, you say? If you can't find the buttons to change your report's tabular settings, click the Arrange tab, and look at the Table section (far left), also shown in Figure 17-3. There are lots of choices available, and my advice is that you experiment with different layouts, and when you like what you see on-screen, print. If you hate what you've done, just keep clicking the Undo button (up on the Quick Access toolbar) until the report is back at its pre–I Don't Like That state.

If you hate the report entirely, just right-click it in the left panel that lists the components of your database and choose Delete from the resulting pop-up menu. When a prompt appears, asking whether you really want to delete the report, just click Yes. Remember, all you had to do was click the Create tab and then click Report to make this thing — so how bad would it be to start over?

Rearranging columns

Not only can you pair up your report's fields vertically, stacking them to keep relevant fields together, but you can rearrange your columns so that (a) your report's readers see what they want to see first (assuming they read from left to right) and (b) you can horizontally pair up things that relate to each other. As shown in Figure 17-4, all you have to do to rearrange columns is drag the headings — and then go back for the data, dragging from the first record, and all the records come with it. When you release your mouse, the fields — the headings and then the data — are rearranged.

Sizing columns to fit the data

One thing that can be very appealing about a quick report on a single table is the ability to put the entire report on a single page (if you have only 20 or 30 records) or on a series of pages that include all the table's fields on each page (for large databases with hundreds or thousands of records, but not a whole lot of fields per record). This can be difficult on a report that has a lot of fields or uses all the fields in a table because rarely do they fit across an 8½-x-11-inch sheet of paper. Sometimes you can fit them all across a sheet of paper — if you resize the fields, narrowing them so they're no wider than they have to be to display the widest entry in the column.

The easiest way to do this to narrow the columns manually. You can widen all the columns in one fell swoop, but that requires working in Design view, which is discussed way over in Chapter 18. This way is quicker for now.

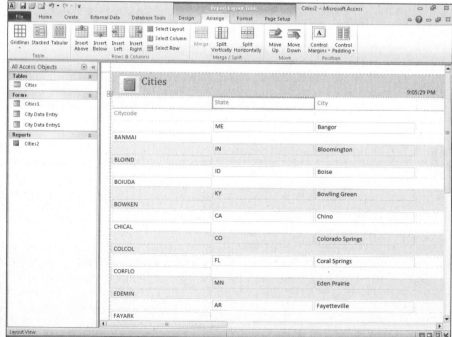

Figure 17-4: The State field will now precede City in left-to-right order of fields.

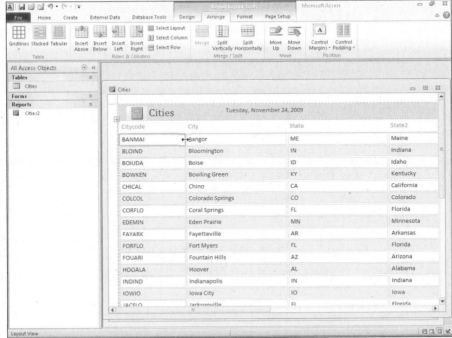

Cities   Tuesday, November 24, 2009

Citycode	City	State	State2
BANMAI	Bangor	ME	Maine
BLOIND	Bloomington	IN	Indiana
BOIUDA	Boise	ID	Idaho
BOWKEN	Bowling Green	KY	Kentucky
CHICAL	Chino	CA	California
COLCOL	Colorado Springs	CO	Colorado
CORFLO	Coral Springs	FL	Florida
EDEMIN	Eden Prairie	MN	Minnesota
FAYARK	Fayetteville	AR	Arkansas
FORFLO	Fort Myers	FL	Florida
FOUARI	Fountain Hills	AZ	Arizona
HOOALA	Hoover	AL	Alabama
INDIND	Indianapolis	IN	Indiana
IOWIO	Iowa City	IO	Iowa
JACFLO	Jacksonville	FL	Florida

Figure 17-5:
Click and drag to widen or narrow your report's columns, one at a time.

To adjust columns manually — the one column that's taking up too much room or each of them, one at a time — simply click the column's heading and then use the two-headed arrow that appears when you mouse over the column's right seam to move the seam to the left to make the column header narrower. Then, using the same two-headed arrow, snag the first record in that column and drag it to the same width as you've just set the heading. The dragging process is shown in Figure 17-5.

The query advantage

The fact that Access lets you base a report on a query is wonderful. When you build a report on a table, you get a report containing each and every record in the table. But what if you want only a few of the records? Access makes it easy to create a query and then base the report upon that query. (Chapter 12 shows how to make a query.)

The advantages don't stop there. If you create a query based on multiple tables, Access neatly organizes your results into a single datasheet. This allows you to use the quick, one-click Report tool to report on multiple tables — essentially duping Access into giving you a quick report on more than one table because the tables are part of a single query, and that single query is your Report source. (If you're unclear on the process of creating a query on multiple tables, take a look at Chapter 12.)

Starting the Report Wizard

So you've decided to take things step by step, perhaps because you want to include multiple tables and/or queries in your report. Or maybe you're still deciding what the best path is, and want to see what's involved in the process.

The Report Wizard is simple. It requires a few more steps and decisions from you than the Report tool does, but it's much more flexible than the instant Report tool. Here goes:

1. **In your database window, click the Ribbon's Create tab and then click the Report Wizard button. (It's right there in the tab's Reports section.)**

   The Report Wizard dialog box appears, listing all the fields in the active table. As shown in Figure 17-6, the dialog box offers

   • A drop-down list from which you can choose other tables and queries

   • Two columns of Selected and Available fields, which you use to determine which fields from the selected table(s) will be used in your report.

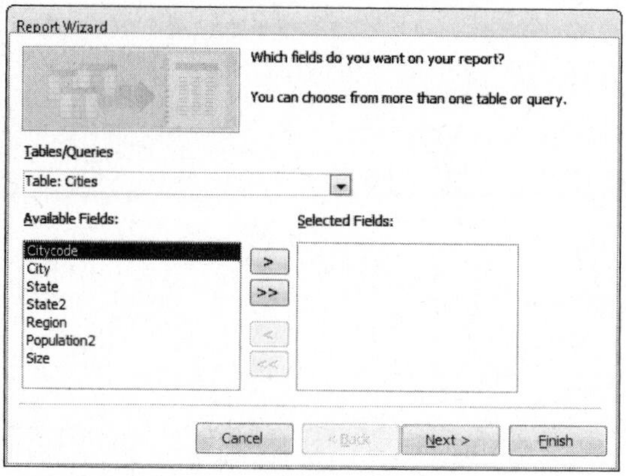

Figure 17-6:
The Report Wizard starts by offering you tables and the fields within them to use in your report.

2. **Use the Tables/Queries drop-down list to choose the table you want to start with.**

   The fields from the table you select appear in the Available Fields box.

3. **Add fields to your report by double-clicking them in the Available Fields box.**

   By double-clicking, you add the fields to the Selected Fields box, and they become part of the report. You can also click a field once and then click the button with a > symbol on it, as shown in Figure 17-7.

Figure 17-7:
Add fields
by double-
clicking
them or by
using the
buttons
between the
Available
and
Selected
Fields
boxes.

4. Repeat Steps 2 and 3 for each table and/or query in the database that you want to include in the report.

If, at any point, you want to add all the fields in a given table or query, just click the >> button to add all the Available Fields to the Selected Fields list.

5. Click Next to move on to the next page of the Report Wizard (see Figure 17-8) then click Next again.

Clicking Next twice bypasses grouping issues, which, for a simple report, are often unnecessary. To explore this step of the Report Wizard in greater detail, check out Chapter 19.

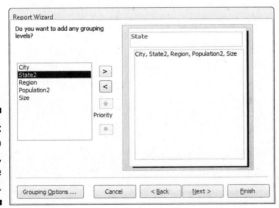

Figure 17-8:
No need to
linger here,
just move
along.

6. **Choose a sort order for your report — typically sorting on the field folks will use to look up information in the report — as shown in Figure 17-9.**

   For example, if your report documents a list of volunteers, Last Name might be a good choice. A report on product sales would be useful in Product Number or Product Name order. You can sort by more than one field, choosing up to four fields to sort by and either Ascending or Descending for the sort order on each field. Figure 17-9 shows the City field chosen for sorting in Ascending order.

Figure 17-9:
Sort by the most important field in the table, or the one that will make the most sense to your report's readers.

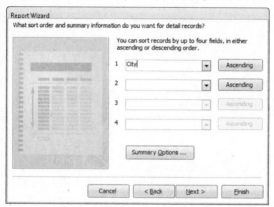

Sorting is best done on fields that have either very few entries or a lot of duplicate entries:

- In a name and address list, sorting by Last Name (which may have very few duplicates) will put the list in an order for which there's very little opportunity for subsequent sorting — because the unique records in Last Name don't create any groups that can be sorted further.

- If you sort that name and address list by City or State (which may have lots of duplicate entries), a subsequent sort can be done on Last Name, putting each group of people living in the same city or state in last-name order.

- To choose between Ascending (the default) and Descending sort order, you'll either leave the Ascending button alone (for A–Z sorting) or click it to change it to Descending (for Z–A sorting).

TIP

You probably don't want to use Justified unless your report has very few fields per record.

7. Click Next to display your options for Layout and Orientation.

8. Choose a Layout and an Orientation from the two sets of radio buttons and click Next.

- Layout options (Tabular or Columnar) are simple — you either want to see your report as a list (Tabular) or in sections (Columnar), in which each record appears in a section on its own. Justified is similar to Tabular, but groups the fields in a sort of stacked jumble.

- Orientation decisions (Portrait or Landscape) are generally easier if you envision the report in your head — are there more fields than will fit across a sheet of 8.5-inch-wide paper? If so, choose Landscape to give yourself 11 inches of paper (or 10 inches, to allow for the smallest margin possible) across which your fields will appear.

  Figure 17-10 shows a Tabular format chosen at this stage of the Report Wizard and allows the user to set up the layout and orientation for that report.

Figure 17-10:
Choose your report's layout in terms of field structure and orientation.

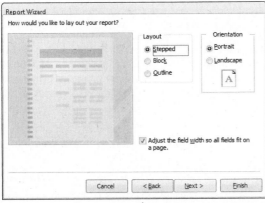

If you leave the Adjust the Field Width So All Fields Fit on a Page option checked, you run the risk of data being chopped off in the report and rendering the report unusable. If you have more than four or five fields, and if any of your fields have very long entries, turn this option off.

9. **Click Next.**

   A default name for your report now appears in this next step in the wizard, as shown in Figure 17-11.

Figure 17-11:
Name your report, or accept the table-name-based moniker that Access applies by default.

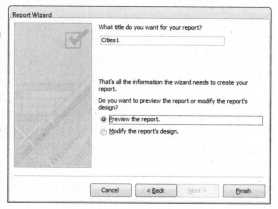

10. **Give your report a name.**

    Type a name in the long box at the top of the dialog box. At this point, you also need to decide how to finish things up — with a Preview of the report, or by leaping right into Design view to make more changes to your report's appearance and content. (This part of the process is covered in Chapter 18.) For now, choose to Preview the Report, which is the default.

11. **Click Finish.**

    The report appears in a Preview window, at which point you can print it or save it for future use. (Press Ctrl + S, or click the Save button and give the report a name, when prompted, to take care of the saving business.) After you've saved it — or if you have no need to save it or continue viewing it — you can close it by right-clicking the report's tab and choosing Close from the pop-up menu. If you haven't chosen to save, you'll be asked if you want to close without saving.

    Figure 17-12 shows a preview of a report that lists a series of Cities, and shows which State and Region they're found in, along with Population data for each city.

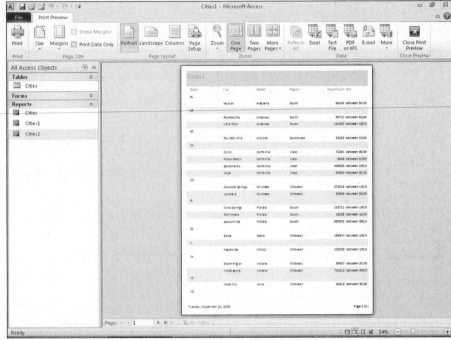

Figure 17-12:
Even a simple report with few fields can look important .

Previewing Your Report

When you're in Print Preview mode (which results from having clicked Finish to complete the Report Wizard process, as described in the steps in this chapter's previous section), you can't do a whole lot with your report except print it. But Print Preview shows exactly what your document looks like. Table 17-1 shows the tools Print Preview provides to help with your inspection.

Table 17-1		Print Preview Tools
Tool	*What It Is*	*What It Does*
	Print button	Opens the Print dialog box.
	Size button	Allows you to choose a paper size for your report.

(continued)

Table 17-1 *(continued)*

Tool	What It Is	What It Does
Margins	Margins button	Allows you to set Normal, Wide, or Narrow Margins for your report.
Show Margins	Show Margins	Click the check box to display or hide the margins.
Print Data Only	Print Data Only	Click the check box to include only your data in the report.
Portrait	Portrait button	Converts your report to Portrait mode.
Landscape	Landscape button	Converts your report to Landscape mode.
Columns	Columns button	Opens the Page Setup dialog box with the Columns tab chosen, allowing you to set up a columnar report.
Page Setup	Page Setup button	Opens the Page Setup dialog box with the Print Options tab chosen, allowing you to customize your printed output.
Zoom	Zoom button	Click this button to choose a percentage view (from 10% to 1000%) or to Fit to Window.
One Page	One Page	Previews one page of your report at a time.
Two Pages	Two Pages	Previews your report two pages at a time.
More Pages	More Pages	Click this to choose to preview four, eight, or twelve pages at a time.
Refresh All	Refresh All	Refreshes the report to display the latest data in the table(s) included in the report.
Excel	Data buttons	Exports your report to any of the following: Excel, a text file, a PDF or XPS file, or an e-mail message; click the More button to choose Word or other options.
Close Print Preview	Close Print Preview	As you might have guessed, this closes the Preview window.

TIP

Another way to see a Print Preview — say, for a report you created a while ago and you don't remember what it looks like on paper — is to open the report (double-click it in the left panel to open it) and then click the File tab. From there, click the Print command, and choose Print Preview from the resulting choices.

Zooming in and out and all around

In Figure 17-12, we see our report. In your preview (assuming you're working along with me here or have tried this on your own) you may be able to see the entire page of your report. The parts you can see look okay, but how can you commit to printing if you don't know how the whole page looks? In Figure 17-13, which doesn't show the entire page (the bottom of the page isn't visible), you can click your mouse when the pointer turns to a magnifying glass — as it will when you mouse over the page. You can also use the Zoom tool to choose a lower zoom percentage.

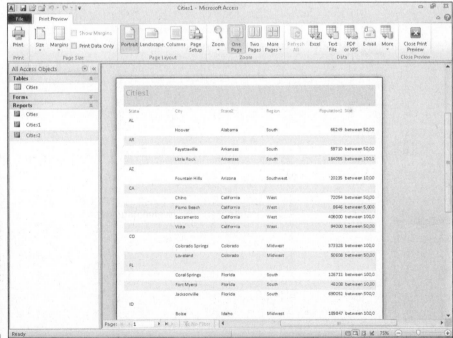

Figure 17-13:
When you view the whole page, the report is too tiny to read, yet you can't see all the content, either.

When you move your mouse pointer over the preview of your report, your pointer changes into a magnifying glass. Use this magnifying glass to zoom in to the report and check individual sections:

- Just click what you want to see, and Access swoops down, enlarging that portion of the report so you can see it clearly.

- Click again, and your view changes back to the previous setting.

Clicking any of the page-number buttons (One Page, Two Page, More Pages) sets the Zoom view to the Fit View setting. When you have two pages showing, the odd-numbered page is always on the left, unlike book publishing, which puts the odd-numbered page on the right (unless the typesetting department is having a very bad day).

If you use the Zoom section of the Ribbon's Print Preview tab rather than one of the page-number buttons, Access offers quite the selection of Page View options, as you see in Figure 17-14. Set your system to show 1 page or 2 pages — or click the More Pages button's drop-down list to choose up to 12 pages per screen (of course, you won't be able to read anything at this setting, but at least you can see how the whole report lays out).

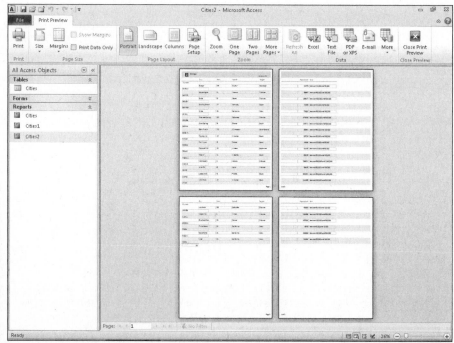

Figure 17-14:
Preview up to 12 pages of your report at a time — here, just four are required.

Pop goes the menu

You can right-click anywhere on the Print Preview screen to see a pop-up menu that gives you the choice of switching the zoom or viewing a specific number of pages, as shown in Figure 17-15. When you click the Zoom button drop list in the Zoom section of the Print Preview tab, you get a similar pop-up menu offering various zoom percentages, from 10% to 1000%.

Other than the Zoom submenu, the following useful commands are available when you right-click the Print Preview screen:

- ✔ **Report View, Layout View, Design View, or Print Preview:** These four options appear at the top of the pop-up menu and give you lots of ways to look at your report.

- ✔ **Zoom.** Enter or choose a zoom percentage.

- ✔ **One Page and Multiple Pages:** If you choose to see Multiple Pages, you must tell Access exactly how many pages by using the submenu that appears when you make that pop-up menu selection. Drag through the grid (it appears as 6 blocks to start with) and the grid expands as you drag. Release your mouse button when the grid shows the number of pages you want displayed.

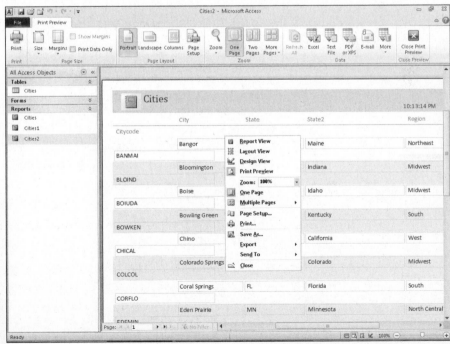

Figure 17-15: Choose the view you want to use or how many pages you want to see at once.

✔ **Page Setup:** This opens the handy Page Setup dialog box.

✔ **Print:** This opens — yep, you guessed it — the Print dialog box.

✔ **Save As:** Choose this command to save your report with a new name and choose what type of object to save it as — Report is the default.

✔ **Export:** Choose this command to save your Access report in a format used by another program. Your choices include exporting as a Word document, PDF (Portable Document Format) file, text file, XML document, or HTML document.

✔ **Send To:** Choose this command and then select an e-mail recipient to send the report to.

✔ **Close.** This closes Print Preview and prompts you to save your changes, if any, to the report's design.

Beauty Is Only Skin (Report) Deep

After looking at your report in the Print Preview window, you have a decision to make. If you're happy with how your report looks, great! Go ahead and print the document. However, a few minutes of extra work does wonders for even the simplest of reports.

Start with the basics in the Page Setup dialog box. To get there, right-click anywhere on the report and choose Page Setup from the pop-up menu. (This command and others hidden away in the pop-up menu are briefly explained in the preceding section of this chapter.)

Use the Page Setup dialog box to fine-tune your report in terms of its Print Options, Page, and Columns settings. You can adjust margins, change orientation, and control how many vertical columns your report content is divided into — all from within this handy dialog box.

The Print Options tab

The Print Options tab of the Page Setup dialog box controls the width of the margins in your report — no surprises here.

Figure 17-16 shows your margin options. The page has four margins, so the dialog box includes a setting for each one (Top, Bottom, Left, and Right).

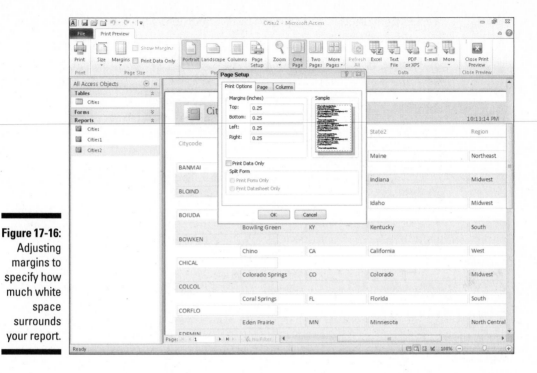

Figure 17-16:
Adjusting
margins to
specify how
much white
space
surrounds
your report.

Here is how you set or change margins:

1. **Double-click in the appropriate box (Top, Bottom, Left, or Right) and type a new setting.**

   When you double-click the box, the current entry is selected. Access automatically uses whatever Windows thinks is your local unit of measurement (inches, centimeters, or whatever else you measure with). On the right side of the dialog box, Access displays a sample image, which shows you how your current margin settings work on a page. After editing one margin, you can press Tab to move through the remaining fields (Bottom, Left, and Right, if you started out in Top), and you can adjust each one.

2. **Make all the changes you want to your report's layout, and then click OK.**

3. **Look at your report in Print Preview to check your adjustments.**

   If you need to tweak the report, simply go back to Page Setup and play with the options until everything looks just right.

The last item on the Print Options tab is the Print Data Only check box. (I guess the programmers couldn't think of anywhere else to put this box because it has nothing to do with margin settings.) If you select this option by checking its box, Access prints only the data in your records; field headings won't appear on the printed document. Use Print Data Only if you plan to use preprinted forms. Otherwise leave it alone because your report looks pretty odd without any field labels.

The Page tab

The Page tab of the Page Setup dialog box tells Access about the sheet of paper on which you plan to print your report — including its size and layout — as well as what printer you keep the paper in. You make some of the most fundamental decisions about how your report looks from the Page tab of the Page Setup dialog box. (See Figure 17-17.)

Figure 17-17: Use the Page tab to choose a printer, page size, and more.

The Orientation box sets the direction that your report prints on paper:

- ✔ Portrait (the way that this book and most magazines appear) is the default choice.
- ✔ Landscape pages lie on one side, giving you more horizontal room (width) but less vertical space (height).

Deciding whether to use Portrait or Landscape is more important than you might think:

- ✔ For tabular reports, landscape orientation displays more information for each field, thanks to the wider columns. Unfortunately, the number of records you can view per page decreases in the process. (After all, that piece of paper is only so big.)

✔ Columnar reports don't do very well in a landscape orientation because they usually need more vertical space than horizontal space.

Your other choices for the Page tab are determined by your printing capabilities:

✔ The Size drop-down list in the Paper section of the tab enables you to choose the size of the paper you want to use. (Refer to Figure 17-17.)

✔ The Source drop-down list gives you the option to

- Use your regular paper feed (the Automatic choice).

- Use another automatic source, should your printer be equipped with multiple trays.

- Feed your paper manually into the printer.

✔ The last part of the Page tab lets you choose a specific printer for this report.

Most of the time you can leave this setting alone; it's useful only if you want to force this report to always come from one specific printer at your location. You can choose either

- **The Default Printer option:** Access uses whatever printer Windows says to use.

- **The Use Specific Printer option:** You choose the printer yourself.

If you click the Use Specific Printer option, the Printer button comes to life. Click this button to choose from among your available printers.

The Columns tab

You get to make more decisions about your report's size and layout on the Columns tab, as shown in Figure 17-18.

Figure 17-18:
The Column
Layout
area of the
Columns tab
enables you
to format a
report with
vertical
columns.

The Columns tab of the Page Setup dialog box is divided into three sections:

- ✔ **Grid Settings:** Controls how many columns your report uses and how far apart the different elements are from each other.
- ✔ **Column Size:** Adjusts the height and width of your columns.
- ✔ **Column Layout:** Defines the way Access places your data in columns (and uses an easy-to-understand graphic to show you as well).

The default number of columns is one column to a page, but you can easily change the setting to suit your particular report. Just keep in mind that with more columns, your report may show less information for each record. If you use so many columns that some of the information won't fit, Access conveniently displays a warning.

If the number of columns you select fits (or if you're willing to lose your view of the information in some of your fields), click OK to see a view of how your document looks with multiple columns.

The Grid Settings section of the Columns tab also adjusts

- ✔ **Row Spacing:** Adjusts the space (measured in your local unit of distance) between the horizontal rows. Simply click the Row Spacing box and enter the amount of space that you want to appear between rows. Again, this setting is a matter of personal preference.
- ✔ **Column Spacing:** Adjusts the width of your columns. If you narrow this width, you make more room, but your entries are more difficult to read.

The bottom section of the Columns tab, called Column Layout, controls how your columns are organized on the page. You have two options here:

- ✔ **Down, then Across:** Access starts a new record in the same column (if the preceding record has not filled up the page). For example, Record 13 starts below Record 12 on the page (provided there's enough room), and then Records 14 and 15 appear in the second column.
- ✔ **Across, then Down:** Access starts Record 13 across from Record 12, and then puts Record 14 below Record 12, and Record 15 below Record 13, and so on.

If your columns don't look exactly right the first time, keep trying. Small adjustments to the row and column spacing produce big changes throughout a long report. The on-screen preview gives you an easy way to check how the report looks — and prevents you from killing multiple trees in the quest for perfection.

Chapter 18

Dazzling Report Design

In This Chapter

▶ Understanding report sections

▶ Using text boxes and labels

▶ Previewing your changes

▶ Putting AutoFormat to work

▶ Drawing lines and boxes

▶ Adding pictures

*T*he Report Wizard does most of the dirty work of report creation. However, it has its shortcomings. Most of the Report Wizard's shortcomings have to do with text — sometimes the text is cut off, it's not aligned properly, it's too small, it's too big — you get the idea.

Along the way, you may not like the Report Wizard's color choices or design elements as well. Don't despair. (Hopefully, you're never at a point in your life where you'll despair over an Access report, but I have to throw some drama in here somewhere.) Design and Layout views hold the key to unlocking the report of your dreams. (I know — who *isn't* dreaming about Access reports?)

In this chapter, I discuss some of the most popular report Design and Layout View tasks. With this knowledge, you can create professional-quality reports and be the envy of the office.

Taking Your Report In for Service

Design and Layout views are the places to be for tweaking reports — but which view to use and when? Usually your best options are as follows:

✔ **Design view:** Great for those situations where you want to add new elements (stuff like lines, titles, and subtitles) to the report.

Figure 18-1 shows a report in Design view.

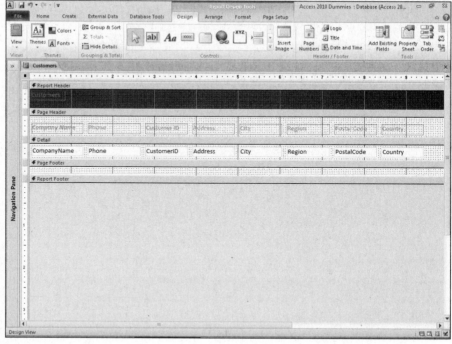

Figure 18-1:
Design view
is best for
adding new
design
elements to
your report.

✔ **Layout view:** A better choice for when you want to format existing elements. (Layout view shows you actual data as it will appear on the printed page.)

Figure 18-2 shows the same report in Layout view.

You have many ways to change report views. Here are some of the most common:

✔ **After creating a report with the Report Wizard:** The wizard asks whether you want to

   • *Preview the report*

   • *Modify the Report's Design*

   Click the Modify the Report's Design option to send the wizard's creation straight into Design view.

✔ **While a report is print previewed on the screen:** Use the row of View buttons on the lower-right corner of your screen:

   • *Design view* is the last button from the right

   • *Layout view* is the second-to-last button from the right.

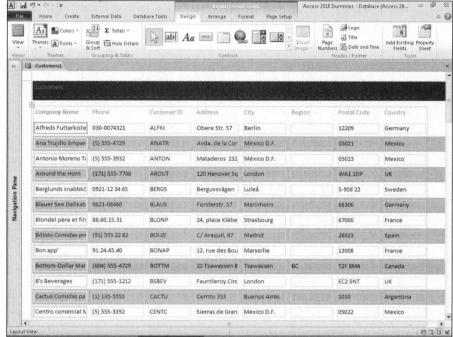

Figure 18-2:
Layout view
is best for
modifying
exiting
report
elements.

✓ **To open a report in Design or Layout view from the Navigation pane:**
Follow these steps:

1. Right-click the report you want to work on.

A shortcut menu pops up.

2. Select Design View or Layout View from the shortcut menu.

Report Organization

Access provides the following design tools to control the *layout* of your report —
where the report data appears on the printed page and where the pages break.

Structural devices

When you look at a report in Design or Layout view, Access displays a ton of
markers (called *controls* by Access) that are grouped into several areas (called
sections by Access). Together, these design elements make up the layout of your
report — and determine where the report data appears on the printed page.

Controls

In Design or Layout view, *controls* show the following:

- ✔ Where Access plans to put the report elements (such as text, lines, or logos) on the printed page.
- ✔ How the program plans to format each element.

Access uses three kinds of controls for text, depending on what information the report includes:

- ✔ **Text boxes:** Boxes that display a particular field's data in the report.

  Most fields you want to include in the final report are represented as a text box in Design view. (The exception is a Lookup field, which is represented on the report as a combo box.)

- ✔ **Combo boxes:** Report combo boxes do not act the same way as form combo boxes. On a report, you'll see the value of the combo box but will not see the drop-down arrow toward the right end of the combo box.

- ✔ **Labels:** Plain, simple text markers that display a text message on the report.

  Sometimes labels stand alone (for example, "Ken Cook Enterprises – Monthly Sales"). Often they accompany a text box to show people who read the report what data they're looking at ("Customer ID," or "Product," for example).

Sections

The *sections* (report headers, for example) determine *where* and *how often* the elements will print.

The report design in Figure 18-3 displays the most common sections (in the order of their appearance on the page).

Chapter 19 shows how to slice, dice, and make julienne fries out of your sections. The following information is a summary of the report sections.

Headers

Access provides a pair of header sections for the top of reports.

The header section you use depends on whether you need to print information at the *beginning* of the report or on *every page:*

- ✔ **Report Header:** Anything in the report header prints just once at the very start of the report — the top of the first page.

  Typically, a report title appears in the report header.

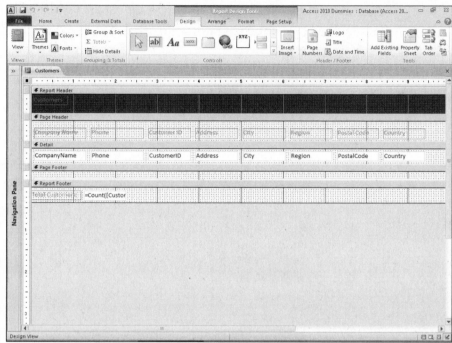

Figure 18-3:
Common
report
sections.

✔ **Page Header:** Information in the page header prints at the top of every page.

On the report's first page, the page header appears *below* the report header.

Typically, the page header contains column heading labels. You can also add design elements such as lines or shaded rectangles to the page header to separate the data rows from the column headings.

Detail

The Detail section displays the essence of the report — the actual database records. The Detail section appears only once in Design View. However, the Detail section is *repeated* for every record in the actual report as seen in Layout View.

The report automatically fits as many Detail sections (records) as possible between the header and footer sections on each page of your report.

The data in the Detail section usually fills the majority of each report page.

Footers

Access provides a pair of footer sections for the bottom of reports.

The footer section you need depends on whether you need to print information at the *end* of the report or on *every page:*

- **Page Footer:** When each page is nearly full, Access finishes it off by printing the page footer at the bottom.

  Common page footer elements are the date and page number.

- **Report Footer:** At the bottom of the *last* page, immediately following the page footer, the report footer is the last thing that prints on the report. This information prints only once.

  Typically, the report footer contains summary formulas that calculate grand totals for numeric columns (such as total dollar sales).

Page breaks

By default, Access fills each report page automatically with as many records as possible, and then starts another page. But Access does provide a couple of ways that *you* can control how reports start new pages:

- **Grouping.** Places like records together.

  For example, you are printing an order report by month and you want each month to start at the top of a page. If you group the report by month and add a group footer, you can tell Access to start a new page after each month's footer prints.

  For more about putting records into groups, see Chapter 19.

- **Page Break control.** Starts a new page from the point where the control is placed in the Report layout.

  The following sections show how to add and remove page breaks.

Grouping is much more efficient in controlling page breaks than the Page Break control. Only use the Page Break control if you can't get the pages to break the way you want with grouping.

Inserting a page break

Here's how to add a page break in Design view:

1. **On the Design tab of the Ribbon, click the Page Break button in the Controls group. (See the Ribbon in Figure 18-4.)**

   The mouse pointer changes to a crosshair with a page next to it.

Page Break button

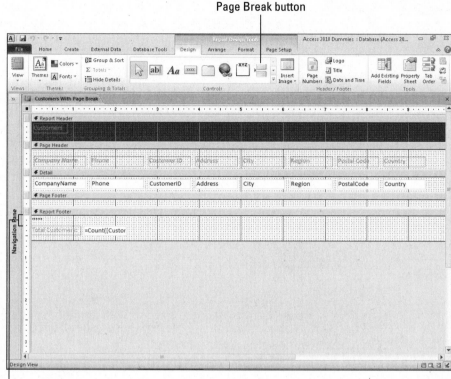

Figure 18-4:
The Page
Break
control in all
its glory.

Page Break control

2. **Position the crosshair wherever you want the page break and then click.**

   A small horizontal line appears on the left side of the report. What you are seeing is actually the *selected* Page Break control. Click somewhere away from the line and that line will become a series of dots, as shown in Figure 18-4. From now on, a new page always begins at the spot of the marker.

Removing a page break (or any other control, for that matter)

If you want to remove a page break, just follow these steps:

1. **With the report in Design view, click the Page Break marker — those series of dots you can see in Figure 18-4.**

   Selection markers appear around the Page Break control.

2. **Press the Delete key on the keyboard.**

   Goodbye, Mister Page Break!

This will not remove any page breaks that are *automatic* or created with *grouping*. Manual deletion will only get rid of page breaks created using the Page Break control.

Formatting This, That, and the Other

You can change almost any existing item in a report's design with the help of the Format tab, which is shown in Figure 18-5. With the Format tab, you can change item properties such as fonts, colors, and borders.

Figure 18-5:
The Format
tab on the
Ribbon.

The Format tab is visible only while a report is in either Layout or Design view. Because you can see the results of formatting changes better in Layout view, the upcoming steps use that view.

To adjust items in your report with the tools on the Format tab, follow these steps:

1. **Click the down arrow at the bottom of the View tool on the Ribbon and select Layout View from its drop-down menu.**

   The report displays in Layout view and the Format tab appears on the Ribbon.

2. **Click the Format tab to select it.**

   The Format tools appear on the Ribbon.

3. **Click the item you want to format.**

   A thick border appears around the item, as in Figure 18-6.

4. **Click the button for the formatting effect you want.**

   The appropriate buttons will be enabled for the item you've selected. There are two kinds of buttons:

   • **Toggle buttons** (like *Bold*): They are either on or off.

   • **Pull-down arrows** (like *Font*): Offer many available choices.

Customers label

Company Name	Phone		Customer ID	Address	City	Region	Postal Code	Country
Customers								
Alfreds Futterkiste	030-0074321		ALFKI	Obere Str. 57	Berlin		12209	Germany
Ana Trujillo Empar	(5) 555-4729		ANATR	Avda. de la Co	México D.F.		05021	Mexico
Antonio Moreno Ta	(5) 555-3932		ANTON	Mataderos 23	México D.F.		05023	Mexico
Around the Horn	(171) 555-7788		AROUT	120 Hanover S	London		WA1 1DP	UK
Berglunds snabbk	0921-12 34 65		BERGS	Berguvsvägen	Luleå		S-958 22	Sweden
Blauer See Delika	0621-08460		BLAUS	Forsterstr. 57	Mannheim		68306	Germany
Blondel père et fil	88.60.15.31		BLONP	24, place Kléb	Strasbourg		67000	France
Bólido Comidas pr	(91) 555 22 82		BOLID	C/ Araquil, 67	Madrid		28023	Spain
Bon app'	91.24.45.40		BONAP	12, rue des Bc	Marseille		13008	France
Bottom-Dollar Mai	(604) 555-4729		BOTTM	23 Tsawassen	Tsawassen	BC	T2F 8M4	Canada
B's Beverages	(171) 555-1212		BSBEV	Fauntleroy Circ	London		EC2 5NT	UK
Cactus Comidas p	(1) 135-5555		CACTU	Cerrito 333	Buenos Aires		1010	Argentina
Centro comercial I	(5) 555-3392		CENTC	Sierras de Gra	México D.F.		05022	Mexico

Figure 18-6: The Customers label is selected.

I cover these options in detail later in the chapter.

Repeat Steps 3 and 4 for all of the items you want to modify.

If you make a mistake while formatting, click the Undo button on the Quick Access toolbar or press Ctrl+Z. Your mistake will be whisked away to cyber-neverland.

The following sections step through some of the most common formatting tasks. Just follow the instructions, and your report will look like a million bucks in no time. (Now if you could only *sell* it for a million bucks!)

Adding color

A little color can help keep report readers awake as they browse through 300 pages of data.

These buttons change the color of labels and text boxes in your report:

- ✔ **Font Color:** Changes the color of text in a text box or label marker.
- ✔ **Background Color:** Changes the control's background color, but not the text.

These buttons are located in both Layout and Design view on two different Ribbon tabs. You can find them in the Font group on the Format tab or the Text Formatting group on the Home tab.

Taking control of your report

In addition to Label, Text, and Combo Box controls, more controls are available in Design view by using the tools from the Controls group of the Ribbon's Design tab.

Some controls work with specific types of fields. For example, a check box can graphically display the value of a Yes/No field.

Some of these controls can be a bit complicated to set up. However, Access includes several control wizards to take the pain out of the process. These wizards walk you through the steps for building your controls in the usual

wizardly step-by-step process. Just answer the questions, and the wizard does the rest.

A control's wizard *usually* pops on-screen automatically after you place the control in the report. If you create a new control but the control's wizard doesn't show up to help, be sure that the Use Control Wizards button is turned on. Click the More button (pictured in the top figure below) on the Controls group drop-down list to see the Use Control Wizards button. If it's on, the Use Control Wizards button will have a colored border around it (pictured in the bottom figure below).

Click here to find the Use Control Wizards button.

Here is a list of the report controls covered in this book and where you can find information on them:

✔ The Line, Rectangle, Page Break, and Image controls are covered elsewhere in this chapter.

✔ Using controls to create summaries in your report is covered in Chapter 19.

I think you'll find these buttons are easier to work with in Layout view.

When a text control is selected, the buttons will show you the current font and background colors for the control. To change colors, follow these steps:

1. **Click the control to select it.**

   The control has a thick border around it.

2. **Click the arrow to the right of the Font Color or Background Color button.**

   The menu of colors appears.

3. **Click the color you want to use.**

   The colors are divided into sections:

   - *Theme:* Colors that the experts at Microsoft have determined work well together.

   - *Standard:* All colors that have been created for you.

   - *Recent:* All colors that have been used in the current Access session on the report

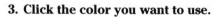

If you make the text and background colors the same, the text seems to disappear! If this happens, just click the Undo button on the Quick Access toolbar to bring back the original color setting.

Relocation, relocation, relocation

Don't like that column where it is? The position of your report title got you down? Your line won't stay in line? You can easily move just about any element (text box, label, line, and such) in a report.

- Most elements can be moved in Layout view. You see your data in Layout view, so I recommend that you start there.

- If you have trouble in Layout view, switch to Design view. For example, I find lines easier to work with in Design view.

The amount of space between the controls determines the space between items when you print the report:

- Increasing spacing gives your report a less crowded look.

  This is appropriate if you have only a few columns on your report and you want to spread them out to fill up the width of the page. For example, a report that shows annual sales by product might have a column for the product description and a column for both the unit and dollar sales. Spread out the three controls to fill up the page width.

- Decreasing the space enables you to fit more information on the page.

  This is appropriate when you have many columns on your report and you want to fit them all on the width of one page. For example, a report that shows dollar sales by month may have 14 columns — 1 for the product description, 12 for the months, and a Total column. Crowd the 14 controls together to fit the page width.

Moving a single control

To move a line, box, label, or text box, follow these steps:

1. **Point the tip of the mouse pointer to the item you want to move.**

2. **Press the left mouse button.**

   The mouse pointer changes to a four-headed arrow.

3. **Drag your item to a new position.**

   As you move the mouse, the four-headed arrow drags an outline of whatever object you selected.

4. **Release the mouse button when the item is in the right place.**

   If you make a mistake while moving, click the Undo button on the Quick Access toolbar or press Ctrl+Z. This will put the item back where it started.

To move a text box and its corresponding label, follow these steps:

1. **Click the text box to select it.**

   The border thickens around the text box, indicating that it's been selected.

2. **Press and hold the Ctrl key then click the corresponding label.**

   The border thickens around the both the text box and the label, indicating that they're both selected.

3. **Follow Steps 3 and 4 in the previous procedure to move both controls.**

Moving a group of controls

In a columnar report, you can move an entire group of controls in the Detail section. Here's how:

1. **Click one of the controls in the Detail section.**

   A thick border appears around the item and a Select All box (the little guy containing a four-headed arrow) appears toward the upper-left corner of the group of controls. (See Figure 18-7.)

2. **Roll the mouse over the box icon containing the four-headed arrow.**

   The mouse will change to a four-headed arrow.

3. **Drag the group of controls to a new position.**

   All the controls in the group will move at one time. Everything stays in alignment.

Click here to select all controls in the section.

| Customers | | | | | | | |

Company Name	Phone	Customer ID	Address	City	Region	Postal Code	Country
Alfreds Futterkiste	030-0074321	ALFKI	Obere Str. 57	Berlin		12209	Germany
Ana Trujillo Empar	(5) 555-4729	ANATR	Avda. de la Cor	México D.F.		05021	Mexico
Antonio Moreno Ta	(5) 555-3932	ANTON	Mataderos 231	México D.F.		05023	Mexico
Around the Horn	(171) 555-7788	AROUT	120 Hanover Sq	London		WA1 1DP	UK
Berglunds snabbkc	0921-12 34 65	BERGS	Berguvsvägen	Luleå		S-958 22	Sweden
Blauer See Delikat	0621-08460	BLAUS	Forsterstr. 57	Mannheim		68306	Germany
Blondel père et fils	88.60.15.31	BLONP	24, place Klébe	Strasbourg		67000	France
Bólido Comidas pre	(91) 555 22 82	BOLID	C/ Araquil, 67	Madrid		28023	Spain
Bon app'	91.24.45.40	BONAP	12, rue des Bou	Marseille		13008	France
Bottom-Dollar Mar	(604) 555-4729	BOTTM	23 Tsawassen B	Tsawassen	BC	T2F 8M4	Canada
B's Beverages	(171) 555-1212	BSBEV	Fauntleroy Circ	London		EC2 5NT	UK
Cactus Comidas pa	(1) 135-5555	CACTU	Cerrito 333	Buenos Aires		1010	Argentina
Centro comercial N	(5) 555-3392	CENTC	Sierras de Gran	México D.F.		05022	Mexico

Figure 18-7:
Use the
Select All
box with the
four-headed
arrow in it
to move a
group of
controls.

One size does not fit all

The Report Wizard as well as the basic Report button do their best to size
your report items properly. Very often, however, neither gets it right. A
column will be too narrow or too wide, using the space on the page ineffi-
ciently. Do you throw your hands in the air and curse at the computer gods?
Of course not. You can size any control to your exact needs.

I find that sizing works best in Layout view; you can see the data in the controls as you're sizing them. You can also size your controls in Design view.

Follow these steps to size a control:

1. **Select the item you want to size by clicking it.**

   The item will have a thick border around it.

2. **Roll the mouse pointer to the edge of the selected item.**

   The mouse cursor changes to a two-headed arrow. See Figure 18-8 for a
   picture.

3. **Drag your item to its new size.**

   As you drag with the mouse, the two-headed arrow drags an outline of
   whatever object you selected to show you its new size.

Company Name	Phone	Customer ID	Address	City	Region	Postal Code	Country
Alfreds Futterkiste	030-0074321	ALFKI	Obere Str. 57	Berlin		12209	Germany
Ana Trujillo Empan	(5) 555-4729	ANATR	Avda. de la Cor	México D.F.		05021	Mexico
Antonio Moreno Ta	(5) 555-3932	ANTON	Mataderos 23	México D.F.		05023	Mexico
Around the Horn	(171) 555-7788	AROUT	120 Hanover S	London		WA1 1DP	UK
Berglunds snabbk	0921-12 34 65	BERGS	Berguvsvägen	Luleå		S-958 22	Sweden
Blauer See Delika	0621-08460	BLAUS	Forsterstr. 57	Mannheim		68306	Germany
Blondel père et fils	88.60.15.31	BLONP	24, place Kléb	Strasbourg		67000	France
Bólido Comidas pr	(91) 555 22 82	BOLID	C/ Araquil, 67	Madrid		28023	Spain
Bon app'	91.24.45.40	BONAP	12, rue des Bc	Marseille		13008	France
Bottom-Dollar Mar	(604) 555-4729	BOTTM	23 Tsawassen	Tsawassen	BC	T2F 8M4	Canada
B's Beverages	(171) 555-1212	BSBEV	Fauntleroy Circ	London		EC2 5NT	UK
Cactus Comidas p	(1) 135-5555	CACTU	Cerrito 333	Buenos Aires		1010	Argentina
Centro comercial I	(5) 555-3392	CENTC	Sierras de Gra	México D.F.		05022	Mexico

Figure 18-8:
Two-headed mouse arrow at the edge of the Company Name label control.

4. **Release the mouse button when the item is the right size.**

   The item stretches or shrinks to its new size.

   Labels can be scaled to the exact size required to display all of the text. To do this, follow Steps 1 and 2 in the previous procedure and then double-click instead of drag. Like magic, Access figures out the correct size for the item and sizes it accordingly.

Spaced-out controls

The spacing of columns is a common problem in tabular reports. The Report wizards tend to butt columns up against each other, sometimes making data difficult to read. If this is the case for you, you can use the Control Padding tool located on the Arrange tab of the Ribbon to space everything out a bit.

This adjustment can be done in either Layout or Design view, but I think you'll find Layout view is easier.

Follow these steps to add space between your columns in Layout view:

1. **Click one of the controls in the Detail section and then click the Select All box that appears. (Refer to Figure 18-7.)**

   The labels and text boxes for all the columns are selected.

2. **Switch to the Arrange tab on the Ribbon, if necessary, by clicking it.**

   The Arrange tools appear, including the Control Padding tool located in the Position group. (See Figure 18-9.)

Figure 18-9:
The
Ribbon's
Arrange
tab that
includes
the Position
group.

The position group

3. **Click the drop-down arrow in the lower-right of the Control Padding tool.**

   Four padding choices drop down.

4. **Select one of the last three choices to add spacing between the columns.**

   The first choice (None) will butt all of the controls up against each other so if your goal is to add padding, you'll want to avoid that one.

   Check your changes in Print Preview (see "Sneaking a Peek," later in this chapter). Sometimes adding too much space between columns pushes one or more of them off the page. If this happens, experiment with the different choices on the Control Padding tool until everything fits correctly.

Borderline beauty

Organizationally speaking, lines and borders are great accents to

✔ Draw your readers' eyes to parts of the page.

✔ Highlight sections of the report.

✔ Add some pizzazz.

The Format tab on the Ribbon contains three commands that work with lines:

✔ Shape Outline

✔ Line Type

✔ Line Thickness

You can use these commands on a line control to change the appearance of the line or on label and text box controls to add a border to the control. The three tools are within the Shape Outline tool in the Control Formatting group on the Format tab.

Coloring

The Shape Outline tool changes the color of lines that mark a text box's border and lines you draw on your report by using the Line tool.

This button works just like the Background Color and the Font Color buttons for text.

To change the color of a line or other control border, follow these steps:

1. **Click the item to select it.**

   The item has a thick border around it.

2. **Click the drop-down arrow next to the Shape Outline button.**

   A drop-down display of color choices appears, as shown in Figure 18-10. The colors are divided into sections:

   - *Theme:* Colors that the experts at Microsoft have determined work well together.

   - *Standard:* All colors that have been created for you.

   - *Recent:* All colors that have been used in the current Access session on the report.

   Note: The Shape Outline button hangs out in the Control Formatting group of the Ribbon's Format tab.

3. **Click your color choice from the myriad options.**

Thickening

In addition to colorizing lines and control borders, you can also adjust their thickness:

1. **Click a line or other control to select it.**

2. **Click the Shape Outline button to reveal its choices.**

   Near the bottom of the Shape Outline drop-down list is the Line Thickness button.

3. **Click Line Thickness to reveal a submenu of options, as shown in Figure 18-11.**

4. **Click the thickness option you want.**

   Like magic, your line or border thickness changes.

   If you make a mistake, click the Undo button on the Quick Access toolbar or press Ctrl+Z to undo your mistake.

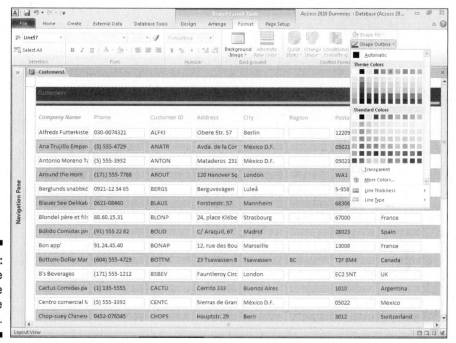

Figure 18-10:
The palette of Shape Outline colors.

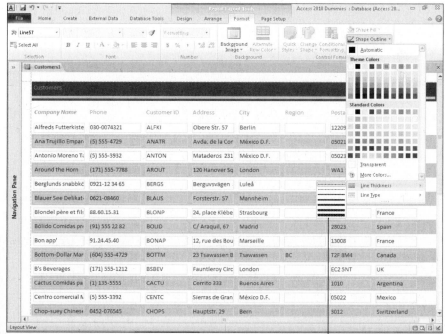

Figure 18-11:
The seven Line Thickness options.

Determine the width

Changing the type

You can change the type of line displayed by your line control or other control border. The Line Type button handles that job for you. Eight choices are available under this button, as shown in Figure 18-12. Don't know what I mean by line type? Well, think dotted, dashed, or solid.

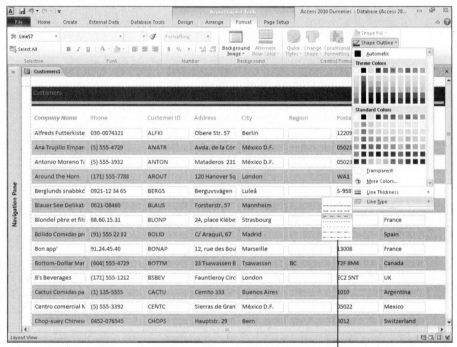

Figure 18-12:
The eight line type options.

Determine the type

To change the line type of a control, follow these steps:

1. **Click the control whose line type you want to change.**

2. **Click the drop-down arrow next to the Shape Outline button to display its options.**

3. **Click Line Type (the very last choice) to reveal a submenu of line types.**

4. **Click the line type you want.**

Tweaking your text

You must select the text you'd like to tweak before using any of the formatting tools. With Access labels, all of the text in the label must be formatted the same way. You cannot format one word differently from another. The same is true with the contents of a text box – unless the text box is tied to a Memo field with its Text Format property set to Rich Text (see Chapter 3 for details).

Fonts

You can change the font or the font size as follows:

1. **Select the text you want to change.**

2. **Click the drop-down arrow to the right of the Font or Font Size list box.**

    Both list boxes are found in the Font group of the Ribbon's Format tab.

3. **Make a selection from the drop-down list that appears.**

To turn on or off the bold, italic, or underline characteristics, select a control and click the appropriate button from the Font group on the Ribbon's Format tab. The characteristic *toggles* (switches) between on and off each time you click the button.

Alignment

You can control the alignment of the text within labels and text boxes. To change the alignment of the text for a label or text box, follow these steps:

1. **Select the control.**

2. **Click one of the three alignment buttons found in the Font group of the Ribbon's Format tab.**

    Figure 18-13 shows the alignment buttons. Pictured from left to right:

    - Align Text Left
    - Center
    - Align Text Right

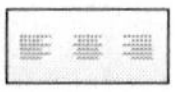

Figure 18-13:
The three alignment buttons.

Make sure your reports follow these simple rules for your reader's pleasure:

- ✓ Align numeric data and dates to the right so the numbers line up correctly. Use the Number group of tools on the Ribbon's Format tab to help keep your numbers tidy.

- ✓ Align text to the left.

- ✓ Align your column headings to the data in the column:

    • Text column headings should align left.

    • Number column headings should align right.

Sneaking a Peek

Neither Layout view nor Design view give you a perspective on how the report will look on the printed page. So where can you go to see how the report will print?

Access provides a command called Print Preview that does the trick. To preview your report, click the Print Preview button from the set of four View buttons on the lower-right part of your screen. (The Print Preview button is the second from the left with the magnifying glass on it.)

Figure 18-14 displays a report in Print Preview. Here's how to navigate it:

- ✓ **Zoom:** Click anywhere on the report to zoom in or zoom out.

    To zoom to a specific percentage of actual size, click the drop-down arrow on the Zoom tool in the Zoom group on the Ribbon's Print Preview tab and then select your size.

- ✓ **Page buttons:** Find these on the lower-left part of the Print Preview screen.

    • The right arrows move to the next or last pages.

    • The left arrows move to the first or previous pages.

    • Type a page number in the Current Page box (the one with the number in it), and Access will take you to that page.

- ✓ **Page Size group** (on the Ribbon): The buttons change page margins and paper size.

- ✓ **Page Layout group** (on the Ribbon): The buttons change page orientation.

✔ **Zoom group** (on the Ribbon)**:** The buttons change the number of pages that appear in Print Preview.

✔ **Close Print Preview button** (on the Ribbon)**:** Exits Print Preview.

For details on setting margins, paper size, and page orientation, see Chapter 17.

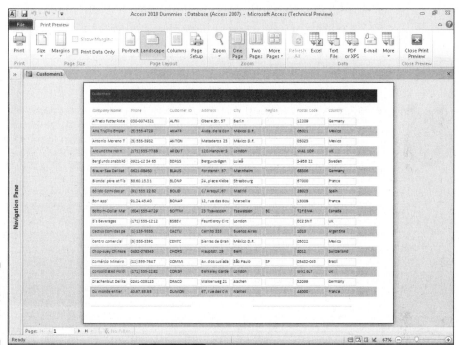

Figure 18-14:
A report in Print Preview.

Getting a Themes Makeover

When you want to change the look of the entire report in a few easy clicks, check out the Themes button. When you click this button, Access offers several different format packages that reset everything from the headline font to the color of lines that split up items in the report.

The Themes button is available in either Layout or Design view on the Design tab of the Ribbon.

Follow these steps to apply a theme to your report:

1. **Open the report in Design or Layout view.**

   Select your report in the Navigation pane then use the View tool on the Design tab to accomplish this task.

2. **Select the Design tab on the Ribbon, if necessary.**

   The Design tools appear, including the Themes group.

3. **Click the drop-down arrow on the Themes button.**

   A palette of formatting choices drops down with a variety of color schemes, as depicted in Figure 18-15.

4. **Click the theme you want.**

   Access updates your report with the new look.

   If you don't like any of the prebuilt themes on the drop-down list, use the Colors and Fonts buttons in the Themes group on the Ribbon to design your own. If you like what you created, click Save Current Theme (via the Themes tool drop-down menu) to record your creation for posterity.

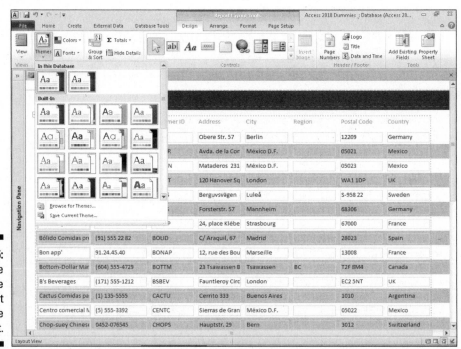

Figure 18-15:
Choose the look you like and apply it to the entire report.

Adding More Design Elements

Use the controls we discuss in this section to enhance the appearance of your report. You'll see suggestions for the control's use in each section.

Drawing lines

An easy way to make your report a bit easier to read is to add lines that divide the sections. Lines can only be *added* in Design view.

You can use the various Shape Outline tool (discussed earlier in this chapter) to dress up your lines.

You must switch to Design view to add lines.

Straight lines

To add straight lines to your report, follow these steps:

1. **Click the Line tool (the one with the diagonal line on it) in the Controls group of tools on the Design tab. (You many need to click the down or scroll arrow on the right edge of the Controls tool to find the Line tool.)**

   Your cursor changes to a crosshair with a line trailing off to the right.

2. **Repeat these steps for each line you want:**

   a. Click where you want to start the line.

   b. Drag to the location where you want to end the line.

   c. Release the mouse button.

Rectangular boxes

The Rectangle tool draws boxes around separate items on your report. Rectangles can only be *added* in Design view. Follow these steps:

1. **Click the Rectangle tool (the one shaped like a rectangle with a light gray interior) in the Controls group of tools on the Design tab.**

2. **Repeat these steps for each rectangle you want:**

   a. Click where you want to start the upper-left corner of the rectangle.

   b. Drag the rectangle shape down to the lower-right corner.

   c. Release the mouse button.

Pretty as a picture

You can add some flair to a report by adding a logo. This, of course, also helps identify that the printed document is from your organization. Use the Logo tool to add a logo to the report. After you click the tool, you will be prompted to select a logo file. By default, Access will place the logo on the upper-left corner of the report.

The Logo button places an Image control on your report. You can find this control on the Design tab's Controls tool.

Adding a logo

You can add a logo in both Layout and Design views.

Pages that contain logos take longer to print. Use your logos wisely:

- ✔ *Headers* and *footers* are the best places for logos.
- ✔ The *Detail* section is not a good place for logos.

  In the Detail section, you get one copy of the logo for *each* record on the report. This could greatly slow the printing of your report.

  Should you have a report title on the upper-left corner of your report, move the title to the right to make room for the logo before you insert the logo.

If you want to add a logo to your report, switch to Design or Layout view and follow these steps:

1. **Select the Design tab on the Ribbon, if necessary.**

   The Design tools appear, including the Header/Footer group.

2. **Click the Logo button from the Header/Footer group.**

   The Insert Picture dialog box opens.

3. **Navigate to the folder that contains your logo, and select the logo file. (See Figure 18-16.)**

4. **Click the OK button.**

   The logo is placed on the upper-left part of the report.

After you add a logo, you can size, move, or delete the logo as described earlier in this chapter.

Figure 18-16:
The Insert
Picture
dialog
box with
a logo file
selected.

Hitting the Office links

You can do a lot with Access, but sometimes you may want to use a different program because Access cannot do what you need. For example, you may need to calculate a median on a report. Access does not contain a built-in median function. To resolve this issue, you can export your data via the Excel Office Link button to Excel and use Excel's Median function to perform your calculation.

Access provides tools for converting reports to file formats that can be opened and modified in other programs (including other Office programs):

1. **In the Navigation pane, locate and then right-click the report.**

2. **Choose Print Preview from the shortcut menu that appears.**

   The Data group of tools on the Print Preview tab has a tool for each file format to which you can export your data.

3. **Click the tool for your desired format.**

   An Export dialog box will appear.

4. **Use the Browse button to assist you in entering a file name in the File Name box.**

   The File Name box should contain a path and file name when you're finished.

5. **Check the Open the Destination File after the Export Operation is Complete check box.**

   Do this so you won't have to remember where you stored the exported file and what you called it.

6. **Click the OK button to begin the export process.**

   The report will be exported to your selected file format then opened in the exported format's application.

Chapter 19

Headers and Footers and Groups, Oh My!

In This Chapter

▶ Placing your records in ordered groups

▶ Resizing your report's sections

▶ Customizing your report's layout

▶ Using headers and footers exactly as you need them

▶ Expressing yourself through footers

▶ Inserting date and time information

The Report Wizard takes much of the stress and decision-making out of creating reports. This is also true of the Report tool, which asks no questions at all and just turns your table into a report — bang, zoom, no fuss, no muss. The Report Wizard is almost that simple; it asks just a few simple questions that you won't have any trouble answering.

Well, *maybe* no trouble. A few of the questions, which I address in this chapter, may give you a moment's pause, if only because you may not understand what's being asked or how your answer can affect your report. Given that this book is all about eliminating any stress or concern for the Access user, my goal, is to explain those questions — and to help you make the Report Wizard even more wizardly.

In addition to simplifying the already-simple Report Wizard, this chapter also covers the use of two very convenient and powerful report features — headers and footers. These stalwart additions appear at the top and/or bottom of your reports, performing whatever role you dictate — from eye candy to outright informers. They can be very spare and simply tell your readers what the name of the report is, or they can be really useful and tell people when the report was created, when it was last printed, or that the data within it is proprietary or confidential. What you include in your headers and footers is entirely up to you.

A Place for Everything and Everything in Its Place

The secret to successful report organization lies in the way you set up the information included in the report. Access enables you to choose how your fields are laid out on the report, enabling you to achieve the most effective layout for the data in question.

A report is effective when the reader can glance at it and see exactly what information is offered:

- ✔ What data is included
- ✔ How much detail is available
- ✔ Where to look on the page to find specific pieces of information

Achieving an effective layout is simple; the automatic reporting tools in Access create a very basic, no-confusion-here layout by default.

Layout basics

Reports come in two layouts, *Columnar* or *Tabular*.

The layout that's right for your report is totally subjective. You can preview your report in both layouts and make your decision accordingly.

In either layout, each of the fields you choose to include in your report appears in two parts:

- ✔ Fields
- ✔ Labels (a name for the field, essentially)

The fields and labels are paired and laid out in either Columnar or Tabular format.

This chapter shows how you can take the default layouts that Access's automatic reporting features give you and tweak them by working in Design view. You can drag labels and fields around to achieve a completely custom report layout.

Here's the skinny on how Columnar and Tabular layout options look and work:

- ✔ **Columnar layout:**

  - Field descriptions print with every record's data (side by side), as shown in Figure 19-1.

    The layout behaves this way because both the field descriptions and data area are in the report's Detail section.

  - The report title prints only once, at the very beginning of the report (because the title is in the Report Header section).

- ✔ **Tabular layout:**

  - Field descriptions (labels) print once per page in the Page Header section, as shown in Figure 19-2.

  - The data areas are in the Detail section.

  - The title prints, only at the top of the report.

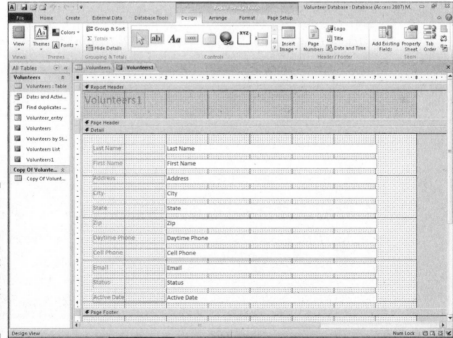

Figure 19-1: In a columnar report, labels are to the left of the fields and repeat for each record.

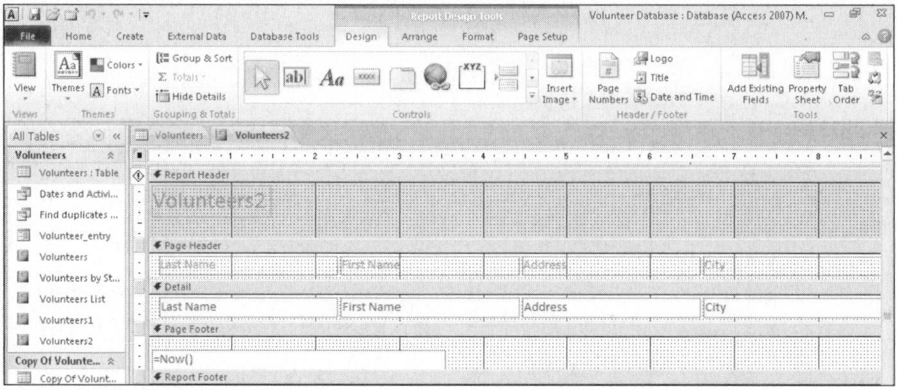

Figure 19-2:
In a tabular
report,
the labels
become
column
headings.

Sections

Reports are divided into sections. The information that appears in each section is dictated by your chosen layout.

Understanding the section concept is a prerequisite for performing any serious surgery on your report — or for running off to build a report from scratch. Otherwise your report groupings don't work right, fields are out of place, and you end up with a very frustrating, unfriendly report that neither you nor anyone else will want to read (or be able to use effectively).

REMEMBER

The most important point to understand about sections is that the contents of each section are printed *only* when certain events occur. For example, the information in the Page Header is repeated at the top of each page, but the Report Header prints on only the first page.

Getting a grip on sections is easy when you look at the *innermost section* of your report first and work your way outward, like so:

✔ **Detail:** Access prints items in this section each time it moves to a new record. Your report includes a copy of the Detail section for each record in the table.

✔ **Group headers and footers:** You may have markers for one or more *group sections.*

In Figure 19-3, information in the report is grouped by State. (You can tell by the section bar labeled *State Header* — the section bar identifies which field is used for grouping.)

Group sections always come in pairs:

• The *group header* section is above the Detail section in the report design.

• The *group footer* is always below Detail.

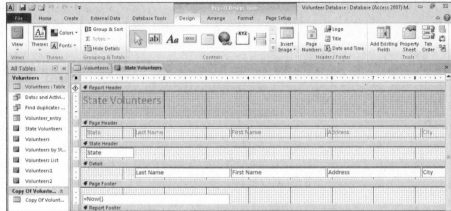

Figure 19-3:
Grouping
volunteer
records by
State.

Information in these sections repeats for every unique value in the groups' fields. For example, the report shown in Figure 19-3 reprints everything in the State Header for each volunteer in the database. Within the section for each state, Access repeats the information for each volunteer who belongs to the organization.

✔ **Page Header and Page Footer:** These sections appear at the top and bottom, respectively, of every page. They're among the few sections not controlled by the contents of your records.

Use the information in the Page Header and Footer sections to mark the pages of your report.

✔ **Report Header and Footer:** These sections appear at the start and end of your report. They each make only one appearance in your report — unlike the other sections, which pop up many times.

Here's what you can do with headers and footers:

✔ The Report Header provides general information about the report. This is a good place to add the report title, printing date, and version information.

✔ The Page Header contains any information you want to appear at the top of each page (such as the date or your company logo). If your report layout is set to Tabular, the column headings (field names) for the data included in the report are found in this section.

✔ The headers for each group usually identify the contents of that group and the field names.

✔ The footers for each group generally contain summary information, such as counts and calculations. For example, the footer section of the Department group may hold a calculation that totals the minimum bids.

✔ The Page Footer, which appears at the bottom of every page, traditionally holds fields for the page number and the report date.

✔ The Report Footer in your report can be a good place to put things like these:

- Confidentiality statements.
- Information regarding the timeliness of the data in the report.
- The name(s) of the report's author(s).
- An e-mail address or phone number to contact the person who made the report.

Grouping your records

When the Report Wizard creates a report for you, it includes a header and footer section for each group you want. If you tell the Report Wizard to group by the State field, for example, it automatically creates both the State Header and the State Footer sections. You aren't limited to what the wizard does, though. If you're a little adventuresome, you can augment the wizard's work with your own grouping sections.

Before making any big adjustments to the report, take a minute to save the report (choose Save from the Quick Access bar). That way, if something goes wrong and the report becomes horribly chewed up, just close it (click the X at the end of the report's tab) without saving your changes. Ahhh. Your original report is safe and sound.

Reporting, step by step

When Access produces a report, what does it do with all these sections? The process goes this way:

1. Access begins by printing the Report Header at the top of the first page.

2. Access then prints the Page Header, if you choose to have the Page Header appear on the first page. (Otherwise Access reprints this header at the top of every page except the first one.)

3. If your report has groups, the Group Headers for the first set of records appear next.

4. When the headers are in place, Access prints the Detail lines for each record in the first group.

5. After it's finished with all the Detail lines for this group, Access prints that group's Group Footer.

6. If you have more than one group, Access repeats Steps 3, 4, and 5 for each group.

7. At the end of each page, Access prints the Page Footer.

8. When it finishes with the last group, Access prints the Report Footer — which, like the Report Header, appears only once in a given report.

The key to creating your own grouping sections is the Group, Sort, and Total panel — which is available after you've created a report with the Report Wizard or while you're in Design view working on a customized report. To display the panel (shown in Figure 19-4), click the Ribbon's Design tab and then click the Group & Sort button in the Grouping & Totals section.

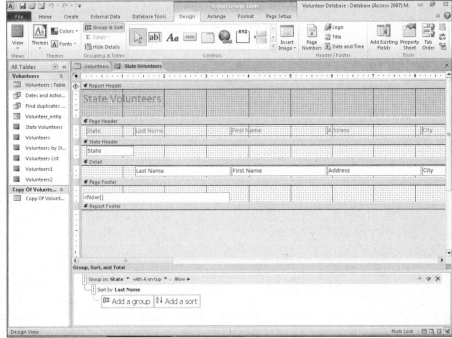

Figure 19-4:
The Group, Sort, and Total panel lets you view and add sorts and groups.

This panel allows you to control how Access organizes the records in your report — augmenting the sorting and grouping you may have already set up, whether through the Report Wizard dialog box or while building a report from scratch in Design view.

You can completely customize how your report's records are grouped and sorted and sort by multiple fields quickly and easily. The next set of steps shows you how.

To build your own groupings and add sorting with the Group, Sort, and Total panel, follow these steps:

1. **Click the Design tab (within the Report Design Tools tab group, shown in Figure 19-4).**

2. **Click the Group & Sort button in the Grouping & Totals section.**

   The Group, Sort, and Total panel appears beneath your report's sections.

3. **View any existing grouping or sorting, each represented by a Sort By or Group On bar, as shown in Figure 19-5.**

    The tree-like display shows the hierarchical groups and sorting currently set up for your report.

4. **Click Add a Group (you may need to scroll down within the Group, Sort, and Total Section, as shown in Figure 19-6); when the pop-up menu appears, select a field by which to group.**

    Access displays a list of available fields you can choose and use to group your report's records.

5. **Click Add a Sort and select a field by which to sort from the pop-up menu.**

    Again, a list of fields appears. You can click a field to choose a new field on which to sort your records. If you can't see these boxes (Add a Group and Add a Sort), scroll down, using the scroll bar on the right side of the workspace.

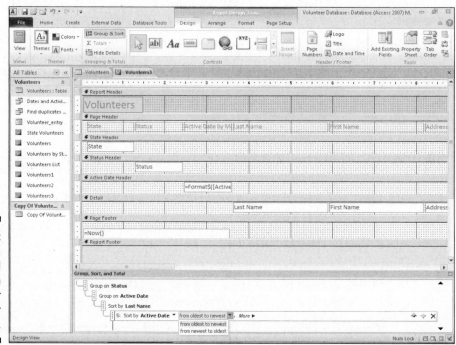

Figure 19-5:
Choose a
new field
by which
to group or
sort your
records.

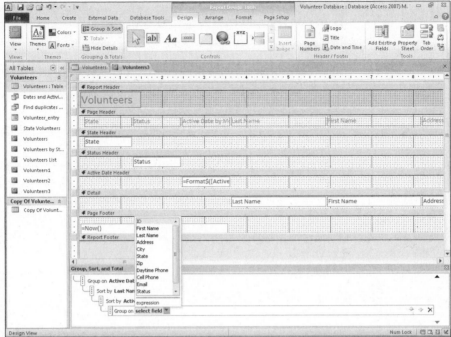

Figure 19-6:
Choose the field you want to use for further grouping of your records in the report.

If you've already sorted by a field within the report, your subsequent sorting will be applied to the sort already applied. Here's an example using the employee database: If you already elected to sort by `Department` (say, while you were setting up the report in the Report Wizard), that sort will appear in the panel. If you click Add a Sort, your next logical field on which to sort might be `JobTitle` or `LastName`. The resulting sort would then put the list — already in order by Department — in further order: putting the departments in order by field chosen for the added sort. All the `Accounting` department people will be ordered by that second field, all the `Operations` people, and so on. It's a lot like the phone book (remember those?) — all the records in that book are in order by last name, and for those listings with the same last name, the records are in order by first name. If the first names are the same, a third order — by `Street` — is applied; if there are two John Smiths, the one on Elm Street comes before the one on Walnut Street.

6. **To change the settings for an existing group or sort, click the Group On or Sort By bar and change the sort order or pick a different field by which to sort.**

Your sorting and grouping options are determined by the nature of the existing sort or group. Where the sort is based on Active Date (refer to Figure 19-5), you can choose From Oldest to Newest or From Newest to Oldest. In Figure 19-6, your Group By options are legion — ranging from First Name to Last Name to City to Zip and beyond.

7. **Close the Group, Sort, and Total panel.**

You can close the panel after you've finished using it by

- Clicking the X in its upper-right corner.

- Clicking the Group & Sort button again (in the Grouping & Totals section of the Design tab).

To remove a group, click the X on the far-right end of the Group On or Sort By bar (visible in Figure 19-6). There is no confirming prompt; when you click that X, your group or sort is gone. Of course, you can re-group or re-sort by using the Add a Group or Add a Sort buttons.

So you want more?

In addition to adding and removing groups and sorts with the Group, Sort, and Total panel, you can also make the following adjustments/selections:

- ✔ **On the Sort By bar, click More** and view a list of options, including "by entire value," "with no totals," "with title" (click the "click to add" link to insert a title), and options for adding headers and footers for the sorted records.

  To hide these options, click Less.

- ✔ **On the Group On bar, click More** to make the same choices as to how to group the records, whether or not to include totals, and how to use headers and footers.

  Click Less to hide the options on the bar when you've finished using them.

  If you don't see the More button, be sure to click the Group On bar to activate it.

With the appropriate fields in the correct header, footer, and detail sections, you've successfully finished the biggest step in building your report. Now you're down to the little things — tweaking, adjusting, and touching up the details of how your report presents itself. The properties described in the following sections govern the visual aspect — the look and feel — of your report.

Some of the stuff in the coming paragraphs looks a little technical at first glance because these settings dig deep into the machinery of report-making. Don't let the high-tech look scare you. By organizing your headers, footers, and detail rows, you've already conquered the hard part of building the report. This other stuff's just the window dressing.

Customizing Properties

In an amazing stroke of usability, Access keeps all property settings for your report in a single panel — the Property Sheet, which appears to the right of your report in Design view (as shown in Figure 19-7, which shows the daunting All tab). But before you can start using the Property Sheet, you have to have it on your screen:

✔ To start adjusting the details of any component of your report, either

- Double-click the item you want to modify.

- Right-click the item and choose Properties from the pop-up menu that appears.

- You can also display the Properties panel by clicking the Property Sheet button, found in the Tools section of the Design tab. The Design tab is one of four tabs available in the Report Design Tools section of the Ribbon.

When displayed, you can widen the Property Sheet panel by pointing to its left side. Your mouse pointer turns to a two-headed arrow; click and drag to the left — essential if you want to use the second column in the panel (which shows values and settings for each property).

✔ To display the Property Sheet for the report, double-click the little box where the two rulers meet, just to the left of the Report Header.

✔ You can also double-click any part of the report to display the Property Sheet, focused on the part you double-clicked.

When the Property Sheet appears, its title bar indicates which part of the report you're about to tweak. You can also click the drop-down list (which repeats the name of the currently displayed portion of the report's properties) and choose a different component to work with.

The Property Sheet is very long and a bit scary-looking — but don't worry about it. Regardless of which report component you choose to tweak (or if you're looking at the properties for the entire report), some of the settings won't need to be tweaked, and you'll probably have no idea *how* to tweak them anyway. And that's fine at this stage of the game. Seasoned Access users often leave many of these properties in their default state, because default settings are the defaults for a reason — they're effective in most situations (and suit most users' needs) without adjustment.

The Property Sheet has five tabs along the top of the list of properties — *Format, Data, Event, Other,* and All (which was the active tab in Figure 19-7). The only tab that's really worth looking at is Format; the others are really only of interest to programmers, and All is just plain frightening because it lists every possible property you can adjust.

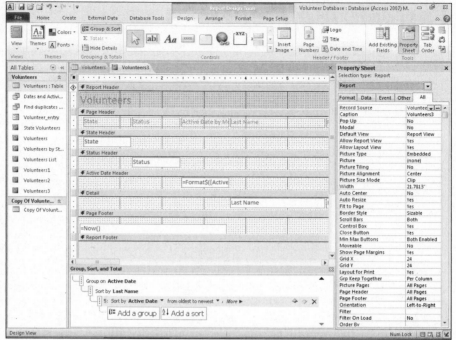

Figure 19-7:
Double-click
any piece of
the report
to see that
item's
properties.

So, with the Format tab clicked, as shown in Figure 19-8, feel free to tweak away. Change the caption, decide whether you want scroll bars on the report when viewed on-screen, decide which pages should have a header or footer, and so on. Most of the properties' names are pretty self-explanatory, so you should be fine.

If you're at a loss as to what one of the properties does or means, click the setting to its right and see the drop-down arrow appear (as shown in Figure 19-9); then you can use the drop-down list to see the options for the chosen property. In many cases, seeing those options clarifies what the property is and does. (Note that if there's a numerical value in the column, no drop-down arrow appears — instead, you can simply edit the value.)

Controlling report and page headings

To adjust when various headings appear in your report, start with the Property Sheet. After the panel appears (open it by double-clicking the report component of your choice), try these settings:

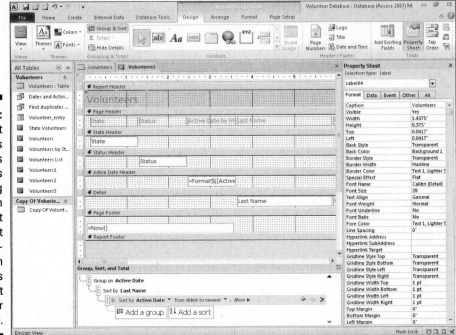

Figure 19-8: The Format tab's properties list varies depending on which report component you're working with (here it's the Report Header label).

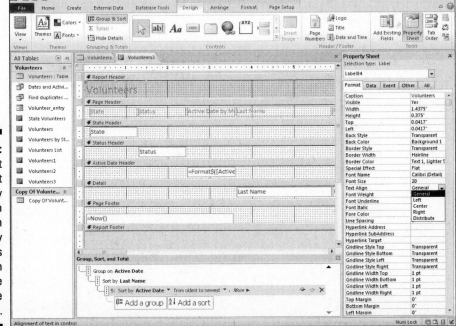

Figure 19-9: Find out more about a property (Text Align is shown here) by using its drop-down list to make alternative selections.

✔ The default setting for both the Page Header and the Page Footer is Yes (or All Pages when Report is selected at the top of the Property Sheet) — meaning that Access prints a header and footer on every page in the report.

Choose Display When to tell Access to

- Always show the header

- Show the header when the report is printed

- Only show the header on-screen

The Keep Together option allows you to decide if a given part of the report should be kept with the adjacent parts. The default is Yes, with your alternative being No. Note that this option is not listed in the Property Sheet for the Page Header and Page Footer.

✔ The Page Header section of the Property Sheet panel comes with a bunch of options, too. Double-click the Page Header to display the PageHeaderSection panel, as shown in Figure 19-10.

✔ Click the Format tab on the Property Sheet for the following options:

- **Visible:** Controls whether the Page Header appears at all.

- **Height:** Access sets this property automatically as you click and drag the section header up and down on the screen.

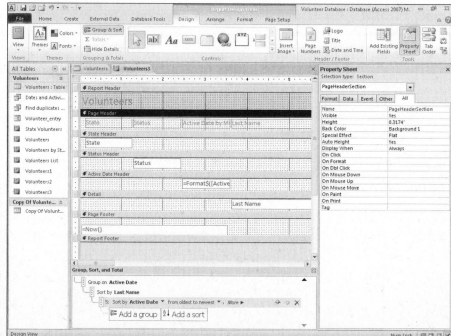

Figure 19-10:
Use the Property Sheet drop-down list to display PageHeader Section properties.

To specify an exact size (for example, if you want the header area to be *precisely* 4 centimeters tall), type the size in this section. (Access automatically uses the units of measurement you chose for Windows itself.)

✔ **Back Color:** If you want to adjust the section's color, follow these steps:

1. *Click the currently selected color.*

2. *Click the small gray button with three dots (the Ellipsis button) that appears to the right of the entry.*

   This button displays a color palette.

3. *Click your color choice.*

   Let Access worry about the obnoxious color number that goes into the Back Color box.

✔ **Special Effect:** This property adjusts the visual effect for the section heading, much as the Special Effect button does for the markers in the report itself — though in this case your choices are limited. Click the Special Effect box and then click the down arrow to list what's available. Choose Flat (the default setting), Raised, or Sunken.

✔ **Auto Height:** This option is set to Yes, but you can choose No if you'd prefer not to have an automatic height setting applied to your page heading.

✔ **Display When:** This is set to Always by default, but allows you to choose from Print Only or Screen Only, should those options appeal to you.

Adjusting individual sections

If you want to change the format for just one section of the report, double-click the header for that section to display its GroupHeader properties in the Property Sheet, as shown in Figure 19-11. (You can also choose the associated GroupHeader item from the drop-down menu at the top of the Property Sheet panel.

If your report doesn't include any groups, GroupHeader won't be in the list of components for which you can view properties, nor will there be a Group heading to double-click in Design view.

If your report does have a group (or groups) in it, you can tweak 13 different Group Header settings. The settings you're most likely to want to adjust include the following:

✔ **Force New Page:** This option controls whether the change for that group automatically forces the information to start on a new page. When you set this option, you can determine whether this page break occurs

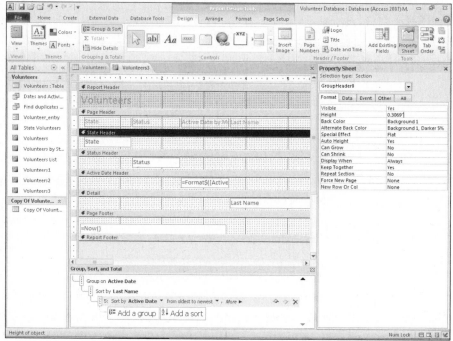

Figure 19-11:
Choose a
section of
your report
to adjust
by double-
clicking the
section.

- Only before the header
- Only after the footer
- In both places

or

- None, to insert no page break at all.

You can control the way in which section beginnings and endings are handled for multiple-column reports (such as having the group always start in a separate column). You can control whether

- The group is kept together (Keep Together)
- The section is visible (Visible)

✔ **Can Grow:** The section expands as necessary, based on the data in it.

Can Grow is particularly useful when you're printing a report that contains a Memo field:

1. *Set the width of the field so it's as wide as you want.*

2. *Use the Can Grow property to enable Access to adjust the height available for the information.*

✔ **Can Shrink:** The section can become smaller if, for example, some of the fields are empty.

To use the Can Grow and Can Shrink properties, you have to set them for both the section and the items in the section that can grow or shrink.

✔ **Repeat Section:** Controls whether Access repeats the heading on each page when a group is split across pages or columns.

Itemized adjustments

Double-clicking works for more than sections. When you want to adjust the formatting of any item of your report — a field, a label, or something you've drawn on your report — just double-click that item in Design view. Access again leads you to the Property Sheet, from which you can do all manner of technical nitpicking.

Customizing headers and footers

Although Access includes several default settings for headers and footers, those settings aren't personalized or imaginative. You can do much more with headers and footers than simply display labels for your data. Why not build expressions in these sections — or insert text that introduces or summarizes your data? (Now, *that's* a header or footer that impresses your friends, influences your coworkers, and wins over your boss. In a perfect world, anyway.)

A good header on your report's shoulders

How you place the labels in the report's header sections controls how the final report both looks and works, so you really need to put some thought into your headers. You want to make sure that all your headings are easy to understand and that they add useful information to the report.

When you're setting up a report, feel free to play around with the header layouts. Experiment with your options and see what you can come up with — the way the information repeats through the report may surprise you.

For example, when you use a wizard to create a grouped report, Access puts labels for your records in the page header by default. Figure 19-12 shows such a report in action. Notice that the State heading is printed above the state's abbreviation. This appears at the top of each and every page because that label is in the Page Header section.

If you want to promote other labels to the page header, simply drag those labels to the Page Header section. You can do this in Layout view (as shown in Figure 19-13). Also in Figure 19-13, Status is now to the left of State, which both appear in the page header.

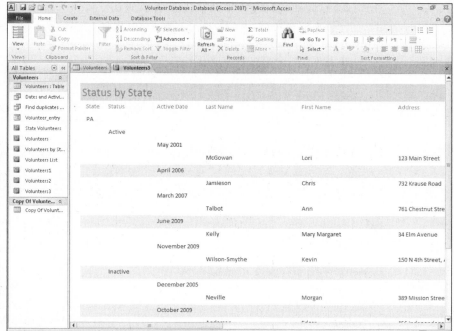

Figure 19-12:
The Status
by State
report, with
the State,
Status,
Active Date,
Last Name,
First Name,
and Address
in the page
header.

Figure 19-12:
The Status
by State
report, with
the State,
Status,
Active Date,
Last Name,
First Name,
and Address
in the page
header.

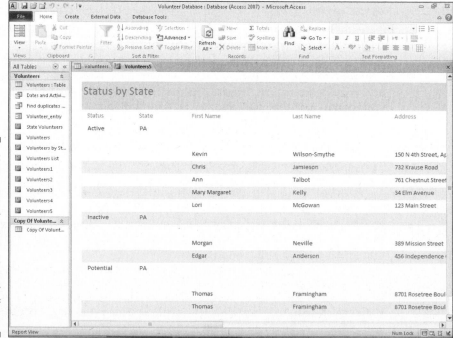

Figure 19-13:
Status and
State share
the Page
Header
section;
a change
in Status
repeats the
State for
this group of
volunteers.

Solid footing with page numbers and dates

Access can insert certain information for you in either the header or the footer. Most notably, Access can insert

- ✔ **Page numbers.** Insert them by using the Page Number command found in the Header/Footer section of the Design tab.

- ✔ **Dates.** Click the Date and Time command, also found in the Header/Footer section of the Design tab.

And this is page what?

If you click the Page Numbers button on the Header/Footer section of the Ribbon's Design tab, the Page Numbers dialog box appears (as shown in Figure 19-14).

Figure 19-14: Control your report's page numbers.

The Page Numbers dialog box has several options for your page-numbering excitement:

- ✔ **Format:**
  - *Page N:* Prints the word *Page* followed by the appropriate page number.
  - *Page N of M:* Counts the total number of pages in the report and prints that number with the current page number (as in *Page 2 of 15*).

- ✔ **Position:** Tell Access whether to print the page number in the Page Header or the Page Footer.

- ✔ **Alignment:** Set the position of the page number on the page.

  Click the arrow at the right edge of the list box to see your options.

- ✔ **Show Number on First Page:**
  - Select this option to include a page number on the first page of your report.
  - Deselect this option to keep your first page unnumbered.

To change how the page numbers work on your report, follow these steps:

1. **Manually delete the existing page number field.**

   To delete the field, click it (you should be in Report view at the time) and press the Delete key.

2. **Click the Page Numbers button in the Header/Footer section of the Design tab.**

3. **Set up new page numbers.**

Time-stamping your reports

Click the Date and Time button — in the Header/Footer section of the Ribbon's Design tab — to display the Date and Time dialog box (shown in Figure 19-15).

The most important options are

- ✔ Include Date
- ✔ Include Time

Select the exact format of your date and/or time from the set of choices. The dialog box displays a sample of your settings in the section cleverly marked *Sample*.

Date and Time
☑ Include Date
⦿ Sunday, November 29, 2009
○ 29-Nov-09
○ 11/29/2009
☑ Include Time
⦿ 1:54:17 PM
○ 1:54 PM
○ 13:54
Sample:
Sunday, November 29, 2009 1:54:17 PM
OK   Cancel

Figure 19-15: Choose dates and times here.

Including the date and time makes a *huge* difference with information that changes regularly. By printing the information at the bottom of your report pages, Access automatically documents when the report came out. It never hurts to include a date stamp (or a time *and* date stamp) in report footers.

You probably noticed the Logo and Title buttons in the Header/Footer section of the Design tab, too. The Logo button opens an Insert Picture dialog box, where you can choose an image to add to the report (such as your company logo or a photo of the people or objects your report is about). The Title button inserts the report's name (the name that appears on the report's tab, which is not necessarily what you've typed in the label (Status by State, as shown in the report we've created in this chapter).

When inserted, the logo or title can be dragged to any position on the report. Figure 19-16 shows an image on the report, to the right of the report's header.

As shown in Chapter 18, you can add images (like your logo) to any report, and not just by adding them to a header or footer. Check it out!

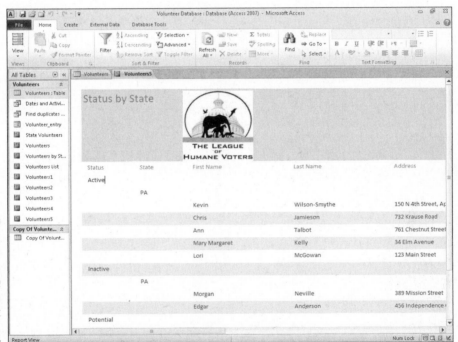

Figure 19-16:
Your organization's logo is a great addition to the report header.

Chapter 20

Magical Mass Mailings

- -

In This Chapter

▶ Creating labels fast, with minimum hassle

▶ Formatting labels for specific situations

- -

*T*he Report Wizard (covered in Chapters 17 and 19) is just the tip of the Access report iceberg. If you're so inclined, you can use Access to generate useful printouts that you probably never thought of as reports — mailing or product labels. So grab your basket (and your little dog, too) because we're off to see the wizard again, as Access provides friendly and magical helpers to see you through.

Massive Mailings with the Label Wizard

So you have 5,000 catalogues, newsletters, or some other mailable items printed and ready to go out to your adoring (or soon-to-be adoring) public. You also have a big Access database full of names and addresses. How can you introduce these two and get them started on what will surely be a wonderful relationship? Although e-blasts have become even more common as ways to mass-"mail" your clients and potential customers, there are still marketing and informative items that (a) require printing and (b) have to be put in the actual mail.

With the Access Label Wizard, your sheets of labels and your database will be hooked up in no time flat. With the Label Wizard, you can (almost instantly!) generate labels that work with just about any commercial label product on the market. If your local stationery or office-supply store carries them, Access can print your data on them. All you need to know is what kind of label you have, which data should go on the labels, and who's going to slap the labels on the mailings after you've finished your part of the job.

The names and addresses on labels are just part of the story. You can also print product labels, with product names, numbers, and inventory locations on them, helping your warehouse personnel find and put away products. If you have the data — whatever it might be — and the blank labels, you can bring the two together to print labels for just about any purpose.

Microsoft engineers put the specifications for hundreds of labels from popular label manufacturers right in the Label Wizard. If you happen to use labels from Avery, Herma, Zweckform, or any other maker listed in the wizard's manufacturer list — it's a long, long list, so yours is probably in there — just tell the wizard the manufacturer's product number. The wizard sets up the report dimensions for you according to the maker's specifications. Life just doesn't get much easier than that.

Before firing up the Label Wizard, decide on the information you'll need for the labels:

- ✔ The Label Wizard uses the active table's fields by default.
- ✔ You can create a query that includes only those fields you want to print, drawing those fields from the tables that currently house them.

Chapters 11 through 14 show the procedures for creating queries. It can be as simple as selecting the table that contains the data destined for your label, querying for all the records, and choosing to include only some of the fields. Or you can query for certain records — again, specifying which fields to include — and you're good to go. Call it one more great reason to check out the query chapters — especially Chapter 12 for the basics — before you embark on this process.

Of course, if your label information can all be found in a single table, make sure that table is open — and follow these steps to build a label report:

1. **In the database window, click the Ribbon's Create tab and then make your way over to the Reports section of the tab.**

   The Create tab's many tools appear, including the Report and Report Wizard buttons we discuss in Chapters 17 and 19.

2. **Click the Report section's Labels button to start the Label Wizard.**

   The Label Wizard dialog box opens, as shown in Figure 20-1.

3. **Click the Filter by Manufacturer drop-down list and select your label manufacturer.**

   Access assumes you have Avery labels; if you do, there's no need to perform this step — just move on to Step 4.

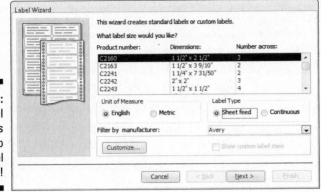

Figure 20-1: The Label Wizard is prepared to make label magic!

4. **Scroll through the list of label types and find your label's product number — and when you locate it, click it to select it.**

   The three-column list includes Product Number, Dimensions, and Number Across information.

   Find the product number on your package of labels in the list. If you don't see it, check the packaging for an equivalent product number that the manufacturer recommends. If you buy a generic or store brand of labels, often the Avery equivalent is printed right on the packaging; you can look for that number in the list.

5. **Click Next.**

   The Label Wizard asks you for your font choices, as in Figure 20-2.

Figure 20-2: Choose font, size, weight, and text color for your labels.

6. **Choose the font, size, font weight (to determine whether you want your text to be light or very bold — click the drop list to see your choices for the font you've chosen), and the text color you want for your labels; then click Next.**

   The next page of the Label Wizard appears; here's where you choose which fields from the active table you want to include in your labels.

7. **Double-click the first field you want to include on the labels.**

   As shown in Figure 20-3, when you double-click a field in the Available Fields box, it appears on the right, in the Prototype Label box.

8. **After the field name appears in the Prototype Label box, type a space after it so there's a space between the first field and the second one.**

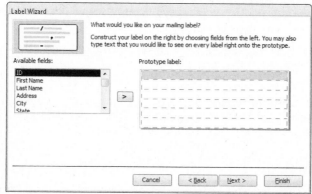

Figure 20-3:
Choose
your fields
from the
Available
Fields box.

9. **Double-click the next field to insert into your label and place a space or press Enter after the field (to advance to the next line), as in Step 8.**

   Continue double-clicking fields to add them to the Prototype — being careful to put spaces between fields and to press the Enter key to move to a new line in the Prototype box, as needed. Figure 20-4 shows a completed address label.

10. **Click Next.**

    Now the dialog box changes to offer choices for sorting your labels.

11. **Select the field by which to sort your labels — such as by last name or by Zip code.**

    As shown in Figure 20-5, you can sort by more than one field; the order in which you add fields to the Sort By box dictates the sort order.

Figure 20-4:
Space your fields and place them on separate lines. Don't forget commas and other symbols that may have to be included between the fields.

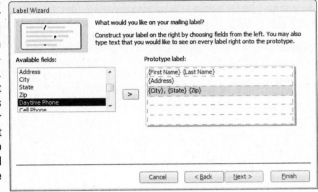

Figure 20-5:
Choose the field(s) you want to use to sort your labels.

If you plan a bulk mailing with discounted postage, check with your local postal authority for details about how to organize your mail. Post offices often want the mail pre-sorted by Zip code; check first because each post office may handle things differently. Rather than drive your friendly postal workers over the edge, bring your mail sorted the way *they* want it.

12. Click Next.

The next step in the wizard process appears, as shown in Figure 20-6.

13. Type a name for your Labels report.

14. Leave the default option chosen (See the Labels as They Will Look Printed) and click Finish.

The Labels report appears on-screen, as shown in Figure 20-7, and you can print as desired (by using the Print command, as usual). You can also save your work for future reprintings of the same report.

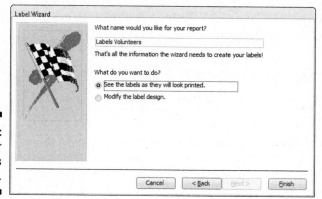

Figure 20-6:
Name your
Labels
report.

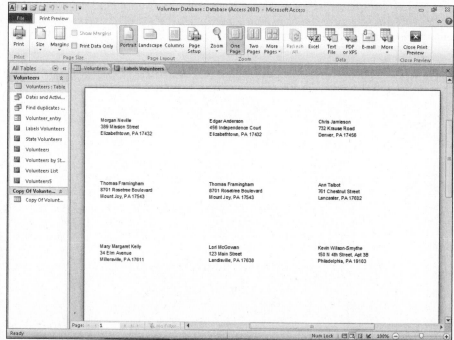

Figure 20-7:
You can
print your
labels now
and save
them for
later.

So you want to create a chart?

In previous versions of Access, charting (or graphing, depending on your terminology preference) tools were part of the action: You could transform your data into a bar, pie, or other lovely chart, suitable for any presentation purpose or venue. Sounds great, right? Well, in Access 2010 (actually, since Access 2007), the Chart Wizard no longer exists. If you want to create a chart, you have to use either of the following programs from the Microsoft Office suite:

✓ **PowerPoint, the presentation application in Microsoft Office:** If you want to use PowerPoint, you can use the datasheet that appears automatically in a PowerPoint chart slide, and you can type your chart data (such as department names and total salary expenses for a given time period) into that datasheet. Alternatively, you can paste your data from an Access table into the PowerPoint chart.

✓ **Excel, the Microsoft Office spreadsheet application:** You can paste or import your Access table data into Excel and then use Excel's charting tools to create a chart based on those numbers.

If you're feeling discouraged about Access' reduced charting capabilities, don't be. Access isn't really the place to build charts. If you have Office, then you already have much better charting tools in PowerPoint and Excel; these two applications use charting more naturally than a database application ever could. A PowerPoint presentation is a perfect place for charts — as is an Excel workbook, where rows and rows of numeric data are often better explained with pictures, in the form of a nice, clear pie chart. Because you can easily use your Access table data to populate a PowerPoint datasheet or an Excel worksheet (and therefore base a chart on the data), you could say that the charting capability has simply been confined to the applications where it belongs.

Part VI
More Power to You

The 5th Wave   By Rich Tennant

©RICHTENNANT

"Yes, I know how to query information from the program, but what if I just want to leak it instead?"

In this part . . .

Power. It's, well, powerful. It's "the ultimate
aphrodisiac" — it's coveted by everyone, in one
form or another, and (lucky for you) Access makes it
easy to grab some and take control of your data.

Part VI gives you more power in the form of the Access
Analyzer, a tool that tunes up your database for better
performance. It also gives you more power by showing
you how, in Chapter 22, to create navigational interface
tools to help users find their way around your database —
and to also control what people see, which tables they
can edit, and how they work with your database, overall.
If you've got people doing data entry for you — or using
your database on their own for any reason — this will be a
really powerful weapon in your Access arsenal.

Chapter 21

Making It All Better with the Analyzer Tools

In This Chapter

▶ Converting a flat file to relational tables with Table Analyzer

▶ Documenting your database

▶ Fine-tuning your database with Performance Analyzer

*T*he Access Analyzer tools promise to help you set up, document, and fine-tune the performance of your database. Sound too good to be true? Well, like most software tools that promise the blessings of automation, the Analyzer tools do some things well — and others not so well.

Here is what the Analyzer tools promise to do:

✔ Convert flat files into relational databases automatically.

✔ Document the database and all its parts (including tables, queries, forms, and reports).

✔ Analyze the structure of your tables to make sure everything is set up in the best possible way.

So which Analyzer tool makes good on its promise? That would have to be the Database Documenter. To do manually what the Database Documenter does would take the average person hours, if not days. If you're using the Analyzer tools for the other two tasks, they don't quite deliver on their promises — but they do have merit, so we cover them as well.

Convert Your Flat Files to Relational Tables with Analyzer

Doesn't this sound great? The Table Analyzer promises to take a messy flat-file table (such as an imported spreadsheet) — with all its repetitive data — and convert it to an efficient set of relational tables. But, as the bromide goes, promises made are promises broken. Unless your flat file follows some strict rules, the Table Analyzer won't quite get it right. I would love to tell you what those rules are, but only Microsoft knows the mysterious rules of the Table Analyzer.

A *flat-file* database is one in which all of the data is in one file. Access is a relational database that allows data to be stored in multiple tables for more efficiency.

Sometimes you get a perfect set of relational tables, and sometimes the Table Analyzer doesn't suggest a new table when it should or suggests a new table when it shouldn't. My advice to you is to give it a try and see what happens. Best case, it works right and you've just saved yourself a boatload of time. Worst case, it doesn't work right and you wasted a few minutes of your time.

The Analyzer works best with a flat-file table that contains plenty of duplicate information. For example, imagine a flat-file table for a video rental store. Each record in the table contains customer and movie data. If the same customer rents six movies, the table contains six separate records with the customer's name, address, and other information duplicated in every one. Multiply that by 1,000 customers, and you have precisely the kind of flat-file mess that the Analyzer loves to solve.

With that thought in mind, here's how to invoke the Table Analyzer Wizard:

1. **Open your database and select the table you'd like to evaluate from the Navigation pane.**

2. **Click the Database Tools tab.**

   The Analyze group of tools appears on the Ribbon as shown in Figure 21-1.

3. **Click the Analyze Table button from the Analyze group.**

   The Table Analyzer Wizard dialog box appears (see Figure 21-2).

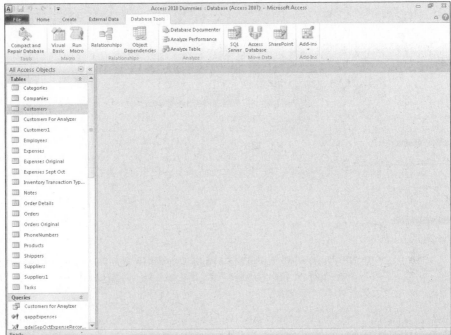

Figure 21-1: Starting an Analyzer tool.

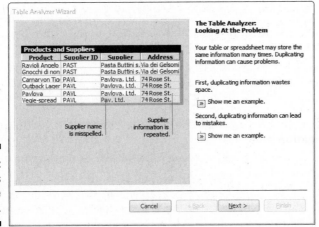

Figure 21-2: Here comes the Table Analyzer.

4. **Read the first two screens if you want (they're strictly educational); click Next after each one.**

   Another Table Analyzer Wizard screen appears, as shown in Figure 21-3.

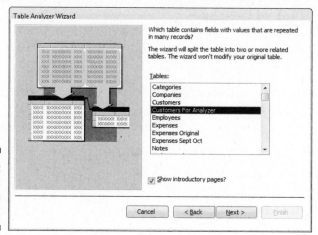

Figure 21-3:
Select a
table to
analyze.

5. **The name of the table you selected in the Navigation pane should be selected in the Tables list. If it is not, click the name of the table you'd like to convert.**

6. **Click Next.**

   In the dialog box that appears, the wizard asks whether you want to just let the wizard do its thing (the wizard will decide how the flat-file table should be arranged into multiple tables) or if you want to decide which fields go to what tables.

7. **Click the Yes option (if it's not already selected) to give the wizard full power in deciding the fate of your table; then click Next.**

   If the wizard recommends that you not split your table, click the Cancel button and pat yourself on the back for a job well done. This message means that the wizard thinks your table is fine just as it is.

   If the wizard does split your table, it will analyze your table and show you its findings. The results look like those shown in Figure 21-4.

8. **Make sure the information from your flat-file table is grouped correctly into new tables:**

   • *If the information is grouped correctly,* name the tables by double-clicking each table's title bar and typing a new name in the resulting dialog box.

   • *If the information is not grouped correctly,* use your mouse to drag and drop fields from table to table — and then double-click each table's title bar to rename the tables.

   • *If you want to create a new table,* drag a field into any open space between or around the existing tables. The wizard will create a new table window containing the field. Double-click the new table's title bar to rename the table.

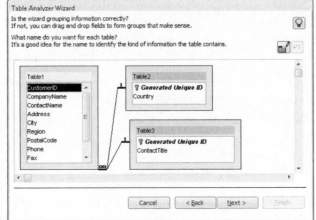

Figure 21-4:
The Table
Analyzer
makes its
decision.

9. **When you're finished arranging and naming your tables, click Next.**

   The wizard automatically selects a key field for each table that it thinks needs a key field. Should the wizard select a field incorrectly as a key field, you can correct the error.

10. **If the wizard does not designate a key field properly, you can:**

    - *Designate an existing field as a key field* by selecting the field and clicking the Set Unique Identifier button (looks like a key).

    - *Change a key-field designation* by selecting the proper key field and then clicking the Set Unique Identifier button (looks like a key).

    - *Add a key field* by clicking the Add Generated Key button (contains a plus sign and key).

11. **Click Next for the final step in the process.**

    The wizard offers to create a query that looks and acts like your original table. If you have reports and forms that work with the flat file, they'll work with the new query.

At this point in the process, you may not see the last screen of the wizard as described in Step 13; the wizard may tell you that some of your data might be incorrect and that you should correct it. For example, if you have a Country field in your table and there are two entries such as USA and UAS, the wizard will ask you for — or suggest — a correction for the error. You definitely should correct this type of error. Unfortunately, I've found that the wizard is often not very good at identifying such errors. (It might suggest that you change Belgium to Brazil, for example.) My advice is to take a quick peek at the data for actual errors and move on — because the suggested "corrections" are often incorrect!

12. **Choose Yes to have the wizard create the query or No to skip query creation.**

    `Yes` creates a query that runs against the new tables. The query looks and acts like the original table. The original table is renamed with an `_OLD` slapped on the end, and any reports and forms use the query (instead of the original table) automatically. `No` generates the new tables but leaves the original table with its original name.

13. **Click Finish to exit the wizard.**

    The wizard completes the process of splitting the flat-file table into a set of relational tables.

The Table Analyzer is unlikely to split a flat-file database *correctly* into a properly designed relational database — especially if the flat file is complicated. You're much better off bringing the database to a qualified human and letting him or her properly redesign it as a relational database — or figuring out how to do that yourself!

Record Database Object Details with the Database Documenter

In the world of database development, the last thing on the to-do list — if it's done at all — is database documentation. You're probably asking yourself, "Why do I need to create a mountain of paper to tell me about my database?" Well, if you're the developer of that database and something were to happen to you — say, you're promoted or you leave the company — someone else would take over responsibility for the database — and be up a creek without a clue. A well-documented database is easier to maintain than one that is not documented.

Why is this important step rarely done? Because it takes time and money — both of which are in short supply for most businesses. Enter the Database Documenter. It browses through everything in your database and records the minutest of details about each item, be it a table, field, form, query, or report. The Database Documenter collects information so obscure that I'm not even sure the programmers know what some of it means.

The Database Documenter is fast and easy. All you have to do is turn it on and it does the rest. Before you know it, the timely and costly job is done!

Here's how to document your database:

1. **Open your database and select the Database Tools tab.**

   The Analyze group appears on the Ribbon.

2. **Click the Database Documenter tool in the Analyze tool group.**

   The Documenter dialog box appears.

3. **In the Documenter dialog box, click the All Object Types tab, as shown in Figure 21-5.**

Figure 21-5:
Click the
All Object
Types tab
and then
click
Select All.

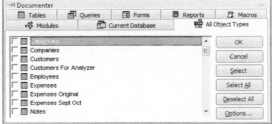

4. **Click the Select All button to document every object in your database, then click OK to start the process.**

   The Documenter begins by examining all the objects in your database, starting with the tables and moving on to the queries, forms, reports, and so on.

   During the process, your forms and reports may appear on-screen for a moment — that's normal.

   The process can take a while, depending on the size and complexity of the database you are documenting. So you might want to run the Documenter before a coffee or lunch break. There's nothing more satisfying than "working" on a break. When the Documenter finishes, it creates a lengthy report about your database, as shown in Figure 21-6.

5. **Click the Print button on the Ribbon to get a paper copy.**

   Access doesn't care a whit about trees or how much paper costs, so it generates hundreds of documentation pages about your database. For a small-to mid-size database, this can be 500 to 1,000 pages of information. If you really want everything documented, and don't want a couple of reams of paper describing your database, consider saving the report and then referring back to it later. To store the report electronically, right-click the report while it is in Print Preview and choose, Export⇨ Word RTF File. Select the destination folder and file name then click the OK button. The resulting exported file can be opened in Word when needed.

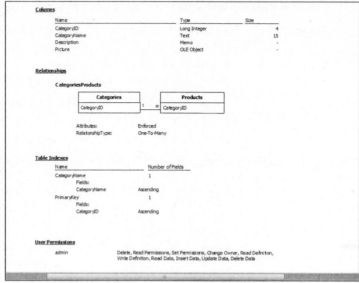

Figure 21-6:
This page of
the report
shows
some table
information.

If you run the Documenter and find that it has generated too much detail, you can control what is documented — thereby reducing the detail (and number of pages) in the resulting report. The following instructions remove specified object properties (such as field properties like the Field Size property) from the Documenter's report:

1. **From the Database Tools tab, click the Database Documenter tool in the Analyze tool group.**

   The Documenter window opens.

2. **Click the Database Documenter tool in the Analyze tool group.**

   The Documenter window opens.

3. **Click the All Object Types tab.**

4. **Click the Select All button.**

   Steps 2 and 3 tell the Documenter that you want to document all objects in the database.

5. **Repeat these steps for each object type (tables, queries, forms, reports) in the Documenter window:**

   a. *Click the tab for the desired object type (like the Tables tab).*

   b. *Click the Options button in the Documenter window.*

      The Print Definition dialog box for the object selected will appear. (Figure 21-7 shows the Print Table Definition dialog box.)

c. *Uncheck all the check boxes in the Include for <object type> section.*

In the Print Table Definition dialog box, for example, this section will be labeled Include for Table.

d. *In the remaining Include For sections, select the second radio button — the one below Nothing (as illustrated in Figure 21-7).*

In the Print Table Definition dialog box, for example, these sections are labeled *Include for Fields* and *Include for Indexes*.

e. *Click the OK button to close the Print Definition dialog box.*

6. **Click OK in the Documenter window to start the documentation process.**

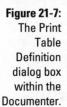
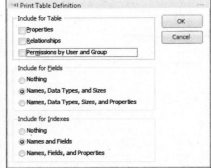

Figure 21-7:
The Print
Table
Definition
dialog box
within the
Documenter.

Improve Database Performance without Steroids

The Performance Analyzer is an Access tool that reviews each database object you designate and makes suggestions on how to improve the object's performance. It might, for example, tell you to break up a complex form that loads slowly on-screen into several smaller forms that will load faster. Use the Performance Analyzer to (a) locate problem objects that are affecting database performance and (b) improve those objects. This procedure, in turn, improves performance.

Like the Table Analyzer, the Performance Analyzer is far from perfect. When you run it (and you should), be sure to review its recommendations carefully *before* implementing them.

Here's how to use the Performance Analyzer:

1. **Make sure all database objects (such as forms and reports) are closed so the only remaining window is the Navigation pane.**

2. **Click the Database Tools tab on the Ribbon.**

    The Analyze tool group appears.

3. **Click the Analyze Performance tool from the Analyze tool group.**

    The Performance Analyzer dialog box appears.

4. **Choose the database objects (such as forms and reports) that you want to analyze.**

    I recommend clicking the All Object Types tab and then clicking the Select All button. The Performance Analyzer dialog box is similar to the Documenter dialog box (refer to Figure 21-5).

5. **Click the OK button to run the Performance Analyzer.**

    You'll see a dialog box flash on-screen, listing each database object as it's analyzed. Eventually, the results of the analysis appear in a dialog box.

6. **Select each result (as shown in Figure 21-8) and review the comments.**

    If Access can make the changes for you, the Optimize button is enabled. Otherwise, use a pencil and paper and jot down any good thoughts that Access may offer. Sadly, Access does not provide a way to print the Performance Analyzer's results — hence the pencil and paper.

7. **To implement a task from the results list, select it and click the Optimize button.**

    The Optimize button won't be available for all recommendations — only for those tasks that Access can implement.

    After Access performs the task, a blue check mark appears next to the task on the list.

8. **When you've completed your review of the Analyzer's suggestions, click the Close button to exit the Performance Analyzer dialog box.**

If you're not sure that a result should be implemented, don't implement it. Ask your local Access expert for his or her opinion before implementing such a result.

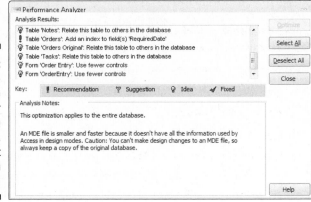

Figure 21-8:
Access supplies some tips for improving your work. Implement with caution!

Chapter 22

Hello! Creating an Interface to Welcome Database Users

In This Chapter

▶ Plugging into a Navigation form

▶ Testing your Navigation form

▶ Keeping the Navigation form running smoothly

▶ Opening a database to the Navigation form

*I*f you plan for others to use your database, you may want to provide them with navigation tools so they can easily find their way around your database (especially if they know nothing about Access). You might even want this luxury for yourself. It's much easier to move around a database with a navigation system in place. Fortunately, the Navigation form provided with Access 2010 makes it easy to build such a system. The form uses a familiar Web-type interface to view various database objects. This chapter explains all there is to know about making your database user-friendly via the Navigation form.

To see a Navigation form in action, download the sample files at `www.dummies.com/go/access2010`. Open the file Access 2010 Dummies.accdb and open the Home form.

The Comings and Goings of a Navigation Form

Before you create your Navigation form, take a few minutes to plan out your database navigation. How do you want you and your users to navigate to the various forms and reports you've created? Access provides several layouts for Navigation forms; which one you choose depends on what you need done:

- ✔ **If you have a simple database with a few data-entry forms and several reports, use one of the simpler layouts such as the Vertical Tabs, Left layout.**

- ✔ **If your database is more complex, you may need to categorize forms and reports. Use a multi-level layout such as the Horizontal Tabs and Vertical Tabs, Left layout.**

  For example, you might have a series of sales reports and a series of inventory reports. You may want two tabs across the top of your form — one for each series of reports. When you click a tab across the top, the associated reports for that tab show up down the left side of the form.

  This multi-level scheme can make the object you (and your users) are looking for easier to find.

Whatever you decide, you can always modify the design of your Navigation form at any time. (We discuss Navigation form editing later in the chapter.)

Creating a Navigation form

Here's how you build a Navigation form:

1. **Open the database file that will contain the Navigation form.**

2. **Click the Create tab on the Ribbon.**

   The Forms group appears toward the center of the Ribbon.

3. **Click the Navigation tool on the right side of the Forms group.**

   A drop-down list of Navigation layouts appears, as shown in Figure 22-1.

4. **Select a layout from the drop-down list.**

   The selected Navigation form appears in Layout view, ready for action. (See Figure 22-2.)

   The Navigation form does away with the old Switchboard Manager in earlier versions of Access. It's much easier to set up and use.

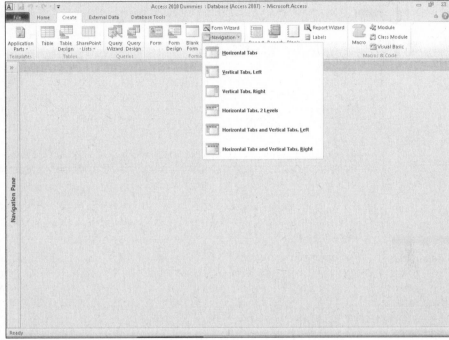

Figure 22-1:
Your
Navigation
layout
options.

5. **Show the Navigation pane, if necessary. (If you don't see it, press the F11 key.)**

   Your database objects appear.

    Don't confuse the Navigation *pane* with the Navigation *form*. The former is a special type of form that you create from a command on the Ribbon; the latter is the built-in window that displays your database objects.

6. **From the Navigation pane, drag an object that you want your users to open on top of an [Add New] tab on the Navigation form.**

   The object's name appears in place of the Add New tab; the object itself appears in the middle of the form. (See Figure 22-3 for an example.)

7. **Repeat Steps 5 and 6 for each object you'd like added to the Navigation form.**

8. **Save the form using the Save button on the Quick Access toolbar.**

   The form will appear in the Navigation pane along with all other database forms. (See "Displaying the Navigation Form at Startup," later in this chapter, for instructions on launching the form automatically when the database opens.)

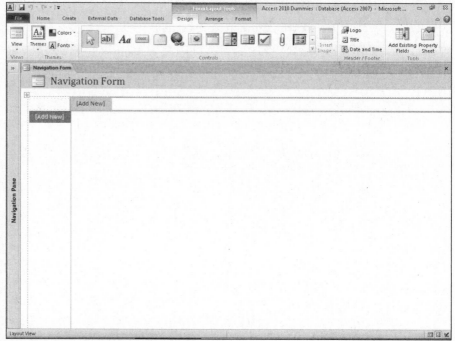

Figure 22-2:
The
Navigation
form, ready
to go.

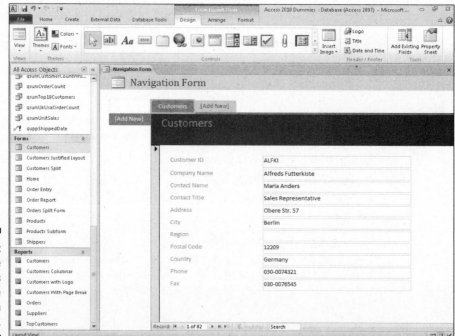

Figure 22-3:
Adding the
Customers
form to the
Navigation
form.

If you find your Navigation form filling up due to the many forms and reports you have, you can create several Navigation forms — and have one Navigation form call another. It's not that unusual; I've created databases containing well over 50 reports. In this instance, I might create a Reports Navigation form and call it from my main Navigation form. Just take care to arrange your forms and reports in a way that makes intuitive sense.

Am I in the Right Place? Testing Navigation Forms

After you've created your Navigation form, be sure to test it before turning your database loose on your users. You'll want to test for two qualities:

- ✔ The legitimacy of the commands you've added. Can you navigate to each form and report you'd like your users to see?
- ✔ The intuitive usability of your Navigation form. Is it easy to find everything?

Put yourself in the shoes of someone who knows nothing about Access. Could you figure out how to run a report or enter a new order with your Navigation form? If the answer is no, then you'd better make some modifications. If the answer is yes, pat yourself on the back for a job well done!

Present your Navigation form to someone who knows nothing about your database or Access. See if your "tester" can perform the basic tasks you'd like your users to perform — without any special instructions. Use your tester's feedback to tweak your Navigation form if necessary.

Of course, to do any testing, you'll want to see the form as your users will. Here's how:

1. **From the Navigation pane, double-click your Navigation form.**

   Your Navigation form opens in Form view. Figure 22-4 shows a sample horizontal and vertical tab Navigation form.

2. **Click a tab button to launch one of your forms or reports.**

   The form or report signified by the tab label should run. If it does, then you've done everything right! If it doesn't, you need to make some modifications — which I discuss in the next section.

3. **Repeat Step 2 for every tab you've created.**

   If everything checks out, your Navigation form is ready for launch.

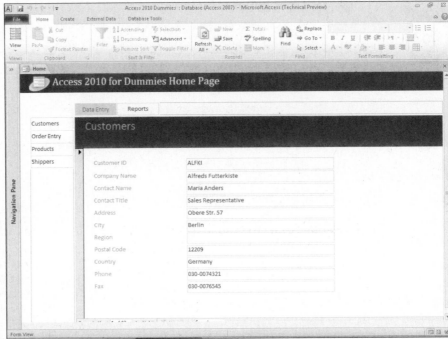

Figure 22-4:
A sample
Navigation
form with a
tab row and
column.

Maintaining the Navigation Form

Almost without fail, a Navigation form will need modifications. You may (for example) have to tweak that form to

- ✔ Correct mistakes or omissions made during initial Navigation form creation.
- ✔ Open new database objects (such as a new report).

See the "The Comings and Goings of a Navigation Form" section, earlier in the chapter, for more on creating Navigation forms. I'll just concentrate on editing, deleting, and moving items here.

Edit a Navigation form item

If a tab is misspelled or does not perform the expected command, you need to know how to fix that command. If the form title itself is mislabeled, you can fix that as well. Here's how:

1. **Show the Navigation pane, if necessary.**

   The Navigation pane appears, showing a list of all database objects.

2. **Right-click the Navigation form you'd like to edit from the Navigation pane and choose Layout View from the resulting shortcut menu.**

   The selected Navigation form opens in Layout view.

3. **To edit the Navigation form or tab name, double-click in the Navigation Form Name or Tab Name box and make your edits.**

4. **Click Save on the Quick Access toolbar to save your edits.**

Delete a Navigation Form tab item

If a Navigation Form tab is no longer needed, it's a snap to send that critter off to cyber-heaven.

Here are the steps for deleting a Navigation Form tab:

1. **Show the Navigation pane, if necessary.**

2. **Right-click the Navigation form you'd like to edit from the Navigation pane and choose Layout View from the resulting shortcut menu.**

   The selected Navigation form opens in Layout view.

3. **Select the tab you'd like to delete by clicking it.**

   A thick border will appear around the tab.

4. **Tap the Delete key on the keyboard.**

   The tab and its corresponding form or report are removed.

5. **Click Save on the Quick Access toolbar to save your changes.**

Move a Navigation Form item

If the tab order on a Navigation form is not quite right, it's easy to rearrange the tabs. You can move items up or down on a vertical set of tabs, and left or right on a horizontal set to put them in whatever order you deem appropriate. So let's get moving!

1. **Show the Navigation pane, if necessary.**

2. **Right-click the Navigation form you'd like to edit from the Navigation pane and choose Layout View from the resulting shortcut menu.**

   The selected Navigation form opens in Layout view.

3. **Select the tab you'd like to move by clicking it.**

   A thick border appears around the tab.

4. **Drag the selected tab into its new location.**

   A vertical or horizontal bar (depending on the orientation of the tabs) follows the tab as you drag.

5. **Release the mouse button when your tab has reached its new home.**

   The tab moves into its new position.

6. **Click Save on the Quick Access toolbar to save your changes.**

Displaying the Navigation Form at Startup

The last step in implementing a Navigation form is to have that Navigation form open when the database opens. Your users might find it inconvenient to have to locate the Navigation form and open it themselves, wouldn't you say? So you'll have to do it for them — automatically. Does this sound too good to be true? Well, it isn't. You can actually do it, and it's easy. Here are the steps:

1. **Click the File tab on the upper-left part of the screen.**

   Backstage view appears.

2. **Click Options on the menu in the left side of the screen.**

   The Access Options dialog box appears.

3. **Click Current Database from the list on the left.**

   The Current Database options appear. Note the Application Options section near the top of the dialog box.

4. **Select your Navigation form from the Display Form drop-down list, as shown in Figure 22-5.**

   I called my Navigation form "Home." Quite charming, don't you think?

Want to control the Title Bar name and icon that appears on-screen when you launch your database? Complete the Application Title and Application Icon text boxes; they're located near the top of the Current Database options.

Display form

Figure 22-5:
The Home
form
launches
automatically when
this database is
opened.

Hide the Navigation pane from your users by removing the check from the Display Navigation Pane check box located further down in the Current Database options. Doing so forces them to use your navigation system, thereby keeping them out of database objects you don't want them to mess around with.

5. **Click the OK to save the change.**

   A message box appears indicating you must close then reopen the database to see the change take effect.

6. **Click OK in the message box window.**

7. **Close the database file and then reopen it.**

   The Navigation form opens automatically for the entire world to see.

Part VII
The Part of Tens

The 5th Wave   By Rich Tennant

"Once I told Mona that Access was an 'argument' based program, she seemed to warm up to it."

In this part . . .

What the heck is a *Part of Tens*? If you asked that
question, too, the first time you picked up a
Dummies book, you're not alone. We asked too. One of
us may have said it out loud in the bookstore, drawing
unwanted attention. (We'll be discreet about which of us
tends to do that sort of thing.)

Anyway, what we found out is that the Part of Tens is a
section of the book that has fabulous lists of 10 things
related to the book's topic. If this were a book called
Avoiding Jail For Dummies, there might be a list of Ten
Ways to Dispose of the Evidence or Ten Ways to Fool a
Polygraph.

Although such a book is probably even more useful than
this one to (ahem) certain readers, this is a book about
Access 2010 — so we're offering Ten Common Problems
and Ten Uncommon Tips.

Chapter 23

Ten Common Problems

. . . .

In This Chapter

▶ Normalizing tables

▶ Resolving data-entry problems

▶ Consoling query woes

▶ Solving invalid validation

▶ Tuning up performance troubles

▶ Importing spreadsheet data with less mess

▶ Dealing with corruption

. . . .

Yes, even so-called "experts" have problems with computers. I've chosen ten of the most common Microsoft Access problems and presented them to you in this chapter — with their solutions, of course!

Don't despair if your problem is not on my list. I find many solutions to my computing problems by searching the Access newsgroups online. Chances are, if I'm having the problem, someone else has already had it and figured out the solution. That's why the newsgroups are a valuable resource. The Appendix on this book's Web site lists a few more valuable help resources.

Speaking of valuable resources, check out the ten problems in this chapter.

That's Just Not Normal

One of the hardest things to do (yet most important when building a database) is building the table structures properly. This process is known as *normalization*. A properly normalized database should never have just one table containing redundant information. Consider the following table:

Customer	*Address*	*City*	*State*	*Zip*	*Telephone*
Jones	125 Main Street	Jonestown	NJ	08000	609-555-1234
Jones	125 Main Street	Jonestown	NJ	08000	609-555-7890
Smith	1542 Jones Hwy	Laramie	WY	82051	307-555-5412
Wilson	78 Smith Circle	Jones	CA	90000	451-555-8645

Do you see the redundant information? Right you are. It's the customer name and address. What is causing the redundancy? Right again! It's the two phone numbers for customer Jones. The correct way to normalize this table would be to split it into two tables — one for customer name and address information and the second for phone numbers. This would eliminate the need to repeat the second Jones record in the Customers table.

If you're having trouble normalizing empty tables, fill each table with five to ten records. Viewing the tables with data usually makes it easier to spot normalizing issues.

Here's how to get started normalizing your tables:

1. **Examine each table as it is currently structured.**

   Are you repeating any information unnecessarily (as we saw with the address and customer name earlier)?

2. **If you have duplicate information, determine why you are repeating it (for example, the multiple phone numbers for one customer).**

3. **Break the one table into two tables to eliminate the redundancy.**

4. **Repeat Steps 1–3 for each table until all redundancy is eliminated.**

You may find that splitting one table into two still does not eliminate all redundancy in a table. In that case, keep splitting the tables until all redundancy is gone.

You Type 73.725, but it Changes to 74

Automatic rounding can frustrate the living daylights out of you, but correcting it is easy. By default, Access sets all number fields to accept *long integers*. As you may remember from your high school math days, an integer is a negative or positive *whole number*. To accommodate long integers, you change the field-size setting so it accepts decimals. Here's how:

1. **Open the table in Design view and then click the field that's not cooperating.**

2. **On the General tab of the Properties area at the bottom of the screen, click the Field Size box.**

3. **Click the down arrow at the end of the box, and then select Single, Double, or Decimal from the drop-down menu that appears.**

4. **Save the table and your automatic rounding problem is over.**

 For details about the difference between Single, Double, and Decimal field sizes, press the F1 key while in the Field Size property box. The Help screen gives a detailed description of each field size, the numbers it will hold, and the amount of space reserved for that size.

The Words They Are A-Changing

Sometimes those "helpful" features in Access can become a nuisance. One such feature is called AutoCorrect. You may be familiar with it from Microsoft Word, where it is often a great thing. Databases, however, often contain acronyms, part numbers, and the like. AutoCorrect can have a field day with such "words." You may not even realize it as you enter your data.

You have two choices to resolve this problem.

- ✔ **Undo AutoCorrect's effects as they occur.** Press Ctrl+Z right after AutoCorrect has botched your data entry. Access puts the data back to the way you typed it. Unfortunately, for this to work you actually have to notice that Access has changed what you entered.

- ✔ **Turn AutoCorrect off entirely.** To turn off AutoCorrect, follow these steps:

    1. *Click the File tab in the upper-left corner of the Access screen.*

       Backstage view appears.

    2. *Click the Options button in the menu down the left side of the screen.*

       The Access Options dialog box appears.

    3. *Click Proofing from the list on the left.*

       Your proofing choices appear.

    4. *Click the AutoCorrect Options button.*

       The AutoCorrect dialog box appears.

    5. *Uncheck some or all of the check boxes in the AutoCorrect dialog box.*

You can disable some or all of the AutoCorrect features, depending on what AutoCorrect is doing to annoy you at present. Uncheck the Replace Text as You Type option if you no longer wish Access to "fix" your "spelling errors" for you.

6. *Click OK two times to save your changes.*

You can now type your problem text correctly, without AutoCorrect's interference, and have it stay as you typed it.

Was There and Now It's Gone

I've heard this one a lot over the years: "The database deleted my record!" Well, I've got news for you: The database doesn't do anything without us humans commanding it. And humans can make a couple of mistakes:

- ✔ **Accidental deletion:** There are several ways to delete a record accidentally. Usually a keyboard shortcut for Delete is pressed, such as Ctrl+Shift+– or Ctrl+X.

  The Undo command (Ctrl+Z) will not reverse the deletion of a record.

- ✔ **Data error:** A record may *appear* deleted if someone inadvertently changes a particularly vital piece of information. For example, suppose the record in question contains an order date of 12/15/09, and someone inadvertently changes the date to 12/15/06. The order date isn't what's expected, so the record may seem to have been deleted.

If a data error makes the record seem deleted, there are several possible fixes, as I outline in the following sections.

Undo

Don't panic. Before doing anything else, press Ctrl+Z. That's the Undo command. If the record comes back, you're in luck. Undo reverses data-entry errors that may cause the record to appear deleted. However, this will only work if you Undo right after the data-entry error takes place.

Search for the missing record

If you try the Undo command and the record doesn't come back, there's still a chance that a data-entry error is hiding it by putting it where you don't expect it to be. Open the table that contained the record and search for it in some way other than you normally would. Look for anything out of the ordinary on similar records. Here are some examples:

✔ If you normally search for orders by date, search by client. See whether an order similar to the missing one exists for that client *and* has an unusual date (say, the same month and day as the missing order but with the wrong year).

✔ Try looking at all orders on the date in question to see whether the client on each order seems to be correct. It could be that the client was changed inadvertently on the missing order.

Backup recovery

If you can't find the record anywhere, copy the record from a backup of the database file.

This solution works only if you've backed up your database since the record was originally added. If you back up at night and the record was entered during the same day it went missing, that record will not be in your backup.

You Run a Query, but the Results Aren't What You Expect

Query-writing is an art form. Even the experts spill their paint every now and then. Here are some common solutions to unexpected query results:

✔ **Check criteria for accuracy.** A single misplaced keystroke is all it takes to turn your query into a dud. Check your criteria for spelling or syntax errors — and then run the query again.

✔ **Try the Unique Values property.** Ever see two copies of each record in your query results when you were expecting just one? A quick fix often comes from using the Unique Values property. This property tells Access to stop with the doubling, already — and, if the query results contain a group of exact duplicates, to return only one row from the group. Here's how to use this property:

   1. Open the problem query in Design view.

   The Design tab on the Ribbon appears.

   2. Click the Property Sheet button from the tab's Show/Hide Ribbon group.

   The Property Sheet window opens to the right of the query grid.

   3. Click in the grey area between the field lists in the top half of the query grid.

The Property Sheet should now display Query Properties. (Look right under the Property Sheet's title bar to confirm this.)

4. Click in the Unique Values row of the Property Sheet.

A drop-down list arrow appears at the end of the Unique Values row.

5. Select Yes from the drop-down list and run the query.

The doubling should disappear.

✔ **Correct the selection logic.** Juggling a bunch of AND and OR connections in a query can quickly mess up even the hardiest of database designers. Chapter 13 has tips on untangling the mess.

✔ **Fix table joins.** If your query results show *way* too many records, and the query uses two or more tables, improper joining is the likely cause. Flip back to Chapter 4 for more about joining one table to another.

✔ **Check table join types.** If your query involves two or more tables, and you get fewer records than you expected, incorrect table joins are the likely cause. For example, if you have an order entry database and run a query listing all customers and their orders, by default, you would see only those customers who have placed an order. To see all customers, whether or not they've placed orders, do the following:

1. In the Design view, right-click the join (the line connecting the two tables) and choose Join Properties from the menu that appears.

2. Examine the types of joins offered and choose the one that says something like "Include ALL records from 'Customers' and only those records from 'Orders' where the joined fields are equal."

The actual text you see differs according to the names of your tables. To query aficionados, this is called an *outer join*. Very cool.

3. Click OK and run the query.

You should now have all records from the Customers table whether there are corresponding records in the Orders table.

If your query involves several criteria, some calculated fields, and numerous joins, try breaking the task into several smaller steps instead of trying to solve the problem all at once. The step-by-step approach lets you focus on each piece, one at a time, making sure each works perfectly before moving on to the next one.

If your query still doesn't work no matter what you do, ask someone else to take a look. I've often wrangled with a tough query problem for hours, shown it to someone else, and heard those magical words: "That's simple. Just do this." And the problem is solved. Getting a fresh pair of eyes on the problem often solves things fast.

The Validation That Never Was

Validations are a great feature in Access that we discuss in great detail in Chapter 6. But validations can cause problems if they're not used properly. The biggest concern is a validation rule that *can't* be valid. For example, suppose someone wants to limit a particular field so it accepts entries between 0 and 100. To accomplish this feat, the person creates a validation that says <0 AND >100. Unfortunately, that rule won't work — ever! The person mixed up the symbols and created a rule that accepts only a number that's both less than 0 *and* greater than 100. No such number exists — but Access isn't smart enough to know that.

Don't let this problem happen to your validations. To avoid such errors, write your rule on paper and then test it with some sample data. Be sure to include examples of both good and bad entries to make sure that the rule works just the way it's supposed to.

The Slowest Database in Town

An Access database may end up on the shared drive of a business so it's available to everyone who needs it. The problem with placing the entire Access database on the shared drive is that it often runs slowly on each user's workstation (that's a fancy word for an individual computer). The complaints start rolling in and you don't know what to do.

The solution to this problem lies in splitting the Access database file into two separate files:

- ✔ **Front end:** Contains all the database objects *except* the tables.

  The front end resides on the user workstation.

- ✔ **Back end:** Contains just the tables.

  The back end resides on the shared server.

  The front end is linked to tables in the back end. (See Chapter 8 for more on table linking.)

All you're really sharing is the data— so the data is all that should go on the shared drive. By setting things up this way, the only information that *must* travel across the network is the data requested by the user. Such a setup dramatically speeds database performance.

Splitting the dataset is not as hard as you might think. Access makes it a snap with the Database Splitter Wizard. Follow these steps to split your database:

1. **Back up the database you'd like to split.**

   If anything goes wrong (unlikely, but hey, you can never be too safe when it comes to data!), you can try again with the backup copy.

2. **If necessary, move the database you'd like to split to a folder on your shared drive.**

   This step allows the Database Splitter to set up table links properly for you.

3. **Open the database file you'd like to split from the shared folder.**

   Make sure you have a backup copy of this database before going any farther. Also make sure all database objects are closed.

4. **Click the Database Tools tab on the Ribbon.**

   The Move Data group appears on the Ribbon. It contains a tool called Access Database.

5. **Click the Access Database tool.**

   The Database Splitter wizard dialog box appears.

6. **Click the Split Database button and let the wizard do its thing.**

   You will be prompted for a back-end database filename. Enter a name, sit back, and watch the fun unfold before your very eyes.

7. **Copy the front end file (the original file you split) to each user workstation.**

   Have each user open the file from his or her workstation — and see how they marvel at the improved speed of the database!

Your Database File Is as Big as a Whale

As time goes by, you find your database file growing larger and larger. This is a result of deleting objects and records over time. If for example, you create a query and then later delete it because it is no longer needed, Access doesn't automatically remove the space occupied by that query from the database file. The same is true for records. As you delete records from a table, the space that those records occupied in the database file remains. Eventually, the file can become four or five times the size required to hold the data and objects within it.

Why should you care if the file size increases? Here are a few reasons:

> ✔ **A smaller database file runs faster.** Performance is a key component to happy database users. You want your forms to load quickly and your queries and reports to run as fast as possible.
>
> ✔ **A regularly compacted database is more stable.** If the database is used often, compacting regularly helps keep file and table corruption from occurring.
>
> ✔ **A regularly compacted database recovers disk space.** I think we all know that's a good thing.

The Compact and Repair command removes the excess. It is good practice to compact your database regularly (once a week is usually fine). Always compact it after making any design changes. Here's how:

1. **Open the bloated database and click the Database Tools tab on the Ribbon.**

   The Tools group appears at the very left of the Ribbon.

2. **Click the Compact and Repair Database button from the Tools group.**

   The status bar (lower-right of your screen) displays a progress bar that notifies you of how the compact process is progressing. When the progress bar disappears, compacting is complete — and you'll be left with a much trimmer (faster and more stable) database file.

Want the database file to compact each time you close it? Follow these steps:

1. **Click the File tab on the Ribbon.**

   Backstage view appears.

2. **Click the Access Options button in the menu bar down the left side of the screen.**

   The Access Options dialog box appears.

3. **Click Current Database from the list on the left.**

   Options for the current database appear.

4. **Check the Compact on Close check box.**

5. **Click OK to save your changes.**

6. **Click OK from the resulting message box.**

7. **Close the database and note the lower-right status bar.**

   The database is compacting before it closes!

You Get a Mess When Importing Your Spreadsheet

It's common practice to upgrade a collection of spreadsheets to an Access database after the spreadsheet solution no longer suits your needs. It's also common to find the imported spreadsheet (now table) data in a state of disarray. The easiest way to solve this problem is by cleaning up the spreadsheet *before* you import it. Here are a few tips for a tidy import:

- ✔ **Double-check information coming from any spreadsheet program to be sure that it's *consistent* and *complete*.** Above all, make sure that all entries in each column (field) are the same data type (all numbers, all text, or all whatever).

- ✔ **Remove any titles and blank rows from the top of the spreadsheet.** An ideal spreadsheet for import will have field names (column headings) in Row 1 and data starting in Row 2.

- ✔ **Make sure your spreadsheet column headings are short and unique** so Access can easily translate them to field names during import.

We're Sorry; Your Database File Is Corrupt

It started out as a day just like any other. However, on this day, you are getting an error when you open the front end of your split access database. You can't seem to open any forms or reports. It's funny how a few little messages can ruin your day. You start wondering if you backed up the data file last night and when the file was actually corrupted. Then you start wondering how you'll get out of this mess.

Fear not. There is a simple solution to a corrupt database. Here are the steps:

1. **Browse to the folder that contains the back-end file.**

2. **Double-click the file to open it.**

   Access will launch and attempt to repair the file. You should see a repair progress bar on the right part of the status bar. If all goes well, the file opens.

3. **Close the back-end data file.**

4. **Reopen the front-end file and everything should be working normally.**

If, after following the preceding directions, the corrupted file still does not open, you have a serious problem that could take some effort to clean up. The next step is to resort to a backup copy of the database. Check what data is missing between the backup and your recollection of the corrupted file. Yes, you'll have to re-enter any missing data. Sorry!

If you don't have a backup, all hope is not lost. You can buy software that is designed specifically to repair corrupted Access database files. Try searching the Web for **"repair corrupt Microsoft Access database files"**. Make sure the software works with Microsoft Access 2010.

Chapter 24

Ten Uncommon Tips

In This Chapter

▶ Documenting everything

▶ Cutting the excess from your fields

▶ Storing numbers as numbers

▶ Validating your data

▶ Naming your tables well

▶ Dodging deletion distress

▶ Thinking about the best, planning for the worst

▶ Keeping your data ducks in a row

▶ Sending out an SOS

Technical experts — the geeks/gurus who really know Access — might be annoying (perhaps simply because they exist and know way more about databases than a human should) but they're important. They're important to average Access users because they provide invaluable advice — and they're important to Access itself because they drive the way Microsoft continuously improves its products. They're the people who test Office products before said products hit the shelves, and they're the ones who write books (like this one and more advanced books for more advanced users).

So the people who develop databases for a living are an essential resource to the average user, to the "power user," and to the software manufacturer as well. This chapter is a compilation of some of the best advice gathered from a host of Access experts. Knowing they were offering suggestions for new users, nothing you read here is going to make your head spin or make you doubt that after reading this book, you really can use Access. On the contrary — the advice found here will help you be more confident and effective in your use of Access because you'll have given your efforts the right amount of planning and organizing — and you'll have solid plans for moving forward with your development and use of the databases you build with Access.

So here's the sage advice — in ten quick bites.

Document Everything as Though You'll be Questioned by the FBI

Don't skimp on the time spent documenting your database. Why? Because you'll be glad later on that you *didn't* skimp. You'll have all your plans, your general information, and all your ideas — those you acted on and those that remained on the drawing board — ready the next time you need to build a database. You'll also have them to refer to when or if something goes awry with your current database. You accidentally deleted a saved query? No problem. Refer to your documentation. Forgot how your tables were related? Check the documentation and rebuild the relationships.

So what should this glorious documentation include? Well, everything. But here's a list to get you started:

- **General information about the database:**
  - File locations (with specific network paths, not just drive letters)
  - Explanation of what the database does
  - Information on how it works

- **Table layouts:**

  Include field names, sizes, contents, and sample contents.

  If some of the data comes from esoteric or temporary sources (say, the shipping report that you always shred right after data entry), note that fact in the documentation.

- **Summary of reports:**
  - Report names
  - An explanation of the information on the report
  - A list of who gets a copy of the report when it's printed

     Jot down the *job title and department* in the documentation as well as the current person in the position.

  If you need to run some queries before creating a report, document the process. (Better, get a friendly nerd to help you automate the work.)

- **Queries and logic:** For every query, provide a detailed explanation of how the query works, especially if it involves multiple tables or data sources outside Access (such as SQL tables or other big-time information-storage areas).

✔ **Answer the question "Why?":** As you document your database, focus on *why* your design works the way it works. Why do the queries use those particular tables? Why do the reports go to those people? Granted, if you work in a corporate environment, you may not *know* why the system works the way it does, but it never hurts to inquire.

✔ **Disaster-recovery details:**

* The backup process and schedule

* Where backup tapes are located (you *are* making backups, right?)

* What to do if the computer isn't working

If your database runs an important business function — such as accounting, inventory, point-of-sale, or order entry — make sure that a manual process is in place to keep the business going if the computer breaks down — and remember to document the process!

If you need help with any of these items, *ask someone!* Whether you borrow someone from your Information Systems department or rent a computer geek, get the help you need. Treat your documentation like insurance — no business should run without it.

Every 6 to 12 months, review your documentation to see whether updates are needed. Documentation is useful only if it's up to date *and* if someone other than you can understand it. Likewise, make sure you (or your counterparts in the department) know where the documentation is located. If you have an electronic version, keep it backed up and have a printout handy — something you'll be glad you did if you or someone else attempts to recycle your database parts using the Application Parts feature, new to Access 2010.

Keep Your Fields as Small as Possible

As you build tables, make your text fields the appropriate sizes for the data you keep in them. By default, Access sets up text fields to hold 50 characters — a pretty generous setting, particularly if the field holds measly two-letter state abbreviations.

Forty-eight characters of extra space wouldn't be anything to write home about, but multiply that space across a table with 100,000 customer addresses in it, and you get 4.8 MB of storage space that's very busy holding nothing.

Adjust the field size with the Field Size setting on the General tab in Design view.

Use Number Fields for Real Numbers

Use number fields for numbers used in calculations, not for text pretending to be a number. Computers perceive a huge difference between the postal code 47999 and the number 47,999. The computer views a postal code as a series of characters that all happen to be digits, but the *number* is treated as an actual number that you can use for math and all kinds of other fun numeric stuff.

When choosing the type for a new field with numbers in it, ask yourself a simple question: Are you *ever* going to make a calculation or do anything math-related with that field?

  ✔ If you'll calculate with the field, use a *number* type.

  ✔ If you won't calculate with the field, store the field as *text*.

Validate Your Data

Validations can help prevent bad data from getting close to your tables. Validations are easy to make, quick to set up, and ever-vigilant (even when you're so tired you can't see straight). If you aren't using validations to protect the integrity of your database, you really should start. Flip to Chapter 6 and have a look at the topic.

Use Understandable Names to Keep Things Simple

When building a table or creating a database, think about the database file, field, and table names you use:

  ✔ Will you remember what the names mean three months from now? Six months from now?

  ✔ Are the names intuitive enough that someone else can look at the table and figure out what it does, long after your knowledge of Access puts your career on the fast track?

Windows allows long filenames. Use them. You don't need to get carried away, but now you have no excuse for a file called *10Q1bdg5*. Using *2010 Q1 Budget Rev 5* makes much more sense to everyone involved.

This becomes even more important as you start using the tools for putting your Access tables and databases online and sharing them via SharePoint — potentially you're bringing millions of users "to the table." Also, with Access 2010's new Application Parts feature, the components of your databases can be recycled to help speed the creation of a new database. You don't want mysterious names for the parts of your database to spread to a new database— to create nightmarish mysteries there, too — right?

Delete with Great Caution

Whenever you're deleting field values from a table, make sure you're killing the values in the right record, check again, and *then* — only when you're sure — delete the original. Even then, you can still do a quick Ctrl+Z and recover the pestiferous thing.

Why all the checking and double-checking? Because after you delete a field value *and do anything else in the table,* Access completely forgets about your old value. It's gone, just as if it never existed. If you delete a record from a table, the record is really gone — because there is no Undo available for an entire record. If that record happened to be important and you didn't have a current backup file when the record went away, you're out of luck. Sorry!

Back up, Back up, Back up

Did I make that clear enough? Back up your work! There's no substitute for a current backup of your data — particularly if the data is vital to your personal or professional life. Effective strategies often include maintaining backup copies at another location in case a disaster destroys your office, be it a home office or an office at your employer's location.

If you're thinking that you've never needed a backup before, so why bother, think about floods. Think about newscasters saying that an area currently underwater has never flooded before. Picture people's lives floating down the street. Whether you're faced with a real disaster of hurricane proportions, a fire, or your computer's hard drive deciding to die (and that does happen — even if it has never happened to you before), you'll be much happier if you have a backup of your database.

Think, Think, and Think Again

You know the carpenter's slogan, "Measure twice, cut once"? The same can be said for thinking when it comes to your database. Don't just think about something, come to a quick conclusion, and then dive in. Wait, think it through again, and then maybe think about it a third time. *Then* draw a conclusion and begin acting upon it. With all the power Access gives you, coupled with the capability to store thousands of records in your database, a relatively simple mistake can be quite costly because of the potential ramifications in terms of data loss or an un-undo-able action taken in error.

Get Organized and Stay Organized

Although the suggestions to get organized and to keep it simple may seem to be at odds, these two pieces of advice are really companions. Keeping things simple can often be a way to avoid the need for a lot of organization after the fact. While you probably got tired of hearing your parents remind you that "there's a place for everything, and everything in its place" (or if they're less poetic, *"Clean your room!!!"*), they were right.

If you keep your database organized, you'll save yourself time and grief. A well-planned, well-organized table will be easier to query, report on, and include in a form. It'll also sort and filter like lightning.

Yes, you can get *too* organized. In fact, overorganizing is altogether too easy. Temper your desire to organize by cultivating another passion: working with as few steps as possible. On your computer, limit the number of folders and subfolders you use — a maximum of five levels of folders is more than enough for just about anybody. If you go much beyond five levels, your organization starts bumping into your productivity (and nobody likes a productivity loss, least of all the people who come up with those silly little slogans for corporate feel-good posters).

There's No Shame in Asking for Help

If you're having trouble with something, swallow your ego and ask for help. Saying "I don't know" — and then trying to find out about what you don't yet know — holds no shame. This rule is especially important when you're riding herd on thousands of records in a database. Small missteps quickly magnify and multiply a small problem into a huge crisis. Ask for help before the situation becomes dire.

Not sure how to ask for help? Check the Appendix on this book's Web site. This little chapter helps you get help through the installed Office suite, through Microsoft's online help, and through third-party sources that offer help on the Web 24/7. Crying "Uncle!" has never been easier.

Index

• *Symbols* •

& (ampersand), 120
* (asterisk), 67
@ (at sign), 120
: (colon), 67
- (dash), 67
$ (dollar sign), 67
" (double quotes), 67
= (equals), 226
€ (euro symbol), 122
! (exclamation point), 67
/ (forward slash), 67
> (greater-than), 120, 226
>= (greater-than-or-equal-to), 226
< (less-than), 120, 226
<= (less-than-or-equal-to), 227
<> (not equal to), 227
% (percent), 67
? (question mark), 67
; (semicolon), 67
' (single quote), 67

• *A* •

Access
    adding icon, 28
    benefits of using, 12–21
    file formats, 158
    navigating, 37–58
    new features for 2010, 21–25
    opening, 26–28
    starting points, 28–34
Access Options dialog box
    adding buttons to Quick Access toolbar,
        49–51
    displaying navigation forms at startup,
        396–397
    ScreenTips, 54–55
accessibility, 11

accessing
    context-sensitive tools, 47–48
    panels, 47–48
    panes, 47–48
    table properties, 116–118
action queries
    Append query, 283, 288–291
    Delete query, 283, 291–293
    overview, 283–284
    Update query, 283, 284–288
ad hoc queries
    overview, 236–240
    running queries, 242–243
    saving queries, 242
    sorting results, 240–242, 243
    table relationships, 239
    troubleshooting, 244
adding
    Access icon, 28
    buttons to Quick Access toolbar, 49–51
    color in reports, 327–329
    hyperlinks
        in fields, 183–184
        to forms, 188–193
    indexes, 95–97
    logos to reports, 342–343
    records, 103–105
    report design elements
        drawing lines, 341
        logo, 342–343
        space between columns, 332–333
    tables, 73–76
    Total row to queries, 257–258
adjusting
    reports
        items, 326–327
        margins, 315
        sections, 359–361
        views, 320–321
    text, 337–338
    types of lines, 336

Advanced Filter/Sort tool, 222, 224–229

alignment (report), 337

Alt key, 57–58

ampersand (&), 120

Analyzer tools

  converting flat files to relational tables, 378–382

  improving database performance, 385–387

  overview, 378

  recording database object details, 382–385

AND. *See also* OR

  combining with OR, 252–254

  multiple levels, 249–250

  using, 246–249

Append dialog box, 289–291

Append query

  creating, 288–291

  overview, 283

Application Parts feature, 22

applying formatting, 119

ASCII files, 159

asterisk (*), 67

at sign (@), 120

Attachment fields, 64

AutoCorrect feature, 403–404

AutoForm tools, 142–144

automatic reporting

  creating one-table reports, 298–303

  customizing reports, 314–318

  overview, 297–298

  previewing Report Wizard, 309–314

  starting Report Wizard, 304–309

automatic rounding, 402–403

AutoNumber fields, 84

Avg function, 256

• *B* •

Background Color button, 327

backing up tables, 170–171

Backstage View, 21, 41

backup recovery, 405, 417

benefits

  creating large databases, 12–13

  databases with user forms, 16–17

  multiple tables, 13–15

  special reporting, 18–21

book

  conventions, 2

  icons, 6

  organization, 3–5

Boolean logic, used in queries, 246–254

borders (report), 333–336

building

  Append queries, 288–291

  calculated fields, 268

  charts, 373

  consistent corrections, 172–174

  databases

    overview, 12–13, 69–73

    with multiple tables, 13–15

  Delete queries, 291–293

  formulas, 269–270

  indexes, 94–95

  input masks, 127–128, 130–133

  label reports, 368–372

  lists, 264–265

  navigation forms, 390–393

  one-table reports, 298–299

  primary keys, 83–84

  relationships, 90–92

  table relationships, 87–93

  Update queries, 284–288

  Yes/No format, 126

buttons

  adding to Quick Access toolbar, 49–51

  Background Color, 327

  Columns, 310

  Data, 310

  Excel Office Link, 343

  Filtered, 228

  Font Color, 327

  Landscape, 310

  Margins, 310

  Page, 338

Page Setup, 310
Portrait, 310
Print, 309
removing from Quick Access toolbar, 51–52
Size, 309
Themes, 339–340
Toggle Filter, 228
using, 44–45
Zoom, 310

• C •

calculated fields
  complex calculations, 270–276
  creating, 268
  defined, 267
  Expression Builder, 277–281
  overview, 64–65, 267
  simple calculations, 268–270
capitalization in text/memo fields, 119–120
changing
  reports
    items, 326–327
    margins, 315
    sections, 359–361
    views, 320–321
  text, 337–338
  for text/memo fields, 119–121
  types of lines, 336
charts, 373. *See also* databases; tables
check box, 151
clicking tabs, 43–44
Close Print Preview, 310
codes (formatting), for input masks, 130
colon (:), 67
color
  adding in reports, 327–329
  lines, 334
Columnar layout (reports), 346–347
Columns button, 310

columns (report). *See also* fields
  rearranging, 301–302
  sizing, 302–303
  spacing, 332–333
Columns tab, 317–318
combo box, 151
commands
  Compact and Repair, 409
  Filter, 210–212
  Find, 204–208
  Find and Replace, 173–174
  Open, 40
  Recent, 40
  Replace, 172–173
  Selection, 212–213
  Undo, 114, 404
Compact and Repair command, 409
comparison operators, 226–227
complex calculations
  multiple, 271
  nested calculation, 271–272
  order of operations, 271
  parameter queries, 272–275
  text formulas, 275–276
Conditional Formatting feature, 23
context-sensitive menus, 56
context-sensitive tools, 47–48
controlling
  form controls, 150–154
  relationships, 90–92
  report headings, 356–359
controls
  defined, 150
  deleting, 153–154
  moving, 151–152, 330–331
  reports, 322, 328
  sizing, 152–153
  types, 151
conventions, explained, 2
converting flat files to relational tables, 378–382
corrupt files, 410–411

Count function, 256, 262–263
creating
    Append queries, 288–291
    calculated fields, 268
    charts, 373
    consistent corrections, 172–174
    databases
        overview, 12–13, 69–73
        with multiple tables, 13–15
    Delete queries, 291–293
    formulas, 269–270
    indexes, 94–95
    input mask, 127–128, 130–133
    label reports, 368–372
    lists, 264–265
    navigation forms, 390–393
    one-table reports, 298–303
    primary keys, 83–84
    relationships, 90–92
    table relationships, 87–93
    Update queries, 284–288
    Yes/No format, 126
criteria
    establishing with OR, 250–252
    selecting for filters, 225–227
Crosstab Query Wizard, 236
currency fields
    data format in, 121–123
    overview, 64
customizing, workspace
    adding buttons to Quick Access toolbar,
        49–51
    data forms
        Layout view, 149
        managing controls, 150–154
        overview, 148
        themes, 150
    footers, 361
    headers, 361
    minimizing Ribbon, 52–53
    overview, 48
    removing buttons from Quick Access
        toolbar, 51–52

reports
    Columns tab, 317–318
    itemized adjustments, 361–365
    overview, 355–356
    page headings, 356–359
    Page tab, 316–317
    Print Options tab, 314–316
    report headings, 356–359
    sections, 359–361
repositioning Quick Access toolbar, 48–49
ScreenTips, 54–56

• D •

dash (-), 67
data
    editing
        automating with queries, 174–180
        creating consistent corrections, 172–174
        overview, 169–172
    entry of
        defaults, 136–137
        input masks, 127–133
        minimizing errors, 119, 404
        Required property, 133–134
        validation, 134–136
    errors, 404
    exporting, 164–167, 343
    filtering, 210–217
    finding, 204–208
    importing, 156–164
    linking, 156, 159
    overview, 60
    publishing to Web, 194–199
    redundant, 68
    sorting, 208–209
    storing from external sources, 162
Data Bars feature, 23
Data buttons, 310
data forms
    adding hyperlinks to, 188–193
    customizing
        Layout view, 149
        managing controls, 150–154

overview, 148
themes, 150
embedding Web content in, 187–193
generating
AutoForm, 143–144
Form Wizard, 144–147
overview, 141–143
managing controls, 150–154
reasons for using, 142
views, 149
Database Documenter, 382–385
databases. *See also* tables
adding tables, 73–76
building, 12–13, 69–73
creating with multiple tables, 13–15
documenting, 382–385
field types and uses, 62–67
file formats, 155–159
flat compared with relational, 67–69
flat-file, 18, 67–69
improving performance, 385–387
maintenance
inserting records and fields, 103–108
modifying field content, 109–110
opening tables for editing, 100–103
overview, 99
renaming fields, 110–112
renaming tables, 112–113
naming, 30–32
opening existing, 29
overview, 62
planning, 14–15
recording object details, 382–385
relational
compared with flat databases, 67–69
converting flat files to, 378–382
relationship types, 85–87
rules of relationships, 85
removing tables, 73–74, 76–77
special reporting, 18–21
starting
from scratch, 29–32
with templates, 32–34

technical terms, 59–62
with user forms, 16–17
date fields, 64, 123–125
dBASE format, 158
Decimal format, 123
Default Value property, 116, 136–137
defaults, for primary keys, 83
Delete query
creating, 291–293
overview, 283
deleting
buttons from Quick Access toolbar, 51–52
controls, 153–154
fields, 108
indexes, 95–97
navigation form tab items, 395
page breaks in reports, 325–326
records, 404
tables, 73–74, 76–77
tips for, 417
delimited text file, 159
design (reports)
elements
drawing lines, 341
logo, 342–343
formatting
adding color, 327–329
borders, 333–336
moving elements, 329–331
overview, 326–327
sizing, 331–332
spacing columns, 332–333
text, 337–338
organization
customizing properties, 355–365
grouping records, 350–354
layouts, 346–348
overview, 345–346
page breaks, 324–326
sections, 348–350
structural devices, 321–324
overview, 319–321
Print Preview, 338–339
themes, 339–340

Design view, 319–320, 322
designing
  filters, 224–227
  input masks, 130–131
Detail section (reports), 323
dialog boxes
  Access Options
    adding buttons to Quick Access toolbar, 49–51
    displaying navigation forms at startup, 396–397
    ScreenTips, 54–55
  Append, 289–291
  Documenter, 383–385
  Edit Hyperlink, 186
  Edit Relationships, 91–93
  Enter Field Properties, 112
  Enter Parameter Value, 274
  Export, 165–167, 343
  Export-HTML Document, 195–198
  Find and Replace, 172–174, 205–208
  Get External Data, 160–163
  Insert Hyperlink, 192
  Insert Picture, 189–190, 343, 365
  Label Wizard, 368–372
  New Database, 71
  New Query, 176
  New Query Wizard, 232
  Open, 101–103
  Page Setup, 316–317
  Paste Table As, 170–172
  Performance Analyzer, 386–387
  Report Wizard, 304–308
  Save As
    AutoForm, 143–144
    building databases, 73
    saving queries, 242
  Show Table
    adding records, 288
    Delete query, 291
    queries, 237
    selecting tables, 89–90
    Update query, 284–287
  Table Analyzer Wizard, 378–382

disabling AutoCorrect, 403–404
displaying
  filler spaces, 120
  navigation forms at startup, 396–397
Documenter dialog box, 383–385
documenting
  databases, 382–385
  importance of, 414–415
dollar sign ($), 67
double quotes ("), 67
drawing lines in reports, 341
duplicate records, 175
duplicate values, 96

• *E* •

Edit Hyperlink dialog box, 186
Edit Relationships dialog box, 91–93
editing
  data
    automating with queries, 174–180
    creating consistent corrections, 172–174
    overview, 169–172
  hyperlinks, 186–187
  labels, 153
  navigation form items, 394–395
  tables, 100–103
embedding Web content in forms, 187–193
Enforce Referential Integrity, 92
Enter Field Properties dialog box, 112
Enter Parameter Value dialog box, 274
entering
  data
    defaults, 136–137
    input masks, 127–133
    minimizing errors, 119, 404
    Required Property, 133–134
    requiring, 133–134
    validation, 134–136
  default values, 136–137
  input masks, 131–133
  Layout view, 149
  validation rules, 135–136

equals (=), 226
errors (data-entry), 119
establishing criteria with OR, 250–252
Euro symbol (€), 122
Excel (Microsoft Office), 18, 157, 373
Excel Office Link button, 343
Exchange, 158
exclamation point (!), 67
Export dialog box, 165–167, 343
Export-HTML Document dialog box,
    195–198
exporting. *See also* importing
  data, 164–167, 343
  data via Excel Office Link button, 343
  formats, 164–165
  query data, 165–167
  table data, 165–167
Expression Builder, 277–281
Expression function, 257
eXtensible Markup Language (XML), 157

F

features
  AutoCorrect, 403–404
  File tab, 37–38
  new and improved, 21–25
Field list (Filter window), 223
fields. *See also* calculated fields; columns
    (report)
  adding hyperlinks, 183–184
  Attachment, 64
  AutoNumber, 84
  calculated
    complex calculations, 270–276
    creating, 268
    defined, 267
    Expression Builder, 277–281
    overview, 64–65, 267
    simple calculations, 268–270

currency
  data format in, 121–123
  overview, 64
data formats, 118–126
date, 123–125
defined, 15
deleting, 108
filtering by content, 210–212
hyperlink, 64, 183–184
inserting, 105–108
key, 68
Lookup, 64
memo, 64, 118–121
modifying content, 109–110
multivalued, 86–87
naming, 66–67, 416–417
number
  data format in, 121–123
  overview, 64
  tips on, 416
overview, 60–63
prohibited symbols, 67
Relationship, 64
renaming, 110–112
Rich Text, 64
selecting
  for filters, 225–227
  for Summary instruction, 265–266
size of, 415
sorting
  on more than one, 209
  by single, 209
text, 118–121
time, 123–125
types, 63–66
types and uses, 62–67
Yes/No, 125–126
file:// protocol code, 183
File tab
  as new feature, 21, 37–38
  overview, 46–47

File Transfer Protocol (FTP) software,
    198–199
FileMaker, 61
files
  corrupt, 410–411
  flat, 378–382
  formats
    database, 158
    defined, 155
    spreadsheet, 157
    translating, 156–159
  troubleshooting size, 408–409
filler spaces, 120
Filter command, 210–212
Filter window, 223
Filtered button, 228
filters
  compared with queries, 221–222
  criteria used in, 220
  designing, 224–227
  disadvantages of, 221
  filtering by
    excluding selections, 217
    field content, 210–212
    form, 213–216
    selection, 212–213
  overview, 210–217, 220–221
  running, 227–229
  Selection, 217
  unfiltering in forms, 216
Find command, 204–208
Find Duplicates Query Wizard,
    176–180, 236
Find and Replace command, 173–174
Find and Replace dialog box, 172–174,
    205–208
finding
  data, 204–208
  records, 404–405
First function, 257
flat-file databases
  compared with relational databases,
    67–69

converting to relational tables, 378–382
  defined, 18
flat-file system. See flat-file databases
Font Color button, 327
fonts (report), 337
footers
  customizing, 361
  reports, 324, 348–350
foreign key, 85
Format property, 115
Format tab (reports), 326–327
formats
  decimal, 123
  exporting, 164–165
  field data, 118–126
  General Number, 122
  Percent, 123, 124
  Scientific, 123
formatting
  applying, 119
  codes
    for input masks, 130
    for text/memo fields, 119–121
  hyperlinks, 185
  options for reports, 300–301
  reports
    adding color, 327–329
    borders, 333–336
    moving elements, 329–331
    overview, 326–327
    sizing, 331–332
    spacing columns, 332–333
    text, 337–338
forms
  adding hyperlinks, 188–193
  data
    adding hyperlinks to, 188–193
    customizing, 148–154
    embedding Web content in, 187–193
    generating, 141–148
    managing controls, 150–154
    reasons for using, 142
    views, 149

defined, 16

filtering by, 213–216

Form Wizard

  data forms, 144–147

  overview, 142–143

navigation

  creating, 390–393

  deleting tab items, 395

  displaying at startup, 396–397

  editing items, 394–395

  maintaining, 394–396

  moving items, 395–396

  overview, 389–390

  testing, 393–394

 unfiltering in, 216

formulas

 creating, 269–270

 text, 275–276

forward slash (/), 67

FoxPro, 61

`ftp://` protocol code, 183

FTP software (File Transfer Protocol), 198–199

functions (Total row), 256–257

• G •

General Number format, 122

generating. *See also* creating

 data forms

  AutoForm, 143–144

  Form Wizard, 144–147

  overview, 141–143

  reasons for using, 142

Get External Data dialog box, importing, 160–163

greater-than (>), 120, 226

greater-than-or-equal-to (>=), 226

Group By function, 256, 258–260

Group, Sort, and Total panel, 351–354

grouping

 records in reports, 350–354

 in reports, 324

• H •

headers

 customizing, 361

 page, 323, 356–359

 reports, 322, 348–350

help, 419

hiding filler spaces, 120

highlighting missing text, 121

HTML (HyperText Markup Language), 157, 194

HTML, XHTML, and CSS For Dummies (Tittel & Noble), 194

`http://` protocol code, 183

hyperlinks

 adding

  in fields, 183–184

  to forms, 188–193

 defined, 182

 editing, 186–187

 fields in tables, 64, 183–184

 formatting, 185

 inserting images as, 189–192

 overview, 182–183

 protocol codes, 183

 testing, 187

 typing, 185–186

HyperText Markup Language (HTML), 157, 194

• I •

icons

 Access, 28

 explained, 6

images, inserting as links, 189–192

importing. *See also* exporting

 data, 156–164

 defined, 156

 overview, 159–160

 spreadsheets, 158–159

 steps for, 160–163

 text files, 159

 troubleshooting, 163–164, 410

improving database performance, 385–387
indexes
  adding, 95–97
  creating, 94–95
  listing, 95
  overview, 93–94
  removing, 95–97
input mask
  creating, 127–128, 130–133
  defined, 127
  Input Mask Wizard, 128–129
  overview, 127–128
Input Mask property, 115
Insert Hyperlink dialog box, 192
Insert Picture dialog box, 189–190, 343, 365
inserting
  fields, 105–108
  images as links, 189–192
  page breaks in reports, 324–325
intranets, 184
invoking Table Analyzer Wizard, 378–382
isolationist tables, 68

• J •

junction tables, 87

• K •

key field, 68
keyboard shortcuts, 56
keys. *See also* primary keys
  Alt, 57–58
  foreign, 85

• L •

label, 151, 153
label reports, 368–372
Label Wizard, 367–373
Landscape button, 310
Last function, 257

Layout view
  controls, 322
  of data forms, 149
  reports, 320
layouts (reports), 346–348
less-than (<), 120, 226
less-than-or-equal-to (<=), 227
lines
  coloring, 334
  drawing in reports, 341
  thickening, 334–335
linking
  data, 156
  fields, 68
  overview, 159
links
  adding
    in fields, 183–184
    to forms, 188–193
  defined, 182
  editing, 186–187
  fields in tables, 183–184
  formatting, 185
  inserting images as, 189–192
  overview, 182–183
  protocol codes, 183
  testing, 187
  typing, 185–186
list box, 151
listing indexes, 95
lists, creating, 264–265
logos, adding to reports, 342–343
Lookup fields, 64
lowercase letters, 120

• M •

mailto: protocol code, 183
maintenance, database
  inserting records and fields, 103–108
  modifying field content, 109–110
  navigation forms, 394–396
  opening tables for editing, 100–103

overview, 99
renaming
  fields, 110–112
  tables, 112–113
troubleshooting, 114
managing
  form controls, 150–154
  relationships, 90–92
  report headings, 356–359
many-to-many relationships, 86–87
Margins button, 310
margins (report), 315
mass mailings, 367–373
Max function, 257
Memo fields, 64, 118–121
menus. *See also* Ribbon
  context-sensitive, 56
  report, 313–314
  Start, 27
Microsoft Exchange, 158
Microsoft Office
  Excel, 18, 157, 373
  PowerPoint, 373
  Themes feature, 22
Microsoft Outlook, 158
Microsoft SQL Server, 61
Min function, 256
minimizing
  data-entry errors, 119
  Ribbon, 52–53
Modify Fields tab, 112
modifying
  field content, 109–110
  relationships, 92–93
  table properties, 116–118
More Pages, 310
mouse, 56–57
moving
  controls, 151–152, 330–331
  navigation form items, 395–396
  report elements, 329–331
multivalued fields, 86–87

• *N* •

naming
  databases, 30–32
  fields, 66–67, 416–417
navigating
  Access, 37–58
  Alt key, 57–58
  mouse, 56–57
  on-screen tools
    accessing panes, panels, and context-sensitive tools, 47–48
    buttons, 44–45
    clicking tabs, 43–44
    File tab, 46–47
    overview, 42–43
    Quick Access, 46–47
  overview, 37–41
  Quick Access toolbar
    adding buttons to, 49–51
    removing buttons from, 51–52
    repositioning, 48–49
  Ribbon, 52–53
  ScreenTips, 54–56
navigation forms
  creating, 390–393
  defined, 103
  deleting tab items, 395
  displaying at startup, 396–397
  editing items, 394–395
  maintaining, 394–396
  moving items, 395–396
  as new feature, 23
  overview, 389–390
  testing, 393–394
nested calculations, 271–272
New Database dialog box, 71
New Query dialog box, 176
New Query Wizard dialog box, 232
news:// protocol code, 183
No fields. *See* Yes/No fields
Noble, Jeff (author)
  HTML, XHTML, and CSS For Dummies, 194

normalization, 401–402
not equal to (<>), 227
number fields
    data format in, 121–123
    overview, 64
    tips on, 416

• O •

ODBC (Open DataBase Connectivity), 158
Office 2010 and SharePoint Productivity
    For Dummies (Williams), 194
Office (Microsoft)
    Excel, 18, 158, 373
    PowerPoint, 373
    Themes feature, 22
on-screen tools
    accessing panes, panels, and context-
        sensitive tools, 47–48
    clicking tabs, 43–44
    File tab, 46–47
    overview, 42–43
    Quick Access tools, 46–47
    using buttons, 44–45
One Page, 310
one-table reports, 298–303
one-to-many relationships, 86
one-to-one relationships, 86
one-way link, 162
online capabilities
    embedding Web content in forms,
        187–193
    hyperlinks, 182–187
    publishing data to Web, 194–199
    Web, 181–182
Open command, 40
Open DataBase Connectivity (ODBC), 158
Open dialog box, opening databases,
    101–103
opening
    Access, 26–28
    existing databases, 29
    tables for editing, 100–103
operators (comparison), 226–227

OR. *See also* AND
    combining with AND, 252–254
    establishing criteria with, 250–252
    using, 246–249
Oracle, 61
order of operations, 271
organization
    reports
        customizing properties, 355–365
        grouping records, 350–354
        layouts, 346–348
        overview, 345–346
        page breaks, 324–326
        sections, 348–350
        structural devices, 321–324
    tips, 418
organization of this book, 3–6
Outlook (Microsoft), 158

• P •

page breaks (reports), 324–326
Page buttons, 338
page headers, 323, 356–359
Page Setup button, 310
Page Setup dialog box, 316–317
Page tab, 316–317
panels
    accessing, 47–48
    Backstage View, 21, 41
    Group, Sort, and Total, 351–354
panes, accessing, 47–48
parameter queries, 272–275
parameters, 273
Paste Table As dialog box, 170–172
percent (%), 67
Percent format, 123, 124
Performance Analyzer, 385–387
placeholder character, 129
planning databases, 14–15
Portrait button, 310
PowerPoint (Microsoft Office), 373
pre-built database templates feature, 22

previewing, reports
  menus, 313–314
  Print Preview tools, 309–311
  zooming, 311–312
primary keys
  creating, 83–84
  defined, 81
  overview, 81–83
Print button, 309
Print Data Only check box, 310
Print Options tab, 314–316
Print Preview
  reports, 338–339
  tools, 309–311
properties
  Default Value, 116, 136–137
  Format, 115
  Input Mask, 115
  report
    itemized adjustments, 361–365
    overview, 355–356
    page headings, 356–359
    report headings, 356–359
    sections, 359–361
  Required, 116, 133–134
  table, 115–116
  Validation Rule, 116
Property Sheet, 355–356
protocol codes, 183
Publish options, 24–25
publishing
  data to Web, 23, 194–199
  tables, 195–199
punctuation in text/memo fields, 120–121

 • _Q_ •

queries
  action
    Append query, 283, 288–291
    Delete query, 283, 291–293
    overview, 283–284
    Update query, 283, 284–288
  ad hoc
    overview, 236–240
    running queries, 242–243
    saving queries, 242
    sorting results, 240–242, 243
    table relationships, 239
    troubleshooting, 244
  advantages of, 303
  Append
    creating, 288–291
    overview, 283
  automating editing process with, 174–180
  Boolean logic, 246–254
  compared with filters, 221–222
  creating lists, 264–265
  criteria used in, 220
  Delete
    creating, 291–293
    overview, 283
  exporting data, 165–167
  filter tools, 220–229
  overview, 219
  parameter, 272–275
  running, 242–243
  saving, 242
  Select
    importance of relationships, 230
    overview, 229–230
    tips, 231
  sort tools, 220–229
  sorting results, 240–242, 243
  summary, 265–266
  Total row, 255–264
  troubleshooting, 244, 405–406
  Update
    creating, 284–288
    overview, 283
Query Grid (Filter window), 223
Query Wizard, 231–236
question mark (?), 67
Quick Access toolbar
  adding buttons to, 49–51
  overview, 46–47
  removing buttons from, 51–52
  repositioning, 48–49
Quick Launch bar, 28

• R •

rearranging columns in reports, 301–302
Recent command, 40
recording database object details, 382–385
records
  adding, 103–105
  deleting, 404
  duplicate, 175
  grouping in reports, 350–354
  overview, 61
  searching for, 404–405
Rectangle tool, 341
redundant data, 68
Referential Integrity enforcement, 92
Refresh All, 310
relational databases
  compared with flat databases, 67–69
  converting flat files to, 378–382
  defined, 13
  relationship types, 85–87
  rules of relationships, 85
Relationship fields, 64
relationship tables, 87–93
relationships
  creating, 90–92
  managing, 90–92
  modifying, 92–93
  relationship with Select queries, 230
  rules of, 85
  types, 85–87
Relationships window, 88
Remember icon, 6
removing
  buttons from Quick Access toolbar, 51–52
  controls, 153–154
  fields, 108
  indexes, 95–97
  navigation form tab items, 395
  page breaks in reports, 325–326
  records, 404
  tables, 73–74, 76–77
  tips for, 417

renaming
  fields, 110–112
  tables, 110–113
Replace command, 172–173
Report Wizard dialog box, 304–308
reporting, automatic
  creating one-table reports, 298–303
  customizing reports, 314–318
  overview, 297–298
  previewing Report Wizard, 309–314
  starting Report Wizard, 304–309
reports
  adding
    color, 327–329
    logos, 342–343
  adjusting views, 320–321
  controls, 322, 328
  customizing
    Columns tab, 317–318
    itemized adjustments, 361–365
    overview, 355–356
    page headings, 356–359
    Page tab, 316–317
    Print Options tab, 314–316
    report headings, 356–359
    sections, 359–361
  design
    elements, 341–343
    formatting, 326–338
    organization, 321–326
    overview, 319–321
    Print Preview, 338–339
    themes, 339–340
  footers, 324
  formatting options, 300–301
  headers, 322
  label, 368–372
  mass mailings, 367–373
  menus, 313–314
  organization
    customizing properties, 355–365
    grouping records, 350–354
    layouts, 346–348

overview, 345–346
sections, 348–350
previewing
menus, 313–314
Print Preview tools, 309–311
zooming, 311–312
Report Wizard
special reporting with, 18–21
starting, 304–309
sections, 322–324
sizing, 331–332
time-stamping, 364–365
zooming, 311–312
repositioning Quick Access toolbar, 48–49
Required property, 116, 133–134
resources
online cheat sheet, 57
SharePoint, 25
World Wide Web Consortium, 194
restrictions for primary keys, 83
Ribbon. *See also* menus
defined, 37
as improved feature, 22
minimizing, 52–53
overview, 42–43
Rich Text fields, 64
rounding (automatic), 402–403
rows. *See* records
rules
for primary keys, 82–83
of relationships, 85
running
filters, 227–229
Find Duplicates Query Wizard, 176–180
queries, 242–243
Query Wizard, 231–236
Simple Query Wizard, 231–236

• S •

Save As dialog box
AutoForm, 143–144
building databases, 73
saving queries, 242

Save options, 24–25
saving queries, 242
Scientific format, 123
ScreenTips, 54–56
searching
for data, 204–208
for records, 404–405
sections (report), 322–324, 348–350, 359–361
Select queries
importance of relationships, 230
overview, 229–230
tips, 231
selecting
criteria for filters, 225–227
fields for filters, 225–227
fields for Summary instruction, 265–266
starting points, 28–34
tables, 89–90
Selection command, 212–213
selection, filtering by, 212–213, 217
semicolon (;), 67
setting(s)
margins in reports, 315
tables, 115–118
Shape Outline tool, 334, 335
SharePoint, 24–25
Show Margins check box, 310
Show Table dialog box
adding records, 288
Delete query, 291
queries, 237
selecting tables, 89–90
Update query, 284–287
showing
filler spaces, 120
navigation forms at startup, 296–297
simple calculations, 268–270
Simple Query Wizard, 231–236
single quote ('), 67
Size button, 309
sizing
columns in reports, 302–303
controls, 152–153

sizing *(continued)*
  fields, 415
  files, 408–409
  reports, 331–332
software, FTP (File Transfer Protocol),
    198–199
sorting
  data, 208–209
  on more than one field, 209
  query results, 240–242, 243
  by single fields, 209
spacing
  report columns, 332–333
  in text/memo fields, 120–121
special reporting with databases, 18–21
speed, troubleshooting, 407–408
spreadsheets. *See also* databases
  file formats, 157
  importing, 158–159
SQL Server (Microsoft), 61
Start menu, 27
starting
  new databases from scratch, 29–32
  Report Wizard, 304–309
  with templates, 32–34
starting points, 28–34
startup, displaying navigation forms at,
    396–397
State Header, 348
StDev function, 257
storing data from external sources, 162
structure of reports, 321–324
subform, 151
Sum function, 256, 260–261
summarizing (Query Wizard), 236
Summary instruction, 265–266
switchboard, 103
symbols, prohibited in fields, 67

● *T* ●

Table Analyzer Wizard dialog box, 378–382
Table Events feature, 23
table relationships
  building, 87–93
  managing relationships, 90–93

  with queries, 239
  Relationships window, 88
  selecting tables, 89–90
Table view
  defined, 16
  renaming fields, 111
tables
  adding
    hyperlink fields to, 183–184
    overview, 73–76
  backing up, 170–171
  creating databases with multiple, 13–15
  exporting data, 165–167
  inserting records and fields, 103–108
  isolationist, 68
  junction, 87
  modifying field content, 109–110
  normalizing, 402
  opening for editing, 100–103
  overview, 61, 61–62
  properties, 115–116
  publishing, 195–199
  relational, 68–69, 378–382
  removing, 73–74, 76–77
  renaming, 110–113
  selecting, 89–90
  settings, 115–118
  structure of, 115–117
  troubleshooting maintenance, 114
tabs
  clicking, 43–44
  Columns, 317–318
  File, 21, 37–38, 46–47
  Format, 326–327
  Modify Fields, 112
  Page, 316–317
  Print Options, 314–316
Tabular layout (report), 346–348
Technical Stuff icon, 6
technical terms, 59–62
templates
  defined, 32
  starting with, 32–34
testing
  hyperlinks, 187
  navigation forms, 393–394

text
  changing, 337–338
  fields, 63–64, 118–121
  file formats, 157
  files, 159
  formulas, 275–276
  highlighting missing, 121
  links, 192–193
text box, 151
Theme group tools, 150
Themes button, 339–340
thickening lines, 334–335
time fields, 64, 123–125
time-stamping reports, 364–365
Tips icon, 6
tips, uncommon, 413–419
Tittel, Ed (author)
  HTML, XHTML, and CSS For Dummies, 194
Toggle Filter button, 228
toolbars
  overview, 37
  Quick Access
    adding buttons to, 49–51
    overview, 46–47
    removing buttons from, 51–52
    repositioning, 48–49
tools
  Advanced Filter/Sort, 222, 224–229
  Analyzer
    converting flat files to relational tables,
      378–382
    improving database performance,
      385–387
    overview, 377
    recording database object details,
      382–385
  AutoForm, 142–144
  context-sensitive, 47–48
  on-screen
    accessing panes, panels , and context-
      sensitive tools, 47–48
    clicking tabs, 43–44
    File tab, 46–47
    overview, 42–43
    Quick Access tools, 46–47
    using buttons, 44–45
  Print Preview, 309–311

  Quick Access, 46–47
  Rectangle, 341
  Shape Outline, 334–335
  Theme group, 150
  Zoom, 311
Total row
  adding to queries, 257–258
  Count function, 262–263
  functions, 256–257
  Group By function, 258–260
  overview, 255–257
  Sum function, 260–261
  toolbox functions, 258–264
  troubleshooting, 261
  Where instruction, 263–264
translating file formats, 156–159
triggers, 23
troubleshooting
  AutoCorrect, 403–404
  automatic rounding, 402–403
  backup, 405
  corrupt files, 410–411
  file size, 408–409
  importing, 163–164, 410
  missing records, 404–405
  normalization, 401–402
  queries, 244, 405–406
  record deletions, 404
  speed, 407–408
  table maintenance, 114
  table structure, 401–402
  Total row, 261
  Undo, 404
  validation, 407
Two Pages, 310
two-way link, 162
typing hyperlinks, 185–186

• *U* •

Undo command, 114, 404
unfiltering, 216
Unmatched Query Wizard, 236
Update query
  creating, 284–288
  overview, 283
uppercase letters, 120

user forms, 16–17
using
  buttons, 44–45
  primary keys, 82
  text links, 192–193

validation
  common number-/date-field, 135
  entering rules, 135–136
  importance of, 416
  options, 134
  troubleshooting, 407
Validation Rule property, 116
values
  default, 116, 136–137
  duplicate, 96
Var function, 257
views
  Backstage View, 21, 41
  data forms, 149
  Design view, 319–320, 322
  Layout view, 149, 320, 322
  Table view, 16, 111

Warning icon, 6
Web
  capabilities of Access on, 181–182
  embedding content in data forms,
    187–193
  publishing data to, 194–199
  publishing to, 23
Web sites
  online Cheat Sheet, 57
  SharePoint, 25
  World Wide Web Consortium, 194
Where function, 257, 263–264
Where instruction, 263–264
Williams, Vanessa (author)
  *Office 2010 and SharePoint Productivity For
    Dummies*, 194

wizards
  Crosstab Query Wizard, 236
  Find Duplicates Query Wizard, 176, 180,
    236
  Form Wizard, 144–147
  Input Mask Wizard, 128–129
  Label Wizard, 367–373
  Query Wizard, 231–236
  Report Wizard, 304–314
  Simple Query Wizard, 231–236
  Table Analyzer Wizard, 378–382
  Unmatched Query Wizard, 236
workspace, customizing
  adding buttons to Quick Access toolbar,
    49–51
  minimizing Ribbon, 52–53
  overview, 48
  removing buttons from Quick Access
    toolbar, 51–52
  repositioning Quick Access toolbar, 48–49
  ScreenTips, 54–56
World Wide Web Consortium Web site, 194

• *X* •

XML (eXtensible Markup Language), 157

• *Y* •

Yes/No fields, 64, 125–126

• *Z* •

Zoom button, 310
Zoom tool, 311
zooming reports, 311–312

Business/Accounting & Bookkeeping

Bookkeeping For Dummies
978-0-7645-9848-7

eBay Business
All-in-One For Dummies,
2nd Edition
978-0-470-38536-4

Job Interviews
For Dummies,
3rd Edition
978-0-470-17748-8

Resumes For Dummies,
5th Edition
978-0-470-08037-5

Stock Investing
For Dummies,
3rd Edition
978-0-470-40114-9

Successful Time
Management
For Dummies
978-0-470-29034-7

Computer Hardware

BlackBerry For Dummies,
3rd Edition
978-0-470-45762-7

Computers For Seniors
For Dummies
978-0-470-24055-7

iPhone For Dummies,
2nd Edition
978-0-470-42342-4

Laptops For Dummies,
3rd Edition
978-0-470-27759-1

Macs For Dummies,
10th Edition
978-0-470-27817-8

Cooking & Entertaining

Cooking Basics
For Dummies,
3rd Edition
978-0-7645-7206-7

Wine For Dummies,
4th Edition
978-0-470-04579-4

Diet & Nutrition

Dieting For Dummies,
2nd Edition
978-0-7645-4149-0

Nutrition For Dummies,
4th Edition
978-0-471-79868-2

Weight Training
For Dummies,
3rd Edition
978-0-471-76845-6

Digital Photography

Digital Photography
For Dummies,
6th Edition
978-0-470-25074-7

Photoshop Elements 7
For Dummies
978-0-470-39700-8

Gardening

Gardening Basics
For Dummies
978-0-470-03749-2

Organic Gardening
For Dummies,
2nd Edition
978-0-470-43067-5

Green/Sustainable

Green Building
& Remodeling
For Dummies
978-0-470-17559-0

Green Cleaning
For Dummies
978-0-470-39106-8

Green IT For Dummies
978-0-470-38688-0

Health

Diabetes For Dummies,
3rd Edition
978-0-470-27086-8

Food Allergies
For Dummies
978-0-470-09584-3

Living Gluten-Free
For Dummies
978-0-471-77383-2

Hobbies/General

Chess For Dummies,
2nd Edition
978-0-7645-8404-6

Drawing For Dummies
978-0-7645-5476-6

Knitting For Dummies,
2nd Edition
978-0-470-28747-7

Organizing For Dummies
978-0-7645-5300-4

SuDoku For Dummies
978-0-470-01892-7

Home Improvement

Energy Efficient Homes
For Dummies
978-0-470-37602-7

Home Theater
For Dummies,
3rd Edition
978-0-470-41189-6

Living the Country Lifestyle
All-in-One For Dummies
978-0-470-43061-3

Solar Power Your Home
For Dummies
978-0-470-17569-9

Available wherever books are sold. For more information or to order direct: U.S. customers visit www.dummies.com or call 1-877-762-2974.
U.K. customers visit www.wileyeurope.com or call (0) 1243 843291. Canadian customers visit www.wiley.ca or call 1-800-567-4797.

Internet

Blogging For Dummies,
2nd Edition
978-0-470-23017-6

eBay For Dummies,
6th Edition
978-0-470-49741-8

Facebook For Dummies
978-0-470-26273-3

Google Blogger
For Dummies
978-0-470-40742-4

Web Marketing
For Dummies,
2nd Edition
978-0-470-37181-7

WordPress For Dummies,
2nd Edition
978-0-470-40296-2

Language & Foreign Language

French For Dummies
978-0-7645-5193-2

Italian Phrases
For Dummies
978-0-7645-7203-6

Spanish For Dummies
978-0-7645-5194-9

Spanish For Dummies,
Audio Set
978-0-470-09585-0

Macintosh

Mac OS X Snow Leopard
For Dummies
978-0-470-43543-4

Math & Science

Algebra I For Dummies,
2nd Edition
978-0-470-55964-2

Biology For Dummies
978-0-7645-5326-4

Calculus For Dummies
978-0-7645-2498-1

Chemistry For Dummies
978-0-7645-5430-8

Microsoft Office

Excel 2007 For Dummies
978-0-470-03737-9

Office 2007 All-in-One
Desk Reference
For Dummies
978-0-471-78279-7

Music

Guitar For Dummies,
2nd Edition
978-0-7645-9904-0

iPod & iTunes
For Dummies,
6th Edition
978-0-470-39062-7

Piano Exercises
For Dummies
978-0-470-38765-8

Parenting & Education

Parenting For Dummies,
2nd Edition
978-0-7645-5418-6

Type 1 Diabetes
For Dummies
978-0-470-17811-9

Pets

Cats For Dummies,
2nd Edition
978-0-7645-5275-5

Dog Training For Dummies,
2nd Edition
978-0-7645-8418-3

Puppies For Dummies,
2nd Edition
978-0-470-03717-1

Religion & Inspiration

The Bible For Dummies
978-0-7645-5296-0

Catholicism For Dummies
978-0-7645-5391-2

Women in the Bible
For Dummies
978-0-7645-8475-6

Self-Help & Relationship

Anger Management
For Dummies
978-0-470-03715-7

Overcoming Anxiety
For Dummies
978-0-7645-5447-6

Sports

Baseball For Dummies,
3rd Edition
978-0-7645-7537-2

Basketball For Dummies,
2nd Edition
978-0-7645-5248-9

Golf For Dummies,
3rd Edition
978-0-471-76871-5

Web Development

Web Design All-in-One
For Dummies
978-0-470-41796-6

Windows Vista

Windows Vista
For Dummies
978-0-471-75421-3